Cultural Studies in the C

MW00852839

Jaafar Aksikas
Sean Johnson Andrews • Donald Hedrick
Editors

Cultural Studies in the Classroom and Beyond

Critical Pedagogies and Classroom Strategies

Editors
Jaafar Aksikas
Humanities, History, and Social Sciences
Columbia College Chicago
Chicago, IL, USA

Sean Johnson Andrews
Humanities, History, and Social Sciences
Columbia College Chicago
Chicago, IL, USA

Donald Hedrick
Department of English
Kansas State University
Manhattan, KS, USA

ISBN 978-3-030-25392-9   ISBN 978-3-030-25393-6   (eBook)
https://doi.org/10.1007/978-3-030-25393-6

This Palgrave Macmillan imprint is published by the registered company Springer Nature Switzerland AG.
The registered company address is: Gewerbestrasse 11, 6330 Cham, Switzerland

For our students, former, current, and future
and
To the memories of two great teachers in cultural studies, the late Stuart
Hall and Randy Martin

Acknowledgments

All knowledge is the product of a number of influences, people, and contexts. An edited volume is even more so. Clearly, so many people, most of whom we cannot remember by name, have shaped this volume, and we would like to give our deep thanks to all of them. We would also like to thank the anonymous reviewers for their productive and useful comments and feedback.

In a volume on teaching and pedagogy, it is most fitting here to begin by acknowledging the key impact of our students over more years than we care to remember in shaping many of the ideas and reflections presented here.

We are also grateful to the editors at Palgrave Macmillan for assisting in several crucial ways in the preparation and production of this volume. We are especially grateful to Shaun Vigil and Glenn Ramirez, who were always prompt, meticulous, and tactful in coordinating the production of a complicated collection.

We would also like to thank the following colleagues and friends: Angela McRobbie, Rich King, Ann Gunkel, Eliza Nichols, Debra Parr, Carmelo Esterrich, Lisa Brock, Lawrence Grossberg, Toby Miller, Walter Benn Michaels, and Paul Smith. Our critical conversations with them, along with their constant support and optimism of the will, have been both a sustaining inspiration and a steadying influence over the years.

Finally, we are also particularly grateful to all our contributors and families for their patience as we labored together for a few years on the completion of this volume.

Contents

Notes on Contributors

Jaafar Aksikas teaches cultural studies at Columbia College Chicago in Chicago, Illinois, USA, where he chaired the Cultural Studies Program (2009–2013). He is also the president of the Institute for Global Arab Media, Democracy and Culture and former president of the Cultural Studies Association (2014–2016). His books and co-edited volumes include *Cultural Studies and the 'Juridical Turn': Culture, Law, and Legitimacy in the Era of Neoliberal Capitalism* (2016), *Cultural Studies of/ and the Law* (2014), *Arab Modernities: Islamism, Nationalism and Liberalism in the Post-Colonial Arab World* (2009), and *The Sirah [Epic] of Antar: An Islamic Interpretation of Arab and Islamic History* (2002). His articles have appeared in journals such as *Cultural Studies, Reviews in Cultural Theory, Lateral, Mediterranean Politics*, and *Cultuur en Migratie*. He is also the editor of the *Cultural Studies and Marxism* book series. Aksikas has taught, researched, and published widely in the fields of cultural studies, media and culture industry studies, critical legal and policy studies, American studies, and Middle Eastern studies. He has also served on the editorial boards of *Cultural Studies* and *Lateral* journals. He has received numerous awards, including most recently the George Mason University Distinguished Alumnus in Cultural Studies Award (2017). He has also served as an expert consultant for media and other organizations on issues relating to Middle Eastern and North African cultures and politics.

Lisa B. Y. Calvente is an assistant professor in the College of Communication at DePaul University in Chicago, Illinois, USA. Her primary areas of research are the black diaspora, performance studies, and cultural studies. Her interests lie in the critical interrogation of anti-black and brown racism and the experiences, representations, and theories of the black Diaspora and coloniality. She has won a number of awards including The Woodrow Wilson Career Enhancement Fellowship for Junior Faculty and The Andrew Mellon African American Studies Post-Doctoral Fellowship at Northwestern University. She is co-editor of *Imprints of Revolution: Visual Representations of Resistance* (2016) and contributor to *Souls: A Critical Journal of Black Politics, Culture and Society*, *Cultural Studies*, and *Social Identities: Journal for the Study of Race, Nation and Culture* as well as to multi-author volumes in her field.

Pablo Andrés Castagno is Professor of Political Science and Media Studies at Universidad Nacional de La Matanza, and Visiting Professor of Cultural Studies at Universidad Nacional de Santiago del Estero, Argentina. Castagno works in the academic field to create critical spaces of cultural production through research, teaching, and cultural policy. His writing in Spanish and English has appeared in cutting-edge journals and collected editions, including *Mediations*, *tripleC: Communication, Capitalism & Critique*, *Cultural Studies*, *Historical Materialism*, *Diccionario del léxico corriente de la política argentina* (UNGS 2014), *Marx and the Political Economy of the Media* (2015), and *Cultural Studies and the 'Juridical Turn': Culture, Law, and Legitimacy in the Era of Neoliberal Capitalism* (2016). He received a PhD in Cultural Studies from George Mason University, the Michael Sprinker Essay Prize, and the Fulbright Fellowship.

Andrew Davis is Visiting Assistant Professor of Media Studies in the Department of Communication at Appalachian State University in Boone, North Carolina, USA. His research operates at the intersection of Media & Technology Studies, Cultural Studies, Political Economy, and Critical Theory. His research focuses on the changing nature of power in the context of (on the one hand) the capacities and limits of convergent media technologies and (on the other hand) the changing relationships between transnational corporations and the US nation-state.

Jodi Davis-Pacheco, PhD is a full-time lecturer in the Women and Gender Studies Department at California State University, Fullerton in Fullerton, California, USA. She received her PhD in Cultural Studies at Claremont Graduate University, Claremont, California. She has taught about 5000 students with a pedagogical framework that is reflexive, collaborative, and grounded in feminist principles and humor.

R. Gabriel Dor earned a PhD in Screen Cultures from Northwestern University, a JD from Berkeley Law, and a MA from Goldsmiths, University of London. His research pursues intersections of Jewishness and gender in US popular culture, and his writing has been published in the *Journal of Popular Film and Television*, *Reviews in Cultural Theory*, and *Diva*. He has taught Media and Communications courses at Northwestern, Northeastern Illinois University, and DePaul University. He works in Chicago, Illinois, USA.

Basak Durgun is a visiting assistant professor in the Department of Global and Intercultural Studies at Miami University in Oxford, Ohio. Durgun earned her PhD in Cultural Studies from George Mason University in 2019. She has a dynamic research program anchored in urban ethnography and critical geography. She applies qualitative methods to analyze social and spatial dynamics in global cities and regions directly influenced by urban expansion. Durgun pays particular attention to new social movements and community activism as they transform landscapes and shape the popular, political and scholarly discourses. In her dissertation research, titled "Cultural politics of urban green spaces: The production and reorganization of Istanbul's parks and gardens," Durgun examined how competing social actors—such as the state, urban planning and architecture professionals, social movements, gardeners, and real estate developers—invest in and govern various urban green spaces in Istanbul. Her research has been supported by internal and external grants and fellowships, such as George Mason University Office of the Provost Research and Writing Grants, Institute of Turkish Studies Dissertation Completion Grant, and Mellon Fellowship in Urban Landscape Studies at Dumbarton Oaks Library and Collection. Since 2011, Durgun has taught several undergraduate courses in a variety of programs, such as Cultural Studies, School of Integrative Studies, Global Affairs, Women and Gender Studies, and American Studies. She likes to incorporate experiential learning strategies in all of her courses to create learning opportunities with long-lasting impact.

Liam Grealy is Postdoctoral Research Fellow in the Housing for Health Incubator and the Department of Gender and Cultural Studies at the University of Sydney. His research relates to the history and cultural life of policy in a range of areas, including housing, media classification, higher education, and the governance of youth. He is currently conducting (in collaboration with Timothy Laurie) an ethnographic project around pedagogy in Higher Degree Research supervision meetings across four Australian universities.

Lawrence Grossberg is the Morris Davis Distinguished Professor of Communication and Cultural Studies at the University of North Carolina Chapel Hill in Chapel Hill, North Carolina, USA. He has published ten books and edited another eleven, written over 200 essays and completed dozens of interviews. His work has been translated into eighteen languages. His most recent books are *We All Want to Change the World* (available free online) and *Under the Cover of Chaos.* He has edited the journal *Cultural Studies* for almost thirty years. His work brings together his passions for politics and the popular, always framed by an assumption that good ideas and better knowledge matter. He has researched, thought, and written about a wide range of topics, from rock music and youth culture to modernities, from political economy to contemporary theory, and from left countercultures to right hegemonies. All of his work expresses a commitment to the practice of cultural studies, an analysis grounded in contingency, complexity, and contextuality, with a good dose of humility.

Mark Hayward is an associate professor in the Department of Communication Studies at York University in Toronto, Ontario, Canada. His research focuses on media history and cultural studies. He has published in such journals as *Cultural Studies, Canadian Literature, New Formations,* and *SubStance.* He is the editor of *Communication and The*

Economy and the author of *Identity and Industry: Making Canadian Media Multicultural.*

Donald Hedrick is Professor of English at Kansas State University in Manhattan, Kansas, USA and the founding director of its graduate program in cultural studies, one of the oldest in the country. Awarded there with the Gasche Lifetime Teaching Award and as endowed Donnelly Scholar, Hedrick has published widely in *Shakespeare, Renaissance Studies*, and cultural and architectural theory, and teaches courses in film, popular culture, language, horror and violence, law, and gender. He is the co-author of *Shakespeare Without Class: Misappropriations of Cultural Capital* (2000). Among other grants, he has been awarded fellowships and visiting appointments at Cornell University's Society for the Humanities, at Amherst College, a Fulbright Teaching Fellowship at Charles University in Prague, and the O'Connor Endowed Chair of Literature at Colgate University. His monograph, *Shakespeare and Fun: the Birth of Entertainment Value*, is forthcoming from Bloomsbury Press.

Sean Johnson Andrews is Associate Professor of Humanities and Cultural Studies at Columbia College Chicago in Chicago, Illinois, USA. He holds PhD and MA degrees in Cultural Studies and English Literature, respectively, both from George Mason University, in Fairfax, Virginia. Johnson Andrews does work at the intersection of digital media studies, political theory, global political economy, and cultural studies theories, methods, and methodologies. His work asks questions about the role of the media and communications technologies in producing meanings, powers, and value—and the ability of the politically committed, interdisciplinary, self-reflexive methodology of cultural studies to better conceptualize, critique, and reshape these relationships. He has written on the political and economic implications of media piracy, the importance of contextual intellectual history in understanding the development and deployment of theories (in economics, media studies, and history itself), the changing relationship between the law and culture in the neoliberal age, and cultural studies methodology more generally. His books and co-edited volumes include *The Cultural Production of Intellectual Property Rights: Law, Labor, and the Persistence of Primitive*

Accumulation (2019), *Hegemony, Mass Media, and Cultural Studies: Properties of Meaning, Power, and Value in Cultural Production* (2016), *Cultural Studies and the 'Juridical Turn': Culture, Law, and Legitimacy in the Era of Neoliberal Capitalism* (2016), and *Cultural Studies of/and the Law* (2014). His writing has appeared in *Cultural Studies, The Journal of Historical Sociology, Lateral, The Review of Radical Political Economy*, and *Jacobin*.

Timothy Laurie is Scholarly Teaching Fellow at the University of Technology Sydney in Sydney, Australia. His core research interests include cultural theory, popular music studies, and gender and sexuality studies. He coordinates and lectures on "Communicating Difference," "Digital Media Industries," and "Global Cinema" in the School of Communication. He is conducting (in collaboration with Liam Grealy) an ethnographic project around pedagogy in Higher Degree Research supervision meetings across four Australian universities.

Toby Miller is a research professor of the Graduate Division, University of California, in Riverside, California, USA; Profesor Invitado, Universidad Tecnológica de Bolívar; and Professor in the Institute for Media and Creative Industries, Loughborough University London. The author and editor of over forty books, his work has appeared in Spanish, Chinese, Portuguese, Japanese, Turkish, German, Italian, English, Farsi, and Swedish. His most recent volumes are *El trabajo cultural* (2018), *Greenwashing Culture* (2018), *Greenwashing Sport* (2018), *The Routledge Companion to Global Cultural Policy* (co-edited, 2018), *Global Media Studies* (co-authored, 2016), *The Sage Companion to Television Studies* (co-edited, 2015), *The Routledge Companion to Global Popular Culture* (edited, 2015), *Greening the Media* (co-authored, 2012), and *Blow Up the Humanities* (2012).

Pia Møller obtained her PhD in Cultural Studies from George Mason University and a Masters in Culture, Literature, and Gender from Aarhus University, Denmark. Formerly a lecturer at the University of Wisconsin-Milwaukee, she is now Program Director at a refugee organization in Rochester, New York, USA.

Gilbert B. Rodman is Associate Professor of Communication Studies at the University of Minnesota in Minneapolis, Minnesota, USA. He is the author of *Why Cultural Studies?* (2015) and *Elvis After Elvis* (996); he is also the editor of *The Race and Media Reader* (2014) and the co-editor of *Race in Cyberspace* (2000).

Josh Smicker is Assistant Professor of Communication at Catawba College in Salisbury, North Carolina, USA. His research focuses on the use of digital media technologies (video games, mobile apps, etc.) by the military to manage PTSD, and is exploring the genealogy of discourses of resilience, creative disruption, and "post-traumatic growth." He has presented at numerous national and international conferences, and his work has appeared in various publications including *Social Identities*, *International Journal of Communication*, and *Joystick Soldiers: The Politics of Play in Military Video Games*. He is also a former associate editor of the journal *Cultural Studies*.

Ronald Strickland is Chair of the Humanities Department at Michigan Technological University in Houghton, Michigan, USA. He writes on topics in cultural studies and the cultural politics of higher education. He is also the editor of a special issue of *HUMANITIES* (2018) on "Saving the Humanities from the Neoliberal University."

Megan M. Wood is a PhD candidate and Royster Fellow studying in the Department of Communication at the University of North Carolina Chapel Hill in Chapel Hill, North Carolina, USA. She teaches and researches in the areas of media and cultural studies. Her research broadly explores the interpenetration of culture, economy, and politics with an eye toward rethinking frameworks for understanding power and agency in the present context. Her major research projects have included investigations of the cultural politics of major corporations, the explanatory power of the figure of "the white working class" in light of the political events of 2016, and the implications of surveillance for gendered and racialized bodies in a "post-feminist" media culture. Some of her work can be found published in the journals *Cultural Studies, Communication Studies, Communication & Critical/Cultural Studies, Lateral: A Cultural*

Studies Journal, Review of Communication, Sexuality & Culture, Cultural Economy, the Duke Anthology Feminist Surveillance Studies.

Sindhu Zagoren is an assistant professor in the English Department at the Community College of Philadelphia in Philadelphia, Pennsylvania, USA, where she teaches courses at the intersection of communication studies, media studies, and cultural studies.

Cultural Studies, Teaching and Critical Pedagogy: An Introduction

Jaafar Aksikas, Sean Johnson Andrews, and Donald Hedrick

The present anthology operates with a very specific understanding of cultural studies as an intellectual-political project. We understand cultural studies as the contextualist and materialist study of the complex and multiple relations between cultural forms, ideological practices, political economic processes, and social formations. At the same time, we also acknowledge the wide range of ways in which cultural studies has been developed and practiced and include contributions that engage with both the specificity and complexity of the formations of cultural studies, as well as their multiple institutional contexts and locations, particularly in the US and North America.

The anthology assumes that cultural studies is also fundamentally a critical pedagogical project and that teaching and pedagogy have always been central to its practice, as well as to the kind of political knowledge

J. Aksikas • S. Johnson Andrews (✉)
Humanities, History, and Social Sciences, Columbia College Chicago, Chicago, IL, USA
e-mail: Jaksikas@colum.edu; sandrews@colum.edu

D. Hedrick
Department of English, Kansas State University, Manhattan, KS, USA
e-mail: hedrick@ksu.edu

© The Author(s) 2019
J. Aksikas et al. (eds.), *Cultural Studies in the Classroom and Beyond*,
https://doi.org/10.1007/978-3-030-25393-6_1

and organic intellectuals it has sought to produce since its early forma-tions in post-war Britain. But if critical pedagogy has always been cultural studies' main stage, it is one that most accounts tend to view from the wings, if not from the greenroom. A recent collection by Connell and Hilton (2016), looking at *Cultural Studies 50 Years On*, touches rather tangentially on the pedagogies and practices of the Centre for Contemporary Cultural Studies (CCCS) at the University of Birmingham. In an earlier article, on "The Working practices of Birmingham's Centre for Contemporary Cultural Studies" (2015), Connell and Hilton hint at the way the CCCS posed "challenges to established forms of pedagogy," but even here, they provide more of a narration of the way emergent trends and tendencies in theory and research collided with the interper-sonal and institutional, rather than an account of the actual practice of what occurred when one walks into a classroom, where actual cultural studies teaching and learning take place.

One reason for this may be that cultural studies—while also always essentially a political project—has always been the inverse of Eliot's Prufrock, in that there has never been time for "tea and cakes and ices," for it has always already been in a state of crisis. By this we mean not the productive intellectual crises that are the bread and butter of the field's histories, but rather the more concrete crises of material sustenance itself: of funding streams drying up, institutes being closed, the neoliberal ide-ology of branding, markets, and corporate sponsorship smothering the most productive experiments in critical pedagogical innovation before they could be recorded or even born.

Take Anne Gray's (2003) important essay on "Cultural Studies at Birmingham: The Impossibility of Critical Pedagogy?" as an example of the genre. Here, Gray briefly recollects, with enthusiastic nostalgia, her arrival at Birmingham in 1989. She says she was, "Pleasantly surprised by the attention paid to teaching strategies and the politics of pedagogy more generally" (771). For a couple of pages, she muses further at this meta-level, recalling the viral excitement around critical pedagogy—spreading from Henry Giroux in the US into Europe and beyond; she notes that her account mirrors that of Paul Gilroy's, who also speaks of these heady times, leveling the hierarchies of the university and challeng-ing structures of power and knowledge. But her only account of the actual teaching practices at the Centre is rather thin; we learn only that her classes were "delivered through fortnightly seminars rather than formal lectures and concluded with an assessed group project" and that her specifications for this final group project were similar to those Hall and Hoggart used in 1968, which was "a study of the new Birmingham shopping Centre, the Bull Ring, as a cultural expression of the spirit of the city" (p. 771).

Whether in Chicago, Illinois; Manhattan, Kansas; or Charlottesville, Virginia, there are spaces where one can imagine an assignment like this working, at the graduate or undergraduate level. But despite the fact that we know that students were assessed on this project, and that it was a group project, we are none the wiser about how the prompt was connected to the curriculum for the semester, how students were actually assessed, and which iterations worked better than others and why. And Gray's mode of description of teaching and pedagogy is far from unique in the field. Like many similar accounts, her story of the classroom, of love and friendship, and of discovery and collaboration, remains overshadowed by the story of the institutional struggles against reactionaries and what Franz Hinkelammert called "the ideological weapons of death," namely, the neoliberal capitalist incorporation of the university: Gray's immediate occasion for writing her piece was the sudden closure of the CCCS, so these nostalgic recollections are pitched more as an eulogy and less as a lesson plan. We might know the theoretical precipitate of the classroom conversations and student assignments at a higher level of abstraction, but we rarely get to see the concrete transcripts or rubrics.

Indeed, the whole field has hardly engaged these questions and issues in any systematic manner, and while critical, self-reflexive accounts on our teaching and classroom practices do exist, they largely remain scattered and rare. This collection seeks to help fill this important gap in the field. Though many of the actually existing accounts cannot help but place their classroom and curricular practice in the context of the aforementioned ugly institutional struggles—struggles which have only intensified since Gray's account—we hope that the contributions to this volume help provide that glimpse behind the classroom door, below the first line of the course description, and beyond the first page of the syllabus.

In most actually existing cultural studies work and practice—the radically contextualist war diaries we might call them—cultural studies has produced some robust analyses and studies of cultural formations and practices, and yet, the pedagogical implications of this work remain largely unrecognized. The anthology seeks to combine and highlight the theoretical and practical aspects of teaching by exploring and reflecting on the ways in which cultural studies is taught and practiced at both the undergraduate and graduate levels, especially in the US, but also internationally. It also seeks to be a space where connections among cultural studies practitioners across generations and locations are formed. Because the alliances built by cultural studies practitioners in the US and the Global North are deeply shaped by the Global South/Third World perspectives, we were keen on including the perspectives of teachers and practitioners in and outside of the US, including those who may offer a transnational perspective on teaching and practicing cultural studies. And yet, despite our attempts, the collection does remain largely US-centric and we can only hope that this collection will lead to the production of complementary accounts of teaching and pedagogical practices in cultural studies internationally.

If one of the legacies of Stuart Hall's classic "Legacies" essay is a response to his call for the "modesty of theory," and, responding to his addendum about the need to approach pedagogy more directly and forcefully, cultural studies has nevertheless been relatively sluggish in carrying out the project. In fact, it has been quite some time since important teaching-and-theory books from a cultural studies perspective arrived on the scene, primarily from the flourishing of theory itself, where the weight of attention has been on teaching theory. For instance, the essays in Cary Nelson's collection *Theory in the Classroom* (U Illinois Press, Nelson 1986), while addressing some content, such as popular culture or technical discourse, are primarily devoted to "problematizing interpretation," and therefore especially attend to theoretical "approaches" in the teaching of deconstruction, feminism, or psychoanalysis.

Considerable time has also passed since a collection from a later generation, Amitava Kumar's cultural studies oriented edited collection *Class Issues: Pedagogy, Cultural Studies, and the Public Sphere* (NYU Press,

Kumar 1997), was first published. More pedagogically "thick-descriptive" than previous studies, Kumar's collection did address teaching in the categories of literature, Marxism, and even beyond pedagogy into the practices of the public intellectual and public culture. And yet only one of its sections was on "cultural studies pedagogy," and of all its 21 essays, only 5 or so get down and dirty into real classroom labor and practice (e.g., the syllabus, course design, and countering resistance). The present anthology seeks to incorporate the ongoing concerns and theoretical challenges animating many of these earlier essays and collections across multiple institutional and national contexts, while also focusing attention on actual classroom practices themselves.

We include as wide a range of voices, practices, formats, approaches, positions, and interests as possible, so while the "traditional" academic essay is the predominant format, the collection also includes personal/ critical reflections on classroom activities and experiences, assignments, lesson plans, and exposition of courses and curricula. We intend this volume to stand as a statement about the centrality of teaching and pedagogy to what we do as cultural studies practitioners and teachers. We present here some of the best current practices and reflections on teaching and pedagogy in the field and hope this work will not only inaugurate a new genre in the field—a genre of writing devoted to a sustained engagement with our everyday practices as teachers and learners in the field—but also, and probably more importantly, will help us value, appreciate, and do this type of work more.

As we were reading through the essays in the volume, with a view of grouping them together, it became quickly and increasingly clear than no conventional table of contents or categorization could honor their complex and many overlapping commitments, interventions, and interconnections and the many other possible ways they could be grouped together. We initially considered presenting the essays in their alphabetical order, according to their author's last name, without any further divisions or groupings. However, we also saw value in adopting a fairly general sectional grouping that would help our readers to see interconnections and relationships among the essays more clearly and more productively. We have grouped the essays into three general categories: "Pedagogy and Teaching in Cultural Studies: Critical Groundings,"

"Cultural Studies Pedagogies in Practice: In the Classroom and Beyond," and "Cultural Studies Pedagogies in Context: Some Case Studies."

Part I: Pedagogy and Teaching in Cultural Studies: Critical Groundings

We open the collection with a lead essay (chapter "What Did You Learn in School Today? Cultural Studies as Pedagogy") by Lawrence Grossberg, one of the leading figures in cultural studies in the US and internationally. As the subtitle of the essay indicates, Grossberg jump-starts the conversation by presenting cultural studies not just as a specific intellectual-political project, but also as a specific pedagogical project, "at its heart." He takes an expansive view of pedagogy and teaching, moving beyond the institutional confines and practices of the classroom to include the deployment of the "resources of thinking" to intervene in concrete social and historical conjunctures and transform the ways we understand and act in the world. For Grossberg, cultural studies pedagogy, grounded in cultural studies specific and deep commitments to "complexity, contingency and contextuality," is offered as a wide-ranging, robust, conjunctural conversation about what goes on in our social world, without any certainties or guarantees.

This important intervention is followed by an equally important essay (chapter "We Are All Art Historians Now: Teaching Media Studies and/ as Cultural Studies") by international media and cultural studies scholar Toby Miller (currently the president of the US-based Cultural Studies Association). Here, Miller responds afresh to the question of what cultural studies and cultural studies pedagogy are and should be, but does so by drawing on his more than three-decade experience teaching cultural studies across multiple levels (graduate and undergraduate), disciplines, institutions, locations, contexts, and regions, and especially in the US, Colombia, and Britain. Miller introduces cultural studies as a specific intellectual-critical disposition, across the humanities, social sciences, and the arts, that seeks to analyze societies and cultures (both esthetically and anthropologically) in terms of the dialectic of subjectivity and power.

Cultural studies pedagogy, while bound to rely, at least in part, on traditional disciplines, is fundamentally critical, disruptive, and subversive of the largely functionalist pedagogical trends and tendencies of these dependent disciplinary contexts. But Miller also wonders, with a sense of lament, about what is missed and discarded by this form of exclusively oppositional pedagogy. Miller reflects on the centrality of newer forms of media to the teaching of cultural studies and, under these circumstances, concludes that we might better conceive of ourselves as art historians and rethink our uncritical, unreflexive, and largely institutionally imposed deployment of multimedia technologies in our teaching and pedagogy. Not only that, he calls for more robust forms of cultural studies, where multiple perspectives from critical political economy, textual studies, and critical ethnography and fieldwork are blended together to help us and our students understand the contradictory life of the commodity form and the totality of the media/culture circuit.

These two prefatory efforts are followed by a sharp self-reflexive contribution (chapter "Dear Progressive and/or Queer Students: A Pedagogical Polemic from Your Queer Adjunct Professor") from Jodi Davis-Pacheco, a queer cultural studies activist, writer, and adjunct professor. Written as a letter to her students, Davis-Pacheco's piece provides an excellent introduction to undergraduate students encountering the frameworks and dilemmas of cultural studies and the way they intersect with the newest fronts of the so-called culture wars. In particular, the essay provides a useful perspective on the emergent "call-out culture," which may be familiar to students from their experiences on social media and/or activism. It is a compassionate call for students to meet each other where they are in order to move us all to a common place of critical self-reflection and self-reflexivity.

Davis-Pacheco's essay is followed by the collectively written essay, where Lisa B. Y. Calvente, Mark Hayward, Josh Smicker, and Sindhu Zagoren offer a virtual weather report of university trends toward and effects of corporatization observed less forcefully and systematically some 30 years ago, though forebodings were certainly in the air. Their report is openly pessimistic at the institutional level, seeing two decades of funding loss, precarious employment and declining enrollment, superficial diversity, and the depoliticization, containment, or "kettling" of resistances.

Their own gesture of force against the behemoth advocates Deleuzian "minor" practices, proposing multiple strategies, including robust forms of collaboration and collective work. For them, limits in the form of constructing, carrying out, and evaluating a pedagogy designed for a more particular audience calls for forms of theoretical "modesty" that bring the broader contexts of institutionalization and historical conjuncture to bear on specialized pedagogies.

We conclude this part of the collection with an essay (chapter "The Impossibility of Teaching Cultural Studies") by Gilbert B. Rodman (former Chair of the international Association for Cultural Studies) about the struggles, challenges, or, as his provocative title suggests, the impossibility of teaching cultural studies. In a certain sense, Rodman elaborates on Grossberg's distinction between teaching and learning that takes place within the institutional confines and practices of the classroom, on the one hand; and teaching students to be organic, political intellectuals, who are able to intervene in concrete social formations and to transform the ways they understand and act in the social world they inhabit, on the other. Rodman insists that regardless of who the taught subject is—an undergraduate student, a graduate student or anyone/everyone else—it is impossible to teach students to be political intellectuals or progressive activists and that for our students to become either depends more on what they teach themselves and how they independently nurture their own intellectual and political investments.

Part II: Cultural Studies Pedagogies in Practice: In the Classroom and Beyond

We open this section with a timely intervention by Donald Hedrick (chapter "Cultural Studies as Writing Project, with Trump Assignment"). In this essay, Hedrick teases out what he terms a "micro-legacy" of Stuart Hall's famous talk on the "legacies of Cultural Studies," in Hall's stated allegiance to the "necessary modesty of theory." Exemplifying his position, he sustains discussion of the unacknowledged importance of metaphors, such as "struggle," "hegemony," and "interruption." Applying this claim to the matter of teaching, which Hall doesn't address, Hedrick flips over the privileged status of theory by treating writing and metaphorization, connected to practices of pedagogy, as primary. Trying out this proposal in an imaginative assignment to compare Donald Trump to capital itself, Hedrick attempts a number of parallels: branding, precarity, volatility, communicative capital, value creation, commodification of pleasures, Marx's universal prostitution, inequality production, and the ultimate absence of any social goal. While such an assignment might seem more playful than rigorous, Hedrick reminds us of Hall's claim that metaphors can be life or death matters. Hedrick's sample might open up a thread of possible cultural studies pedagogy through serious, radical, exploratory, and creative imagination.

In another hopeful vein, Ronald Strickland (chapter "Critical Pedagogies in Cultural Studies: On Teaching Marxism Online") offers an exemplary case of a limited but thorough-going pedagogical practice—a course with specific content taught in a specific way, in this case one that would not necessarily work for a regular departmental course offering. Building on the historical example of cultural studies beginnings in educational outreach and adult education, Strickland gives a fine-grained narrative account of spotting an opportunity to improve a graduate seminar, inviting guest lectures, and developing the subsequent filmed talks into an online course with 100,000 views for its Frankfurt School lecture alone. Sometimes resisting the recourse to individualism and a pedagogical consumerist model, Strickland draws from Ranciere's radical questioning of the teacher/student inequality which takes into account prior student knowledge, contending that shared focus on a text rather than on face-to-face learning benefits a "textualized and deprivatized pedagogical scene." As was the case for other essays in this volume, Strickland's story concludes with what might be thought of as a current cultural studies hope, that is, to not acquiesce to the "negative challenges of the current moment."

Basak Durgun (chapter ""Bringing the World to the Classroom": Cultural Studies and Experiential Learning") takes us from the world of experimental online learning to the world of experiential learning. She argues that experiential learning strategies are essential to making visible the structural and institutional political, economic and social injustices, to developing permanent critical thinking strategies and skills, and to promoting a learning environment grounded in social action and movement building. Durgun offers concrete examples of engaged, experiential learning, taken from several classes on identity, representation, and the environment. She outlines the possibility for students, in collaboration with teachers, to build the ability to engage different experiences, critical observation, conceptualization of problems and corresponding solutions through active experimentation and deliberation and critical self-reflexivity. By empowering students to reflect on their own positions and to express those reflections in an open artistic format, this model of learning challenges the conventional "banking" model of education as it attempts to define and meet the key critical goals of cultural studies.

Sean Johnson Andrews (chapter "Teaching Cultural Studies in the Undergraduate Curriculum: From the Abstract to the Concrete, and Back Again") provides a useful, critical self-reflexive account of his experience at the Cultural Studies Program at Columbia College Chicago, one of the more visible undergraduate cultural studies programs in North America. This program must contend not only with the recent transformations in higher education, but, housed as it is in an institution specializing in arts and media education, in the heart of the "creative city" of Chicago, must reimagine its critical theoretical project in the face of local institutional pressures. This essay discusses the core courses in the curriculum and the way they map onto the core assumptions of the field of cultural studies. But it also captures a moment in the life of a constantly changing institutional setting, suggesting a possible curricular configuration for similar institutions, even as it recognizes that the local changes and pressures are likely to transform this program, possibly beyond recognition.

We conclude this section with an important essay (chapter "Cultural Studies in Practice: Toward a 'Thick Description' of a Methodology Course in Cultural Studies") from Jaafar Aksikas (former president of the Cultural Studies Association). Here, Aksikas provides a unique "thick description" of the methodology course in that same bachelor's program in cultural studies at Columbia College Chicago (that his colleague Andrews talks about in the preceding chapter). Like most contributors here, he insists that cultural studies is not just a specific radical intellectual-political project; but is also a critical pedagogical project and practice, and that the work of taking seriously and reflecting critically on, as well as of widely documenting and sharing, our concrete teaching and pedagogical practices at the level of courses and classroom activities will yield some important benefits. He also sees cultural studies pedagogy as an important "way of struggle" in the current moment and presents his essay as primarily a call for the need to produce more systematic accounts and "thick descriptions" of the courses we teach; and secondarily as an intervention in the growing debates around issues of methodology and epistemology in cultural studies. Aksikas refuses to make any claims about the successes and merits of the course and warns against seeing his "thick description" as an ideal to be followed. Rather, he wants us to approach it as a singular example of what might get covered in a cultural studies methodology course, as one experimental response to the key questions: what is cultural studies? And what should it be doing?

Part III: Cultural Studies Pedagogies in Context: Some Case Studies

Moving to the very concrete, Pia Møller (chapter "Critical (Race) Pedagogy and the Neoliberal Arts in Walker's Wisconsin") opens this section with a rather detailed account of what it looks like to teach in the context of Scott Walker's administration of Wisconsin and its proposed revamping of that US state's higher education system, which was only the latest precipitates of old-established structural conditions. Her essay asks how educators can uphold critical teaching practices under administrative micromanagement and declining academic freedoms. Based on her experience teaching in the highly segregated city of Milwaukee, where the predominantly white students resist discussions of race and racism, she also considers what critical race educators can do about white racial bias in the classroom. Møller chronicles the results of several ad hoc techniques she has developed to engage her students critically and intellectually in this hostile and challenging environment.

Pablo Andrés Castagno's essay (chapter "Into the Factory: Teaching Cultural Studies as a Critique of Global Capitalism") provides an important international perspective on cultural studies pedagogy; it develops out of a larger Marxist problematic, which uses the post-industrial site of the Universidad Nacional de La Matanza—in an abandoned Argentinian Volkswagon and Chrysler factory—as a metaphor for the rote education of its 50,000 students. But he also contrasts this with the larger context of leftist political movements in Latin America. Castagno develops critical strategies to engage important debates on radical democracy, particularly in relation to the results of a workshop in which students explore the ways concrete differences in the social forces and social movements do not map readily onto the conventional subjects of political science. Castagno reports that these workshops create the potential for a resuscitation of the pink tide for a new generation, where students produce concrete, transformative knowledge when they analyze the many determinations of empirical reality and the social world.

Andrew Davis (chapter "Teaching Conjuncturally: Cultural Studies as the Practice of Conjunctural Analysis") and Megan M. Wood (chapter "Conjuncturally Teaching: Cultural Studies Pedagogy Beyond Common Sense") both draw on their experience developing and teaching the "Practices of Cultural Studies" undergraduate class at the University of North Carolina-Chapel Hill, the home of one of the most important doctoral programs in communication studies and cultural studies, to provide insightful and timely perspectives about the merits and limits of teaching cultural studies in the undergraduate curriculum at the current historical moment, one marked by deep crises of knowledge, agency, public memory, politics, and more. While these two chapters intersect with many of the contributions in the volume, they are written in immediate dialog with each other and are, therefore, best read together. Davis contends that students benefit most from a course designed—from syllabus selection to reading assignments to student projects—around an understanding of cultural studies as a specific intellectual-political project, one that is grounded in the practice of radical contextualism and conjunctural analysis. Wood's chapter further situates the aims of the course Davis describes within a contradictory conjuncture for the promises of both the university and neoliberal higher education and the ideals of substantive democracy and offers valuable insights into students' experiences in the context of the course. Like Davis, Aksikas, Grossberg and others, she does not approach the question of cultural studies pedagogy narrowly, but suggests that it must extend well beyond formal education and the classroom, seeing cultural studies pedagogy as radically contexualist and conjuncturally specific.

Liam Grealy and Timothy Laurie's essay (chapter "The Ethics of Postgraduate Supervision: A View from Cultural Studies"), grounded in another important international context, with a robust cultural studies tradition, addresses the Australian context of supervision of postgraduates for higher degree research (HDR). Using a critical sociological approach, they study a context beyond the cultural studies practices within the undergraduate classroom. Supervising research involves shaping the teaching practices of others, is more project dependent, serves students requiring more "determinacy" than Hall's allegiance to the field's "indeterminacy," and requires texts not preselected for a field's mastery. Grealy and Laurie, looking toward ways of improvement, examine research on collective responsibility and "learning alliances," always taking into consideration institutional and conjunctural political contexts, precarious employment demands and rewards, and even the possibilities of "joyful" affects for higher research.

R. Gabriel Dor (chapter "Public Pedagogy and Private Programs: Practicing Cultural Studies in Professional Education") introduces a quite different and usually omitted but nationally expanding context of cultural studies as taught for older, returning students in a private university's professional studies outreach program. While acknowledging many of the same cultural studies goals and orientations that Hall, hooks, and Giroux have defended throughout their work, Dor's experience teaching a small (3–13) class of motivated adults benefits from a pedagogy openly prioritizing personal experiences and social relationships in a learning community over short-term mastery of course content, structured around dull power points and standardized exams. Using a variety of methods and essays from media and cultural studies collections, and final projects on a media controversy, the course must still overcome student resistance to high theory and jargon, despite the fact that the students tend to be "disciplined and achievement-oriented learners." Dor hopes that such a personalized approach—"sharing subjectivities"—and a view that cultural studies must "adapt to survive," might counter the growing pessimism and cynicism about cultural studies in the "mass market model of neoliberal education."

A Few Concluding/Opening Remarks

Taken together, the following contributions seek to focus on cultural studies as a pedagogical project that rethinks, and in the process, brings new life to core practices and questions in critical pedagogy and teaching in the humanities, social sciences and the arts. To approach cultural studies in this way is not to address all the pedagogical work that has gone by that name, but to focus on some of the best pedagogical innovations, models, and thinking made available when a range of cultural studies teachers and practitioners are brought together to rethink the very meaning of pedagogy and teaching, and with them the intellectual, political and cultural for our current moment, a moment of deep crisis at all the levels of the social formation. We present here some of the ways we can begin to think about the multiple links, both theoretical and practical, between cultural studies on the one hand and pedagogy and teaching on the other, and invite—even urge—our colleagues in cultural studies to think of even more links and connections. At a time where both the university and cultural studies are everywhere under "existential attacks," paying serious attention to our actual teaching and pedagogical practices acquires renewed urgency; and critical pedagogy becomes, in the words of one of the editors and contributors, an important "way of struggle" against fundamentalist neoliberal capitalism (see Aksikas's chapter).

Works Cited

Connell, K., & Hilton, M. (2015). The Working Practices of Birmingham's Centre for Contemporary Cultural Studies. *Social History, 40*(3), 287–311. https://doi.org/10.1080/03071022.2015.1043191.

Connell, K., & Hilton, M. (Eds.). (2016). *Cultural Studies 50 Years On: History, Practice and Politics* (Rep. ed.). London/New York: Rowman & Littlefield International.

Gray, A. (2003). Cultural Studies at Birmingham: The Impossibility of Critical Pedagogy? *Cultural Studies, 17*(6), 767–782. https://doi.org/10.1080/09502 38032000150011.

Nelson, C. (1986). *Theory in the Classroom.* Urbana-Champaign: University of Illinois Press.

Kumar, A. (1997). *Class Issues: Pedagogy, Cultural Studies, and the Public Sphere.* New York: New York University Press.

Part I

Pedagogy and Teaching in Cultural Studies: Critical Groundings

What Did You Learn in School Today? Cultural Studies as Pedagogy

Lawrence Grossberg

I have devoted my adult life to teaching, more particularly to teaching cultural studies. As much as my passion for cultural studies involves a faith that better ideas, better knowledge, and better stories matter, that they are invaluable to any political project for social change, it also involves a deeply felt recognition that cultural studies is, at its heart, a pedagogical project.

I have always known that teaching is central to cultural studies, not only in the narrow sense of the institutional practices of the classroom,

I am deeply grateful to many of my students who have lovingly forced me to think about my own pedagogy. Most recently, I have to acknowledge how much I have learned from Andrew Davis and Megan M. Wood, whose commitment and intellectual rigor have pushed me further. I want to thank Paul Gilroy for generously sharing his forthcoming essay on Stuart Hall and for many conversations, and Heather Menefee for bringing John Trudell's piece to my attention. I also want to thank Ted Striphas, Jaafar Aksikas, and John Pickles for invaluable criticisms. Finally, I owe a debt I can never repay to Henry Giroux, whose political passion and insight have always made me think about the pedagogy of politics and the politics of pedagogy.

L. Grossberg (✉)
University of North Carolina Chapel Hill, Chapel Hill, NC, USA
e-mail: docrock@email.unc.edu

© The Author(s) 2019
J. Aksikas et al. (eds.), *Cultural Studies in the Classroom and Beyond*,
https://doi.org/10.1007/978-3-030-25393-6_2

but in the broad sense of pedagogy as using the resources of thinking to change the ways people (including ourselves) understand and act in the world. The heart and soul of cultural studies have always been defined by the ways pedagogies enable us to articulate thinking and socio-political change—in classrooms, the arts, popular cultures, and mass media,[1] in all sorts of conversations, intimate, institutional, and public, and in whatever media are available and promising to us. If the very possibilities of cultural studies have always to be understood conjuncturally, then the conjunctural demands *for* pedagogy, and moreover, for particular practices of pedagogy, have to be answered, even if always within the limits of the conjuncture. These questions of pedagogy—and education—have to be embraced as an inescapable part of the effort to construct cultural studies in the present moment, but again, the very question of pedagogy—and my own response to it—has to be understood conjuncturally.[2]

The Centre for Contemporary Cultural Studies (CCCS)—my own introduction to cultural studies—was built on a foundation of teaching, in a variety of forms and practices. As has often been remarked, each of the three major founding figures of British cultural studies—Williams, Hoggart, and Hall—began their careers in extra-mural and adult education (although Hall also taught at a secondary modern school). Hall's first book, *The Popular Arts*, co-authored with Paddy Whannel[3]—was written primarily for school teachers. Williams wrote extensively about how his experiences in adult education pushed him into questions of popular culture and communication on the one hand, and into the broader questions of what was to become cultural studies on the other. Hoggart and

---

[1] After leaving CCCS, I joined an itinerant, anarchist theater commune touring Europe. After returning to the US, I taught what were described as 'troubled' kids at the Bank Street College in New York by helping them use (primitive) video equipment to gain new perspectives on their lives and environs. Without realizing it at the time, these experiences helped me come to terms with cultural studies and its pedagogies.

[2] For my own efforts to analyze the contemporary conjuncture, see *Under the Cover of Chaos: Trump and the Battle for the American Right* (Pluto, 2018) and *We All Want to Change the World: The Paradox of the U.S. Left*. https://www.lwbooks.co.uk/sites/default/files/free-book/we_all_want_to_change_the_world.pdf

[3] Paddy Whannel was the Education Officer of the British Film Institute from 1957 to 1971. His role in the history of film studies and cultural studies, and his passion for education, has yet to be fully told.

Hall have similarly acknowledged the profound impact of their peda-gogical roots and routes.

CCCS was devoted to teaching. I remember Stuart Hall often talking about the Centre's responsibly to teachers, especially to colleges (as opposed to universities) and to what were then called polytechnics, and some of the material they produced and seminars they organized were directed to teachers in such institutions. Many of those studying/working at the Centre were themselves teachers at such institutions. The Centre maintained the interest and commitment to education throughout its history, and published a number of books directly addressing it: *Learning to Labor* (1977), *Unpopular Education* (1981), and *Education Limited* (1991).

But it went much deeper than that. I think for Stuart Hall, being a political intellectual was intimately and inextricably linked to being a teacher in the broadest sense possible. This link between scholarship and teaching, thinking and pedagogy, is one of the things that makes cultural studies uniquely powerful and appealing. It was the passion generated by the belief that both could be effectively made to matter if and only if they were inseparable that made an extraordinary impression on me (and that inaugurated my own passion for teaching, however often I think I fail) and on the audiences of early cultural studies events (in the US).[4] And, I have to admit, it was just this unique relation that I had the great fortune to experience in a number of amazing teachers—Jarold Ramsey, Loren Baritz, and Hayden White (none of whom quite knew that I would later understand them as reaching for cultural studies) in my undergraduate years, and Stuart Hall and James W. Carey as my graduate mentors.[5]

The everyday life of the Centre was in fact deeply and intimately involved with teaching as it tried to create new practices for graduate education—new kinds of seminars, new kinds of collective experiences,

---

[4] I am thinking particularly of *Marxism and the Interpretation of Culture* (University of Illinois, 1983) and *Cultural Studies Now and in the Future* (University of Illinois, 1990).

[5] To this list, I would add Richard Taylor and Paul Ricoeur, who nurtured my love of critical analy-sis and theory with true generosity and open-mindedness, but also the grade school and high school teachers, whose names I have unforgivably forgotten, who taught me to love reading and arguing. Each of my many wonderful teachers had their own expertise, styles, passions, and pedagogies. I could feel their pleasure, their passion, their intensity, and their intelligence in every class and every interaction I had with them. I have learned from some of the very best.

new forms of institutional practices. The Centre was also involved in some undergraduate teaching early on, where it similarly reached for new possibilities. All these experiments sought to enable, even to invent, new relations between 'teachers' and 'students,' new forms of authority, new syntheses of rigor and passion, new ways of distributing and acknowledging expertise while still respecting the broad political commitments (because there were a lot of very real and very passionate disagreements as well) that often bound people together. These experiments were usually compromises—among those present in the Centre, and dependent on what the Centre could get away with behind the back of the administration as it were—that satisfied no one completely, but the more important question was: Did they move the work of the Centre forward? Later they tried to extend this experimental attitude to pedagogy into a taught M.A. program and even a more formal undergraduate program. These extensions brought greater administrative scrutiny, limiting what they could do even more, but they never gave up the effort, even long after Hall left, even after the Centre had become a department (and gone through numerous transformations), until it was finally—arbitrarily? politically?—closed in 2002.

I want in my comments here to talk about cultural studies as a pedagogical project and pedagogy as the practice of a particular sort of conversation, one that is always multiple, complex, fluid, and ongoing, but also one that seeks not consensus but a dissensual 'unity-in-difference,' one that seeks a better understanding of what's going on and better stories of how we get out of this place, elucidating the possibilities of forging forms of strategic cooperation aiming to move toward something more humane. But let me be very clear here that I am trying to rearticulate the very concept of conversation into the present conjuncture, and the present political crises. By conversation, I do not mean to assume a process of rational, deliberative, or persuasive relations (although I do not exclude them as tactical efforts) but a more tortuous process of engagement by which we attempt to move people and to move with them, into new forms of community, new forms of political movements. It is a conversation simultaneously intellectual and political (although these are never equivalent or simply corresponding), discursive and embodied, a conversation into which we enter and attempt to contribute something that will move it along, however slightly, and a conversation that will (hopefully) continue beyond us in ways we could not have predicted.

Such a pedagogy need not appear exclusively under the sign of cultural studies, as if it belonged to cultural studies. I think such pedagogies are actively championed by some formations within feminist, anti-racist, antipatriarchal and anti-heterosexist, post- and de-colonialist, environmentalist, et cetera thinking, but such political commitments do not guarantee the kind of pedagogy I am here articulating as and to cultural studies. After elaborating such a pedagogy, I will address its possibilities in the college classroom and the public arena. I will conclude with some thoughts on the state of pedagogy in the current conjuncture.

Cultural Studies as Pedagogy

This is not the place for me to elaborate, once again, my argument that the specificity of cultural studies begins with commitments to complexity, contingency, and contextuality.[6] I want instead to talk about how such commitments might change the ways we think about pedagogy. And I want to begin by displacing the relation of cultural studies and politics in order to more carefully articulate them. First, although the desire for cultural studies is driven by political concerns in the first instance, and the 'success' of cultural studies is partly measured by its ability to open up new possibilities for struggling against the dominant tides of history and power and imagining possible futures, cultural studies has no guaranteed politics attached to it. It is too easy and too common to assume that the politics of cultural studies is guaranteed to follow certain 'progressive' values and visions. But if cultural studies is both an intellectual and an educative/pedagogical project, if it in fact recognizes that these are inseparable insofar as they are pedagogical, if it is built on a particular understanding of the nature of political struggle and

---

[6] For discussions of cultural studies, see Stuart Hall, *Cultural Studies 1983* (Duke University Press, 2016) and *Familiar Stranger* (Duke University Press, 2017). Also my own *Cultural Studies in the Future Tense* (Duke University Press, 2010); "Pessimism of the will, Optimism of the intellect." *Cultural Studies* 32–6 (2018); and "Cultural Studies in search of a method, or looking for conjunctural analysis." *New Formations*, no. 96/97 (2019), pp. 38–68.

possibility, such assumed guarantees are unwarranted—and conservative articulations of cultural studies are more than simply possible. This is because the pedagogy of cultural studies is defined by its intellectual project and commitments, albeit always deeply colored by its particular political choices. That being said, my own take-up of cultural studies is shaped by my own oppositional politics and by my own progressive commitments in the present conjuncture.

Second, to the extent that cultural studies is always articulated by and to politics, its politics is always conjunctural and pragmatic; it is not interested in attaching itself to some absolutist vision of the 'correct' and 'pure' politics. It has become all too easy and all too common to think that teaching cultural studies means educating students to a proper political experience/interpretation/judgment of the world, so that, in the end, teaching cultural studies comes to mean teaching social justice and the critique of capitalism. A cultural studies pedagogy will talk about how such structures and practices of inequality, injustice, et cetera characterize our realities, but that is only the beginning. Cultural studies is committed to being part of political and social change, but only through the mediation of the production of the best knowledge possible, of creating better maps that might open up alternative strategies leading to better futures, and better stories that might speak to people in ways that win them, however slowly and however compromised, to different political positions. That is to say, part of the uniqueness of cultural studies is that it does not presume to have a pre-constituted constituency; rather, it recognizes that politics works precisely by assembling new political constituencies. The differentiation between maps and stories is a tactical and unstable one. Maps tell stories, and stories provide maps. Maps provide the backstories as it were, vital information if we are to understand where we are and how we got here as the foundation for the strategic stories we imagine and tell. But this means, at the very least, finding a way out of the distinction between knowing and sharing/showing, between research and education, for as I will argue, they are both always imbricated within the same pedagogical conversations.

In such efforts to tell better stories, that is, to join in and contribute to the conversation in ways that enable us to keep thinking (and strategizing), one must take account of the nature of ongoing struggles—the forms, strategies, and effectiveness of all sides engaged in contemporary struggles for power. One has to move beyond what is see-able and say-able to discover the complexities that too often go unnoticed and unre-marked, the practices by which they are inaugurated and maintained, the contradictions that make their apparent taken-for-grantedness always contingent, and the ways that people are recruited into supporting them, often unknowingly (without assuming they are dopes, duped, or even worse, morally reprehensible).[7] But understanding contemporary com-plexities always demands knowing the history—both intellectual and political—that has both grounded and often been erased in the current conjuncture.

Cultural studies attempts to reconstruct the obvious, the taken-for-granted, not merely to change the ways we judge them, or even just to bring them into consciousness, but to problematize them, to problema-tize the larger contexts and temporalities that hold them in place and make them seem reasonable, unavoidable, or just the way the world is. It seeks not merely to make the invisible visible, to give voice to the unsaid and silenced, but to create the conditions for understanding why and how the world continues to be made in such (inhumane) ways. And for that, it offers a pedagogy that enables people to think about their lives and the contexts that make those lives possible. Therefore, it has to be concerned with what our intellectual and political practices communi-cate to those who we are attempting to reach and move.

Finally, cultural studies refuses the illusion that it is political activism or even politics by other means. Again, I am not denying that cultural studies is political; on the contrary, it seeks to provide better 'intel' for activisms—although these are never so neatly separate, being always in conversation and contestation—and therefore perhaps to enable more effective tactics and strategies. I believe the political engagement and mis-sion of cultural studies were prefigured in Stuart Hall's understanding of the (British) New Left, which was actually formulated originally by young

---

[7] I find it helpful to remember Foucault's observations that revolutions are defined and accom-plished not by the vanguard leading it but by those watching it from the sidelines as it were, trying to decide their own place and response.

émigrés in the UK.[8] The New Left called for: (1) a new analysis of the political, economic, and social relations and dynamics of 'our times,' which would (2) take culture seriously. Such work would provide the ground on which to (3) reinvent a new conception of socialism (and an expanded understanding of politics), what we would think of today in terms of economic *and* social justice, embracing freedom, equality, and difference together. This vision of political possibilities can only be realized if we (4) inaugurate a popular politics that connects with people's lives, that starts engaging with people where they are, and that makes questions of everyday life and agency central. It would not only embrace democracy, but heterogeneity, seeing the political struggle not as a battle between two warring camps but as a struggle to create unities-in-difference, new forms of social, cultural, and political assemblages. Finally, all of this depends upon (5) embracing another way of thinking, one that rejects any and all binary choices between oversimplified options (e.g., the old and the new, the left and the right, party politics and movement politics, the good guys and the bad guys) in favor of seeking a third, more complex position defined neither by a simple compromise nor by a dialectical synthesis. In political terms, Hall often described this as a strategy of "one foot in, one foot out," that is, as a partial connection, a tempered commitment. If I may oversimplify for a moment, I would suggest that the first two are the decisive purview of cultural studies, the next two are the point at which cultural studies reaches out to political struggle, and the final one is what provides the condition of possibility for all four and points us to the pedagogy attached to or imagined within this broader project.

There are three aspects as it were to this pedagogy.[9] First, it is a pedagogy of the conversation, not an ideal conversation but a real conversation built upon the ever-present possibility of being wrong and the reality

---

[8] Stuart Hall, "Life and Times of the First New Left." *New Left Review* II, no. 61 (January–February 2010), 177–96.

[9] This image of cultural studies as pedagogy puts it in conversation with other projects that articulate the intellectual, political, and pedagogical through notions of complexity, contingency, and contextuality. I am, however, not claiming that such sympathetic interlocutors are all simply versions of or equivalent to cultural studies. One powerful and influential example is Wendy Brown's *States of Injury* (Princeton University Press, 1995).

that conversations will change everyone involved. It is not merely the liberal conversation of pluralism (teaching the debates) or the postmodern conversation of sheer multiplicities.[10] It is a conversation embodying the democratic principle that all voices have a right to be heard, but qualifying that principle insofar as it recognizes that not all voices are equal or have equal authority, and that such judgments have to be made contextually by balancing the claims of various experiences and forms of expertise. Further, obviously, not all voices can win the day as it were, and no voice is guaranteed assent or leadership by virtue of its social position or moral virtue. The point of the conversation is not victory but moving the conversation forward, intellectually and strategically. The point of the conversation is to find a livable and useful order in the chaos, to find an organization of the multiplicities that is both possible and better (according to some epistemic and political values, which are themselves to be decided within the conversation). Cultural studies believes that conversations can move people, hopefully toward better—albeit always contextual—truths and possibilities. It is always a matter of finding the best available truths of the situation. Of course, failure is always an option—especially these days—but it becomes almost a foregone conclusion if we enter the conversation with the certainty of our own truths and values.[11] Certainty is what ends the very possibility of conversation. Certainty arises from simply affirming what we already know, from whatever it is that seems obvious to us, from whatever it is that we are willing (even required) to take for granted—whether epistemically, politically, or even morally. Certainty makes it almost impossible, offering no incentives—reinforced in the contemporary political and intellectual cultures—to admit that one might be wrong and to change one's position.

Second, cultural studies' pedagogy rejects any absolutism, the result of the articulation of certainty and simplicity. Cultural studies recognizes the necessary and specific complexity of determinations, contradictions, and agencies that define any context, as well as the possibilities of seeking

---

[10] I do not intend to re-assert the accusations made against 'the left' of illiberalism, brainwashing, and the denial of freedom of speech.

[11] Stories can always fail; they may fail because the pieces do not come together, or because they end with either a bang or a whimper.

collective strategies for making the future. The conversation that cultural studies calls for is never limited to cultural studies, or to any single, pre-approved set of voices. It is a conversation defined by a logic of yes…but, where the 'ellipsis/but' is not operating in the register of critique or the accusation of evil or complicity or necessary failure. It is not an act of exclusion or refusal. Instead, it is an affirmation, an invitation: yes … and … give me more. It is always about the complexities, the contradictions, the contingencies, the multiplicities, the relations among the many agents and agencies, among the many operations of power, the constructions of unities and differences, the competing possibilities of both order and change.

Third, one always needs to figure out where to enter the conversation, but even more important is how one enters, for there is I believe a distinctive voice of cultural studies. It is a voice predicated on uncertainty, humility, generosity, and, if possible, even a bit of humor (yes, even in the face of despair and monstrosity). But most importantly, it is a voice that recognizes that the task of such a conversation—its greatest contribution—is to enable us to go on thinking, not to settle for some new Absolute, some new Truth. It is a voice that embraces its own necessary incompleteness. Such a conversation is not dialogic,[12] a call and response, since its temporality is always uneven, nonlinear, and fractured. And it must always recognize the real inequalities, some reasonable and many unreasonable, of knowledge, experience, and feeling. Moreover, in conversation, while every contribution has to be received as a gift, not every contribution will be a useful or even appropriate response to what has preceded it. It is a conversation among people who are simultaneously equals and non-equals, where the necessary negotiation of identifying what matters where (e.g., claims of expertise) always constitutes it as reflexive and self-reflective. It is also not a call for a return to reason or civility, because it cannot forget the criticisms of the ways both of these have been imbued with and articulated to particular structures of power. It is a conversation imbued with passion, but a passion always tempered by the call to know better.

---

[12] I am thinking here of the Buberian tradition, rather than the Bakhtinian; the latter is closer to what I have in mind.

Stuart Hall

put it this way ... you have to be sure enough about a position in order to teach a class, but you have to be open-ended enough to know that you are going to change your mind by the time you teach it next week. As a strategy that means holding enough ground to be able to think a position out but always putting it in a way which has a horizon toward open-ended theorization.[13]

John Trudell, a poet and leader of the American Indian Movement, expresses it somewhat differently, talking about the difference between believing and thinking.

You can't do both. Either we're going to believe or we're going to think, and the difference is ... when ... we're thinking, energy is flowing, it's going where it goes, it's flowing. When we believe, we've taken that flowing energy and put it into the box that is limited by the definitions of the belief. So here's energy that should be going and finding its way into the universe so that we can create solutions, being put into the box of belief, and then every solution we attempt to come up with is limited by the box of belief.[14]

The conversation of cultural studies always attempts to convert believing into thinking. Cultural studies offers a voice, a voice courageous enough to speak against the tide, not only of the forces of inhumanity but also against those forces seeking—but often failing—to challenge them and redirect the tides of history. But this means, among other things, that we must know these histories, understanding what is old and what is new, understanding where there are both intellectual and political insights, and where we face failures and dead-ends. It seeks a voice passionate enough to defend itself against the taken-for-granted certainties of both sides, but humble enough to accept that it may be wrong—and always incomplete—and that, at the very least, it will need to change as it

---

[13] Cited in David Scott, *Stuart Hall's Voice*. Durham: Duke University Press, 2017.
[14] John Trudell, "I'm crazy?" U.S. Social Forum 6-24-2010. https://www.youtube.com/watch?v=ctUecTdPEO0

responds to the vicissitudes of the conversation itself and of the changing world in which it lives and which it seeks to reconfigure. This is cultural studies' pedagogical voice—whether engaged in public debate about political strategy or trying to reach students in a classroom. It poses at least two problems: how to get people to think otherwise (other than those embodied in the academy and the media), and how do you provide the "content" that will enable people to enter into the conversation in productive ways.[15]

Cultural Studies in the Classroom

I hope it is clear that I think that research and teaching are inseparable in cultural studies, and so the question of teaching cultural studies in the academy is crucial. Before proceeding, I have to at least acknowledge that there are people—usually not in cultural studies—who criticize its move from 'the new left' into the academy. They usually grab hold of Stuart Hall's statement, latching on to the word 'retreat'[16]:

> We thus came from a tradition entirely marginal to the centers of English academic life, and our engagement in the question of cultural change . . . we first reckoned within the dirty outside world. The Centre for Contemporary Cultural Studies was the locus to which we retreated when that conversation in the open world could no longer be continued; it was politics by other means ... But then, one always has to make pragmatic adjustments to where real work, important work, can be done.

But Hall's statement not only acknowledges the pedagogical impulse always inscribed in cultural studies, it also recognizes the contingent and strategic location of cultural studies. It starts with an awareness of the contingency and multiplicity of potential sites for the inextricable link of

---

[15] The intellectual left has too often failed to provide the intellectual, cultural, and political histories that form the necessary backstory and that might serve as resources for contemporary analyses and strategizing. This is a problem of popular media/journalism as well as of the 'content' of institutional education.

[16] Stuart Hall. "The emergence of cultural studies and the crisis of the humanities." *October* 53 (Summer 1990), 11–23.

pedagogy and knowledge production, but also of the changing availability and limits of such sites. The consequence is that there is always a need for pragmatic and contextual judgments about how to use different sites, for particular projects. While this is not the place for a map of the contemporary epistemic-pedagogical landscape—one would certainly have to include the continuing work of the trade union movement and NGOs, such as those dedicated to matters of law and justice, economic justice, environmental rights, et cetera—I do not mean to ignore the complicated relation between pedagogy and schooling.[17]

I have been teaching classes in cultural studies for a long, long time. Sometimes they have been more advanced, more focused classes, but mostly they have been 'introductory.' Sometimes they have been undergraduate classes, but mostly they have been graduate classes. And mostly, to be honest, I have never felt like I really succeeded, although I hope that at least some of my students would disagree. In fact, I have always found teaching cultural studies to be a somewhat impossible task. I am sure that this is partly my own failure, because some of my students have developed classes that seem more promising than my own efforts. So, what does it mean to teach a class in cultural studies? What are we trying to do when we teach cultural studies?

Unfortunately, the most common answers largely miss the point, even if they are often inscribed into 'textbooks.' Some assume we are teaching students how to read and respond to the current state of power, in particular, to an already defined set of structures and relations of economic and social injustice and inequality. Teaching cultural studies becomes a matter of getting students to see the world in 'politically correct' ways; we teach anti-racism, feminism, heterosexism, the critique of capitalism, et cetera usually within a set of predefined analyses and concepts. Others assume we are teaching students how to read power off of texts, as if meanings were permanently inscribed, often guaranteed by the politics of their origin, assuming an equivalence between discourse, meaning, and power. Just as commonly, cultural studies is reduced to a matter of theory—so we teach some canonical mixture of political and cultural theory,

---

[17] I am indebted to many critical pedagogy scholars, including Ivan Illich, Paolo Freire, Henry Giroux, Peter McLaren, Patti Lather, Mike Apple, Roger Simon, and Cameron McCarthy.

choosing from among the apparent chaos of modern and postmodern schools and authors, constructing some sort of canon from various traditions of critical thought (Frankfurt School, post-structuralism, post-modernism, etc.) or identifying cultural studies with whatever theories they conceive to be the new cutting edge, or simply offering up a list of key concepts (among the latest, biopower, ontology, rhizome), which, like Maslow's famous hammer, will always lead you to find what the tool (concept) tells you to look for. I have to say that many of the theories included in such constructions of a canonical field have, in my opinion, little to do with cultural studies except as interlocutors or positions against which cultural studies has constituted itself, at least in my own contexts of thinking. On the other hand, and more generously, theories and concepts may provide tools and resources useful to cultural studies in particular contexts. Finally, some people make cultural studies into a new (sub-) discipline or set of (sub-) disciplines, defined by some range of objects that have been ignored by or are outside the normal range of vision of existing disciplines (e.g., forms of popular culture, or new technologies, or regimes of power). The result is often that cultural studies becomes a survey of social and cultural activities (that students will find interesting?).

I hope it is obvious that these approaches actually avoid coming to terms with cultural studies. Cultural studies transforms the very organization of knowledge by insisting that its 'object' is the messy, multidimensional context. For cultural studies, the questions that demand to be answered, and the political struggles that need to be addressed, can only be known in the confrontation with the concrete, empirical, and discursive materialities of the context, always mediated by theoretical concepts that are viewed as tools that may or may not prove useful, but that are always likely to have to be adjusted to serve the needs of specific contexts.

So, what is to be done? Cultural studies—I do not claim it is alone—is about how to be a political intellectual rather than the proper politics of theories or theories of politics; it is an intellectual practice/attitude, a way of thinking, and a way of organizing a conversation so as to go on thinking. Teaching cultural studies means making this visible, hearable, maybe even desirable. However much I might agree with the particular ethics or politics on offer, I have trouble with the notion of a teacher as the model of an ethical or political subject who stands as a measure against which students have to judge themselves (usually as failures). As Tony Bennett and others have pointed out,[18] such pedagogies have a long and problematic history, operating by turning ethics or politics into normative systems of judgment. For cultural studies, the teacher is but one intellectual, part of a community, who struggles to find better questions, better tools, better analyses (maps), and better stories, who embodies the tension between—and the possibilities of articulating—rigor, passion, pragmatism, and humility—at the intersection of analysis and politics, in order to go on thinking. At the same time, I have no problem thinking of the teacher as an occasional and circumscribed expert, or as someone positioned to call out others' assumptions and certainties.

The easy part is to get students to understand that culture matters and, in the contemporary world, that popular culture and everyday life matter. The harder part, especially given the current, problematic status of knowledge and the levels of cynicism, is to get them to appreciate that ideas and knowledge actually matter as well. But the hardest part is to get them to know, deep in their bones, that the only way to understand how they matter is to be willing to question and to risk whatever they take for granted, starting with every certainty (no matter how obvious it seems to them), any faith in certainty, the very search for certainty.

Most students have been taught for their entire lives that there is always and only one right answer—often framed within a binary choice, which is to be found by clearing a way through all the messiness, reducing the overwhelming complexity to find the single, simple truth, interpretation, explanation. Such ways of thinking assume that, whatever the question, in the final analysis, it is all about some one thing and even that every question leads to the same thing (e.g., economics, class, patriarchy, racism). They have to be moved (we all do) to give up the assumption that they can know the answers in advance—whether they are guaranteed by theoretical commitments, political investments, or by apparently legitimated empirical generalizations. All of these, to use Hall's phrases, let you off the hook, let you sleep comfortably at night, thinking that the world is neatly wrapped up and explained. At the same time, abandoning 'truth'

---

[18] See, for example, Tony Bennett, *Outside Literature*. London: Routledge, 1990.

to relativism (it's all a matter of perspectives), cynicism (it's all a matter of politics), or the celebration of multiplicity for its own sake (it's all about modernist ontologies) are equally problematic.

Actually, the really, *really* hard part is to realize just how pervasive such ways of thinking are, how commonsensical they appear to be, even in the academy—among both faculty and students. How do you explain to students who have not yet really lived inside the over-disciplined and over-specialized academy what it means to be interdisciplinary?[19] How do you explain to students who have been educated for their entire lives to think in precisely the ways cultural studies criticizes, who have internalized academic habits and norms, why cultural studies thinks it is necessary to disrupt the everyday and structural conditions of labor in the academy? How do you tell students that they have to learn how to ask questions, and how to recognize what an answer looks like? How do you tell students who are seeking academic jobs that cultural studies is trying to teach them how to be an intellectual rather than a professional academic? How can we teach students if we do not take the contingency of the classroom seriously, if we do not engage with the students' own structures of beliefs, involvements, and investments?

They have to learn new ways of figuring out what questions to ask, how to construct the context or problem space within which one is working, which conceptual and empirical tools might help to answer those questions in that context, and how to arrive at a better story, opening up new possibilities of reconfiguring the present for another future. To do this, they have first to learn to think complexity, contingency, and contextuality, to think of a specific social reality as the result of multiple forces and struggles configuring the chaos into an organized structure of relations of power (i.e., there may be conspiracies, but there are always lots of them, as well as other forces, and chance, all working on the same reality). Students have to be gently convinced (we all do) to give up any and all appeals to homogeneity, unity, purity, wholeness, or rather, they have to understand that such realities are always contingent constructions, the results of articulating relations and organizing multiplicities, which yet

---

[19] See my "Seeking interdisciplinarity: The promise and premise of Cultural Studies." In *Cultural Studies 50 Years On: History, Practice and Politics* edited by Kieran Connell and Matthew Hilton. Rowman and Littlefield, 2016, pp. 123–33.

always retain their heterogeneity, their hybridity, their syncretism. Hence, any reality is always the space of contestations and possibilities, of many contradictions, struggles, agencies, and openings. Second, they have to learn to speak provisionally, with humility, accepting the uncertainty and incompleteness that is the very condition of knowledge. And third, they have to learn to recognize that interesting work and effective politics are not only collective and collaborative endeavors, but always risky and difficult.

All this brings me back to the question of how—how do you teach students to think outside the habits of both common sense and the academy? How do you teach cultural studies? Over the years, I have tried many ways: traversing political and theoretical literatures, constructing canons, creating genealogies, rehearsing different questions and problematics, staging arguments, et cetera. Increasingly, I have learned to teach cultural studies from my students. Somehow this seems appropriate. I have come, in recent years, to approach the task simultaneously in two ways.

First, I have learned from some recent graduate students (Adam Rottinghaus, Andrew Davis, and Megan M. Wood) who have serially and collectively designed an exemplary and effective undergraduate class, to emphasize, from the very beginning, that the practice of cultural studies is conjunctural analysis.[20] Conjunctural analysis might be figured as the construction of a context by mapping the lines of determinations and structures of relations that intersect at a particular point of entry (and hence, the conjuncture can be mapped by following these lines out from that starting point). The very practice of conjunctural analysis is the organizing principle that defines the structure of the class and the particular tools—theoretical concepts and research techniques—the students will need to carry out closely monitored collective and collaborative research projects. They learn cultural studies in the conduct of cultural studies itself. My own observation and experience suggests that this works better in undergraduate classes than graduate seminars. Without being too cynical, graduate students are often too involved in self-professionalization (aided by their departments no doubt), too dedicated to defining their

---

[20] See the contributions of Davis and Wood in this volume.

own individualizing (if not star-making) niche, and too unwilling to take the risk of giving that all up and really stepping outside their comfort zone. On the other hand, undergraduates for the most part have no disciplinary comfort zones to be transgressed.

Second, whether or not there is a canon of cultural studies, and to what extent such a canon can be or has to be 'diversified,' there are certainly particular authors who have had powerful and dispersed influences within and sometimes across different contexts. The question is not so much whom to read but how to read them: to figure out how they are an expression and response to their own context, and how they have been and can be taken up in different contexts. This is in line with Thomas Kuhn's notion of paradigm exemplars, which tell the scientist how to do normal science within a specific paradigm. The problem is that there is no "normal" cultural studies, or at least, what constitutes 'normal' cultural studies is less a matter of theoretical revolutions than of conjunctural specificities. It is impossible to say what cultural studies would or should look like in any particular context; this is the paradox of contextuality. But it is not impossible that particular exemplars of cultural studies can be understood and even appropriated into other contexts (because, as Kuhn himself later admitted, paradigms are not completely incommensurable). Hence, the second strategy is to learn to read cultural studies contextually, to understand any genealogy as embodying the project of cultural studies itself.

If I were able to start over, I would try to develop a classroom pedagogy of cultural studies that articulates these two efforts: doing a cultural studies of cultural studies' exemplars alongside the very attempt to do cultural studies. It is, I hope, a challenge that others are taking up and will take up as both the need for cultural studies and the risks and difficulties of professing and practicing cultural studies continue to grow.

Cultural Studies as Public Pedagogy

As I have said, cultural studies is a pedagogical project in any context, but these days it seems vital that we bring it into the public arena. However, rather than attempting to offer a template for such engagements, I want to take my own advice and offer instead a particular example of public pedagogy—the particularities of which may well be forgotten by the time anyone reads this.[21] There has been much controversy and struggle recently, in the US, over the presence of Confederate symbols and monuments in the South. One of the most visible has been on my own campus—Silent Sam. Silent Sam (the name appeared in the 1960s) is a commissioned, bronze statue of a confederate soldier erected in 1913 through the efforts of the United Daughters of the Confederacy, with private funds. It stood at 'the front door' of the campus of the University of North Carolina in Chapel Hill until August 2018, when protestors pulled it down after a year of protests. This act of 'removing' Silent Sam was, to some extent, predetermined by the lack of foresight and courage demonstrated by the university administration, who seemed more concerned with a reactionary Board of Governors and wealthy alumni/donors. This was not the first demonstration against Silent Sam; there was an intermittent history of such protests since the 1960s. In 2009, a graduate student re-discovered a speech made by Julian Carr at the dedication ceremony, a particularly ugly speech that defended and advocated white supremacy and described—even celebrated—his own recent, brutal treatment of a black woman not far from where the statue stood.

Protestors—most of whom were students, many students of color—asserted that this speech defined the meaning of Silent Sam, that it had always been and continued to be a paean to slavery and white supremacy, on a campus that had never truly come to terms with its own history in relation to the Confederacy, slavery, segregation, and racism. They argued that Silent Sam was a key site defining the history and landscape of a university that still refused to face up to the problems

---

[21] I think that similar questions and conversations need to be raised, for example, around the Me Too movement. There have been numerous interesting attempts to start such a conversation by JoAnn Wypijewski, Margaret Atwood, and many others. I have no doubt that such conversations are continuing—although they are also too often simply ignored or the authors castigated—but they seem too hidden to affect the actual course of events. These questions might interrogate the place of law and legal protections (including the ways colleges handle complaints of sexual assault), demands of punishment, the possibilities of personal change, forgiveness and redemption, the relation of suffering (and rage) to politics and the utility of shame and humiliation, the embrace of Twitter politics, and, most importantly for me, the question of how one changes what is clearly a sexist and heteronormative culture.

and challenges of racism. Their passion and willingness to act was inspiring, and many of their arguments about the still-hidden history of the university and its current policies were compelling. At the same time, much of their rhetoric was framed in a language that transformed the feminist maxim 'the personal is political' into a much more problematic belief that the political is personal. It was a language of victimage and suffering, measured in terms of feelings of comfort and safety. So one commonly heard descriptions of the feelings of sadness, discomfort, danger, and anger that people of color felt as they walked by Silent Sam. It is important that we do problematize these claims, and not assume that the meanings and resonances of these terms can or should be taken for granted, without denying their personal realities; they are no doubt expressions of highly complex but unarticulated experiences and commitments.

Many professors, graduate students, alumni, and staff supported the demand to remove the statue and continued to support the protestors after they had torn the statue down; some joined the protests at various moments. Some demanded that the protestors not be punished in any way. Many professors have spoken of and used the protests as a pedagogical opening, particularly in relation to the history of slavery and Jim Crow, and their continuing legacies in contemporary racisms and the recent 'mainstreaming' of white supremacy. They asked: How are these differences, these inequalities, these acts of violence and suffering, but also the struggles against racism, inscribed in our histories and on our landscapes, on campus and more generally?

My own relation to the protests was, I admit, more ambivalent. On the one hand, especially given the increasing visibility and voice of white nationalists and white supremacists in the current context, and the all too common retreats into cynicism, such courageous acts of resistance bring a moment of optimism into an increasingly desperate political situation. And such small victories are often necessary. On the other hand, they have to be understood in the context of larger—conjunctural and strategic—struggles. I thought the pedagogy of the struggle was quite limited and the questions that were raised were all too predictable (even if still important). I was concerned that we had not learned the important lessons from recent past struggles.[22] I wondered if the faculty had not abdicated its responsibility to initiate (or bring the discussion of the protests into) another conversation, which is perhaps just as salient in the present context.[23] That conversation would start by locating the current resurgence of racisms and the rise of white nationalism and supremacism

---

[22] A few years ago, students, staff, and faculty protested against the name of an academic building (Saunders Hall) after a man who had been a leader of the KKK. The protestors had wanted to rename it after Zora Neale Thurston who, in her later life, had been a member of the faculty of the North Carolina College for Negroes (now North Carolina Central University) in Durham. The result was that the name was changed—to Carolina Hall, as innocuous a name as one can imagine, and a small education presentation was mounted in the entrance hall. And the Board of Governors of the university declared a ten-year moratorium on renaming campus buildings.

[23] I know, through my own conversations, participation, and research, that some versions of the sorts of conversation I am calling for in the paper do take place. I also know that I am overgeneralizing to some extent in the following comments and that there are important exceptions to my criticisms. Nevertheless, my sense is that these conversations often take place locally, around the tactical choices for a particular struggle or event, or among particular dimensions and communities of resistance (e.g., Black Lives Matter), or even just among friends. Often, they assume that real conversations can take place through social media. In some locations, such as the Social Forums, they are taking place in larger communities and contexts. But such conversations do not generally include the full range of voices (including intellectuals/experts, and those with longer histories of experience of opposition). I do not think they do enough to invite and embrace disagreements. I do not often see a willingness to risk the possibility that their certainties may not be right or, at least, may not define the best strategic options. I do not see them questioning the relations between analyses and strategies, and between strategies and tactics.

Moreover, given the context of the continuing victory of the conservative/capitalist agenda, and the recent victories and voices of reactionary right formations, these conversations cannot remain only local or uni-dimensional (and I do not think intersectionality solves the latter problem) or limited to pre-defined political communities and struggles. There has to be a way to make the conversation national and even regional—and that requires us to move beyond our assumption that we already know what is going on in these larger contexts. While the right has, for 60 years, found ways to manage, organize, strategize, and even at times control (the Tea Party has destabilized its ability to do this) its own internal chaos, the opposition continues to operate with what I might call an imagined anarchic unity. Again, I am not calling for homogeneity and consensus, but for better maps and stories, for strategic thinking and a cooperative politics that articulates the many struggles, that recognizes but is not ruled by heterogeneity, difference, and dissensus: unities-in-difference.

And perhaps most controversially, I think such conversations have to involve serious self-criticism. Given the ongoing successes of conservative/capitalist efforts to redirect and reshape the political culture of the nation, they have to be willing to ask why, despite the real battles that have been won, the progressive, oppositional forces seem to be losing the war or, at the very least, seem to have to fight the same battles over and over. We need to recognize and celebrate what feminisms, anti-racism, anti-militarism, environmentalism, et cetera have accomplished but we also need to be able to ask, critically but in solidarity, about the limits of the politics of the last 50 years or more. At the very least, can we not start by admitting that we have often failed to change the culture within which racisms, sexisms, consumerisms, militarism, xenophobias, exclusionary nationalisms, et cetera continue to assert or re-assert themselves—in popular culture, politics, and everyday life?

in the struggles over political culture that have defined the US (at least) since the 1960s. Understanding these struggles would require us to consider the ongoing and significant victories of right-wing politics as at least in part the result of long-term strategic conversations, alliances, and actions. But it would also require us to reconsider the successes and the failures of liberals, progressives, leftists—both in terms of party politics and social movements—and to ask why such heterogeneous forces have largely been unable to mount an effective opposition to or to stop the increasingly conservative and even reactionary directions of US society. It would do just what cultural studies tries to do: to offer better stories about what's going on, so that one might find better ways of actually affecting the tides of change. It would raise some very different—and difficult—questions about the struggle itself, its assumptions and tactics, in the present conjuncture, not in order to criticize what has been done (there is little point to that) but to open up the possibilities for thinking in the future. In the present climate, I feel it necessary to say: I offer these questions (and I do not claim to know the answers, or that cultural studies has answers already formed, even if it sometimes sounds as if I think I do) to enter into or, perhaps, to initiate a conversation.

1. What are the strengths and limits of symbolic politics *in this context*? What can it win, and what might be its unintended consequences? How is it articulated to other struggles against racism and the larger reactionary and conservative rights? How is it even articulated to the deeply inscribed racisms of the university, which continues to think of diversity as a marketing strategy, which continues to pay its service workers significantly less than a living wage?

2. Are meanings so singularly and transparently inscribed upon texts (monuments) and landscapes, once and for all time? Have there not always been multiple, contested meanings of Silent Sam for different audiences? Even at the dedication ceremony in 1913, there were other speeches that seem to have challenged Carr's white supremacism. What does it mean to claim the power to close the struggle over meaning, to demand that one's experience—often offered in the name of an assumed collectivity—is fully determining? The struggles

over contested meanings demand something other than declarations of certainty and self-righteousness.

3. Ought we to raise questions about going beyond the deconstruction (in this case, quite literally) of specific histories in order to construct multiple counter-histories, to rewrite the landscape as it were as a more complicated field of struggle. Rather than 'settling' for the absence of Silent Sam, how might we endeavor to commemorate the overwhelming presence of black histories?[24]

4. Does the fact that politics has become increasingly affective—that it works on and through structures of feelings, mattering maps, et cetera—justify the claim that the primary stakes of politics are affective?[25] What's the relationship between affect as a landscape of struggle and strategy, a set of political demands, and the certainty that determines truth and politics in the last instance? What are the implications of a politics based in personal experience or feelings of suffering, discomfort, and danger? Progressive intellectuals and activists, especially feminists, have argued before about the dangers of a politics of victimage and comparative suffering. Aren't appeals to feelings, like any other form of certainty (because they are not challengeable), more likely to close the conversation prematurely? Might we not, following Fanon for example, use our multiple histories of suffering and our common capacities to both feel and abhor suffering, to forge new assemblages, new unities-in-difference?

5. Did the discourse of the protestors adequately capture the complexity of race and racisms in the US? While I do believe that many if not most people raised in the US have racist thoughts and even habits, I think that many if not most of them perform their racism non-consciously and without consenting to it. At the very least, there are many different ways people enact and consent to the many different forms of racism. Not all people who may still accept, even unwittingly, the effects of racism are white supremacists. It

---

[24] For example, circling the statue or perhaps the entire quadrangle on which it stood, with remembrances not only of slaves but of civil rights struggles, of musicians and artists, of scientists and intellectuals, of leaders and politicians.

[25] For a discussion of affect, see my *We Gott Get Out of this Place* (Routledge, 1992), *Cultural Studies in the Future Tense*, and "Pessimism of the will, Optimism of the intellect."

does matter how one thinks about difference[26] and racism—whether one recognizes its complexity and conjunctural specificities. And it is not merely a matter of intersectionality but of the multiplicity and syncretism of any identity/identification.[27] The work of building an innovative and effective movement against racism has to reject the simple binary that says people are either committed anti-racists (in already defined terms) or at least complicit in racism, or simply racists. It is in the middle, where people are ambivalent, uncertain, not self-conscious, or apathetic, that the real challenges lie.[28]

6. If politics involves constructing constituencies and popular consent, trying to win fragmented and contradictorily invested subjects to the possibility of new positions and of different organizations of the space of possibilities, then how do we create and continue conversations toward democracy and justice? Is asserting that everyone who does not automatically agree with you, who might even oppose or resist you at the beginning, is the enemy, likely to be an effective strategy? Is configuring the political field as a simple binary division between camps, us and them, victim and privileged, a useful way of organizing the struggle? Or are such strategies (e.g., despite denials, they often fall into black suffering, white privilege) too simple, too certain, destined to close the conversations? Certainly 'privilege' is never as simple as it sometimes seems, (It is worth recalling that the

---

[26] I am thinking here of the absolutely crucial work on race and racisms by such thinkers as Stuart Hall and Paul Gilroy. Both argue that race and racism have to be understood as always syncretic, fractured, multiple, processual, and contextually specific. Additionally, Gilroy has argued persuasively that race as a political category (as opposed to a cultural discourse) is always and only constructed in the struggles of racism and raciologies. See the collection of Hall's essays on race, forthcoming from Duke University Press, and Paul Gilroy's *Against Race* (Harvard University Press, 2002), a rather misleading title. For a popular version of these arguments, see Asad Haider's *Mistaken Identities* (Verso, 2018). There is, additionally, in recent literatures, the question of what one might call the ontology of difference—as negation, positivity, singularity, exception, positionality, ambivalence, displacement, et cetera.

[27] As often happens, I think there is a gap between how the concept is introduced (in this case, by authors like Kimberle Crenshaw) and how it is taken up by others in a variety of contexts.

[28] One way to think about the range and specificity of racisms is to start with the notion of whiteness as a 'norm' in US society. But as Foucault and others have taught us, norms can take many forms and operate in many ways, always contextually.

white supremacists marching in Charlottesville were shouting anti-Semitic slogans).[29]

7. While politics might be grounded in moralities and feelings, how they are articulated in any conjuncture is a strategic question. One might suggest that, in recent memory, the civil rights movement, for very conjunctural and tactical reasons, strongly equated politics and morality, but one can also ask whether such an equivalence is the best strategy in the present context. Is the answer somehow obvious, or already sewn up? We must ask: Is the equation of politics and morality, the reduction of politics to a moral struggle between good and evil, a viable strategy? What is the best—contextual—articulation of morality and politics today? What are the differences and relations among moral witness, pedagogy, and strategic politics?

8. What is the meaning, goal, and practice of civil disobedience in the contemporary context of struggle? Can such forms of resistance demand that actions have no risks (such as arrest) or consequences beyond those intended?

9. What other histories and geographies—of fear, threats, silencing, protests, et cetera—might be brought into the current conversation?

10. Finally, in summary, and perhaps most importantly, at least from my own perspective on cultural studies, what sort of understanding of the importance of culture and of how cultures can be changed are being enacted here?[30]

It is reasonable to ask why such pedagogical conversations are not taking place, or at least, why they are not particularly and publicly visible, and why it sometimes feels that they are impossible, or that they have largely been silenced. It's all too easy to blame the current reactionary turn and the longer-term conservative shift on some singular conspiracy, or on some fraction of capital or on the stupidity or racism of anyone who does not share our position, or on technology (while with the other face, hoping the technology will unleash some liberatory and cooperative

---

[29] Many Jewish intellectuals, myself included, have received death threats recently. I would hope that my comments here are taken, not as coming from a simple position of privilege, but as a gift offered on the basis of research, thinking, conversations, and, yes, experience.

[30] See, for example, Ted Striphas, "Known-unknowns." *Cultural Studies* 31 (2017).

General Intellect).[31] It's a lot easier than considering the changing contours and conditions of intellectual production, and the changing cultural economies of the academy as, perhaps, still the major site of intellectual and pedagogical labor.[32] It's a lot easier than coming to terms with the conjuncture, its complexity and contradictions. And it is certainly a lot easier than having to look at the ways our own tactics and strategies, our own discourses and conversations, are part of the context, part of the calculation as it were, which is not to say that they are to blame for or even complicit in the dominant configurations of power.

I know too many intellectuals and teachers who have succumbed to the weariness that results from feeling that we have had these arguments and struggles many times before and yet they seem to have been forgotten and their results erased. Perhaps some (myself included?) are afraid of being attacked for what are seen as 'politically incorrect' or even complicitous positions, as expressing some form of the privilege of the dominant, or as dinosaurs representing some old mealy-mouthed liberalism. For example, I know that many people who both support anti-racist struggles and have questions about contemporary tactics increasingly feel the pressures of what my friend Ted Striphas calls a "public compulsion to perform 'being-in-line'" as a condition of inclusion in a political community.

Perhaps some of us hear echoes of the memories of our own college struggles in the 1960s, and we are afraid that we sound too much like the professors in that decade who opposed the many new social movements. But such concerns have to be faced and addressed in the context of the changing conjuncture and the changing fields of political struggle. Those liberal professors in the 1960s operated in an affective landscape of optimism, which they shared in some ways with the social movements, but while they thought things were getting better and would inevitably continue to do so, the movements thought 'not so much.' Today, we speak

---

[31] While I agree with those who are increasingly pessimistic about whether the changes in the political and cultural economies of the university have virtually eliminated the possibility of doing the sort of work/teaching I am advocating, I think there are too many who seem to think that technology will transform both the micro-practices of research/writing and the constitution of intellectual communities.

[32] See my "Tilting at Windmills: A Cynical Assemblage of the Crises of Knowledge." *Cultural Studies*, 32–2 (March 2018).

from within a much more overpowering landscape of pessimism. Those liberal professors did not understand the crucial role of social movements, nor did they have to face the overwhelming failure of the political establishment and the cynicism that has resulted (partly the product of the very forces that benefit from cynical disinvestment); they did not understand the absolute centrality of culture in contemporary politics, or the possibilities of a popular politics. Things have meanings and effects only in context, and as contexts change (and also, in part, do not change), so do the possibilities of tactics, strategies, and even conversations. That is the difference, for me, that cultural studies makes. Cultural studies is not liberalism by another name, but it does say that these are risks we must take.

Teaching in the Conjuncture

In concluding, I want to consider some broader questions about pedagogy, education, and teaching in the present conjuncture. But any discussion has to begin by acknowledging that as culture has become a primary battleground of political struggle, even the condition of possibility for further political struggle, the very possibility and status of knowledge has been called into question and with it the legitimacy of the academy. But the legitimacy crisis of the academy is not only the result of partisan struggles (and our own intellectual arguments and failures[33]), but also of the dissolution of that which separates us from journalists and documentarians on the one hand and activists on the other. At least part of the academy seems increasingly to be competing with these other groups, while often saying pretty much the same things.[34] We no longer seem able to answer the question: What is it that we as academics can or should

---

[33] Ibid.

[34] As Megan M. Wood has pointed out to me, the internet has given rise to the almost immediate production of 'crowd-sourced' syllabi that respond to the immediate demands of the situation, such as Trump's election, or the white supremacist and anti-Semitic rally at Charlottesville, VA, in August 2017. The problem is that all too often, such 'syllabi' respond to these immediate events by presenting you with everything you need to read to reaffirm what you already think you know, reinforcing the conditions of certainty. They almost always presume to know in advance the questions that need to be posed.

do? Cultural studies might suggest that this is, in part, a matter of the temporality of the academy—both in terms of its work and its focus. I have elsewhere distinguished between three political-historical temporalities: the situation, the conjuncture, and the epoch.[35] The situation is the time of the 'now,' the immediate moment, and it is often experienced with the greatest sense of urgency. And it is, I believe, the realm of the journalist and the documentarian and, often, of certain kinds of activisms (deposing Trump, winning elections, saving immigrant families, etc.). These are obviously important struggles and require particular kinds of knowledge and stories. The epoch stands at the other extreme—the relations of power that have been established, however fluidly, over centuries. It often defines the concern—or at least the moral foundation—of many activists who seek to overthrow capitalism, overturn patriarchy, put an end to racism, reconstitute the environmental ways of living of modernity, et cetera. Epochal struggles also require particular—different— kinds of knowledge and stories. As I have suggested already, cultural studies is concerned with the conjuncture—with the changing relations of power constituted, usually over decades, by the articulations of many different forces and contradictions. Unlike the situation, which is impossibly overdetermined, and the epoch, which demands abstracting particular forces from the complexity of determinations, the conjuncture is constituted precisely as an intellectual and political site where we can grasp and transform the complexity into manageable stories and effective strategies.[36] But as a result, the work of cultural studies takes time: it cannot operate at the speed of popular media (and hence, it must be wary of adapting itself to these new technologies), nor can it take the time required to produce the sweeping panorama of social history. It knows that it must take the time to negotiate the complexity but that it must also limit that time, so as to offer its carefully considered maps and sto-

---

[35] See my "Cultural Studies in search of a method, or looking for conjunctural analysis."

[36] Thus, when I say that the task of telling better stories about the conjuncture demands that we embrace the complexity, I do not mean to suggest that the work of conjunctural analysis is simply a matter of amassing more and more empirical detail; rather it is about finding structure in the complexity, order in the chaos. If we are committed, as I believe cultural studies is, to a popular politics that speaks to people where they are, then we will have to find ways of telling stories that people can both understand and care about. We need to find ways of telling simple stories that capture the complexity. Isn't that just what the best story-tellers—the best historians—do?

ries, aiming to both suggest possible interventions and continue the conversation and transform the conjuncture.

So, with the aim of continuing the conversation, let me admit that teaching has always been something of a mystery to me, despite over six decades as a student and close to five trying to be a teacher. I love teaching, although sometimes I hate it. Sometimes I know I have succeeded, sometimes I know I have failed, but most of the time I really just don't know. In fact, I am not sure I know what I mean by success and failure, or how to judge or measure it. Do we buy into current metrics that reduce quality to outcomes, but absolve ourselves of possible guilt by simply changing the outcome we desire? Instead of making students into consumer goods or potential employees, we define our desired outcomes in political terms, making the classroom into a tool of political recruitment.[37]

Yet I know that, like everything else we do, a teacher is certainly not in control of the outcomes (at least not those that matter beyond the immediacy of students' 'performances'). We can never guarantee what our students take away from our classes or interactions—in part because we don't know where they are starting from or where they are going. (I remember early on in my career reading somewhere in Roland Barthes that the one thing a professor should never do is to look at his or her students' notes.) I often find that my own understanding of success changes from class to class, from year to year, and from decade to decade. But is 'success' even the most relevant question to be asking?

---

[37] When I taught my graduate seminar in cultural studies in Spring 2017, I proposed using the class to at least think out what a conjunctural analysis might look like, one which begins with the moment of Trump's selection, but seeks to open up to and construct the conjuncture. In addition to trying to introduce the students to the project of cultural studies, the students were divided into groups defined by their own (common) interests, to research some of the vectors that one might follow out of the election into the larger contexts. I keep asking myself if it was a success. Unfortunately, perhaps predictably, a majority of the students were unable to leave aside their own research questions and professional identities. On the other hand, for some of the groups—on race and class, for example—the work actually led them to change the questions they posed, and as a result, they actually learned and taught things they/the class did not already know. Some of this work has been published and contributes to the conversation that I keep hoping will emerge. In addition, I should acknowledge that the class certainly helped me write my own book (*Under the Cover of Chaos*. London: Pluto, 2018).

There are so many questions one can ask about teaching, especially in the current conjuncture. Struggles over education have taken on a whole new importance and passion—and have become part of the popular political agenda—since the Cold War and the rise of the New Right, which is not to say that education has not been a political touchstone in a highly divided, partisan nation before. New conservatives like William Buckley and Allen Bloom understood not only that education was ideological but, perhaps even more importantly, that culture mattered. ("Politics is downstream from culture," as Breitbart noted.)[38] While the left tends to think politics precedes culture and therefore understands culture almost entirely in ideological terms, the right is actually more attuned to the need for more conjunctural understandings of culture, enabling them to foreground the politics of affect (feeling) as perhaps the key linchpin in the struggle to redefine and reorganize the political field (and the relations of common sense and political positions). And they have made education one of the major sites of partisan struggle at every level, from institutional finances, to curriculum, to teaching practices.

Partly as a result of the politicization of education, but only partly, teaching has become ever more precarious in a variety of ways. It is increasing devalued and disrespected in the public (and governmental) arena, and I am not sure about how it is viewed in the academy. While teaching is, in one sense, the public face of the academy, it still remains less valued for many within the academy. When I began teaching, an administrator in my department warned me that students "just got in the way" of an otherwise enjoyable job, and further warned me not to put too much time into my teaching because strong course evaluations might speak against my tenure case. I doubt that anyone would say that today, at least not in public. But do we actually take teaching as seriously as our research today? We continue to act in ways that prioritize research as both the true locus of passion in the profession and as the criterion of judgment for success. I have rarely heard a young scholar suggest that he or she had to devote their full attention to teaching in order to gain tenure.

---

[38] Buckley famously refused to support Goldwater's presidential campaign in part because he suggested that the right had not done the analytic and educative work necessary to create a new constituency enabling the country to be moved to the right in particular ways.

But the solution is neither to privilege teaching over research nor to pretend that we can achieve some real balance between them. As long as we think we can separate our research and teaching (even if we are teaching our research), I do not think such valuations will change. But there is an important difference between seeing the articulations of our teaching and research, and defining our teaching by our research, rather than by the need to introduce students to broad bodies of knowledge and multiple ways of thinking.

Whether one grasps this relation depends upon how we understand the point of education. Are we training students to be good workers, good citizens, or good people? Everyone claims to be teaching students to think, but they define thinking in very different ways (and adding 'critical' does little to clarify the differences): thinking as an ability to adapt to the changing demands of an evolving economic sector; thinking as the embodiment of certain processes of rational decision-making; thinking as the inculcation of particular habits of moral and political judgment. If the first reduces education to matters of economic survival and corporate power, the second assumes that social life is a process of rational decision-making, while the third position makes education a project of constructing 'proper' subjects (where each particular moral-political project defines its own propriety, its own sense of adequacy or, in some cases, inadequacy). In this third, increasingly visible, vision of teaching, teaching is too easily measured by our own sense of political self-satisfaction, by the appreciation of those (resisting and insurgent) groups whose politics we support, and by how much we have strengthened or transformed the pedagogical subjects.

I suppose it is already clear that I have problems with the over-politicization or, better, the too quick and easy politicization of pedagogy, with the idea that we are supposed to make our students better moral/political subjects. I am not sure that teaching—or politics—should be reduced to a matter of subjectivity or that the role of teaching is defined by moral and political concerns. More importantly, I have trouble with an all too easy articulation of knowledge and politics; knowledge is no more transparent, and its politics no more guaranteed, than any other discourse. We do not know what we know without the extraordinary labors embodied in conversations. From the other side, I wonder whether many academics, especially those working in public institutions, are capable of justifying their actual research or teaching programs, or at least of explaining why the public should be paying for them to teach students, for example, how to overthrow capitalism. This is not a call for the legitimation of the humanities or of critical thinking, or of the cultivation of capacities; nor is it a call for abandoning the effort to enable students to see the world differently, to question their own—and others'—certainties. It is a question about the ways we understand and represent our own pedagogies and the potential contributions of higher education.[39]

In recent years, many serious debates about pedagogy have been displaced onto the question of different practices of teaching, and the 'atmosphere' of the classroom. One can distinguish many styles of teaching, and the many forms of authority to which they can be articulated: on the one hand, lectures, discussions, skills training (often claiming to instill in them the capacity to learn, making them into permanent students as it were), and 'active learning'; and on the other hand, various forms of elitism (from expertise to absolute hierarchy), representation (speaking for those who cannot or are not allowed to speak), dialogics (empowering others to speak), and egalitarianism. Too often, these forms of classroom practice and authority are presented as exclusive choices, rather than recognizing that one might have to adopt different practices in different contexts, for different questions. At the same time, the relations between these two dimensions of pedagogical practice are often assumed in advance, for example, assuming that active learning is in some sense egalitarian, making students into co-producers.

It would be easy to look back at the early efforts of the CCCS as experiments in active learning, but that would be too simple, too decontextu-

---

[39] Recent attacks on critical academic research—such as recent scandals of 'grievancy studies'—have to be taken more seriously and answered. I would think an adequate response needs to address at least: (1) the changing history of such attacks, from the Sokal affair (an attack on forms of social constructionism) to 'political correctness'; (2) an analysis of the deleterious effects of the current political economy of the academy, and its changing metrics of success, emphasizing that these are both imposed on the humanities and even the university, and also derived from more externally-funded scientific research; (3) the paradoxical absence of attacks on the bench sciences given their histories of much more serious scandals; and (4) a serious reflection on the state of critical humanities and social science research, and its response both to number (2) and to the demands of the current moment, including a discussion of the ways it is shaped by ever-narrowing forms of over-specialization in terms of objects, theories, and politics.

alized, ignoring the often necessary assertion of expertise and authority, as well as the simple fact that such practices were necessary in the context of trying to invent something which, to a large extent, did not yet exist. Often, the requirements of such a transformative vision of education are presented as if they depend upon a particular understanding of the class-room environment as 'comfortable' and 'safe,' defined largely by the pro-tection of the subjugated, the victims. This has led, recently, to the absurd demand that students not be required to do or hear anything (e.g., public speaking) that makes them uncomfortable. But I do not mean to argue about complicated issues by reduction ad absurdum. We have to engage the competing claims, not by pitting one certainty against another but by asking questions and challenging certainties.

Nowhere is the need for the kinds of unruly and unfinished conversa-tion constitutive of cultural studies more necessary than around the ques-tion of 'free speech' and the silencing of some voices on college campuses. Such silencing can take many forms—and they are not all equal or equiv-alent: simple refusal of the right of access to spaces; disruptive actions that make speech impossible; violent protests that make the occasion of speech unsafe; forms of intimidation that undermine some peoples' abil-ity to voice their position, et cetera. We need to question both the bases and the political effects of various demands and actions. Are there incon-sistencies in the ways people appeal to free speech and anti-discrimination (only partly justified by the first amendment and anti-discrimination laws), and do these matter? Should we take serious claims of the univer-sity as a unique site for the expression of ideas seriously despite its fail-ures? How do we take into account the history of voices that have been silenced in the past, and the possibilities of which voices might be silenced in the future? Who has the right—and what is the basis of such a claim—to decide which voices are to be allowed and which denied? Do assertions of moral certainties (often couched in the forms of political judgments) and personal feelings provide compelling and adequate grounds for deci-sions to silence particular voices, and might such appeals work for differ-ent moral and political positions? In what ways does the academy already silence many voices—especially voices of precariously positioned minorities? Do we understand how and where such silencing is experi-enced? Should we separate—temporarily, so that we can more effectively re-articulate them—concerns about the different kinds of venues (e.g., public lectures versus classrooms), the voices of those invited to campus and those of members of the university community, the distribution of various resources, et cetera? What are the complex relations among the freedom, the willingness, and the ability to speak? And what are the conditions of possibility, in various contexts, of speech, including the construction of specific affective landscapes and interpersonal expectations? How much do we need to consider the effects of our actions outside the university, where the apparent denial of the right to speak to various conservative and reactionary speakers has become primary evidence for the accusation of 'political correctness,' a very tactical appeal aimed at constructing intellectual elites and progressives as extremists unworthy of popular political support? Are we, however unintentionally, providing succor to the increasingly extremist right by giving them exactly what they want, a powerful point of articulation for their chain of equivalences that define 'the enemy'? Do we have the luxury—or would it be a better political tactic—to deny them an audience and the publicity that they seek? Again, whatever my opinions on these matters may be, my argument is that we need to have intelligent conversations around these concerns, however passionate and uncomfortable such conversations may be. However, at this point, I want to recall that Stuart Hall once said,

> . . . I do think you have to create an atmosphere which allows people to say unpopular things. I don't think it is at all valuable to have an atmosphere in the classroom which is so clearly, unmistakably anti-racist that the natural and 'commonsense' racism which is part of the ideological air that we all breathe is not allowed to come out and express itself. . . That experience has to surface in the classroom even if it is pretty horrendous to hear—better to hear it than not to hear it.[40]

To repeat myself, cultural studies as pedagogy is all about discomforting not only students, but ourselves and our colleagues as well. Progressive pedagogies have too often been quite happy to discomfort the 'other side,' without attending to their own assumptions and certainties.

---

[40] Cited in Paul Gilroy, "Race is the prism," his introduction to the forthcoming collection of Stuart Hall's essays on race and racism, Duke University Press.

Returning to the matter of various pedagogical practices, I believe that one cannot separate these options, that they always interpenetrate each other, that teaching is always a hybridized endeavor. One cannot escape elitism and uneven power, even in contexts of active learning and social justice classrooms. The notion that one can eliminate them is an illusion which, if ever realized, would render the role of the professor irrelevant or reduce it to that of a facilitator.[41] And from the other side, one cannot escape the activity of the student even in the most hierarchical and authoritarian contexts. In the final analysis, we have to remember that one does not produce knowledge ex nihilo and the conversation of knowledge does not begin anew in every classroom. One does not magically become a producer of knowledge; there are real conditions of possibility that include not only learning how to produce knowledge within a particular paradigm, but also what tools are available and how to use them appropriately (contextually), and what claims to knowledge already define the discursive spaces one is operating in. Again, I would point to the efforts of my students (mentioned above) to teach cultural studies not by simply having students do it, as it were, not by making them co-producers, but by carefully and closely guiding their activity, by both providing them with the tools and knowledge they need in order to proceed, and carefully directing and even constantly surveilling their efforts. That is to say, teaching cultural studies by teaching the practice of cultural studies, by getting the students to engage with and in cultural studies—as a conversation marked by collaboration and humility on the one hand, and authority, rigor, judgment, and expertise on the other, as a conversation that does not assume it knows the questions or the answers in advance.

Teaching is a conversation, but not a democracy; research is a conversation, but not a democracy. In fact, for cultural studies, they are part of the same conversation, an ongoing pedagogy seeking better maps and better stories. In conclusion I can only repeat what I have said about the conversation that is cultural studies' pedagogy: it is a conversation that started before we or our students entered into it, and will continue (hopefully) long after we leave the classroom and the academy. It is a conversa-

---

[41] At the very least, should we think about sharing our salaries with the students?

tion that seeks not truth but, rather, to go on thinking, in a context that recognizes the real inequalities, some reasonable and many unreasonable, of knowledge, experience, and feeling. It is a conversation constantly negotiating the terms and practices of equality and inequality, where one can never predict in advance what difference (including expertise) will matter where. It is a conversation imbued with passion and tempered by humility.

Many people (myself included) are deeply frightened by the increasing power of a reactionary right with its re-articulations of nationalism and hatreds. Many are disturbed by the recognition that these developments are the unanticipated consequences of strategic political thought and struggles—led by shifting alliances among re-imagined conservatisms and fluid assemblages of corporate/capitalist interests—to reshape modernity and the forms and futures of the nation-state. But there is another dimension that should trouble us: the failures of the liberal and progressive forces to effectively stem these tides of change. Do we not need to accept the limits of our own thinking and strategies? And in the current conjunctural struggles, for me, the most troubling expression of this troubling situation is the fact that those who should be bound by common bonds of political desire are increasingly unable to establish the conditions for convivial forms of agonistic conversation and cooperation beyond the urgency—often lived as panic—of the most immediate and personal threats.

It is hard, maybe even impossible. For at the very least, we have to begin by learning, within the possibilities and constraints of the current conjuncture, how to constitute such a conversation (just to remind you, a conversation that is an engagement, always complex, multiple, fluid, and ongoing, not predefined or limited by principles of rationality or ideological struggle). Like any conjunctural effort, it will require us to question where we begin, the very questions we ask. The sort of conversation I have in mind cannot be conceptualized in terms of the problem of 'audiences' (so that we distinguish teaching and research as addressing different audiences) but as part of an ongoing process of constructing commonalities alongside difference, forging new figures and possibilities of unities-in-difference. But while pedagogy is always political, it is not politics in the last instance. I am suggesting that such conversations provide the conditions of possibility for finding more effective political struggles. While the answers emerge from the conversation, the conversation can never guarantee its own outcome at the beginning or by a formalist appeal to the process itself. The point of such conversations is not just to produce better stories, or even to simply produce new 'communities' and alliances, but to organize and create new kinds of organizations and movements and long-term infrastructures, which are necessary to transform the culture and with that the field of political possibilities. For that reason, the conversation cannot be endless; one must, however temporarily, take the pedagogical conversation into the realities of political decisions—strategies and tactics. It is always a risky effort and it does take time. I believe it is worth the effort, no matter how much or how often we fail, or how desperate we may feel. Paradoxically, we cannot afford to refuse to take the time we need. We do not have the time to abandon the effort.

We Are All Art Historians Now: Teaching Media Studies and/as Cultural Studies

Toby Miller

This chapter is based on my experience of teaching cultural studies over 30 years. For what it's worth, I've taught at grad and/or undergrad levels in many countries as a visitor, but most of the time in the US, Colombia, and Britain. I worked at private and public US research schools for two decades, and know it best. In disciplinary terms, I've taught cultural studies 'inside' sociology, cinema studies, American studies, anthropology, women's studies, English, journalism, social communication, management, film and media studies, and Latin American and Caribbean studies.

The chapter does three things, based in part on those experiences. It makes some Olympian claims about cultural studies' content and location, looks into ways of teaching the media as core components, and concludes that we are all art historians today—but probably shouldn't be.

T. Miller (✉)
University of California, Riverside, Riverside, CA, USA

© The Author(s) 2019
J. Aksikas et al. (eds.), *Cultural Studies in the Classroom and Beyond*,
https://doi.org/10.1007/978-3-030-25393-6_3

Olympian Remarks

In general, I understand cultural studies to refer to esthetic and anthropological ways of analyzing societies, in terms of subjectivity and power. In this formulation, art represents and creates ritual and vice versa through institutions and discourses. They construct identities, which in turn form them: femininity, for instance, is generated through the census, fashion, sports, religion, science, philosophy, the psy-function, and so on, but also structures those entities and norms in processes of stealth, deliberation, struggle, policy, administration, and conformity, inter alia.

In the colleges I know, cultural studies is generally a tendency functioning within longer established disciplines, rather than an area of study with its own departments. There are national and international professional associations dedicated to it,[1] but cultural studies rarely stands alone as an undergrad major or doctoral degree named and taught as such. We tend instead to be an irritant or alternative within things entitled literature, communications, sociology, or anthropology—and generally when connected to studying the media. An indicative list of some of these congruent associations, both marginal and mass, niche and prominent, is as follows:

Broadcast Education Association	Association for Education in Journalism and Mass Communication
National Communication Association	International Communication Association
North American Society for the Sociology of Sport	American Sociological Association
Society for Cinema and Media Studies	Organisation of American Historians
American Anthropological Association	European Communication Research and Education Association
American Journalism Historians Association	Asociación Latinoamericana de Investigadores de la Comunicación
Association for Chinese Communication Studies	Association of Internet Researchers
Associação de Investigadores da Imagem en Movimento	Federación Latinoamericana de Facultades y Programas de Comunicación Social

(continued)

---

[1] Consider the Inter-Asia Cultural Studies Society, the Canadian Association of Cultural Studies, the Association for Cultural Studies, the Cultural Studies Association of Australasia, and the Cultural Studies Association (US).

(continued)

Modern Language Association	Global Communication Research Association
Australian and New Zealand Communications Association	Southern African Communication Association
International Association for Media and History	Canadian Communication Association
International Association for Media and Communication Research	Union for Democratic Communications
Chinese Communication Association	Media, Communication, and Cultural Studies Association

The table above indicates the centrality of media and communications to cultural studies. It also signals the need to engage cultural studies in varying contexts, unlike monistic domains such as *bourgeois* economics or Anglo political science, which are dominated by rational choice theory and experimental method and governed by corporate service and state obeisance.

National and disciplinary educational systems and the availability of publications in the language of instruction also color how and where cultural studies 'occurs.' For instance, in US communications, teaching cultural studies generally means integrating into the curriculum under the sign of qualitative and/or critical methods and theories and working in English. The precise forms of integration depend on the department— whether it was born from rhetoric/speech communication (generally down the spine of the Midwest, as an initiative from the Reform Era dedicated to instructing the immigrant white working class in Ohio English) or from mass communication (wherever Marxism has been thwarted and products sold in the US since the 1930s). Within those spheres lies the division of administrative versus critical research first named by Paul Lazarsfeld in 1941 as he admiringly differentiated himself from Max Horkheimer. It has remained peskily persistent ever since (Smythe and Van Dinh 1983; Splichal and Mance 2018).

In Colombian communication studies, finding a place for students to make sense of cultural studies means signaling one's relationship to the 'four fields' (not unlike US anthropology). Those fields derive from the intersection of developmentalist (US) and critical (Latin American) para- digms. They include journalism, quantitative method, organizational communication, and semiotics. But unlike the US, faculty and students frequently define themselves across these domains, doing policy-oriented and quantoid work as well as textual analysis and political economy.

It follows that cultural studies pedagogy depends in part on disciplines, subfields, and languages. One thing is pretty constant: how publishers, universities, and disciplines organize textbooks and omnibus survey courses and select materials for exegesis and application (follow 1.1.1.1 for a feminist reading of the text; take steps 2.2.2.2 for post-colonialism; move on to 3.3.3.3 for an explanation of media-effects research). Perhaps, as a consequence, students and the pedagogic police[2] alike generally expect a narrative that situates knowledge within a recognizable narrative trajectory: an equilibrium is disrupted by a disequilibrium, before a new equilibrium is peacefully established.

This is a familiar story of *données* displaced by disturbance, followed by new norms gently and logically appearing. The new equilibrium is forged as untruths are abandoned and proofs accepted in the inexorable onward march of the market in ideas[3]—"we used to think this was the truth. Then we discovered it wasn't"; "we once believed x was the magical agent propelling history forward; now we know you need to add 'y' in order to get there." This functionalist form of knowledge dominates carefully unfurled histories of cultural studies and its influences.

I am reminded of Graeme Turner's critique of introductory courses inaugurating professorial authority via prolixity. They disempower students by negating clarity and advancing obscurantism through readings that presume an "improbably high level of theoretical sophistication … problematising established theoretical positions that the students have yet to understand." As a consequence, "the class turns into an exegetical performance in which the knowledge of the teacher dominates" and "the student's own cultural capital is given lip-service but implicitly undermined" (2009: 180).

This is particularly unfortunate in places where heavy workloads for faculty and students preclude luxuriating in the clover of academic dis-

---

[2] I've not experienced much curricular policing in Colombia or the US by contrast with the UK and Australia, where an abject faculty appears to accept control by the bureau with barely a whimper, in keeping with the baleful drive to satisfy daddy state and mommy corporation/mommy state and daddy corp.

[3] *Abrams v. United States*, 250 U.S. 616 (1919), dissenting opinion by Oliver Wendell Holmes, Jr., joined by Louis Brandeis. Of course, their minority view was the right one, but its rhetoric, as per that of Milton and Mill that informed it, accepts a plutocratic norm.

course so accessible in fancy schools (Caesar 1991). Students beyond those comfy cloisters often struggle with both high-theoretical language and such Jewish Bible/Old Testament formulations as "x theory begat y theory begat etc"—the tritely triumphant genealogies of orthodox pedagogy.

A pity in my eyes, and a reason why the way I have done these things sometimes infuriates students who want a tale of that kind rather than one of ongoing disruption and difference in an awkward interplay of dominant, residual, and emergent theories and subjects, where what is discarded may be of greater value than what is heralded (Ross 2012; Smith 2011).

I try to explain how cultural studies differs and draws from other forms of knowledge to which students are becoming accustomed. I base instruction on their own media experiences, which can inform and be informed by cultural studies. That's been especially helpful in teaching hundreds of people at one time or if students are reading beyond their first languages. When I am unfamiliar with their social worlds, this also encourages a less charismatic model of authority (Weber 1946: 245–52)—one operates as a naïve inquirer rather than a donnish or activist expert.

In the case of many hundreds of students gathered in a room, I tend to ask them each week what they think about a given topic, invite them to discuss it with their neighbors for ten minutes, reconvene in a plenary, ask for contributions, write those up on a board, spend a moment organizing them, and then make that the structure of our lecture. In smaller classes, I do similar things, but with more attention to readings and specific debates. This generally works well, though it is difficult with and for folks who are unfamiliar with the liberal theory of knowledge and expect faculty to disclose 'correct' answers rather than relativize such things or involve students in a joint search for them.

Below, you'll see a set of binary opposites distinguishing cultural studies from its neighbors/others. This table was generated some time ago in the hope that the heuristic value of an admittedly tendentious picture would override its conceptual imprecision—that it might provide a means of provoking *Ostranenie* and *détournement* (Miller 2001: 8). The table has helped some people with limited time for internecine debates to get a sense of where cultural studies sits within and across universities and disciplines.

Cultural Studies

What it is	What it isn't
Ethnography	Physical anthropology
Textual analysis of the media	Literary formalism and canon formation
Social theory	Regression and time series analysis
Political economy	Neoclassical economics
Critical geography	Town planning
Psychoanalysis	Rational choice and cognitive psychology
Postmodern art	Art history
Critical architecture	Engineering and quantity surveying
Environmentalism	Industrial development
Feminisms	Human biology
Queerness	Deviance
Globalization	Nationalism
Post-colonialism	World literature
Continental philosophy, structuralism, and post-structuralism	Analytic philosophy
Popular music	Classical musicology
Social semiotics	Formalist linguistics
Fashion	Technical design
Cultural and social history	Political history
Critical public health	Medical training
Critical legal studies and critical race theory	Legal reasoning and formalism
Subcultural theory	Interest group study

The next question often posed is: when and where does cultural studies appear? Origin myths abound, in terms of both histories and locations.

I've not seen a stronger, less parochial account in English than Richard Maxwell's (2000). He largely excludes Asian references, which have become very influential recently,[4] but highlights that cultural studies began in the Global South at the same time as the North and within Nairobi, Rio, and Santiago social movements, *favelas*, and revolutions as much as Birmingham seminars, Newtown bars, or Illinois armchairs.

---

[4] In teaching the diagram, I have added more Asian references and various other topics and names.

Maxwell systematizes things through diachronic and geographical axes attuned to political and theoretical movements—to life beyond, as much as within, academia. This materially adds to, and unsettles, the dominant logics of who, what, when, where, and how that are generally served up in Anglo- and Asian-centric formulations.

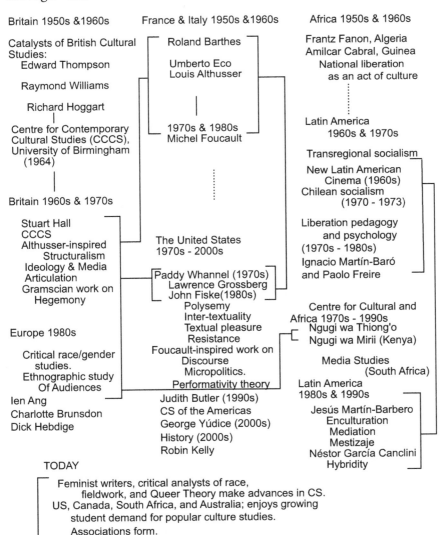

Britain 1950s &1960s

Catalysts of British Cultural Studies:
  Edward Thompson

Raymond Williams

Richard Hoggart

Centre for Contemporary Cultural Studies (CCCS), University of Birmingham (1964)

Britain 1960s & 1970s

Stuart Hall
CCCS
Althusser-inspired
Structuralism
Ideology & Media
Articulation
Gramscian work on
Hegemony

Europe 1980s

Critical race/gender studies.
Ethnographic study Of Audiences
Ien Ang
Charlotte Brunsdon
Dick Hebdige

TODAY

France & Italy 1950s &1960s

Roland Barthes

Umberto Eco
Louis Althusser

1970s & 1980s
Michel Foucault

The United States
1970s - 2000s
Paddy Whannel (1970s)
Lawrence Grossberg
John Fiske(1980s)
  Polysemy
  Inter-textuality
  Textual pleasure
  Resistance
Foucault-inspired work on
  Discourse
  Micropolitics.
  Performativity theory
Judith Butler (1990s)
CS of the Americas
George Yúdice (2000s)
History (2000s)
Robin Kelly

Africa 1950s & 1960s

Frantz Fanon, Algeria
Amilcar Cabral, Guinea
National liberation
  as an act of culture

Latin America
  1960s & 1970s

Transregional socialism

New Latin American
  Cinema (1960s)
Chilean socialism
  (1970 - 1973)

Liberation pedagogy
  and psychology
(1970s - 1980s)
Ignacio Martín-Baró
and Paolo Freire

Centre for Cultural and
Africa 1970s - 1990s
  Ngugi wa Thiong'o
  Ngugi wa Mirii (Kenya)

Media Studies
  (South Africa)
Latin America
1980s & 1990s

Jesús Martín-Barbero
Enculturation
Mediation
Mestizaje
Néstor García Canclini
Hybridity

Feminist writers, critical analysts of race, fieldwork, and Queer Theory make advances in CS.
US, Canada, South Africa, and Australia; enjoys growing student demand for popular culture studies.
Associations form.
Cultural Policy Studies and Creative Industries Studies emerge.

It is possible to review Maxwell's diagram teleologically, as a triumphant emergence over the decades—a cloudburst from anonymity into success. But the story is of course more awkward. And this should be no surprise. In the UK and the US, the troubled introduction into universities of the natural sciences in the nineteenth century and politics, philosophy, English, and sociology in the twentieth century indicates how academic life is routinely disrupted when new economic formations call up new intellectual ones. For the appearance of all these disciplines represented responses to socioeconomic transformations—industrialization, state schooling, class mobility, and public welfare (Fox 2003; Whittam Smith 2008). Their latter-day equivalent in cultural studies reacts to the triumph of post-industrial/ternary/services/cultural sectors, thereby addressing new areas of economic activity and the expansion of democracy, engaging new human rights and subjectivities, generally in urbanizing and immigrant contexts. As a consequence, it invites/experiences calumny as well as cool denunciation as much as annunciation.

Like those older but once insurgent disciplines, cultural studies in the Anglo world emerged under different conditions of scholarly existence from those applying now. Meaghan Morris makes the point well in her account of university life in the 1960s and 1970s by contrast with today:

> the difference between a good course and a disaster could depend on how much charisma and enthusiasm the students as well as the teacher brought to class. ... Not only were classroom evaluations, progress reports and performance reviews unknown, but so was research productivity; lazy, drunken, and socially challenged academics could enjoy jobs for life. However, this system was not ... a taxpayer-funded orgy of self-indulgence; ... it was organised by an ethic of caring and public responsibility rather than ... contract and surveillance

In grad contexts, particularly for folks seeking to become academics, I run some kind of line between the laissez-faire world of wannabe charisma and the saturnine surveillance of everyday governmentality. So, I explain to doctoral students how journals work, as they are the coin of the realm, along with grants, across so many universities. Grants indenture research students to a bench-science model of fulfilling the career goals of full professors. Journals expect them to conform to the norms of professional associations.

In the US, the virtual exclusion of cultural studies from the Federal grants that make for big science and biggish social science means we mostly rely on the research infrastructure provided by schools themselves. In other Anglo countries, the availability of such funds rewards mundane research into apolitical topics, thereby facilitating more and more grant-getting, tying doctoral students to professors' agendas, and increasing the studious avoidance by faculty of the actual work of university teaching.

Britain's redoubtable legion of second- and third-rate schools in particular forces doctoral students to list efforts to get published in their annual reports. They want these wandering mendicants/freeway faculty/roads scholars to justify publishing choices (much as they do with a largely compliant, gutless professoriate). In Latin America, where there are many great journals in Spanish and Portuguese, governments are putting faculty under intense pressure to publish in English—something that scientists are used to, but folks in the humanities and social sciences are not.

It's important that people subject to English/Australian graduate education or Latin American governmentality who seek to work within those hegemonic strictures and structures understand the grand binary that determines the status of knowledge in publishing; for it divides cool, unreliable journals from boring, efficient ones (hint: US tenure committees peopled by botanists and economists feel less comfortable with the former than the latter).[5]

I'm on the relevant sub-panel[6] of the British Government's Research Excellence Framework for 2020, which will undertake surveillance of faculty publications nationally and award departmental grades that lead to public esteem, campus power, and some funding. Seeking to satisfy this Framework takes up vast resources in universities and induces intense anxiety among the professoriate. It also takes effect elsewhere, as per Hong Kong's emergent mimetic Research Assessment Exercise. Australia has a system akin to the Framework. It initially ranked journals within disciplines, designating the great and the good from the downright decadent. This proved unworkable.[7] Although abandoned, it remains a norm

---

[5] I haven't really operated instrumentally—I followed lines of inquiry that appealed and seemed to matter. I was lucky, both interpersonally and conjuncturally.

[6] It is entitled Communication, Cultural and Media Studies, Library and Information Management.

[7] http://www.arc.gov.au/excellence-research-australia

in some universities seeking means of rewarding docile scholars and punishing aberrant ones.

Unlike most disciplinary fields, our sub-panel's very sensible policy has evidently been "You can publish on a toilet roll." Content matters, address doesn't. But persuading universities of this fact is well-nigh impossible, so taken are they with traditional disciplines' insistence that all knowledge worthy of the name appears in English and in journals sponsored by professional associations. Within that dominant logic, monographs and book chapters don't matter. Sokal rules, and *Social Text* sucks (Guillory 2002).[8] And beyond that, of course, university presses are endangered species because libraries have shifted their budgets from buying books to subscribing to databases (Cohen 2018; Miller 2016).

Hence, I present the following binary table, which I drew so that emergent scholars could know the stakes and can act accordingly:

Journals of tendency	Journals of profession
Avowed political project seeking to make interventions, situated in time and space	Avowed truth project seeking a universalist pursuit of knowledge
In-house manuscript reviewers who argue for and against authors' mss along grounds of politics and cohesiveness	External manuscript reviewers who engage in double-blind review of mss in terms of disciplinary competence and falsifiability
Open calls for mss, theme issues, responses to contemporary social questions	Access restricted to members of professional associations, lengthy period of review, and revision
Seeks hegemony of political positions across disciplines	Seeks hegemony over professional success within disciplines
Self-selecting editorial collective	Editors chosen by associations
Prone to inefficiency, sudden bursts of energy and newness, and an eventual sense that the 'moment' of the journal has passed	Prone to efficiency, 'normal science,' and a fate joined to its sponsoring discipline
Examples: *Social Text, Public Culture, Socialist Review, camera obscura, Radical History Review, History Workshop Journal, GLQ, New Left Review, Cultural Studies*	Examples: *PMLA, Cinema Journal, Journal of Communication, American Historical Review, Popular Communication, American Sociological Review*

---

[8] Although then an Associate Professor at NYU, I underwent the equivalent of a tenure review at Duke when I took over the co-editorship of *Social Text* during the crisis, so exercised was the publisher, Duke UP, by the scandal.

Teaching cultural studies to doctoral folks necessitates explaining such tasteless, tedious realities and how they vary across boundaries of various kinds.

Media Teaching

This takes me to a further reality. Opportunities to teach cultural studies at the undergrad level frequently arise because students wish to study and then work in the media, as broadly construed (so it includes boys in basements who rarely wash, and play first-person shooter games; queer-curious girls in the burbs luxuriating in *The L Word*; working-class black Latinos sending baseball tweets; creepy market researchers scanning consumption patterns; cultish Facebook monitors asking visitors "What do you think of Mark?"; and Hollywood's reliance on state subvention and labor exploitation—all such stereotypes are relevant). 'The media' is a *portmanteau* term, covering a multitude of machines, processes, and genres. There is increasing overlap within this multitude, as seemingly black box techniques and technologies, once set away from audiences, become part of public debate and experience.

The question then becomes *what* we teach about the media. One of cultural studies' tendencies has been to counter pessimism over structural, political-economic media matters, such as ownership and control, with optimism about audiences (assuming radical freedoms of reading and interpretation). This often leads to narcissography, with the critic's *persona* a guarantor of audience revelry and Dionysian joy (Morris 1990). Welcome to the 'Readers Liberation Movement' (Eagleton 1982), where everyone is creative and no one merely a spectator: "a consumer on the one hand, but ... also a producer" (Foucault 2008: 226). It is a strange amalgam that eschews political economy and undertakes textual analysis as if it were a participant's observation.

This is how Marwan Kraidy and I have typified these utopian cultural studies tendencies (2016: 17):

• because of new technologies and practices of consumption, concentration of media ownership and control no longer matters—information

is finally free, thanks to multi-point distribution and destabilized hierarchies
* consumers are sovereign and transcend class and other categories
* young people are liberated from media control
* journalism is dying as everyone becomes a source of both news and reporting
* creative destruction is an accurate and desirable description of economic innovation
* when scholars observe media workers and audiences, they discover that ideology critique is inappropriate
* Marxist political economy denies the power of audiences and users and the irrelevance of boundaries—it is pessimistic and hidebound
* cultural imperialism critiques miss the creativity and resilience of national and subnational forms of life against industrial products
* media-effects studies are inconsequential—audiences outwit corporate plans and psy-function norms

There may be both too much leftist functionalism in political economy and too much leftist hope in cultural studies. One tendency lacks conflict; the other amplifies it.

Explaining how these assumptions came to be orthodoxies and what is right and wrong with them gives students some applied knowledge and engages many of their own experiences along with policy and public concerns and shibboleths. That means reaching beyond cultural studies tired denunciations of effects studies to say, "If the media have no effects, what is the point of my writing or speaking?"

It's best, I think, to outline to folks the various ways in which the media have been studied, rather than to denounce the past or assert newness. In the humanities, the media tend to be judged by criteria of inclusiveness, representation, and quality, as framed by practices of cultural criticism and history. The social sciences, by contrast, focus on the languages, customs, spaces, and times of different groups represented or working within the media, as explored ethnographically or statistically.

So whereas the humanities articulate differences within populations through symbolic norms (e.g., providing some of us with the cultural capital to appreciate high culture), the social sciences articulate such differences through social norms (e.g., legitimizing inequality through doctrines of human capital).

The following table offers a typology of the issues, means, and disciplines associated with media studies.

Topics	Objects	Methods	Disciplines
Regulation, industry development, new technology	State, capital, labor	Political economy, neoliberalism	Engineering, computer science, economics, political science, law, communication studies
Genre	Text	Content analysis	Communication studies, sociology
Genre	Text	Textual analysis	Literary/cultural/media studies
Uses	Audience	Uses and gratifications	Communication studies, psychology, marketing
Uses	Audience	Ethnography	Anthropology, cultural/media studies, communication studies
Effects	Audience	Experimentation, questionnaire	Psychology, marketing, communication studies

As noted above, many students desire careers in the media. In Colombia, I'm used to this being about telling the truth. In New York and Los Angeles, it's more about not telling the truth. Put another way, one focuses on journalism, the other on drama. But in Colombia, I've mostly taught doctoral classes, where folks want to do other things with cultural studies, be they pregnant army colonels, feminist medical specialists, self-doubting architecture professors, activist indigenous intellectuals, *mestiza* executives, or combinations of the above. In Gotham, I taught at a renowned film school, which basically was a ticket to film and TV fiction, regardless of our curricula. In Los Angeles, I was in a company town, where the word 'industry' meant only one thing.

So getting messages across that relate to cultural studies requires adjustments and compromises, even as it can operate dynamically with students' experiences and hopes. I seek a way of blending political economy, textual analysis, and ethnography in order to understand the life of the commodity sign. I particularly want screen drama students to understand how the industry operates, given the emphasis in their studies on textuality, technology, and performance; hence, the diagram below, which we devised as part of collaborative work on Hollywood (Miller et al. 2005).

That pragmatic approach aside, I endeavor to ensure that, regardless of their specific instrumental desires, students learn how the media constitute and are constituted by:

- technologies, which form their conditions of possibility
- policies, which determine the field in which they operate
- genres, such as drama, music, sports, and information
- workers, who make texts via writing, performing, and recording
- audiences, who receive the ensuing content; and
- environments, which house their creation, operation, and detritus

We Are All Art Historians Now

If newer forms of media are crucial to teaching cultural studies, why are we all art historians today? Simply put, in terms of both our own internalized desire to obey and the strictures placed on us by the bureau, every class must have slides, courtesy of Power*less*Point*less* (other software is available). Multimedia presentations and learning are *de rigueur*.

This is unfortunate in two ways. First, it indexes the power of the bureau to draw up and police asinine templates for designing syllabi and imparting material. Failed academicians (AKA managers) punish faculty who do not comply. The result is a mindless reiteration of shibboleth after shibboleth, and the awarding of merit certificates for parroting weasel words (anthropomorphism often leads to mixed metaphors) and engaging in the mimetic managerial fantasy that takes clichés from the private sector and applies them to the public (Heffernan 2018; Collini 2018). And second, the real value of art historians using slides in lectures—to permit shared encounters with images—is misapplied in the desire to communicate ideas via typed text. I think it's fine to show graphs or tables as well as pretty pictures—after all, this chapter is littered with diagrams—but I doubt the efficacy of sentence after sentence on screen in lectures in order to satisfy the bureau's banal technological sublime (Nye 1994).

What do students really glean from a mixed-media, multi-platform education? The science available shows that cell phones have a negative impact on learning. For 'low-achieving and at-risk students,' banning their use is "equivalent to an additional hour a week in school, or to increasing the school year by five days" (Murphy and Beland 2015). Cornell's renowned 'Laptop and the Lecture' study showed that lecture attendees remembered lessons best if they did not use laptops during class (Hembrooke and Gay 2003). Subsequent research confirms the risks of technological multitasking with smartphones and the value of taking notes with ink—and not only for those doing so; others get distracted by people typing in ways they do not when surrounded by pen and paper (Sana et al. 2013). Studies even show, paradoxically, that people who engage heavily in media multitasking are worse than others when given a range of tasks to perform simultaneously. Sending texts and engaging with social media seriously diminish such capacities, and learning in general (Lawson and Henderson 2015; Gingerich and Lineweaver 2014; David et al. 2015; Ophir et al. 2009).

In addition, while conventional lectures are often said to be dead, many students in many countries, though not all, tell me they really like them. They want performances and the charismatic authority mentioned by Morris—and they want a figure they can approach afterward to explain what has been said and written in greater detail.

Conclusion

Cultural studies offered Néstor García Canclini 'una salida de emergencia' (an emergency exit) from the irrelevance or complicity of self-serving, sclerotic disciplines (2004: 122). Can it keep up that simple service?

The national, linguistic, and disciplinary differences I've mentioned will probably continue, as will a reliance on the media as a source of undergraduate enrolments. And the creeping commodification and governmentalization of knowledge will seek ever greater control over pedagogy. The lecture won't die, but it will be further technologized and diminished. There will be pressure to fetishize big data and social media as core components of courses.

How do we get around this? For me, the answer lies in meeting the minimum requirements of the bureau without embracing its discourse *tout court*, and doing so in ways that involve critique of the process. That means creating agendas that derive from three audiences: academics, public-interest advocates, and social-movement campaigners. Methodologically, it necessitates considering the who, what, when, where, and how of cultural justice, rather than name-checking theorists. And that means always asking three questions: the *cui bono* conceit of political economy; the what is in the text of social semiotics; and the how it is made sense of from ethnography. Perhaps I've answered the query of what is cultural studies.

Works Cited

Caesar, T. (1991). On Teaching at a Second-Rate University. *South Atlantic Quarterly, 90*(3), 449–467.

Cohen, S. (2018, April 22). When University Presses Close, So Do Our Minds. *Chronicle of Higher Education.* https://www.chronicle.com/article/Scholarly-Publishing-s-Last/243187?cid=at&utm_source=at&utm_medium=en&elqTrackId=e067faa79db341d4aeceac758914b910&elq=2581a3a1dbf54af6815be7a623ae9f35&elqaid=18746&elqat=1&elqCampaignId=8452

Collini, S. (2018, April 24). In UK Universities There Is a Daily Erosion of Integrity. *Guardian.* https://www.theguardian.com/education/2018/apr/24/uk-universities-erosion-integrity-bologna-statement

David, P., Kim, J.-H., Brickman, J. S., Ran, W., & Curtis, C. M. (2015). Mobile Phone Distraction While Studying. *New Media & Society, 17*(10), 1661–1679.

Eagleton, T. (1982). The Revolt of the Reader. *New Literary History, 13*(3), 449–452.

Foucault, M. (2008). In M. Senellart (Ed.), *The Birth of Biopolitics: Lectures at the Collège de France, 1978–79* (Graham Burchell, Trans.). Houndmills: Palgrave Macmillan.

Fox, A. (2003, May 23). Talking About My Generation. *Guardian.* https://www.theguardian.com/education/2003/may/23/highereducation.comment

García Canclini, N. (2004). *Diferentes, desiguales y desconectados: Mapas de interculturalidad.* Barcelona: Editorial Gedisa.

Gingerich, A. C., & Lineweaver, T. T. (2014). OMG! Texting in Class = U Fail :(Empirical Evidence That Text Messaging During Class Disrupts Comprehension. *Teaching of Psychology, 41*(1), 44–51.

Guillory, J. (2002). The Sokal Affair and the History of Criticism. *Critical Inquiry, 28*(2), 470–508.

Heffernan, M. (2018, April 24). Beware University Reputations Tarnished by Business Links. *Financial Times.* https://www.ft.com/content/33adaa9e-43ad-11e8-93cf-67ac3a6482fd

Hembrooke, H., & Gay, G. (2003). The Laptop and the Lecture: The Effects of Multitasking in Learning Environments. *Journal of Computing in Higher Education, 15*(1), 46–64.

Lawson, D., & Henderson, B. B. (2015). The Costs of Texting in the Classroom. *College Teaching, 63*(3), 119–124.

Lazarsfeld, P. (1941). Remarks on Administrative and Critical Communications Research. *Studies in Philosophy and Social Science, 9*(1), 2–16.

Maxwell, R. (2000). Cultural Studies. In G. Browning, A. Halcli, & F. Webster (Eds.), *Understanding Contemporary Society: Theories of the Present* (pp. 281–295). London: Sage.

Miller, T. (2001). What It Is and What It Isn't: Introducing … Cultural Studies. In T. Miller (Ed.), *A Companion to Cultural Studies* (pp. 1–19). Oxford: Blackwell.

Miller, T. (2016). How Green Is This Paper? *Culture Unbound: Journal of Current Cultural Research, 7*, 588–599.

Miller, T., & Kraidy, M. M. (2016). *Global Media Studies*. Cambridge: Polity Press.

Miller, T., Govil, N., McMurria, J., Maxwell, R., & Wang, T. (2005). *Global Hollywood 2*. London: British Film Institute.

Morris, M. (1990). The Banality of Cultural Studies. In P. Mellencamp (Ed.), *Logics of Television: Essays in Cultural Criticism* (pp. 14–43). Bloomington: Indiana University Press.

Morris, M. (2008). Teaching Versus Research? Cultural Studies and the New Class Politics in Knowledge. *Inter-Asia Cultural Studies, 9*(3), 433–450.

Murphy, R., & Beland, L.-P. (2015, May 12). How Smart Is It to Allow Students to Use Mobile Phones at School? *The Conversation.* https://theconversation.com/how-smart-is-it-to-allow-students-to-use-mobile-phones-at-school-40621

Nye, D. (1994). *American Technological Sublime*. Cambridge, MA: MIT Press.

Ophir, E., Nass, C., & Wagner, A. D. (2009). Cognitive Control in Media Multitaskers. *Proceedings of the National Academy of Sciences of the United States of America, 106*(37), 15583–15587.

Ross, A. (2012). Interview with Andrew Ross [by Jon Cruz]. *European Journal of Cultural Studies, 15*(3), 343–359.

Sana, F., Weston, T., & Cepeda, N. (2013). Laptop Multitasking Hinders Classroom Learning for Both Users and Nearby Peers. *Computers & Education, 62*(1), 24–31.

Smith, P. (Ed.). (2011). *The Renewal of Cultural Studies*. Philadelphia: Temple University Press.

Smythe, D. W., & Van Dinh, T. (1983). On Critical and Administrative Research: A New Critical Analysis. *Journal of Communication, 33*(3), 117–127.

Splichal, S., & Mance, B. (2018). Paradigm(s) Lost? Islands of Critical Media Research in Communication Journals. *Journal of Communication, 68*(2), 399–414.

Turner, G. (2009). Cultural Studies 101: Canonical, Mystificatory and Elitist? *Cultural Studies Review, 15*(1), 175–187.

Weber, M. (1946). In H. H. Gerth & C. W. Mills (Eds. & Trans.), *From Max Weber: Essays in Sociology.* New York: Oxford University Press.

Whittam Smith, A. (2008, February 25). Media Studies Is No Preparation for Journalism. *Independent.* http://www.independent.co.uk/opinion/commentators/andreas-whittam-smith/andreas-whittam-smith-media-studies-is-no-preparation-for-journalism-786785.html

Dear Progressive and/or Queer Students: A Pedagogical Polemic from Your Queer Adjunct Professor

Jodi Davis-Pacheco

Dear Progressive and/or Queer Students,

Welcome to our women and gender studies classroom. Take some deep breaths because we have our work cut out for us this semester. I'm not sure if you are feeling it, but it seems like the world has become a pretty toxic place. I mean, sure, the world has always been unjust—but it certainly feels more concentrated and intense as of late. Activists are spread dangerously thin attempting to resist, protest, and defy a conveyor belt of persistent assaults on human rights: bans on refugees entering the US, increased risk of deportation for immigrants, curtailing of reproductive rights, rescinded workplace protections for LGBT people, police brutality, school shootings, an increase in violence against communities of color, and a state-sanctioned campaign against the dissemination of information (i.e., "Fake News"). Many of us feel pushed to our limits, and some of us might even want to throw our hands up because it can be hard to figure out what we can do about it all.

As we begin this new semester together, I thought it necessary to explain a bit about where your professor is coming from and try to

J. Davis-Pacheco (✉)
California State University Fullerton, Fullerton, CA, USA

© The Author(s) 2019
J. Aksikas et al. (eds.), *Cultural Studies in the Classroom and Beyond*,
https://doi.org/10.1007/978-3-030-25393-6_4

illustrate for you how we might make our time together productive. I am supposed to teach you about social justice. In fact, my pedagogical strategies have always used social justice as a guiding principle. But lately, I am afraid to do that—and I think some of you might be too. Which is why failure will be our motivation this semester.

Allow me to explain—I'm not saying you should be motivated by the fear that I might fail you. Instead, I'd like us all to acknowledge that failure is inevitable. An education founded in social justice and critical thinking is a path riddled with complicated histories of identity, oppression, and structural inequalities. We all must begin with an understanding that in order to transform our ways of thinking about the world, we must take risks and that mistakes are inevitable. In short, we are going to make one another uncomfortable and we will confront complicated but necessary ideas.

If you have never taken a class with me before, you should probably know that I am both queer and a feminist—let's just get that out of the way, even though I'm fairly certain you already expected that. I am, after all, the living embodiment of what the talking heads on television warn us about the "liberal university." This means I believe that experiences, identities, and lived realities are informed by the complex relationship between ideology, culture, and power. It also means my courses require a critical examination of identities and their intersectional connections. We will recognize the interlocking and inextricable relationship between different aspects of identity and systems of domination. Additionally, because I am queer identified, any material we cover that relates to non-heterosexual identities will be viewed by some of your colleagues as advancing my personal agenda.

Please let your colleagues know that even though this class is taught using feminist and queer pedagogical strategies, interventions, methodologies, and theories that they do not have to be a feminist or queer person to get a good grade. Pedagogy is how an instructor manages the theory and practice of teaching and how this will influence student learning. Feminist pedagogy informs my actions and teaching strategies by taking into consideration the needs and lived experience of my students while working toward decentering power in the classroom. No one will get a membership card at the end of the semester and there are no uniforms or secret handshakes. That said, please do contact me if you would like to create a handshake.

You should also know that I have been doing this a while. Twelve years, to be exact. In those 12 years of adjuncting at this large public university in a women and gender studies department in a conservative county, I have experienced a lot: I have helped students work through tremendous grief; held students' hands as I walked them to the on-campus counseling center; supported and celebrated my transgender students' transitions; helped homeless students find safe places to sleep; connected food-insecure students to resources on campus; and have been the first point of contact for dozens of students who have been sexually assaulted. I was also a student myself at this large public institution in this conservative county, and I remember professors who did some of the same things for me.

In total, 4500 students have entered my 110 classrooms. All of this experience means I can make some well-informed guesses about who some of you and your colleagues might be.

Reasons Students May Enroll in my Classes (in no particular order):

1. The course has "sex" or "women" in the title.
2. Enrollment is difficult on this campus and this particular course offered an open seat at a good time. It also offers the coveted general education credit.
3. They are international students, students on academic probation, or non-matriculated students who must petition to add courses with an instructor's signature on the first day of classes. I am generally sympathetic to these students and believe education should be as accessible as possible.
4. Students who are LGBTQ+ identified.
5. Women for whom sexism is visible.
6. Women for whom sexism is not visible.
7. Conservative activist students seeking to disrupt the course.
8. Friends of my former students who heard I don't give a midterm or final exam and that I'm funny enough to not be too awful.
9. Student athletes, because of my collaborative relationship with some of the athletic advisers.

10. Students who thought this would be a class about women in history even though that is not in the course title or description.

It might surprise you, but I am generally excited when students enroll because the class fits their schedule or because I would let them in. These students have often never had meaningful conversations about sexual orientation, race, class, sexuality, gender, or sexism. Some of you will get angry that you haven't thought about these issues before this class, and I understand because, for a lot of you, there was no choice but to think about these issues because you suffer through them every day. I'm not asking you to write a thank-you note to students who are beginning this journey for joining us (that's sort of like applauding a father for "babysitting" his child), but I am asking you to enter this room open: open to new ideas, open to expanding on what you already know, and open to the process. It is not my job to criticize students for not having done some of this work already, nor is it yours. Perhaps in an alternate setting I might feel differently, but in this classroom, it is my aim to create an environment that fosters meaningful exchange of ideas. We simply cannot do that when we shut down conversation instead of engaging it further.

I will warn you that someone in this room will be quick to say something that some of us find problematic. It might even be me (I am a fallible human who makes mistakes, after all). The initial reaction of some of my activist-minded/social-justice-oriented students tends to be to publicly call out the mistakes made by their colleagues or me. Call-out culture refers to the tendency among progressives, activists, community organizers, and so on, to publicly name oppressive behavior or language when displayed by others. It's performative, and you might see it anywhere from the comment section of an article posted online to a classroom discussion. My pedagogical strategies this semester require that we do our best to refrain from this impulse and try some other methods instead. Now, before you call me out on my assessment of call-out culture, please understand this: there will always be moments that are worthy of very public call-outs. When someone with a lot of power does or says something that is sexist, racist, ableist, transphobic, and so on, call it out loudly and publicly. But in this room, I urge you to take a moment to find another way. It is my experience that call-out culture in a classroom is a toxic performance that is counterproductive.

Call-out culture, whether it is the intention of the individual or not, is a public scene that can appear as people trying to demonstrate the purity and righteousness of their own politics. However, I am not encouraging you to "call in," the alternative often offered by those who are critical of call-out culture, wherein the individual is asked to speak privately with the individual who has done something wrong in order to address their behavior without making a spectacle. Call-in culture is just as fraught with issues, and the labor of it will still most likely rest on the shoulders of minority students to point out what they have witnessed but in a way that puts the other person's feelings, and the feelings of the group, ahead of their own. I simply want everyone in this room to remember that we are a classroom full of people experiencing complicated overlapping identities with complicated stories and histories. Even students who share an identity will not agree on every issue, and you don't have to look very far to find examples of this. From LGBTQ+ individuals in the military to same-sex marriage, it's clear that even marginalized voices differ. That's because identity is overcomplicated and power structures are difficult to resist. Nothing we discuss in this class will be able to be understood in oversimplified either/or terms.

There is a tendency among progressive student communities to define and attempt to control the boundaries of who can speak on which subject. I understand this impulse; for too long marginalized populations have been unable to tell their own stories or study their own histories and receive support or be heard. It is powerful when an insider does the research, writes the article, teaches the class, or adds to the classroom discussion. It is also powerful when someone who, on the surface, has no vested interest in understanding discrimination or oppression takes the time to do the work.

More often than not, the boundaries of who is on your side and who is not are policed through the use of language and terminology. It is critical that we remember that language, like any other cultural convention, is forever shifting and is nearly impossible to keep up with. I had a professor when I was an undergrad that was famous for kicking anyone out of the room who said something that they found offensive. One day, a student used the term "gay" as an insult toward an idea they didn't like. The professor, angry, pointed their finger and said, "Homophobia will not be tolerated in my class. Pack your things and leave." Some applauded the professor and some became visibly nervous about the call-out that had just happened. That moment stuck with me: why would we kick out a student who used an insensitive yet common slang term? What good did this do? What did students learn from this? Was there something better that could have been done?

Since then I have been in that professor's shoes many times over. I've heard students use some language in class that shocked me and that, so I didn't lose my cool, required some deep breathing to process. What I've discovered is that many of these students haven't been taught that language has any value, power, or meaning. This shouldn't be surprising to those of you that have been paying attention to the current cultural landscape: anyone who elicits any kind of criticism of language, or highlights any example of oppression, is deemed an overly sensitive snowflake and ignored, humiliated, or worse.

Here's where our pedagogical strategies take effect. In this class, we will not kick anyone out of the room for saying the "wrong" thing, we will not call them out in an effort to publicly shame or humiliate them, and we won't expect marginalized voices to do the hard labor of quietly dealing with the moment on their own in a "call-in." Instead we will ask questions because, in my experience, these linguistic lapses are done with very little critical thought and a general acceptance of language as just a set of words. Sometimes it's that students have never heard the terminology that is so comfortable for many of us who exist in queer and/or social-justice-minded groups. Instead of the call-out, I suggest we ask questions that require all of us to reflect on the power and potency of language: why did you use the words you did? What does this say to members of certain communities about your feelings about them? Why do you think that phrase or utterance has become so commonplace in our society? This gives students an opportunity to work through their own thinking while simultaneously questioning the systems that make space for those ideas in the first place.

Finally, we will remember that intersectionality is real and complex, and that individuals cannot be held as representations of the systems from which they benefit. Power is everywhere and it is dispersed and pervasive. The classroom is a concentrated locale for the power relations we experience in the "real world." Power is not only understood in negative terms and it doesn't just exclude, repress, censor, or conceal—it also produces. For example, in this classroom, I might be viewed as the individual wielding the most power. However, after more careful scrutiny, we will see that adjunct faculty in particular work under precarious conditions that do not guarantee employment from semester to semester. One condition of employment for many adjunct faculty are the student surveys conducted at the end of the semester encouraging adjunct faculty to perform for their paychecks—if students rate you negatively you may not be hired back regardless of the reason those ratings came out low. We can begin to see that students also hold a position of power in this room, not only in the professor/student dichotomy but more importantly in producing the way that knowledge is produced in the classroom. If we can begin to see ourselves and our colleagues as works in progress who are coming from different social positions instead of individuals who stand in for the total systems that portions of our identities represent, perhaps we can begin to view one another as whole people more beautifully complex than our identities. After all, if we are going to create the kinds of substantial and meaningful changes we are so desperately in need of, we are going to need some help from each other.

Sincerely,
Your Queer, Feminist, Adjunct Professor

Cultural Studies and (Un)Critical Pedagogies: A Journey Through the Corporatized University

Lisa B. Y. Calvente, Mark Hayward, Josh Smicker, and Sindhu Zagoren

We all met at graduate school and share memories of the advice, recommendations, and challenge that lurked behind the phrase 'do the work.' It was a phrase that was often used by Lawrence Grossberg to explain what could be done, what needed to be done, and what must be done in order to achieve the political and intellectual goals of Cultural Studies. Yet, the question of what 'the work' was, and exactly how it was to be done, always remained open and perhaps unanswerable. Being (and hopefully always remaining) students in search of a response to this question, the passing of time has made clear that 'the work' has both

L. B. Y. Calvente
DePaul University, Chicago, IL, USA

M. Hayward
York University, Toronto, ON, Canada
e-mail: mhayward@yorku.ca

J. Smicker (✉)
Catawba College, Salisbury, NC, USA

S. Zagoren
Community College of Philadelphia, Philadelphia, PA, USA

© The Author(s) 2019
J. Aksikas et al. (eds.), *Cultural Studies in the Classroom and Beyond*,
https://doi.org/10.1007/978-3-030-25393-6_5

aspirational and pragmatic aspects that go beyond simply the completion of a given task. It is aspirational insofar as it calls forth the possibilities and potentials of intellectual research in ways that require recognition of how individual reflection intersects with collective inquiry and dialogue. It is pragmatic insofar as 'the work' was literally labor; it demanded time and energy and that resulted in explanation, clarification, and perhaps even change.

Starting from our own intellectual and personal formations in Cultural Studies, our goal in this chapter is to draw attention to the ways in which the intersection between theoretical and practical work at the heart of Cultural Studies is being challenged and marginalized in the contemporary university. We reflect upon the crisis of the corporatized academy and how it affects Cultural Studies as a knowledge-producing practice both inside and outside academy. Derived from the body of literature on the academy and from experiences of everyday academic life, this chapter analyzes how neoliberal strategies have transformed and depoliticized higher education through the appropriation of difference and the proliferation of professionalism. We underscore how Cultural Studies becomes a target of these strategies and argue that the signifiers of Cultural Studies have been disarticulated from issues of critical praxis, solidarity, and political change within the past two decades. We highlight collaboration as a strategy and mode of working that offers a potential avenue for the continuation of critical pedagogies and research practice. This chapter documents and is a product of the institutional tensions and contradictions that surround the practice of Cultural Studies as it is situated within the contemporary university.

Any Way You Want It: From New Times to Hard Times

Many of us working today in Cultural Studies have seen programs and job positions cut or shifted into other departments. Critical scholarship has fallen by the wayside only to be replaced by work that promotes consumerist models of citizenship among faculty, students, and staff across every level of the academy. The current crisis within the academy is intrinsically tied to a series of larger cultural crises that have eroded rather than fostered collective and sustainable modes of resistance and change. There has been much written about the crisis of higher education, the demise of the humanities, and glut of under- and unemployed PhDs due to the collapse of the job market and the rise in adjunct faculty. Critical analyses of these trends have centered on what is described as the corporatization of the academy in relation to broader social and economic transformations. These include the growth of loans and other forms of debt for students and the reorganization of knowledge production itself to conform to marketing and consumerist imperatives (Soley 1995; Readings 1996; Slaughter and Leslie 1997; Dávila 2008; Giroux 2013, 2014).

While this process has been discussed at length, what is more surprising is that depoliticization and redeployment of some of the language and priorities of Cultural Studies have been central to these trends. The impetus for Cultural Studies was to challenge established cultural hierarchies and academic disciplines within an institution that represented itself as a space of high culture excluding the experiences, peoples, and texts that exist outside of and in opposition to the canon. However, the very spaces that were opened up by Cultural Studies critiques have been appropriated and redeployed by the corporatized academy, which today represents itself as a space that is broadly (and enthusiastically) inclusive and postracial. Curriculum now celebrates, markets, and promotes diversity and multiculturalism, as they are seen as crucial components in sustaining and creating capital investment via student enrollment, external funding, and alumni engagement, as well as sources to draw upon for effective public relations and marketing strategies. Students of color are often called upon to be representatives or at least visual representations of multiculturalism and diversity while virtual students of color have been photoshopped into university promotional material.

The superficial embrace of diversity and multiculturalism masks the systematic, institutional, and interpersonal marginalization that continues to occur on campuses within everyday life. Difference is celebrated, managed, and sustained as difference for the sake of difference in itself. It serves to represent visual variety, but as Richard Iton (2008) has highlighted, it *speaks* only the status quo. Racial difference is replaced by merely the idea of difference, while the material effects of race and racism are systematically displaced and even erased through excessive visibility and cultural recognition (Gray 2013). Arlene Dávila, for example, discusses how one of the common hiring processes of universities is to employ "black immigrants over African Americans, and first- and second-generation blacks, Asians, and Latinos over their native born counterparts." Dávila further argues, "the status of transplanted nationals is ostensibly less of a threat to the U.S. academy, if only because their research, and embodiment (in their person) of race, provide greater room for distance and comfort" (Dávila 2008). The visible markers of race become the tools used to erase the discourses of race and racism.

Racism and inequality that occur in the US are effaced within corporatized university culture. This calculated deployment of 'differences that make no difference' aligns with Hall's claim that "the so-called 'logic of capital' has operated as much *through* difference—preserving and transforming difference (including sexual difference)—not by undermining it" (Hall 1996). However, the loudly proclaimed doctrine of inclusion is not extended to voices, subjects, methods, and topics in the margins that adhere to politics or positions antithetical to the logic of capital as expressed through the corporatized university. Critical discussions about race and ethnicity increasingly dissipate and become remnants of the past. In fact, race, ethnicity, gender, and class are often presented as tropes of past struggles that have been successfully resolved within the diverse corporatized university. The established programs, centers, and departments as well as the 'diverse' body of students, faculty, and staff serve as visual triumphs over these past struggles, indicating that individualized subjects need not worry about systematic and institutional mechanisms of inequality. Ironically, this alleged success enables the defunding of multicultural and diversity programs, centers, and departments as well as the removal of these critical courses from the core curriculum. The dominant sentiment is as follows: students do not need it, so they do not want it.

As the university succumbs to the logic of the market, all departments are under the dominion of 'supply and demand,' left to fight for student enrollment. The university as a neoliberal space subjects students, faculty, and staff to the dictates of this market logic through participation in proper modes of consumption and production (work)—although the latter is not always necessary. Department and university faculty and administrators become predictors of the enrollment market and determine what need to be removed, reduced, expanded, and maintained. Informal conversations and structural decisions around practices of departmental and institutional production, such as hiring, policy changes, curriculum development, and requirements, are all part of the insidious daily reproduction of privilege, racism, and inequality. Research, experience, and even lawsuits have demonstrated that the tenure and promotion processes within the academy privilege whiteness. These processes unfairly scrutinize faculty and research that do not reinforce increasingly micromanaged institutional standards, norms, and priorities.

With this marketized logic applied to the university, concerns of 'supply and demand' and the maximization of capital are at the core of every institutional decision. This reorganization of the university is often justified as a necessary response to budget crises even as the hiring of university administrators has been rapidly increasing. Within this framework, students function as consumers who choose courses and evaluate their instructors through the model of customer service. This consumerist approach to higher education positions faculty primarily as servicers of student-consumer demands. Faculty are subsequently subjected to the regulatory and disciplinary modes of increasingly frequent informal and formal reviews, such as course evaluations, enrollment number maintenance, and even the monitoring of social media like Facebook, Twitter, and Rate My Professor. Within this context, classes are governed and disciplined by trends and fads as well as student enrollment and enjoyment. This management extends beyond the courses offered to include behavior within the classes themselves, as well as readings and assignments. This is most evident in (but not limited to) academic institutions considered 'tuition driven' universities, where the student body is catered to by an institutional discourse, suggesting that their tuition entitles them to only engage with classes, ideas, and knowledge packaged to their liking and acceptance, along the lines of Burger King's motto—you will get it your way.

Student enjoyment, whether actual or purported, and the students themselves become commodities which are used to secure scarce faculty lines and departmental resources. They are also used by the faculty, in the form of increasingly important positive teaching evaluations that determine hirability, tenure, promotion, and salary. Program success is measured primarily by enrollment numbers and completion rates, which in turn serves to attract more students. In order to achieve these benchmarks of success, a number of programs have reduced the requirements for master's and doctoral degrees. The imperatives of supply and demand then produce more graduate students at a faster rate and refocus them away from their own research toward exploitative forms of labor such as teaching introductory, low-level, and even upper-level undergraduate courses. The goal of graduate programs becomes focused on the creation and maintenance of a disposable labor force rather than the production of critical knowledge. The emphasis on professionalization leads to universities reclassifying students as trainees, with the figure of the hirable subject serving as their unachievable ideal. This position as trainee is literalized in the case of graduate students, who are no longer classified as either 'employees' or 'students,' which allows universities to circumvent any minimum wage, health care, and unemployment obligations they would otherwise incur.

The accelerated production of graduate students complements the corporatized universities' attempts to tighten budgets by allowing for a reduction in the hiring of faculty, in general, and the hiring of tenured or tenure-track professors in particular. Newly graduated doctorates from even the best universities in the country are often left to join the exploitative and uncertain world of adjunct faculty, where they may receive even fewer benefits than they did as graduate students. The tenure-track position has become the academic equivalent of a golden ticket. Those who were not fortunate enough to be chosen by the best graduate programs are left with the realization that they have been used for tuition and free labor as they compete for the same positions as those with the networks, sensibilities, and resources developed and available in more well-known programs.

Within this context, we have seen the rise and increasing normalization of 'permadjuncts,' and even more alarmingly, the establishment of 'faculty pools.' These pools allow universities to compile skillset-centered databases of unemployed and underemployed PhDs in order to call upon them to teach individual classes on an ad hoc basis without even the minimal stability provided by a fixed-term or adjunct contract. They then can release them back into the 'pool' when the particular course demand is sated or no longer fashionable or desirable. Junior faculty are similarly regulated by the corporatization of the academy via course demand. Tenure and promotion policies have become stricter and unceasing. In this way, research, teaching, and service expectations also subject the lucky winners of the academic lottery to continuous regulation.

The marketized university establishes multiple spaces of anxiety and generates the ideal hirable subject in the same ways that the fashion-industrial complex produces the ideal desirable woman, an impossibility that one must nevertheless strive to become. Within these spaces of anxiety, individuals become responsible for multiple forms and technologies of self-regulation. These include participation in institutional practices such as professional development workshops, re-certification programs, career counseling, combined BA/MA and accelerated programs as well as a range of commodified techniques that institute self-management, for example, self-help books, seminars and webinars, productivity apps and software, and psychotropic pharmaceuticals. Rather than critically assessing the broader structural transformations and shifting priorities within contemporary capitalism, the blame for slow hiring, un/underemployment, and stagnant wages generating these anxieties shifts onto individuals. Managing these spaces of anxiety provides the impetus for a large number of new administrative positions that are created to oversee the expansion of services to deal with this increasingly anxious university population (such as recreation facilities, financial aid assistance, and psychological and career counseling.) The hirable subject, of course, is never fully realized as the security of employment is always under threat through performance reviews, demands for re-credentialization, and other forms of precarity. Students and faculty at all levels of the corporatized university are subject to anxieties about an uncertain and threatening future.

Given the expansion of spaces of anxiety and institutional contexts that are unsympathetic (or openly hostile) to critical, political, and collaborative academic work, why even carry on? Why continue to try and make space for an intellectual project that is often described as outdated or no longer relevant within the contemporary academy? In spite of institutional resistance and an uncertain future, many of us continue to do the work we believe is required to generate possibilities of political and institutional change. As Grossberg has reminded us by drawing on the works of Gramsci, Althusser, and Hall, "belief is a matter of practice" (1997, 153). The contradictory incorporation of Cultural Studies into the corporatized university exemplifies the multiple challenges faced today by critical scholars. We believe in a vision of Cultural Studies that looks beyond the marketized parameters of success and confines of individual institutions. However, we increasingly see a disarticulated and depoliticized version of Cultural Studies becoming normalized. Understanding the problematic reconfiguration (and sometimes literal rebranding) of Cultural Studies is an important first step before thinking about how to use critical practices to help us continue to create strategies for political and institutional change.

Don't Stop Believing: Cultural Studies and Collaboration as a Minor Strategy

According to Stuart Hall, the impetus for Cultural Studies was to highlight a way in which the masked, taken-for-granted "cultural forms and practices of a society" can be studied through "the maximum mobilization of all the knowledge, thought, critical rigor, and conceptual theorization one can muster, turned into an act of critical reflection, which is not afraid to speak the truth to conventional knowledge" (Hall 1992). Hall argues that Cultural Studies was the "necessary irritant in the shell of academic life that one hopes will sometime in the future produce new pearls of wisdom" (Hall 1992). A little over two decades from when he spoke these words, we remain committed to this vision of Cultural Studies in the U.S. academy, which increasingly stands in opposition to it. If Cultural Studies remains a "commitment to a particular practice of intellectual-political work, and to the claim that such intellectual work matters both inside and outside the academy," then we are now in a moment when those who practice Cultural Studies face an especially difficult struggle. While Cultural Studies parallels other fields with an explicitly political-intellectual project, such as ethnic and gender studies, unlike these fields, it has refused to canonize itself. As an interdisciplinary project, Cultural Studies is often housed within and between other fields and departments, making it especially susceptible to budget cuts. This produces an institutional environment where Cultural Studies as envisioned and practiced in the past quite literally has no place in the academy.

Within the contemporary context, the engagement with popular culture has been depoliticized and reappropriated to serve the interests of the corporatized university. Popular culture appreciation courses reduce culture to a series of individual texts, disarticulating cultural formations and their connection to broader political and economic contexts. This parallels the incorporation of a depoliticized version of diversity into the corporatized university's mission and reduces critical understandings and knowledge formations around issues of identity such as race, class, and gender into forms of difference that make no difference. The institutional commodification of certain elements of Cultural Studies *qua* various disconnected 'popular culture studies' serves as an entry point for a broader devaluation of the kinds of knowledge and research practices that were initially articulated together as part of a larger political-intellectual project. This is most apparent in classes that center on histories or 'appreciation' of various components of popular culture—video games, hip hop, television, and so on. These courses are often composed of, and justified by, publications that analyze these topics in a similar fashion, adapting key academic slogans and phrases while rarely going beyond a textual reading of the object of analysis. Courses and faculty that are visible, popular, or productive in ways that align at least partially with the metrics of value established by the university become incorporated into its structure.

This particular image of Cultural Studies as 'popular culture studies' is presented and then disparaged both by those who seek to recover the security that came with elite knowledge and by those who seek to transform the university primarily into a site of applied knowledge and skills acquisition. From a certain perspective, these are echoes of long-standing debates that simply rehash arguments about the irrelevance and frivolity of teaching courses about popular music, art forms, and cultural practices. The article in the newspaper about academic conferences that takes the tone "can you believe this is what they do!" sounds a counterpoint to professional complaints that scholars of popular culture should "do some real research" (Wente 2015). As a result, Cultural Studies is marginalized and minimized both inside and outside the humanities and social sciences. It is perceived to be merely an ornamental (or 'boutique') specialty that can be easily assimilated into the traditional liberal arts disciplines, like literary studies or sociology, or jettisoned completely and replaced by programs that provide more 'job-ready' skills. As Cultural Studies, Ethnic Studies, and Gender Studies programs are drained of their monies and politics, departments and colleges continue to build curriculums primarily based on what will be cost-effective and profitable. The undermining and exhaustion of Cultural Studies from within is accompanied by the pressures to increase the number of science, technology, engineering, and mathematics (STEM) graduates with every directive and funding initiative issued by governments and the private sector.

Cultural Studies' consignment to the fringes of the academy resulting from these corporatized logics and priorities can be compared to the 'kettling' or 'corralling' used to contain and exhaust protest. Kettling functions as a mode of control precisely through soliciting and encouraging movement; as protestors are directed into certain spaces, their own forward movement and positioning ultimately enable their containment. Kettling, like the relegation of protesters to 'free speech zones' at the periphery of secured events, permits opposition but only in ways that modulate and manage the embodied interventions into spaces of power, making pacification and appropriation possible. In making this comparison, we are expanding the analogy between military strategy and class struggle developed by Gramsci. Making use of concepts from military strategy, Gramsci described the forms through which class struggle took shape. In particular, he drew attention to the difference between an all-out 'war of manoeuvre' that brings class struggle out into the open and a 'war of position' that describes the slow underground struggle between classes. Gramsci's analysis was well suited to the Fascist-Capitalist context he was struggling against and remained relevant to the Liberal-Capitalist context to which British Cultural Studies was attempting to respond in the 1970s. Yet, the present moment has further refined these techniques, developing new modes of containment for the management of opposition and resistance.

As with Kettling, those aspects of the project of Cultural Studies that cannot be assimilated, but cannot simply be eliminated, are contained. This has been done in ways that align them with the competitive individualism that organizes the corporatized university. While this containment of Cultural Studies may seem like the end of its life as an effective mode of protest in the university, it is preferable to the total exclusion of Cultural Studies faculty and the elimination of Cultural Studies programs. Within the context of the neoliberal academy, those of us who specialize in Cultural Studies must respond to these institutionalized processes designed to exhaust the critical and transformative potential of intellectual work. These responses are literally strategies of survival in an academic environment that is actively hostile toward critical practices. Given the glut of doctoral programs and graduates, as well as the accelerated rate of adjunct hires alongside diminishing faculty lines, these are strategies both for the survival of Cultural Studies and also for the economic survival of the potentially hirable subject.

Some of these strategies of survival are decidedly pyrrhic in the vision of the future they put forth. Those who specialize in Cultural Studies are forced to adapt to the institution's curricular demands and priorities rather than teach to their expertise. Faculty, especially at the adjunct and junior levels, are corralled into teaching courses that are disciplinarily bound to technological skills for the hirable subject as Cultural Studies courses are dropped from curricula. This results, for instance, in 'choosing' to teach an excessive number of lower level courses like public speaking at a variety of institutions as a strategy to maintain academic employment and avoid the deeper pitfalls of debt. Those teaching with a Cultural Studies orientation can either expunge the critical elements from their teaching in order to keep their positions or add emphases beyond course requirements, often at a lot of risk and for very little reward.

Such practices force the hirable subject to make the modern equivalent to Pascal's wager. The belief in the possibility of an ultimate reward as a *hired* subject in the form of a tenure-track Cultural Studies position, coupled with the fear of losing that possibility forever after years of specialized training, justifies and sustains ongoing participation in underpaid and precarious academic labor. The decision to pursue such a strategy to economically and academically survive can perhaps explain why people actively engage in institutional initiatives that they don't actually believe in or, in fact, actively despise. It is tempting to seek out strategies and subject positions that offer uncorrupted alternatives to the spaces of anxiety that constitute the contemporary university. However, it is no longer possible to build an 'optimistic' vision of the future that rests on either a pure space of resistance outside of institutional boundaries or a return to a mythologized ideal of the university. Moving forward requires building on the ambiguities within and beyond the contemporary university through a series of practices and strategies that are, to borrow a concept from Deleuze and Guattari, 'minor' in nature (1975). Such strategies require inhabiting institutional spaces differently; it entails recognizing the ways in which techniques of containment and exhaustion are interwoven with aspirational and transformative desires and practices.

In light of this current situation, the practice of 'doing the work' of Cultural Studies looks markedly different than it once did. We see rigorous collaborative work as a good example of a minor strategy that traverses institutional and affective borders. By collaborative work, we do not mean corporatized and semi-marketized partnerships that reinscribe normative power relations between the university and the communities it purportedly serves. Instead, a critical understanding of collaboration requires a disruption of formalized hierarchies and binaries, such as private versus public and politics versus professionalism. Collaborative work can challenge institutional hierarchies and redefine intellectual labor, making them inclusive of public processes that seek to expand new ideas rather than police the discipline. This type of collaboration can generate alternative understandings of knowledge production and authorship that are not tied to individualized notions of ownership and property. Authors take up collective research and writing not primarily to advance individual careers, but instead to produce critical political work which is made stronger, and is in fact only possible, through shared intellectual labor. Collaborative work also challenges the dominant mode of a peer review process that primarily serves to regulate and discipline intellectual production through the myth of meritocracy and anonymity. Such co-writing processes become political acts and produce collective knowledge that challenge dominant notions of professionalism, individual authority, and self-promotion. Instead, these practices can produce the type of intellectual labor that opens up the possibilities of social and political intervention and change, which lie at the heart of Cultural Studies.

However, lack of institutional support for interdisciplinary and collaborative projects that do not reinforce the marketing goals of the corporatized university or the hirable subject have severely limited the structural possibilities of doing this kind of work. The result is that such efforts are often treated as 'labors of love' that require a significant commitment of time and energy on the part of all participants. These forms of labor are not institutionally recognized or rewarded (in the form of payment, course credit, teaching credit, etc.) besides the presumed benefit of 'expanding one's network.' Scholars that want to pursue this type of work are forced to negotiate their commitments of time and energy in ways that easily translate into the neoliberal self-management practices of becoming hirable subjects. If such efforts produce written work, this too is undervalued by the corporatized university, which emphasizes solo-authored pieces as the primary criterion for hiring, promotion, and tenure.

In light of these constraints, the contemporary struggle of Cultural Studies is to resist forms of incorporation and processes of exclusion from a position of containment. This context requires practices and pedagogies that recognize the material context within which they operate, while struggling against individualization and neoliberal management. We started this essay by recalling the imperative to 'do the work' that first inspired our commitment to the project of Cultural Studies. The analysis of the contemporary university we have provided here requires a reconsideration of how to fulfill this challenge. In light of this, it is important to remember that 'doing the work' did not entail the realization of some predetermined goal or output. 'The work,' in this sense, was not a thing or a product in the way that one might talk about 'a work of art.' 'Doing the work' was about transforming social relations, modes of knowledge production, and forms of pedagogy both within and beyond the classroom. And so the work goes on.

Works Cited

Dávila, A. (2008). *Latino Spin: Public Image and the Whitewashing of Race*. New York: New York University Press.

Deleuze, G., & Guattari, F. (1975, 1986). *Kafka: Toward a Minor Literature* (Dana Polan, Trans.). Minneapolis: University of Minnesota.

Giroux, H. A. (2013). *America's Education Deficit and the War on Youth: Reform Beyond Electoral Politics*. New York: Monthly Review Books.

Giroux, H. A. (2014). *Neoliberalism's War on Higher Education*. Chicago: Haymarket Books.

Gray, H. (2013). Subject(ed) to Recognition. *American Quarterly, 65*(14), 771–798.

Grossberg, L. (1997). *Dancing In Spite of Myself: Essays on Popular Culture*. North Carolina: Duke University Press.

Hall, S. (1992). Race, Culture and Communications: Looking Backward and Forward at Cultural Studies. *Rethinking Marxism: A Journal of Economics, Culture, & Society, 5*(1), 10–18.

Hall, S. (1996). What Is This "Black" in Black Popular Culture? In D. Morley & K.-H. Chen (Eds.), *Stuart Hall: Critical Dialogues in Cultural Studies*. London: Routledge.

Iton, R. (2008). *In Search of the Black Fantastic: Politics and Popular Culture in the Post Civil Rights Era*. Oxford: Oxford University Press.

Prichep, D. (2013). A Campus More Colourful Than Reality: Beware That College Brochure. Article, npr.org

Readings, B. (1996). *The University in Ruins*. Cambridge, MA: Harvard University Press.

Slaughter, S., & Leslie, L. L. (1997). *Academic Capitalism: Politics, Policies, and the Entrepreneurial University*. Baltimore: The Johns Hopkins University Press.

Soley, L. C. (1995). *Leasing the Ivory Tower: The Corporate Takeover of Academia*. Boston: South End Press.

Wade, L. (2009). Doctoring Diversity: Race and Photoshop. *blogpost*, thesocietypages.org

Wente, M. (2015, June 1). Adventures in Academia: The Stuff of Fiction. *The Globe & Mail*.

The Impossibility of Teaching Cultural Studies

Gilbert B. Rodman

As my title suggests, I want to argue for a hard truth. You can *not* teach people how to do cultural studies. You. Just. Can't.

To be sure, many of us routinely do things that seem to give the lie to that statement, insofar as we teach courses filled with books and articles that (1) attempt to define cultural studies, (2) make claims about how cultural studies should be practiced, and/or (3) are themselves examples of cultural studies research. I have taught such a seminar myself multiple times over the past 20 years, so I know the genre pretty well.[1] It's taken me a long time to accept the central claim I'm making in this chapter.

But we should be honest with ourselves. At best, the kind of courses I've just described expose students to a range of cultural studies texts and

---

[1] At the University of South Florida, this seminar was officially called "Contemporary Cultural Studies." At the University of Minnesota, its formal name is "Critical Communication Studies." Syllabi for all those courses—as well as compressed, four-week version of the course I taught at the University of Turku in 2015—can be found online at http://www.gilrodman.com/syllabi

---

G. B. Rodman (✉)
University of Minnesota, Minneapolis, MN, USA
e-mail: gil@gilrodman.com

© The Author(s) 2019
J. Aksikas et al. (eds.), *Cultural Studies in the Classroom and Beyond,*
https://doi.org/10.1007/978-3-030-25393-6_6

maybe—if we're lucky—they inspire some (but by no means all or even necessarily most) of those students to embrace cultural studies as a project they want to take up themselves. But this is not the same thing as teaching those students how to do cultural studies.

In part, my argument hinges on a crucial slippage of meaning in how we typically think about "teaching." On the one hand, the word describes routine practices of pedagogical labor: for example, crafting syllabi, writing and presenting lectures, leading seminar discussions, grading papers and exams, and so on. All that labor implies the presence of other people (i.e., our students), but none of it guarantees anything about what those people actually get out of our courses. When we say things like, "I'm teaching my cultural studies seminar next semester," we're making claims about *our* labor that have no necessary bearing on what corporatized universities have come to describe as "learning outcomes." In this sense—and this sense only—we can teach cultural studies, insofar as we make something called "cultural studies" the central focus of courses that we offer. But, in the end, this is nothing more than a descriptive—and trivial—claim about the content of our syllabi.

On the other hand, we also use the word "teaching" in ways that are entirely about the impact our pedagogical labor has on students. Ideally, after all, the people who take our courses are not the same at the end of their time with us as they were when it began. In this sense of the term, "teaching" primarily refers to "learning outcomes" (though not in the corporatized sense of that term): it's a process that changes the people on the other end of it so that they have new knowledge, or new skills, and/or new ways of seeing the world. If students aren't transformed in some way by the time they've spent in our classrooms, then we haven't taught them anything. In theory, some of those changes are the result of the pedagogical work described the first sense of the word, but the actual relationship between our labor and our students' transformations is rarely as straightforward as we would like it to be.

Put a slightly different way, the semantic slippage at the core of my argument is the one between "teaching a course" and "teaching our students," and we need to remember that many of our students, independently of anything we may (or may not) do well on our side of the desk, will not learn anything like what we aim to teach them. More crucially, the converse is also true: the fact that people learn how to do cultural studies does not necessarily mean that they've been transformed because someone else has taught them all (or even most) of the tricks of the cultural studies trade. What we do in our classrooms undoubtedly matters—especially insofar as our mistakes can make it harder for students to learn anything—but, in the end, what our students actually learn depends more on *their* labor than it does on ours.

To this point, much of what I've described applies to almost any subject that one might teach. But cultural studies isn't a traditional form of academic work (and, arguably, it isn't necessarily academic at all, but that's too big a debate to take on in the space available here) and the ways that it differs from more conventional disciplines make it especially difficult to teach. For the rest of this essay, then, I want to focus on three facets of the problem at hand that are specific to cultural studies: (1) teaching undergraduates, (2) teaching graduate students, and (3) teaching anyone/everyone else.

Teaching Undergraduate Students

As I've argued elsewhere (Rodman 2015, 93–94), there is no such thing as teaching cultural studies to undergraduates—at least not in the US (and maybe not anywhere, but I'll limit my argument here to the national context I know best)—because cultural studies is a *political* project as much as (if not more than) it is an intellectual one. And, in the vast majority of cases, undergraduates don't enter our classrooms prepared to invest in political activity. To be sure, there are individual exceptions to that rule—and thankfully so—but they remain exceptions. Few of us who teach undergraduates in the US have the luxury of being able to assume that our classrooms will be filled with students who are ready to *think* politically, much less to engage in overtly political work.

Readers of this essay who work in US higher education can test this out for yourselves—though you do so at your own risk. Prepare a new undergraduate course with the expectation that most of the students in that course will be (1) politically aware, (2) politically engaged, and (3) politically progressive (because, even though there are somehow people who still resist this notion, cultural studies really *is* a leftist project [Rodman 2015, 43–49]). Compile a reading list and craft assignments that will only work well if the class as a whole is willing and able to take a left-leaning, activist approach to the subject at hand. If you're reading this book, there's a good chance that you're capable of designing such a course. The odds are also good that you'll enjoy the process and that it's a course you'd be excited to teach.

The odds are even better, though, that you will struggle to make such a course to work in practice—and that's *not* because of any faults you may have as an instructor. There's a fair chance—especially if you need someone else's approval to teach a new course, and doubly so if you're not protected by the magic sword and helmet of tenure—that someone higher up the food chain at your institution (e.g., your department chair, an associate dean) will balk at approving a new course that requires students to engage in overtly political work. More crucially, though, even if you clear that hurdle, there's a good chance that your students won't cooperate. A tiny handful will be as excited as you are by the experiment, a few more might be open to the prospect of becoming more politically engaged, but a significant number of them will simply be unprepared to take on an overtly political project—and there's a genuine risk that a vocal minority will be actively upset and belligerent about what they see as your efforts to impose a political agenda on them.[2]

To provide a concrete example: one of the undergraduate courses I teach on a semi-regular basis is something I call "Media Outlaws."[3] It's a course about media pranksters, activists, and hackers: "ordinary" people, with no inside connections to mainstream media institutions, who

---

[2] If there are major exceptions to this pessimistic vision, they involve the various "identity"-based disciplines—for example, Women's Studies, African American Studies, and so on—that already have political agendas at their core. Even in these departments, though, there is often pressure (both from administrators and from students) for instructors to steer clear of pedagogy that looks like political "indoctrination." Instructors are encouraged to teach students *about*, for example, feminist activism rather than to teach students *how* to engage in such activism themselves. Similarly, courses that require students merely to read and analyze "minority" literature as aesthetic texts—rather than to take up the pointed challenges that such literature often poses to hegemonic cultural and political norms—don't ruffle administrators' feathers as much as courses that require students to read and produce critical analyses of institutional racism.

[3] Syllabi for the different iterations of this course can be found online at http://www.gilrodman.com/syllabi

nonetheless manage to use mainstream media against itself for purposes of political critique, resistance, and rebellion. I originally designed the course as an excuse to teach *The Yes Men* (a 2003 documentary made by an activist group of the same name), but it also includes readings on Adbusters, Anonymous, Negativland, and other "culture jammers." I have the luxury of teaching on a (relatively) progressive campus in a (relatively) progressive metropolitan area in a (relatively) progressive state—so there aren't a lot of bible-thumpers or entrepreneurial libertarians in my classrooms to begin with who would be resistant (or even antagonistic) to the course's subject matter. It's a situation about as tailor-made for left-leaning, politically engaged undergraduate teaching as I can imagine in a US context and yet, routinely, I still get students in the Outlaws class who are surprised—and even shocked—that we're reading authors who not only think the world isn't already a happy, egalitarian utopia, but also actually want to *change* the world.

In a different universe, I could teach this course as a four-month-long workshop on grassroots activism, where the bulk of the work that students do builds on and feeds into the various political projects that they were planning (or already engaged in) before they ever enrolled in my class. In practice, I can't even pretend to aim for such a goal. For any given group of 25 students who start the semester, I can assume that 4–5 of them will drop the course, another 3–4 will never quite warm up to the idea that capitalism (or white supremacy, or patriarchy, etc.) needs to be resisted, 12–15 will be sympathetic to at least one of the political causes at stake in our readings but still not see the value in engaging in resistance (because "nothing ever changes anyway," or because activism makes them uncomfortable, or because they believe that someone else should do the work involved), which will leave a *very* tiny handful of students who get to the end of the course and are willing to go out and (try to) change the world themselves.

Perhaps not coincidentally, the one semester when I came closest (which, to be clear, still wasn't the same as "close") to seeing more than just a handful of students inspired to become activists themselves was the fall of 2016, when the US presidential election helped to underscore the systemic nature of the political problems at stake in the course with great urgency and clarity. At the same time, however, this was also an iteration of the course that highlighted some of the more troubling contradictions in how pedagogy has been institutionalized. The student who was the most dramatically transformed that semester was also the group's most epic failure—at least when viewed in conventional ways. This student was quite explicit about what (he thought) the course had done for/to him, even going so far as to write on the course blog: "You've radicalized me, Gil." And he was clearly thrilled to find himself activated this way. At the same time, and for reasons that weren't necessarily related to the course at all, he also ultimately found himself incapable of doing the quantity and quality of written work he needed to do to earn a passing grade. From my perspective, he was one of the most impressive success stories I've ever had in an undergraduate classroom: someone who was visibly, deeply transformed by the course (though I would maintain that he understated his own role in that process, while overstating mine). From a more traditional perspective, however, he wasn't a success story at all: he was just another student who failed.[4]

To bring this back to the main issue at hand, we can teach our undergraduates any number of things that are valuable to the practice of doing cultural studies—how to engage in specific types of critical analysis, how to use particular research methodologies, how to write better essays, and so on—but we can't really teach them one of the main things that distinguishes cultural studies from other intellectual practices: that is, how to be political. The vast majority of US undergraduates, after all, don't bring a political head into the game. In fact, they often actively resist the notion that politics belongs in the academy—and to be fair to them, this is largely because, by the time we see them in our classrooms, they've spent nearly two decades being trained in schools that insist, not only that those institutions are politically neutral and/or objective (even when

---

[4] There isn't enough space here to do the subject the justice it deserves, but this would be a good moment to point out that most traditional measures of both "good" teaching and "good" learning—for example, grades, course evaluations, and so on—are deeply flawed. Outside of contexts where our primary pedagogical goals involve the rote memorization of facts (and maybe not even then), there's usually a vast chasm between what we most want our students to learn and what we can actually assess in a meaningful way.

unavoidably they're no such thing), but that neutrality and objectivity are *supposed* to be the guiding principles of such institutions.[5]

Even in those rare and wonderful moments when, against all odds, we see visible evidence that one of our students has become "woke" (in one form or another), those breakthroughs are *not* the same thing as us having produced a full-fledged cultural studies practitioner. At best, we've set someone on a path that might, eventually, lead them into cultural studies. But they still have a lot to learn, and we haven't taught them to be "woke" as much as we've exposed them to some new ideas and (where applicable) encouraged their enthusiasm for engaging with the world in a new-to-them way.

Teaching Graduate Students

Not surprisingly, graduate students are more likely to arrive in our classrooms with strong critical/political lenses already in place. After all, they typically continue their education beyond their college years because they have a desire to study and/or teach a subject that already interests them. That helps. Still, for most of us, graduate education is constrained by heavy pressures to professionalize our students, and nowhere near enough liberty (for us or for them) to engage in radical forms of intellectual experimentation or collaboration. The dominant messages from university administrations to everyone involved in the process of graduate education—faculty, students, and staff—are all about efficiency and metrics. Get the "best" students (i.e., the ones with the highest GREs and GPAs) into our programs. Get as much teaching labor out of them—for as little money as possible—while they're on campus. Get them through the system as quickly as possible. Lather. Rinse. Repeat. This is not fertile ground for cultural studies to grow in.

It's not a coincidence that the Centre for Contemporary Cultural Studies (CCCS) at the University of Birmingham produced what is

---

[5] This is one of the many lies about education that our students have been told. Some of the others are summed up here: https://www.gilrodman.com/2015/02/01/lies-we-tell-our-students-rerun-sunday/

widely recognized as groundbreaking and innovative work in cultural studies precisely because it was *not* organized or managed in conventional ways. If one reads the personal reflections (Connell and Hilton 2016; Vincent and Grossberg 2013) of people who spent time at the Centre, it becomes clear that even though many of them have different interpretations of what the Centre was about (its goals, its successes, its failures, its legacy), they are in universal agreement about how *unusual* the Centre was compared to other sites of postgraduate education.

When the Centre was founded in 1964, it had no set curriculum, since there was no history within the university of anything called "cultural studies" to draw upon. As such, there was no way for the Centre's faculty to claim—or even pretend—that they had already achieved a mastery of a subject that they would then convey to the students. And so those faculty (Richard Hoggart and Stuart Hall) and several years worth of students had to make the project up together.

Even after the proverbial ball had been rolling for *just* long enough that there might be *some* semblance of a sedimented set of reading lists that newcomers needed to familiarize themselves with, the Centre was still far too marginalized and short-staffed—it never had more than three full-time faculty on staff—to deliver anything that looked like a conventional curriculum. And so, deep into the 1970s, the collective hurly-burly of staff and students all making things up together as they went along was the norm.

Even today, however, there's still a fundamental problem with creating a workable syllabus for a cultural studies seminar: a problem rooted in the linearity of a semester, and in trying to create a sequence of readings that helps cultural studies novices make sense of such a sprawling, heterogeneous, and internally contentious project. It seems to me there are three major options for how to deal with the flow of a cultural studies seminar, but none of them are entirely satisfactory.

First, one could work through the history of cultural studies chronologically—reconstructing the project from the ground up for each new crop of students—though this is undoubtedly too big a project for a single semester, and it requires trying to familiarize twenty-first-century US students with the various political, cultural, social, institutional (etc.) contexts that gave rise to the CCCS in the UK in the mid-1960s—assuming, of course, that one accepts that Birmingham is the place where one needs to start such a history. And that's not a safe assumption at all.[6]

Second, one could begin with examples of strong cultural studies scholarship and then try to backfill the history, debates, theory, and so on that laid the conditions of possibility for those exemplars. But then one runs into the problem of trying to explain how, for example, Jan Radway's *A Feeling for Books* (1997); Paul Gilroy's *Against Race* (2000); Meaghan Morris' *Too Soon Too Late* (1998); Larry Grossberg's *Caught in the Crossfire* (2005); and Carol Stabile's *White Victims, Black Villains* (2006)—five *very* different books, in terms of their subject matter, research methods, and theoretical frameworks—are all somehow part of the same larger project. In the absence of some sort of meta-discourse about what cultural studies is, newcomers to the project will most likely struggle to understand the nature of that larger project very well simply by looking at isolated examples of it—and the ways that multiple examples will diverge from one another will make such an approach more confusing, rather than less (see Rodman 2013).

Third (and this is the approach that I take), one could begin with the meta-discourse about cultural studies—the sizable body of literature that wrestles with the project's definitional questions (what it is, what it should be, and so on)—and then move on to more concrete examples of cultural studies research. But this approach can be frustrating for students, who find themselves struggling to make sense of the abstract debates about the general characteristics of a project that (1) is still very new to them and (2) actively refuses to be defined in straightforward ways. After two or three weeks of this approach, even students who appreciate the reasons why cultural studies has historically resisted efforts to be defined cleanly will often say that feel more lost and confused than when the semester began. All that meta-discourse may capture the actual fluidity of cultural studies accurately, but it also makes it harder for newcomers to the

---

[6] This isn't the place to address in full the long history of cultural studies folks questioning the proper place of Birmingham in the history of cultural studies (see Rodman 2015, 120–157). Suffice it to say that there are multiple legitimate versions of cultural studies' origins, and that the Centre doesn't figure prominently in all of them. Nonetheless, the Centre is an oft-cited choice for cultural studies' birthplace, and—for better or worse—it is (probably) the first site where the term "cultural studies" was adopted and broadly recognized as a label for a particular kind of blending of intellectual and political projects.

project to recognize cultural studies work when they see it or know how to produce cultural studies work of their own.

In different ways, all of these approaches suffer from the fact that cultural studies is—arguably, by design—an unstructured, heterogeneous amalgamation of projects and, as such, it defies almost any attempt to explain it using a linear narrative. Regardless of where one starts to learn about cultural studies, one is beginning somewhere in the middle of a story that is incredibly difficult to follow without knowing something substantial about other bits of the story that one hasn't gotten to yet. Short of trying to work through three (seemingly) different seminar-sized reading lists simultaneously—the cultural studies equivalent of being tossed into the deep end of the pool in order to learn how to swim—one will almost inevitably begin the task of learning cultural studies confused and frustrated.

It doesn't help matters that, at this stage in its history, cultural studies is arguably too big a project to squeeze into a single course—and has been so for a long time now. For example, the graduate seminar introduction to cultural studies that I took from Larry Grossberg in 1988 involved ten books plus two giant coursepacks of photocopied essays. Each of those coursepacks were about two inches thick, double-sided, and most of those pages contained a two-page spread in landscape format on each side. It was far more reading than anyone could tackle in a single semester. Eventually, Larry started teaching that seminar as a two-semester sequence—and then, later, as a *three*-semester sequence—but that expansion of the course's time frame *wasn't* about spreading out that massive reading load to be more manageable: it was about being able to *add* new material to the mix to cover more contemporary cultural studies work.

All that said, I think that it's certainly possible—maybe even common—for students to come into a graduate program knowing little or nothing at all about cultural studies and, four (or five, or seven, or nine) years later, come out the other side being proficient enough to claim (quite legitimately) that they do cultural studies themselves. They've obviously learned something about doing cultural studies during grad school that they didn't know before—and I'm willing to accept that strong faculty guidance can be a vital part of that process—but I'm less convinced that this transformation is about us as teachers anywhere near as much as it is about them as students.

At the end of the day, after all, we still come up against the different senses of "teaching" that I discussed at the start of this essay. Regardless of subject matter, after all, we don't actually teach students anything. They learn. Or they don't. But the change in the state of their knowledge depends more on what they do than what we do. We may put various facts and ideas in front of them. We may present them with ways of seeing and understanding the world that are revelatory to them. But the real work of education is still theirs, not ours. On a good day, we show them doors they hadn't noticed before. Maybe we even unlock and open those doors for them. But they still have to walk through them on their own. To actually learn cultural studies—what it is, how to do it, why it matters—involves going through one of those doors and then living on the other side of it long enough to find and embrace a new way of being in the world. But that last bit is the bit that we, as teachers, can't really do much about.

Teaching Anyone/Everyone Else

The problems I've described above are largely byproducts of the university as an institution. And, arguably, any good cultural studies approach to a question would require us to think *outside* the logics of existing institutions. So what happens if we take the university out of the equation? Can one teach cultural studies more generally? Can one teach outside of (or around, or in spite of) the institution? Maybe. But probably not. The more I've tried to teach cultural studies, the more convinced I am that it's a fundamentally unteachable project. The best I think any of us can do is to give people some things to read, offer some advice and encouragement and constructive feedback, and hope that our students eventually find their own way into the project.

If there really is a way to teach other people how to do cultural studies, it's probably something closer to the old martial arts movie shtick where the young neophyte goes to the old master to learn some ancient, noble art of combat and where said neophyte then spends most of his or her time performing seemingly irrelevant, yet humbling, tasks—making rice, fetching water, raking sand—that help said neophyte to unlearn all the bad habits of the mind and body that the world has already taught him or her. And it is only after endless repetition of those small, supposedly meaningless tasks that the *real* training—or, more precisely, what a misguided outsider would think of as "the real training"—can begin. It's a slow, arduous process, and not everyone can master it.

Some of you are undoubtedly thinking that, in spite of my earlier objections, what I've just described sounds a lot like an extended metaphor for grad school. And so (supposedly) we can—and do—teach people how to do cultural studies all the time. Except, of course, things aren't that simple. After all, the underlying lesson of many (most? all?) of those martial arts films is that the old master doesn't possess a truth that he or she passes on to the pupil. Instead, the pupil must ultimately find the truth inside himself or herself. The Sacred Art cannot simply be passed on from one person to another, like a pebble from hand to hand, even in an extended tutelage by the most skilled master and the most promising of pupils. In the end, the teacher is actually more of a guide—or perhaps a goad (especially if we move back to the graduate school side of my extended metaphor)—but the *real* learning always comes from the student. Always.

Embedded in all those martial arts films is another seemingly implausible truth: that is, that teaching is really all about failure. Those of us who teach for a living rarely admit this, but in our hearts, we know it's true. The only *truly* effective teachers—at least in the second sense of the term described at the start of this chapter—are the ones that live (and apparently thrive) in the imaginations of rabid right-wing pundits: the folks who go off (and also go on and on and on) about the dangers of tenured radicals who indoctrinate their students with the dangerous evils of marxism and feminism and environmentalism and queerness and anti-racism and other unspeakable forms of left-wing poison. *These* mythical teachers march into classrooms and magically transform vulnerable, complacent, God-fearing young people into fire-breathing leftists hell-bent on destroying the nation from the inside out.

Back in the real world, however, anyone who's ever spent more than a week in front of a room of US undergraduates knows how hard it is to get them even to *read* what you've assigned them—much less consider what that reading has to say long enough for it to move their worldview even a millimeter from where it was before. Even the most inspiring teachers, working with the brightest students, routinely tell stories about how many of their young charges sail through their courses without seeming to be affected much by them, one way or another.

I sound crankier than I actually am about my students. But I'm only not-so-cranky in real life because, even as I've maintained high standards, I've learned to lower my expectations for what a "good" semester can actually accomplish. I figure that I've had a successful semester if, out of a class of 30, as many as 3 of them show signs that they've been transformed by the course in positive and significant fashion. I can usually manage to hit that percentage—maybe even exceed it on occasion—but that still means that I fail much more often than not. And I suspect I'm not unusual in this regard.

Let me close with a thought experiment that (hopefully) helps to demonstrate at least a piece of my argument here. Think about the major cultural studies figures who passed through the CCCS, in one way or another, at some point in its brief but influential history: Brunsdon, Chambers, Clarke, Coward, Curti, Dyer, Ellis, Gilroy, Grossberg, Hebdige, McRobbie, Morley, Mort, Williamson. It's a long list of amazing scholars, and it's one of the reasons why Birmingham is accorded (and deserves) a special place in the cultural studies story. And let's assume, just for the sake of argument, that we can single handedly credit Stuart Hall with teaching cultural studies to all these people. It's a grandiose claim (and one that Hall would no doubt have been the first to reject), given what we know about how things worked at the Centre during its heyday, but let's roll with it anyway, while understanding that it *over*states Hall's actual influence.

Now think about all those other people whose names we do *not* know—but whom we can be sure existed, since it's not as if the Centre managed to survive for as long as it did averaging less than a single student per year—who did *not* go on to become cultural studies *anythings*. Then think about how much longer that list of names must be. Hall "taught" those people too—but he "failed" to teach them cultural studies. The list of names we know is a version of what John Clarke has called "the diversity that won" (quoted in Grossberg 1995, 32): that is, the tiny, if chaotic, piece of a larger story that is the main (if not the only) piece that the rest of the world knows anything about. But our list of "failures" is always much longer than our list of successes.[7]

And this suggests, in turn, that our successes aren't ever really *ours*. Whatever we may contribute to them, they still depend heavily on our students. We don't teach them as much as they teach themselves.

Works Cited

Connell, K., & Hilton, M. (Eds.). (2016). *Cultural Studies 50 Years on: History, Practice and Politics.* New York: Rowman & Littlefield.

Gilroy, P. (2000). *Against Race: Imagining Political Culture beyond the Color Line.* Cambridge, MA: Harvard University Press.

Grossberg, L. (1995). Cultural Studies: What's in a Name (One More Time). *Taboo: The Journal of Culture and Education, 1,* 1–37.

Grossberg, L. (2005). *Caught in the Crossfire: Kids, Politics, and America's Future.* Boulder: Paradigm Publishers.

Hall, S. (1992). Cultural Studies and Its Theoretical Legacies. In L. Grossberg, C. Nelson, P. A. Treichler, L. Baughman, & J. M. Wise (Eds.), *Cultural Studies* (pp. 277–294). New York: Routledge.

Morris, M. (1998). *Too Soon Too Late: History in Popular Culture.* Bloomington: Indiana University Press.

Radway, J. A. (1997). *A Feeling for Books: The Book-of-the-Month Club, Literary Taste, and Middle-Class Desire.* Chapel Hill: University of North Carolina Press.

Rodman, G. B. (2013). Cultural Studies and History. In N. Partner & S. Foot (Eds.), *The Sage Handbook of Political Theory* (pp. 342–353). New York: Routledge.

Rodman, G. B. (2015). *Why Cultural Studies?* Malden: Wiley Blackwell.

---

[7]When I presented a very early version of this essay at a conference, Michael Denning suggested that the known successes in the list of former CCCS students above might actually be better understood as the *failures.* These, after all, are the people who wound up in the academy, rather than in the proverbial trenches. I'm not sure I agree with this sentiment entirely. Is Angela McRobbie (for instance) *really* a "failure" because she carved out a successful academic career against all odds? That seems like too harsh an assessment. But part of what I value about Denning's suggestion is the acknowledgment that what counts as a pedagogical success story may not always be the obvious outcome. At least some of our pedagogical "failures" may actually turn out to be successes in ways that we never actually witness.

Stabile, C. A. (2006). *White Victims, Black Villains: Gender, Race, and Crime News in US Culture.* New York: Routledge.

Vincent, H., & Grossberg, L. (Eds.). (2013). Contributions to a History of CCCS. A special issue of *Cultural Studies, 27*(5).

Part II

Cultural Studies Pedagogies in Practice: In the Classroom and Beyond

Cultural Studies as Writing Project, with Trump Assignment

Donald Hedrick

A Micro-legacy from Stuart Hall

Seriously dating myself by acknowledging my attendance at the "groundbreaking" University of Illinois Cultural Studies Conference in 1990, I want to enter the present concerns of pedagogy by way of a circumlocution or detour, not through theory but through a specific, if now canonical, essay by Stuart Hall given at that conference. The essay, "Cultural Studies and its Theoretical Legacies," heard by me live, certainly bears rereading now, but my detour will primarily join something of my first impressions hearing it with a more studied focus now.

As a doubtful choice for addressing pedagogy, the essay notably doesn't come near at all to addressing our topic, instead providing a theoretical view of the field in the earlier days of the Centre for Contemporary Cultural Studies. The accounts by Hall constitute an account of intellectual history, with dominant and emerging forces on the scene of cultural studies: the significance of Gramscian hegemony, the contestatory arrival

D. Hedrick (✉)
Department of English, Kansas State University, Manhattan, KS, USA
e-mail: hedrick@ksu.edu

© The Author(s) 2019
J. Aksikas et al. (eds.), *Cultural Studies in the Classroom and Beyond*,
https://doi.org/10.1007/978-3-030-25393-6_7

of Althusserian structuralism, the "ruptural" emergence of feminism and the "turns" toward poststructuralism and textuality. While Hall appears in the essay to glance toward the 1970 feminist mantra that the "personal is political," his account, unlike those early feminist accounts, is rather about personal intellectual history than about personal life experience.

And yet, my first response to his giving the paper at the time was in some ways thoroughly personal and immediate, indeed responding to the charisma, style and *ethos* of his self-presentation. What connected with the essay's writing at the time, and connects with it for me now, is a running theme of *modesty*, even as he amusingly describes that, while autobiography is a form usually motivated by seizing authority and authenticity, he must instead speak autobiographically "in order not to be authoritative" (277). The essay thus describes not merely the discipline's movements but also Hall's own take on them, his personal intellectual history from an exploratory or trial perspective.

The absence of attention to pedagogy in Hall's essay even struck at least one member of the audience at the time as potentially problematic, for the question she asked at the talk's conclusion (her question helpfully included in the conference collection) was how Hall would apply his consideration of their attempts to create a "public intellectual" to the colleagues and students in "our world" (290). Hall graciously acknowledged the question's implicit critique, apologizing for having appeared to take the topic for granted, and he noted that in all the talking about institutional positions (as we might as well extend to the present) we often fail to ask questions about teaching.

For the present reading of the essay, however, I want to try to tease out several pedagogical implications actually present in the essay and even its stylistics—not merely in ornamental but in constitutive relations to the field of cultural studies. These implications are not accidentally related to the essay's repeated modesty *topos* having been performed, moreover, in a delivery which much impressed me at the time. In self-reflexivity, his intellectual gesture toward the "necessary modesty of theory" is matched by his writing practice in the essay, I propose. I want to try (essay) to envision cultural studies, outside but especially inside the classroom, as in effect a kind of writing practice in itself, as Hall demonstrates in performance. This short analysis attends to what might be thought of not as the "theoretical legacies" but rather as a "micro-legacy" of cultural studies, or at least of Hall's own contributions. It will conclude with a minor, practical intervention by way of illustration: an imaginary assignment about Donald Trump that I will assign to myself to write.

The "modesty of theory" parallels the frequent qualifications of the essay, qualifications that delimit otherwise ambitious claims or theoretical generalizations. Thus, the theory is even a bit demoted in the phrase "detour through theory." Modesty takes the form of qualified claims that we would see in a later essay calling for Marxism "without guarantees." While suggesting more open-endedness in defining the field, Hall modestly limits this open-endedness itself, jocularly cautioning that cultural studies "can't be just any old thing" (278). The schoolmarmish colloquialism itself performs this self-limitation, naming it "modesty."

As a special function of this modesty *topos* about methodology generally, Hall in the essay recurrently notes something that might also seem to be a limiting practice, namely, the field's and his own recourse to and even dependence on *metaphors*. Key concepts for both the field of cultural studies and for the essay's own explication are all addressed as *metaphors:* "struggle." "conundrums," "hegemony" and "interruption."

For "struggle," Hall recounts at length his lengthy integration with Marxism, which he concedes from the start was not a "perfect fit," particularly with his political background in the New Left (279), as might be the case now with those approaching Marxism from any other intellectual/political movements. Marxism's "silences" and "evasions," and especially for him its "Eurocentrism," engage him in a lengthy struggle with Althusser's theory, which he further describes as "wrestling with the angels" for its seriousness, yet indicating with this metaphor he neither dismisses it or lets go, even if without any winner really he nevertheless "warred with" Althusser "to the death" (280). By "conundrum," he signifies opening up undecided theoretical territory, to address what "Marxist theory couldn't answer" or unresolved issues for Gramsci or for "grand theory" (280). For "hegemony," the metaphor opens up questions of class relations by "using the displaced notion of ensemble and blocs" (280). The "production of organic intellectuals" also becomes a puzzle in not knowing in advance where to look for them or with what intellectual movement to identify them. But Hall finds that Gramsci's description of intellectual work entails two dimensions for the metaphor of hegemony, namely, that the work must be both on the forefront of theorizing as well as it must carry out "the responsibility of transmitting those ideas, that knowledge, through the intellectual function to those who do not belong, professionally, in the intellectual class" (281)—a double function we might consider a fair description of a cultural studies understanding of pedagogical practice.

Or, perhaps in the most memorable of the essay's metaphors, the "interruption" of feminism is described as having "broken in" to the Centre: "As the thief in the night, it broke in; interrupted, made an unseemly noise, seized the time, crapped on the table of cultural studies" (282). Announcing that he used the metaphor "breaking in" "deliberately," Hall captures what the intervention looked like given the masculinist *hubris* of the founders—not, as it has been taken (with the lurid "crapping" metaphor), as an instance of Hall's sexism. Their condescending welcome to feminism, by guys who thought themselves "good, transformed men," required such rudeness or perceived rudeness in order to bring visibly to the surface "every single resistance" hitherto hidden (282). The metaphor includes an additional illustration still meaningful, that even though an "interruption" seems to have been welcomed, the proof of real acceptance remains to be seen: "And yet, when it came to the question of the reading list..." (283). The multiple metaphors he uses clarify this point of admiration of feminism even further, as in the allusion to "the day of the Lord will come like a thief in the night" (*1 Thessalonians* 5.2.), or even Bobby Seale's story of the Black Panther Party, *Seize the Time*. Again, the practice of historicizing cultural studies in analysis and self-reflection requires invention and metaphorization and even the creativity of a writing practice.

Throughout the essay, he thus deploys such casual and even colloquial metaphors deliberately. But he does not do this offhandedly, as he also regards metaphor as a serious theoretical methodology; for instance, in explaining the "enormously productive metaphor of hegemony" (267) with the essay's collection of metaphors, Hall even self-reflexively comments on metaphorization itself: "We never produced organic intellectuals (would that we had) at the Centre; it was a metaphoric exercise.

Nevertheless, metaphors are serious things. They affect one's practice" (258).

Italicizing this seriousness in political rather than more narrowly in institutional or disciplinary terms, he again turns to metaphorization in addressing the AIDS crisis as a site of representation, insisting that not only people will die over this question of who is represented, but also, in a remark going further beyond the dire immediacy of the crisis into further crucial consequence, "desire and pleasure will also die if certain metaphors do not survive, or survive in the wrong way" (272). Hall is ultimately thus methodologically modest in turning to a writing device, stylistic or rhetorical, such as metaphor, as elsewhere he uses autobiography counterintuitively "not to be authoritative."

But Hall is hardly modest in attributing to metaphors the highest theoretical and real life consequentiality. An instructive comparison would be the methodological turn of Deleuze and Guattari in their argument that philosophy is foundationally about the construction of concepts (*What is Philosophy?*). Yet their deliberative provocative notion undoubtedly risks what Imre Szeman and Nicholas Brown critique as the "wrong message," that the ceaseless activity of invention by philosophy sends in an age of the impoverished use namely of the term "inventing" (as inventing communities, identifies, etc.), which might also be applied to invention through metaphorization, I would imagine. They claim, on the contrary and admitting how naïve it might sound, that the necessary path of the intellectual is toward Truth. ("Twenty-five," 331). Less ambitiously, Hall's allegiance to and spirit of *invention* requires the writing practice of metaphors for understanding, and therefore for teaching—even for teaching oneself—rather than we imagine to be the more extreme case, say, for Deleuze and Guattari, that creating concepts would have to be carried out in order to enable thinking at all.

In sum, let me suggest that composing metaphors and deliberate metaphorization in advancing theoretical discussion, while constituting the "micro-legacy" of Hall's "theoretical legacies" do at least three things for Hall, which can be applied to considerations of theorizing and practicing cultural studies pedagogy: first, it allows a colloquial, personal deauthorization, as he does also with the autobiographical narrative, in shared or commonplace significance; second, in this very colloquiality, it can be more reification-resistant than direct theoretical vocabulary may be, such as the "concept invention" philosophizing of Deleuze and Guattari; and third, more productively, it allows for a more creative expansion for exploring, testing and generating research and ideas—as it has often done, for instance, in the history of the sciences, from which we recall the importance of the generative concept of Thomas Kuhn's "paradigm shift." We might consider, for instance, how the Althusserian concept of interpellation as "hailing" is really another metaphorical treatment, in this case of the construction of subjectivity, by portraying a dramatized speech act scene of addressing and uptake, the speaker calling forth the subject who, in becoming "interpolated," turns around in response.

In conclusion, unpacking Hall's classic essay for the micro-legacy of metaphorization provides us with a distinctive model of cultural studies as a writing practice with a distinct place for *invention*. As such, it is not that what we do *with* what has been written to produce "cultural studies," but as foundational for or even prior to the cultural studies enterprise of committed knowledge production itself, in order to write in the first place. If all this seems rather apolitical for such a discipline (or even, in one school of thought, an anti-discipline) such as cultural studies, engaged toward political commitment and an effect in the real world, let us try out a "real world" "application" imaginatively, for one of the most politically charged and discursively oversaturated subjects of our current conjuncture: the Presidency of Donald J. Trump.

Trump Assignment

Here then, as a heuristic exercise if not the draft of a cultural studies lesson plan itself, let me attempt a "reading" of President Donald Trump not through a political or even cultural analysis of his relationship to contemporary capitalism, but rather as capital itself. I do not claim that this metaphorization is necessarily as "serious" a one as Stuart Hall's exercise and practices, but it may be more in the spirit of Marx when he ventriloquizes what "commodities would say if they could speak," and it may provide then one kind of instruction.

Apprentice Arenas

Capitalism requires what Marx terms a "competition of capitals." He notes parenthetically, however, that this also entails and produces a "competition among workers" (*Grundrisse* 403, 651). Trump's reality show *The Apprentice* clearly falls into this concept, with Trump himself cast in the role not merely of the "boss' but of capital itself, in demonstrating and in reinforcing by visual example the precarity of *all* workers. The famous staged "firings" of the show, apparently were not usually determined by Trump himself, although portrayed such that he carried out a theatrical role as CEO decider in chief. If it is the case as reported that Trump actually found it difficult to fire people (especially to their face, as his infamous Twitter firing of top government officials testifies), he would stand in for the impersonal logic of capital itself, not as the tough entrepreneur of the promoted market fantasies displaying manly business acumen.

Voice of America

While the capital, especially financial capital, is certainly a global matter, Ha-Joon Chang points out that most companies, despite "transnationalization," remain national companies with international operations, ultimately benefiting the home country (74). The economic premise of "Make America Great Again," despite the problematic and nostalgic "again" in the brand, is transparently Trump speaking as capital, particularly in his difficulty with anything but bilateral trade or other international agreements.

Be Unpredictable

While the stock market is not in itself "capital," it certainly is tied to and reflective of capital, in a way that corresponds to Trump's force as President. While Trump sometimes tries to take credit for stock market upticks (followed by silence when it goes the other way), the fact of his presidency has over time illustrated that it is not the President at the controls of the capitalist machine. On the other hand, his wild political and emotional swings, and pride in unpredictability as a strategy in itself (tied more to the "art of the deal" in real estate negotiations), corresponds to one significant way in the weather of stock market reporting since the explosion of financialization and "casino capitalism" from the 1980s and the Reagan era onward. That era, in fact, marked the invention of a new market index devised to capture and quantify the *volatility* now so pronounced in Trump's "leadership" (using the term quite loosely), namely, the Volatility Index. This now-standard economic index is a perfect match for the most erratic, shifting political leader seen at the head of our state.

Communicative Capital

Jodi Dean's analysis of the role of what she terms "communicative capital" is especially apt here in the broad terms of national communication. The paradox she addresses is the one for which, despite the great quantity of discourse production befitting a supposedly vital democracy, a majority of the dialogue occurs without and hardly expecting any *response*. This nonreciprocity or even blocked communication destroys the possibility of an ideal social logic of communication posited by Habermas, by which public sphere discourse is ideally reciprocal. As Dean concludes, "the more we communicate, the less is communicated" (*Communist* 148, 155). Trump as capital seems to have successfully extrapolated from the less ambitious playbook of George Bush, who in a throwaway comment of populist modesty once remarked that he only read the *headlines* in newspapers. Whether this was true or merely his own politically constructed populist image, he wished to construct (as I strongly suspect it was), the headline as the dominant "voice" of capital would explain Trump's extension and weaponization of the idea by using his Twitter account. These provocative Twitter postings thus invite feelings and expressions but not actual responses (though some appalled readers, of course, have been lured into a kind of response which, like capital, expands endlessly, adding value to the original, and which, like capital, recognizes no barriers).

Jameson once argued that finance capital's subjectivity effect was especially on the *speed* of communication, reducing entertainment value to the image of the 30 second or minute movie trailer as its embodiment ("Culture" 261). Trump's form of advertising is then the personal expression of the Tweet, which, befitting Dean's theorization, distinguishes the message (implicitly requiring response) from what she terms the "*contribution*" ("Communicative" 535). Under this new formation within capitalism, she proposes, "Messages are contributions to circulating content—not actions to elicit responses" (539). To "send" them makes one "*feel political*" (552), in an "exponential expansion" or abundance of communication, mirroring capital's self-expansion, but whose effect is depoliticizing. Or, in terms of capital, Dean writes, "Differently put, the exchange value of messages overtakes their use value." Even more generally applicable and applicable to Trump, her argument adds that "the circulation of logos, branded media identities, rumors, catchphrases, even positions and argument exemplifies this point." The message's success, moreover, is marked not by a response but by "the popularity, the penetration and duration" of the contribution (540). Her description of an entire communicative apparatus under the regime of capital well describes Trump himself, as a newer formation of capital than that envisioned and critiqued by Marx.

Branding

Consider also what is now fully naturalized in the world of consumer capitalism, namely product branding. As all have observed, Trump's product line has wildly veered from real estate to steaks, often under the "Trump" brand as the only unifying feature in their exchange value, his own name as the very brand itself. A function of branding economically, moreover, is that branding of products occurs in self-expansion, with profit diversified among expanding, diverse product lines by which profitability over time invested in the "Trump" brand counts more than profit itself. Marx did, however, anticipate this feature of capital fully exploited by Trump, in Marx' analysis that for capital profitability over time trumps profit itself, or, more explicitly, the logic of capital is that which maximizes the "*conditions* of profitability" (italics added) in various ways, of which the consumerist version is the brand. In its commodification, it works exactly as does the form of the commodity itself, significant only in exchange, whereby surplus value is generated (*Capital* I, 254). Since "Trump" is both identity and commodity, and Trump's most highly advertised and protected "product," it makes sense to carry out this exercise in regarding Trump *as* capital. In effect, Trump's practice follows the political logic of Lenin, who wrote an entire pamphlet about the power and the necessity of the political *slogan*, as we see also in the variety of Trump's go-to lexicon constructions about "fake news" or the like.

Capital Speaks Value

Another aspect of "TrumpTalk" is slightly different than the "contribution" phenomenon Jodi Dean examines as part of the contemporary capitalist expressive culture: the self-valorization of capital through performative speech. As a "competitor capital," for instance, Trump through praise or blame, idolization or insult, can directly, even immediately if he is lucky, raise or lower exchange values, which must as capital be sustained in motion. His speech and speaking style of sales; therefore, count as capital itself, its only true "language" as exchange value. His speech is therefore always engaged with "sportification," and, even when indirectly, is not competitive, part of his "art of the deal's" "truthful hyperbole." In one instructive instance of this, President Trump, when angry at France's vigorous and vocal opposition to his withdrawal from the Paris Climate Accords, made a point of announcing that Paris is overrated as a tourist destination and that "no one" is traveling there any more for a vacation. While this might seem a rather random, petty insult, irrelevant to global climate and greenhouse gas issues, it functions nevertheless in the logic of capital. That is, once again, in the "competition of capitals" (in which one notes that his hotel and golfing industry business is in actual competition with other leisure activities and even nations and places), Trump hoped to have a direct effect of his speech on his own profitability, competing with all other leisure activities such as even tourist travel to the brand "Paris." For Marx, again, this is an important characteristic of capital—namely, that it seeks to maximize profitability over time above an immediate profit.

We might speculate whether the practices we see are more in keeping with his real estate background or with his reality television show background, and which if either would be more historically significant for the regime of contemporary finance capitalism. Real estate would seem the more likely candidate for his preference, as its performative speech would seem, like capital, to have no limits to either the valorization or devalorization (debranding, insult, etc.) of the object to which it is directed. In the expansion of competition, Trump thus valorizes his own industry above others in an always imagined "competition of capitals." Of course, Trump seems hardly to have been elected primarily for his real estate expertize, considering his failures and bankruptcies. Nor did it seem to win voters over because of his personal professional identity, since real estate is generally regarded as one of the least trusted and lowest regarded among occupations, not to mention also the potential nation-wide stigma of being a New Yorker. Italicizing his method of performing profit, would seem to suggest that his election was not so much a vote for an individual, successful businessman, as it was perhaps a vote for capital itself, ever forgiven, even as it consistently displays what David Harvey has explicated as the "madness of economic reason."

Genüssfähigkeit

One of Marx's little known features of the products as a positive feature of capital is the quality of increasing the kinds of pleasures and, especially, the ability to experience them, or *Genüssfähigkeit* (*Grundrisse* 409). This multiplication of pleasures and pleasure-capability, he regarded, perhaps surprisingly, as a civilizing trait of capital's logic (though in Trump's particular character the near limiting case incivility of "compulsory competition" would clearly seem predominant). Interestingly, Trump's entire empire seems to have captured this logic in its range of entertainment pleasures under his brand noted before, from gambling to steaks to visual splendor to golfing to his reality television show *The Apprentice*. The hodgepodge character of the products onto which Trump latches and then drops is another verification that he is less the Wiley entrepreneur (of the current business and university world romanticization of entrepreneurship), but rather as capitalist production itself, which, Marx argues, "is indifferent to the particular use-values its produces, and in fact to the specific character of its commodities in general" (Vol. III, p. 297). In terms of the corresponding nature of wage labor, as again exemplified by the ultimate indifference of *The Apprentice* to actual commodity-related expertize, capital must also be "indifferent to the specific character of its work." Its strategic inconsistency, like Trump's, enacts a necessity "to change according to the needs of capital and let itself be flung from one sphere of production to another" (297). Trump exemplifies in the apparent attraction of his show, moreover, in creating a fantastic identification with capital, "as it drives an unwelcome series of new soldiers of fortune onto the field alongside and against the various individual capitalists already present," widening its basis to "recruit ever new forces from the lower strata of society"—hence, the soon bankrupted Trump University implicit marketing mission. (III. 735).

The latter turns the workplace into what DeBord would think of as just another part of the "society of spectacle," in which *firing* is the consummate money moment of vicarious pleasure for an audience. With the workplace metamorphosed into reality show, Trump acts as a function of late capitalism as it pertains to entertainment value, namely what Theodor Adorno regarded as its logic of "sportification," or its tendency to turn all entertainments into *contests or sports* (89). Thus, the adventures of capital itself turn wage labor and apprenticeship (updated as precarity) themselves into a contest, whose ultimate adjudicator is, or is imagined as, the impersonal market of capital itself. Trump's project of "Trump University," however, does not at least at first glance seem quite to fit this same pattern of entertainment production, perhaps accounting for its eventual failure and bankruptcy. It might, however, share with other entertainments the promotion of a collective, banal fantasy of achieving maximum personal wealth, selling fantasy over know-how for a post-expertize economy, in a psychology mimicking the expansion of capital, for which all obstacles—even the personality of a Presidential candidate—are considered barriers to be overcome. Thus, Trump himself was often by pundits acknowledged to have broken all the barriers of political culture and convention.

The entertainment logic of "sportification," moreover, is the equivalent of what the Marxist scholar Ellen Meiksins Wood regards as a central feature of capitalism's origins, in the historical move from a market economy of opportunities to a specifically capitalist economy of "compulsory competition," when wage labor itself will become compulsory (*Origin* 12). Trump's role in his reality show magnifies what capital has done to wage labor overall, and specifically to teaching in its increasing reliance on adjunct labor, namely a condition of "precarity." Trump's role on the show is both to maximize a sense of precarity's prominence. Trump's "reality" thus mimics "real life" precarity, only for the length of one episode rather than potentially through an entire lifetime. As it has been ironically claimed, under capitalism the only thing worse than being exploited is not to be exploited (Denning 79). Trump himself, moreover, embodies a precarious instability of his own, as he always appears on the verge of collapse in a crisis.

"Universal Prostitution"

Marx considers exchange value under capitalism as leading to a kind of "universal prostitution," whereby everything is exchangeable for everything else. Echoing, and sometimes citing, Shakespeare's famous observation in *Timon of Athens* that money makes "impossibilities kiss," Marx goes on to describe money's transformative powers in language that serves as a perfect character description of Trump, if he exemplified a "philosophy" along with his own maximization of masculine value:

> The extent of the power of money is the extent of my power. Money's properties are my…properties. Thus, what I *am*, and *am capable of* is by no means determined by my individuality. I *am* ugly, but I can buy for myself the *most beautiful women*. Therefor I am not *ugly*, for the effect of *ugliness*—its deterrent power—is nullified by money … I am *brainless,* but money is the *real brain* of all things and how then should its possessor be brainless? Besides, he can buy clever people for himself. Does not my money, therefore, transform all my incapacities into their contrary. (*Economic and Philosophic Manuscripts,* 103).

Yet in our metaphoric exercise, we might expand on the observation for purposes here, namely to assert that Trump not only exemplifies the effect of capital but actually performs as capital itself, by virtue of being the instrumental cause of prostitution *in others*. Clearly he has served as this continually, not merely in his own person in providing hush money to porn stars with whom he had affairs and doubtless others, but as the cause of the very prostitution of what has virtually become "his" party (an ownership of Republicans as property, or more within the metaphor, rather as their pimp), selling out any residual conservativism or any other principles in order to maximize the wealth of himself/itself and that of its allies.

As capital in traditional Marxist terms embodies the inherent contradiction and source of class conflict, Trump as a current form of capital-in-motion both creates and uncreates *every* allied form of conflict, maximizing and exploiting inequalities of every kind and promoting a war of all against all: urban vs. rural; white vs. nonwhite; the 99% vs. the 1%; educated elites vs. the less educated; North vs. South; Western Europe vs. anti-democratic regimes; the U.S. vs. "shithole" countries; television vs. Hollywood, science vs. know nothingism; the U.S. vs. allies and neighbors. Like capital's continual self-expansion, class conflict metastasizes as it historically varies its modes of exploitation.

Speech Acts as Exchange Value

Serious linguists have made attempts to characterize Trump's speech linguistically, with some arguing that his incoherence, loose association, jumping into other topics and ungrammaticality are actually more common in ordinary, everyday discourse than we might like to admit about ourselves (see McWhorter, Sclafani, Lakoff). But let me suggest another reading from a linguistic focus, one that might account for why lies in the Trumpsphere do not seem to be perceived lies, either to Trump himself or even to his presumed "base," as they are termed, of supporters, rendering them slightly less "deplorable." As in the creation of exchange value in the discourse of real estate negotiation, the *illocutionary force* of Trump speech is more often than not less of an *assertion* or claim, as might be expected for instance in standard academic discourse, than it is rather a *bid,* as one might make in a capitalist business, or as in a bid on a piece of property to purchase. To suggest, for instance, an outsized attendance at an inauguration is not on the order of a warranted assertion, which would be appropriately subject to verification and fact-checking as it might be for academia or media, but rather *an offer or a bid,* or even sometimes as a gambling wager: "I'd bet you that…" Thus, in this sense Trump speech and attitude is not as much anti-PC as it is anti-professional-managerial.

These sorts of admittedly everyday speech acts, therefore, exist as and are subject only to exchange value with other, even counter-offers, rather than to factual warrant, serving in this metaphor more like speech with a particular use-value. Our objection or astonishment, especially academic and professional, at his indifference to the warrantability of assertions is probably in one sense beside the point, arguably showing a perspective about language and communication either nostalgic or naïve. When speaking of speech acts technically, moreover, the phenomenon calls to mind many of J. L. Austin's categorized illocutionary acts that are not subject to truth-value tests, or even economic ones, but nevertheless carry out or perform *actions*, that is, "doing things." Such acts (for instance, "I owe you ten dollars") are not subject to verification as "true" or "false" but are (in Austin's stylistic invention) "felicitous" or "infelicitous" given their role within an entire context and their having met stipulated formal conditions (as explicated in speech act theory). Similarly, in his embodiment as capital, Trump once infamously responded to an MSNBC Network interviewer about discrepancies in the value of the real estate he was selling: "I set the value of my properties in my mind." Only capital would talk like that.

The "Marx Ratio" and Radical Inequality

Trump's famous indifference to his workers, as well as to the temporary bands of loyalty that "vanish into air," follows capital's, as Gayatri Spivak notes, that "traffic of exchange … in labor-power as a commodity," which leads not only "to difference but to indifference" (243). Quoting Marx from the *Grundrisse,* she explicates further, "In the developed system of exchange... the ties of personal dependence, of distinctions, of education and so on are in fact exploded, ripped up...; and individuals seem independent (this is an independence which is at bottom merely an illusion, and it is more correctly called *indifference*") (italics added). Like subservience to capital, the loyalty demanded to Trump becomes only one directional. Consider Chomsky's claim (somewhere) that capitalist business is our only national religion. The expansion of both inequality as well as indifference to inequality is underscored by the recent economic and even business attention to inequality—covered perhaps surprisingly in the business sections of the *NY Times*, but therefore guaranteeing it will have no effect on the widespread culture or politics as a "contribution" getting, in Jodi Dean's terms, "no response," changing nothing. Thus, the *Times* published what in another universe would be a scandalous chart of the ratio of top CEO pays relative to their employees' wages, for a large list of Fortune 500 companies—Mattel leading the pack with CEO pay about 5000 times workers' pay ("Highest-Paid").

For the recent radical reduction of corporate tax levels by Congress, Trump spoke more directly as capital when he refused to speak of his win in the usual political euphemisms, by not using Congress's more obscure branding of "Tax Reform and Cuts Act." Instead, Trump boasted of it as simply (and really more honestly) as his "Tax Cuts Act," while explicitly and publically assuring rich friends thereby that with this legislative act he would "make them richer." Thus, Trump does refuse, in perverse honesty, the filter of neoliberalist politics in order sometimes to speak directly, brutally and arrogantly, as capital would speak "unfiltered" if it dared.

In an example of capital's tendency to swallow up its own critique, the business section of the NY Times remarkably featured its front-page story of a proposed "Marx Ratio," accompanied by a sketch of Marx himself (Irwin). Here, the novel statistic consists of the ratio of an individual company's yearly profit to the yearly annual wage of its lowest-paid employee, which virtually captures the nature of surplus value lost to the wage-earning worker. Once again, even an ostensibly anti-capitalist message like this is in Dean's term merely a neutralizing or depoliticizing "contribution" to economic discourse in the air, relegated to Business News and thus one expecting no response, never really entering any truly public sphere. Capital can even, given the right circumstances, get away with speaking the language of capital's critique (as we might surprisingly find Trump himself doing).

What Capital/Trump Wants

The final word on capital confirming its identity with Trump is provided by Fredric Jameson, and perhaps constitutes the most succinct yet comprehensive formulation of the central issue for this pedagogical exercise: "Capitalism itself has *no social goals*" (italics added, cited by Brown and Szeman, "Twenty-five" 333). Often framed as Trump's effective lack of "ideology" in political chat and punditry, the observation certainly encompasses Trump's own history (changing from Democrat to Republican, and many other 180-degree flip flop on policies), but especially to the only real "visions" that emerge, such as tax cuts for the rich, which could only by a serious stretch of language constitute a "social goal." What is finally to be done with money, or even with "jobs" for that matter, is left entirely unexplored and irrelevant. We see in this the irrationality or anarchism of capitalist distribution that David Harvey explores in *Marx, Capital and the Madness of Economic Reason* (Oxford UP 2017). While his Trump's personal style of wealth accumulation might suggest a utopian social goal of leisure if it were radicalized democratically (a gold toilet for every citizen perhaps?), it remains individualized and not for the "general welfare"; the general "99%" public can expect to play in his casinos and on his golf courses, but not to own them. This lack of social goals also accords with his penchant for creating surprises, throwing his competitors offguard, in his deal-making previously and now in policy-making as President.

Conclusion

There's nothing really to conclude here for this fictional pedagogical-metaphoric exercise, except perhaps to note that if actually carried out by students, rather than by myself, it might satisfy an assessment instrument for newly invented Marxist Student Learning Outcomes (MSLO), whose straightforward goal would be to increase critical and effective understanding of capital and capitalism. It might be accompanied, moreover, by treating theory more modestly if not playfully. Perhaps the assignment becomes an example of the usefulness of or need for yet another pedagogy—namely, a pedagogy for teaching oneself. If metaphors seem too flexible in meaning "any old thing," especially metaphors of a radical or transhistorical or incommensurable nature, they may require a modest pedagogy of allowed, albeit forced analogies. Rather than the commanding slogan of "Always historicize," perhaps the more inviting slogan is through invention in cultural studies to "sometimes de-historicize" (Hedrick, "Dumb" 74), even in our "interesting" present conjuncture.

Works Cited[1]

Adorno, T. (1991). *The Culture Industry*. New York: Routledge.

Austin, J. L. (1962). *How to Do Things with Words*. Oxford: Clarendon Press.

Brown, N., & Szeman, I. (2014). Twenty-Five Theses on Philosophy in the Age of Finance Capital. In A. Pendakis, J. Diamanti, N. Brown, J. Robinson, & I. Szeman (Eds.), *Contemporary Marxist Theory: A Reader* (pp. 321–336). New York: Bloomsbury.

Chang, H.-J. (2010). *Twenty-Three Things they Don't Tell You About Capitalism*. New York: Bloomsbury.

Dean, J. (2012). *The Communist Horizon*. London: Verso.

Dean, J. (2014). Communicative Capitalism: Circulation, and the Foreclosure of Politics. In *Contemporary Marxist Theory: A Reader* (pp. 533–554). New York: Bloomsbury.

DeBord. (n.d.). *Society of the Spectacle*. London: Rebel Press.

Deleuze, G., & Guattari, F. (1994). *What Is Philosophy?* New York: Columbia University Press.

Denning, M. (2010). Wageless Life. *New Left Review, 66*, 79–97.

Hall, S. (1992). Cultural Studies and Its Theoretical Legacies. In L. Grossberg, C. Nelson, & P. Treichler (Eds.), *Cultural Studies* (pp. 277–294). Routledge: New York.

---

[1] An earlier version of this essay, "Adorno Does Donald," Was Presented at a Plenary Session of the Cultural Studies Association at Georgetown University, Washington, DC, May 25, 2017.

Harvey, D. (2014). *Seventeen Contradictions and the End of Capitalism*. New York: Oxford University Press.

Hedrick, D. (1997). Dumb and Dumber History: The Transhistorical Popular. In A. Kumar (Ed.), *Class Issues: Pedagogy, Cultural Studies, and the Public Sphere* (pp. 65–76). New York: New York University Press.

Irwin, N. (2018, May 23). Is Capital or Labor Winning? Introducing the Marx Ratio. *New York Times*.

Jameson, F. (1997). Culture and Finance Capital. *Critical Inquiry, 24*(1), 246–265.

Jameson, F. (2009). *Valences of the Dialectic*. London: Verso.

Kumar, A. (Ed.). (1992). *Class Issues: Pedagogy, Cultural Studies, and the Public Sphere*. New York: New York University Press.

Lakoff, G. *Understanding Trump*. https://georgelakoff.com/2016/07/23/understanding-trump-2/

Lenin, V. I. *On Slogans*. https://www.marxists.org/archive/lenin/works/1917/jul/15.htm

Marx, K. (1973). *Grundrisse*. Harmondsworth: Penguin.

Marx, K. (1978). *Economic and Philosophic Manuscripts of 1844. The Marx-Engels Reader*. (Ed. Robert C. Tucker, pp. 66–125). New York: Norton.

Marx, K. (1981). *Capital: A Critique of Political Economy* (Vol. III). London: Penguin.

McWhorter, J. (2017, January 21). How to Listen to Donald Trump Every Day for Years. *New York Times*, SR1.

Sclafani, J. (2017). *Talking Donald Trump: A Sociolinguistic Study of Style, Metadiscourse, and Political Identity*. New York: Routledge.

Spivak, G. (2014). Scattered Speculations on the Question of Value. In A. Pendakis, J. Diamanti, N. Brown, J. Robinson, & I. Szeman (Eds.), *Contemporary Marxist Theory* (pp. 239–260). Bloomsbury: New York.

Szeman, I., & Brown, N. (2014). Twenty-Five Theses on Philosophy in the Age of Finance Capital. In *Contemporary Marxist Theory: A Reader* (pp. 321–336). New York: Bloomsbury.

The Highest-Paid CEO's in 2017. *The New York Times*, May 25, 2018.

Volatility Index (VIX). https://en.wikipedia.org/wiki/VIX

Wood, E. M. (1999). *The Origin of Capitalism: A Longer View* (p. 200). London: Verso.

Critical Pedagogies in Cultural Studies: On Teaching Marxism Online

Ronald Strickland

At Illinois State University in the spring semester of 2000, I taught what must have been the first completely online, credit-bearing graduate seminar in Marxist theory in an American university. In the late 1990s and early 2000s, many educators viewed online courses with suspicion. Online teaching was vaguely associated with the neoliberal disinvestment in public higher education and the corporatization of the academy. But rather than simply to bemoan these developments, I sought to embrace them as opportunities to improve a graduate seminar that I had been teaching in the conventional format. From its inception, I envisioned the online course as an experiment with the goal of expanding intellectual engagement beyond conventional disciplinary and institutional boundaries. The course was structured more or less on the model of a correspondence course, with the internet allowing for participants to see each other's work and interact with each other on a regular basis. I posted weekly reading assignments and written lectures online, then students posted formal responses to an open discussion board, and we all followed

R. Strickland (✉)
Michigan Technological University, Houghton, MI, USA
e-mail: rlstrick@mtu.edu

© The Author(s) 2019
J. Aksikas et al. (eds.), *Cultural Studies in the Classroom and Beyond*,
https://doi.org/10.1007/978-3-030-25393-6_8

137

up with comments and further discussion. In 2007, after offering the course several times, I recorded my lectures as a series of ten-minute videos and uploaded them to YouTube for free public distribution. The YouTube lectures have had a life of their own. As of March 2018, these videos had been viewed, collectively, more than 500,000 times.

The University Without Walls

In Great Britain, there are strong links between the emergence of cultural studies as an academic movement and the history of educational outreach to non-traditional students. Both Richard Hoggart and Raymond Williams tutored and produced lectures for the Workers Educational Association (WEA), a charitable organization founded to promote adult education in the late nineteenth century. The WEA has received major funding from the British government throughout the twentieth century. Stuart Hall taught in the Open University, another British-government-funded project intended to extend the opportunity for higher education to all social classes.[1] Projects like these have functioned to subsidize vocational training for the business sector and to perpetuate existing social power relations. But for progressive intellectuals like Hoggart, Williams and Hall, this structure of "public pedagogy" using mass media technology to reach adult learners was a resource too powerful to concede to corporate interests.

In the US, at least since the end of World War II, traditional "on-campus" higher education has been widely available across the social spectrum. Still, among many faculty of my generation—those who came into the profession in the aftermath of 1968—there was a commitment to get ourselves and our students out of the classroom and into the "real world." We experimented with idealistic "free university" schemes such as extra-curricular courses taught in local community centers and coffee houses. We taught courses in prisons and county jails. And we developed

---

[1] See Cole, Josh (2008). "Raymond Williams and education—a slow reach again for control", the encyclopedia of informal education. [http://infed.org/mobi/Raymond-williams-and-education-a-slow-reach-again-for-control/. Retrieved May 19, 2015].

experimental alternatives like "service learning" courses outside the traditional curriculum. Many of these were grass-roots, faculty-led "off the books" initiatives, conceived in opposition to the formal conventions and institutional structures of the university. Teachers involved in these projects tended to see the administrative bureaucracy of the university as the enemy. Often, when proposals for the projects were submitted, the financial support was not forthcoming, or not ongoing, or not really sufficient. Sometimes no attempt was made to gain financial support for the projects. It was taken for granted that administrative financial support meant a loss of control that would inevitably compromise the value and effect of any radical or progressive initiative. It should come as no surprise that few of these projects lasted long. In order for free extra-institutional courses to be taken seriously, they would have to be taught by university-credentialed teachers; in effect, they would have to be taught by the same faculty who were running the gauntlet of tenure and promotion within the institutional system. Any faculty member who undertook this task would quite probably be moonlighting for no pay at the expense of one's own career advancement and professional status. This was not a sustainable arrangement.

So, during the 1970s and 1980s, some progressive projects, like Women's Studies and African American Studies, found a tenuous foothold within the institutional structure of the academy, while others, like Peace Studies and Working-Class Studies, remained on the margins. Clearly, progressive activism in higher education confronted the limits of an increasingly "corporatized" public higher education. At the same time, a trend emerged on the other side of the political divide in the university's community outreach effort. Institutions established "corporate-university partnerships," "technology transfer programs" and "business incubators." These programs, many of which have been institutionalized and continue to thrive, are typically administration-driven. Sometimes they have been subsidized by corporate donations. The offices may be corporate-style, well-equipped and well-staffed. The disjuncture between the tradition of academic freedom and "disinterested" inquiry, on the one hand, and service to the business and industrial sector, on the other, is evident in the fact that these projects are often managed by non-academic (or non-tenured) staff.

Leveraging Technology for Quality Enhancement

For many Humanities professors in the late 1990s, online teaching seemed to be nothing less than the latest stage in the ongoing corporatization of the academy. Online teaching promised to degrade the learning experience and squeeze instructors into a regimented, assembly-line work regime. Meanwhile, among administrators, there was quite a bit of excitement. With online courses, economic efficiencies of space and faculty time might be realized. Online courses might open up new revenue streams from tuition paid by off-campus students. Visions of classes with one professor teaching hundreds of students at the same time were irresistible, thus confirming the fears of faculty members. Indeed, 20 years on, some evidence can be found to support most of those predictions. Online teaching has become widespread in all kinds of institutions. For-profit online ventures such as the University of Phoenix have carved out a substantial niche for themselves. Several premier universities have begun to offer courses through a delivery system known as the "Massive Open Online Course" (MOOC) and even degree programs referred to as "Massive Open Online Degrees" (MOOD). Some of these are offered through for-profit companies like Udacity and Coursera, which offer the course for free, but charge a fee for a certificate than can be granted when the student passes an online exam at the end of the course. Arizona State University has gained national prominence and expanded its enrollments by promoting a cafeteria-style selection of online courses that can be taken by students who are not seeking a degree. Arizona State and other institutions like Georgia Institute of Technology also offer complete degree programs online, charging tuition at rates much lower than traditional on-campus programs.[2]

In general, these online courses and degrees are focused on delivering basic general education, skills-based training and content knowledge to relatively large groups of students. But, early on, I was intrigued by the potential for an online course with quite a different character. My goal

---

[2] [National Public Radio, August 17, 2014 http://www.pbs.org/newshour/updates/new-degree-program-big-test-mooc-style-higher-ed/ Retrieved February 22, 2015].

was to use the online delivery system to enhance the quality of a limited-enrollment, advanced theory-focused graduate course. I had taught traditional graduate courses in Marxist Cultural Theory under a "Special Topics" rubric in our English curriculum, and I was interested in establishing the course as a regular offering. A regularly scheduled course in Marxist Theory, however, wouldn't have been approved by my department's curriculum committee. The topic would have been considered too narrow, hence the projected enrollment too small. The department couldn't afford to staff such a course on a regular basis. Then a window of opportunity opened up. Faculty members across the university were invited to apply for small internal grants to design online courses, which would be taught regularly so that the university would develop a foothold in the new world of online higher education. I submitted a proposal that was funded and began to offer the Marxist Theory course on a regular basis.

The practical issues of staffing and curriculum were factored into the grant proposal. It occurred to me that in many graduate programs, there were faculty and students working from a Marxist or neo-Marxist perspective, but, at that time, not many departments offered a regular course in Marxist theory. I anticipated that there would be interest in taking the course among graduate students at other universities. So, I wrote into the proposal a request for a remitted-tuition scholarship for up to three graduate students from other universities to take the course for credit. I publicized this opportunity on the Marxist Literary Group's listserv and sent it to colleagues around the country. I asked for a letter of interest and a professor's recommendation from each potential external student and chose three of these applicants for the "scholarship" each time. These were highly motivated and engaged students, and their participation raised the level of intellectual rigor and engagement among all participants. The external students came from a variety of disciplines, including Anthropology, Communications, History and Sociology as well as English, and from institutions across the US and Canada. The contributions of the external students enriched the learning experience of students in our graduate program. With their perspectives from different programs in different geographical locations and institutional settings, they added a significant measure of intellectual and socio-cultural diversity to the course.

In addition to the tuition funding for graduate students from other institutions, my grant proposal included a request for honoraria for scholars from other universities who would participate as "virtual guest lecturers" in the course. I invited Jerry Phillips from the University of Connecticut, Rosemary Hennessy from Rice University and Barbara Foley from Rutgers University at Newark to collaborate with me on the experiment. The guest lecturers would take control of the course for a week, just as though a visiting scholar had been invited to give a guest lecture to a class. In each case, the virtual guest lecturer provided a brief introductory statement and a selection of readings for students. The students would respond to these texts in their weekly position papers, and the guest lecturer would participate in the subsequent discussion and debate in the online discussion forum. Jerry Phillips posted a lecture on Marxism and Utopian Socialism. Rosemary Hennessy engaged students in a discussion of her work on Materialist Feminism. And Barbara Foley provided an essay and a series of discussion questions on Marxism and Critical Race Theory.

Acknowledging the Political at the Scene of Pedagogy

The idea of teaching online appealed to me additionally because I saw it as an opportunity to further my efforts to develop rigorously theorized Marxist/historical materialist pedagogical practices for courses in literary and cultural studies. By the late 1990s, I had written several essays on this topic and had been experimenting with the strategies in my classes for several years. My guiding principle, one that I derived from my reading of Marx, was that a university-level Humanities course should be a site for the production of knowledge, not merely for the transmission of established information. I was influenced by Antonio Gramsci's observation that each class group produces its own "organic intellectuals" and by Paolo Freire's efforts to allow students to exercise self-determination in the educational process. I was also influenced by an essay by Shoshana Felman entitled "Psychoanalysis and Education: Teaching Terminable and Interminable," which argued, from a Lacanian perspective, that conventional pedagogy is structured in such a way that the student is conditioned to mirror the teacher's knowledge, rather than attempting a breakthrough of understanding. In 1990, I published an essay entitled "Confrontational Pedagogy" in which I also argued that the premise of the knowing teacher and the ignorant student was problematic. Students bring a wealth of knowledge into the classroom, and students' knowledge is not without power, supported as they are by the views of family and community. Such engagements between institutionally sanctioned and popular-discourse instances of cultural power are esthetic phenomena, in the broad, post-Kantian sense of the term concerned with the possibility of rational self-government in Modernity. So, my goal is to engage the political esthetic, rather than simply to ignore it.

The politicization of esthetics, it so happens, is a project undertaken by the French philosopher Jacques Rancière, in a series of interviews published as a book entitled *The Politics of Aesthetics* (1991). I was not familiar with Rancière's writing at the time that I formulated my Marxist/materialist pedagogical strategies and developed the online course, but when I later read *The Politics of Aesthetics* and Rancière's earlier book, *The Ignorant Schoolmaster* (1987) I found that he and I had reached many of the same conclusions. In *The Politics of Aesthetics*, Rancière reserves the term "political" for those interventions that disrupt hierarchical order in such a way as to achieve a "redistribution of the sensible" leading to an extension of human equality and emancipation. In *The Ignorant Schoolmaster*, Rancière suggests a way to do this in education. He presents a theory of "universal teaching" for political emancipation based on the experiments of early nineteenth-century French educator Joseph Jacotot. In revolutionary France, Joseph Jacotot had established a reputation as a celebrated professor of various Humanities subjects as well as Mathematics. When, in 1815, he was forced into exile in Louvain after the Bourbon restoration, students there sought to study with him, but many of them knew no French, and Jacotot did not speak Flemish. As a preliminary gesture toward establishing a shared language, he gave copies of a recently published novel, *Les aventures de Télémaque*, in French with a Flemish translation on facing pages. To his surprise, after one month of study with no input from a teacher, the students had learned French on their own. From this experience, Jacotot recognized that traditional assumptions about the relationships among teachers, students and objects of study were deeply flawed. The "transmission" model, which accords primary importance to the teacher, was highly overrated.

In *The Ignorant Schoolmaster*, Rancière deliberately fuses his own voice with that of Jacotot in recounting Jacotot's experiments with universal teaching, so I will combine their names as "Rancière/Jacotot" in describing the theory here. It is founded upon a critique of the hierarchical structure of all conventional "magisterial" pedagogies, which are premised on an assumption of intellectual inequality between teacher and students and the expectation that learners will achieve equality with masters at the end of a period of study. Every conscientious teacher expects the students to improve, and, one hopes, eventually to match the teacher's level of mastery. The hegemonic sensibility of inequality is inherent in the common practice of "explication," in which the teacher explains to the student why the student's response is not quite acceptable, just yet. Typically, the teacher finds some small error or omission in even the best student's work. The achievement of equality is delayed; there is always something left to master. And, when the student finally becomes the professor, this structure of inequality is perpetuated with a new group of students. Universal teaching, by contrast, employs a heuristic principle of equality. What can be achieved, Rancière/Jacotot asks, if one begins not by emphasizing unequal levels of mastery, but by assuming that every human has an equal capacity of intelligence—an equal capacity to achieve understanding through a motivated engagement with the task of learning?

Rancière/Jacotot's universal teaching method involves identifying a topic and an object of focus that students are eager to study—a mathematical procedure, a philosophical concept, a foreign language—and then allowing the students to focus their energies on the object in stages by relating each element of it to other elements of knowledge they already possess. The teacher's role is to provide the structure at the beginning and to verify that the student has focused on the project and produced a substantive result at the end. Differing performances among students, different levels of mastery, are seen as results of different levels of attention, focus and engagement, not differences in innate intelligence. There are obvious limits to this method. For teaching advanced instrumental skills, it would depend upon the students' having a sufficient foundation of previous knowledge to make a beginning. And it runs counter to the unavoidable tendency toward regimentation characteristic of mass education. But we should acknowledge our nagging discomfort with this regimentation. Our constant projects of refining and transforming our syllabi and curricula bear witness to the need to overcome the institutional and conventional barriers that stand in the way of focused engagement on the part of students and teachers.

Within the somewhat relaxed institutional limits of an advanced graduate seminar with self-selected students and a special topic not covered in the prescribed curriculum, my course in Marxist Theory enjoyed some of the same advantages discovered by Jacotot and his students in Louvain. The online format as well as the structure of the course accord with Rancière/Jacotot's egalitarian emphasis. The format de-emphasizes the professor's authoritative role in favor of elevating the textual objects of study and the students' engagement with the texts. In my articles on theorizing pedagogy, I argued for "textualizing" and "de-privatizing" the classroom discourse by requiring the instructor and students to produce "position papers" that would be circulated among participants in advance of the classroom discussion. These position papers are available for critical responses posted to a discussion board in advance of the class meeting, and they provide a framework and starting points for in-class discussions. By introducing elements of formality and asynchronicity, I was addressing some uneasiness with the conventional discussion model of Humanities courses. I wanted to problematize the individualistic ethos of the informal classroom discussion model. In my view, the ideological framework of individualism encourages a "consumerist" attitude about education, in which it is assumed that the student is a consumer who has the right to demand satisfaction from the instructor and the institution. I find this hegemonic structure of individualism especially problematic in the context of public universities, which are partially supported by taxpayers, some of whom live in areas where the public high schools are not very successful at preparing students to gain admission to the institutions their taxes are supporting.

So, in addition to my dissatisfaction with the "master-apprentice" dynamic identified by Rancière/Jacotot, I rejected the simple "producer-consumer" structure of pedagogy. And I mistrusted the typical strategy for de-centering the instructor's authority that was then current—simply declaring that the classroom is a democratic space for open debate. This seemed to me to be a disingenuous evasion of accountability, or an abdication of the instructor's actual responsibility to lead the class. An instructor, after all, has the authority of the institution and the profession at one's back, whatever one says about students' voice. Textualizing the class discourse gives students the opportunity to absorb and reflect on the teachers' statements and positions. It gives each student the opportunity to consider carefully the contributions of other students, to learn from and with each other—possibly even to draw strength in numbers to challenge the instructor's perspectives and interpretations. Further, I wanted to adopt pedagogical practices that acknowledge the collective process of knowledge production. If students have a voice in the production of knowledge and cultural value, it is not merely because they should be respected as individuals or as consumers. Students have a role to play and a stake in the production of knowledge (not merely the transmission of established knowledge) because they represent discourse communities with political and cultural power. Contested social values and attitudes are shaped and transmitted through popular culture, mass media, peer groups and families. A student who advances, for example, a racist argument didn't invent racism by himself or herself. Tribalist, heteronormative and elitist positions like this must be engaged not simply because an individual student is benighted or "wrong" about something, but because the student represents a socio-politically empowered discourse community that shares this perspective. The argument is with the larger community, not with the individual student. So, the issue must be engaged at the level of discourse rather than at the level of the individual student. A textualized and de-privatized class discourse enables that engagement.

One of the ways I typically address such situations is to move the target. Instead of engaging the student directly, I point out that, for example, that some well-known public intellectual or media pundit has made a similar argument. Has the student been reading this writer? Does he or she endorse a political agenda shared with the pundit? This kind of substitution of the discourse (established public intellectual for the individual student) is easier to manage in an asynchronous textual exchange than it is on the spur of the moment in a classroom discussion. Further, there is an egalitarian dimension to the textualized and de-privatized pedagogical scene. The written position papers, submitted by instructor and students, provide a greater opportunity for a reflective, substantive engagement in the discussion. Some students who are typically silent in spontaneous class discussions will come to voice in an exchange of written texts. There is time to consult references, invoking authorities and examples outside the immediate classroom community. Position papers reinforce the understanding that knowledge is produced collectively and must be tested by critical interrogation. And, in general, the level of discussion becomes more substantive and precise. On balance, I welcomed the absence of face-to-face discussions in the online delivery platform as a potential advantage, rather than a disadvantage.

So, with several years' of practical experience in conducting courses on this model, the transition to online delivery was smooth for me. The online teaching experience was a novelty for my guest lecturers, but they also adjusted easily. As anyone who has team-taught a course can attest, the experience can be stimulating and enriching, but also daunting. Most of us are accustomed to the intimacy and spontaneity of privatized classrooms. Without really thinking about it, the instructor may take for granted that whatever one says will not be strongly challenged. In the online Marxist Theory course, with multiple guest lecturers in addition to myself and students from different institutions and in different locations, the stakes were a bit higher. As with email and twitter messages, irony can fall flat and nuances of tone and intention can be misunderstood. But the gains from de-privatizing the classroom in this way are well worth suffering through a little discomfort. From the beginning, in my online courses, I have always used the "lagging-edge" technology. Although course delivery systems such as "Blackboard" were available early on, I began by writing my own html code for the course web pages, supplementing them only with a pre-packaged discussion board program. When the software for face-to-face conversations and group discussions became available, I stuck with the textual interchanges. I was reluctant to adopt the latest technology because I wanted to make sure that students with old computers and slow dial-up internet connections could participate without technical problems. I wasn't particular concerned to replicate the "face-to-face" classroom discussions, so, I still have never used Skype or other synchronous internet communication software. I value the reflection, precision and formality encouraged by slowing things down with asynchronous communication. However, in 2007, I took the plunge into video, recording a series of 15 short lectures and uploading them to YouTube.

Professing Marxism on YouTube

If the online course in Marxist Theory shared some features of Rancière/Jacotot's universal teaching method, the YouTube videos of my lectures are still more in line with the theory. Neither I nor my YouTube interlocutors gain any direct institutional recognition or credit for our efforts; participation is driven by genuinely self-motivated interest and need to solve particular problems or answer particular questions. When I produced my first video lectures in 2007, YouTube content creators still had to get special permission in order to upload videos more than ten minutes long. But I found that longer videos were not necessary, in any case. By carefully scripting my short lectures, and by interweaving them with visual graphics such as diagrams, photographs and other images, tables and relevant text quotations, I was able to compress about one hour's worth of conventional classroom presentation material into a ten-minute video. The ten-minute segment, as it turns out, is a good amount of time for me to present the material and for viewers to process it. When a topic requires more time, it can be organized into two segments. Viewers can repeat lectures or parts of lectures as they find it necessary. In this manner, viewers can absorb material that is densely presented. So, I present the material in a tightly organized package. In recent years, YouTube has relaxed its policy on the length of videos; now, one can upload longer videos without the special permission and there are many college course lectures of one hour or more available. Some of these are excellent—for example, there is a good series of lectures on Marxism by David Harvey. But in many cases, these videos are simple recordings in which a camera has been pointed at an instructor while he or she delivers a classroom lecture. This kind of performance usually doesn't translate well to the small screen. Meanwhile, producing a shortened version of lecture doesn't mean less work is involved. It took me nearly 30 hours to produce my first video. Eventually, I was able to cut the production time, but it still takes me between 10 and 15 hours to produce a 10-minute video lecture.

For my original text-based online Marxist Theory course in the spring of 2000, I wrote eight lectures on the following topics: "Historical Materialism," "Base and Superstructure," "The Labor Theory of Value," "Commodity Fetishism," "Frankfurt School Critical Theory," "Materialist Feminism," "British Cultural Studies," and "Althusser's Concept of Ideology." Seven years later, I adapted these written lectures as scripts for videos on a YouTube channel; I called "Marxism 101," later to be renamed "Cultural Theory On-line." I then added seven more videos on the following topics "The Individual and Society in Modernity," "The Concept of Culture in Modernity," "The Social Function of Art in Modernity," "Economic Relations of Production in Modernity," "Political Conditions of Modernity," "Paradigms of Knowledge Production in Modernity," "Idealist and Historicist Paradigms of Literature" and, most recently, a 30-minute lecture on "Aesthetics, Politics and Cultural Studies." Although the original videos were intended as an introduction to Marxist cultural theory for graduate students, the added videos on various aspects of "modernity" are intended to help undergraduates and lay viewers to make sense of the series.

What interested me in particular about YouTube video lectures was the opportunity to reach a large audience beyond the limits of my university classes. I saw YouTube as a way to realize, at last, the ideal of the "free university"—a pure teaching and learning experience, unbound by institutional constraints. I offer free public tutoring to YouTube viewers who don't get any reward or credit, monetary or otherwise. At the end of each lecture, I post my email address and invite viewers to contact me directly with questions and comments. Of course, I get the occasional message from a student looking for a shortcut to finish a term paper assignment. But most of the correspondents are intellectually engaged, self-motivated learners. I have had stimulating exchanges with artists and activists as well as university instructors, graduate students and undergraduates from many different countries. Among the many institutions where my videos have been used by teachers and students, notably, is the Open University of the Arts, an accredited open-access online educational institution in the UK. This is the sort of egalitarian sharing of academic resources that we hoped for in the aftermath of 1968.

My most widely viewed video is the one on Frankfurt School Critical Theory, which has more than 100,000 views and nearly 200 comments. Sometimes the response to online teaching can be revealing; this number of comments is significantly inflated by rants and slurs against the Frankfurt School from right-wing viewers, including one particularly active proponent of the "Austrian School" economic theory advanced by Ludwig Von Mises. Sometimes I enter into these discussions, but most of the posts are from viewers, and the comments on other videos are generally less vitriolic. Viewers get into discussions with each other, using the videos as occasions to work out their understandings of commodity fetishism, the system of ideology and so on. For example, in one exchange, two viewers discuss the relationship between "Repressive State Apparatuses" (RSA) and "Ideological State Apparatuses" (ISA) in relation to military recruitment in poor communities in the US and the UK. "ButherLi55ett" begins the exchange by disagreeing with an earlier post from another viewer arguing that the RSA is more important than the ISA:

> Owners of capital will do all they can to split working people to keep wages and conditions down and profits up, which isn't some conspiracy or deed of evil men though they might be utter bastards but a requirement within the current mode of production. It's certainly true that not too long ago in certain parts of the Britain it was 'the army or the coal mine' once you got out of high school. Just like the US, the more deprived areas are sucked into the military just not on the same scale.

A few months later, a viewer called Kaleo183rd chimed in with a personal perspective:

> @ButherLi55ett Jea, I mean, I'm Latino, and studying the current context, Non-whites in the US are 2nd class citizens, on the one hand (Even though there is a bourgeois that is Black, Latino in each nation and in the US etc),

But coming from NYC, the are many Latinos/Blacks who sign up, in the military, in spite of the knowledge that they are being screwed by the same system, I don't know too much about the UK but The US military is actively always going to poor neighborhoods.

And ButherLi55ett responds:

@kaleo183rd That's what I meant by the term "economic conscript". Though you added some depth. Workers are indirectly forced to sign up. Of course the state uses propaganda and nationalism too. Especially in the US, where military recruiters go into schools and colleges etc. This I think would be frowned upon in the UK but that's not to say it hasn't happened (but isn't common). And of course there are children 'cadets' though I imagine not on the scale of similar US programs.

As this excerpt suggests, viewers commenting on the videos may or may not have had much exposure to the kinds of texts we are teaching in university courses on Marxist theory. But this exchange exemplifies something that I find especially encouraging about the format. Here are two individuals—one from the UK, one from the US—who found a video on an obscure topic that is nonetheless interesting to them. They may not easily find people who share this interest among their respective friends, family members and co-workers. They share their distinctive perspectives based on local experience with each other. They may learn something new or have a perception affirmed from the online encounter. This kind of teaching, learning and intellectual sharing happens routinely in the "Comments" sections of my Marxism Online YouTube videos, and, while the resulting effect is unmeasurable, it is surely far greater than I could achieve through my classroom teaching.

In addition to the online comments, I also receive many inquiries directly through email, and I try to answer all of these. I'll describe one such exchange, with a student who was preparing for his exams in jurisprudence at the London School of Economics. The student began by noting that Marx predicted that "the next stage after capitalism was communism" and asking the following questions:

How could he know this, were there facts at the time that indicated this and how could he know there was no other penultimate system before communism? It seems that Marx might have got this wrong. Surely today's "Consumerism" is the current base (the superstructure seems to reflect this) and there is therefore still the possibility of the emergence of communism?

I responded, in part, as follows:

There have been different interpretations of Marx's prediction of the inevitability of communism following capitalism [Edouard Bernstein's "Evolutionary Socialism", Rosa Luxembourg's insistence on the necessity of revolt] …. Marx himself seems to have come down on both sides of this issue at different times, but, in my view, Marx saw capitalism as, on the one hand, a progressive, enlightenment-oriented phenomenon--capitalism is better than feudalism--capitalism can foster democratic conditions through modernist developments like urbanization, internationalism (and globalization), scientific and technological advance, etc. On the other hand, Marx thought that he could scientifically predict that capitalism would repeatedly provoke its own crises, … New sources of extracting surplus value must be developed, constantly, or the owners of capital (investors) will not put their existing capital at risk. New sources of surplus value can take various forms: (1) primitive accumulation--conquest and appropriation of foreign territory, for example, or colonialism … . or by discovering oil under the ocean, etc. (2) increases in industrial production achieved through technological and bureaucratic advances--Taylorism, Fordism, automation, etc. … (3) and, interestingly, as you mention, through what might be called "ideological" (Althusser's focus and Foucault's) or "hegemonic" (Gramsci's term) systems and discourses.

These examples of different modes of producing surplus value and the different points at which the capitalist system could break down are followed by a paragraph in which I digress to entertain the possibility of a breakdown of capitalism that would neither be a direct transition to communism nor a further stage in that trajectory. I mention that I find the possibility presented by some speculative science fiction writers of a post-apocalyptic (e.g., post-nuclear or post-fossil fuel) reversion to a repressive authoritarian dictatorial regime or some primitive state of tribal anarchy fairly convincing. Then I returned to the question at hand, of how to understand consumerism in the context of scientific Marxism. I agreed that consumerism cannot be simply reduced to a superstructural effect, while not conceding that the superstructure has replaced the base in the current stage of neoliberal capitalism:

> Quite often, the expansion of surplus wealth or the opening up of new means of accumulating surplus wealth is achieved through a combination of these different realms.... . Having said all this (and I'm sorry I've taken this long to get to this part of your question [about "consumerism" being the new "base"]) I do believe that Marx didn't fully anticipate the rich complexity of modern consumerism as a hegemonic structure, though Marx did foreshadow some of the basic workings of the consumer society in his analysis of the commodity form and his theorization of commodity fetishism.

My full response, in this case, ran to 968 words and required some time for me to produce. And this exchange was followed by more emails from the same viewer that also required thoughtful, substantive answers from me. So, it should be understood that this kind of online teaching involves a lot of work and must be approached responsibly. I feel a sense of responsibility to all the viewers who are watching my videos. I feel a responsibility to the viewer who is asking a sincere question, and to the other viewers who may be reading the question and my response. I feel a responsibility to my colleagues in cultural studies and especially to those colleagues whose knowledge of Marxist theory far surpasses my own. And I feel a responsibility to my university and to the profession at large. I want to teach accurately, effectively and progressively; these stakes are raised exponentially when the audience of potential students—or potential viewers, at least—numbers in the thousands rather than the classroom of 12 or 25.

In recent years, I've taught a for-credit graduate course in Cultural Theory that is required in our PhD curriculum. This course includes but is not limited to Marxist theory, and I use the video lectures to supplement our seminar discussions. But the free, extra-curricular YouTube videos have allowed me to reach a much larger audience, and they have enabled my teaching to have a much greater impact, than I could have imagined previously. From our day-to-day interactions with students, it is undeniable that the digital media revolution presents a profound challenge to Humanities education. But the internet has also made it possible to realize the progressive, post-1968 vision of reaching students beyond the classroom. It would be doubly unfortunate if we were to acquiesce to the negative challenges of the current moment (neoliberalism, technologization, etc.) without taking full advantage of the potential they also sometimes offer for emancipatory education.

Works Cited

Felman, S. (1982). Psychoanalysis and Education: Terminable and Interminable. *Yale French Studies, 63*, 21–44.

Freire, P. (1993). *Pedagogy of the Oppressed* (M. B. Ramos, Trans.). New York: Continuum.

Gramsci, A. (1971). *Selections from the Prison Notebooks* (Q. Hoare & G. N. Smith, Ed. and Trans.). London: Lawrence & Wishart.

Rancière, J. (1991). *The Ignorant Schoolmaster: Five Lessons in Intellectual Emancipation* (K. Ross, Trans. with an Introduction). Stanford: Stanford University Press.

Rancière, J. (2004). *The Politics of Aesthetics: The Distribution of the Sensible* (G. Rockhill, Trans. with an Introduction). London: Continuum.

Strickland, R. (1994). Curriculum Mortis: A Manifesto for Structural Change. *College Literature, 21*, 1–14.

Strickland, R. (1997). Pedagogy and Public Accountability. In A. Kumar (Ed.), *Class Issues: Pedagogy, Cultural Studies and the Public Sphere* (pp. 163–176). New York: New York University Press.

Strickland, R., et al. (1998). Postmodern Pedagogy and the Death of Civic Humanism. *Social Epistemology, 12*, 339–348.

Strickland, R. (1990). Confrontational Pedagogy and Traditional Literary Studies. *College English, 52*(March), 291–300.

Strickland, R. (1993). Teaching Shakespeare against the Grain. In J. Davis & R. Salamone (Eds.), *Teaching Shakespeare Today* (pp. 168–178). Urbana: NCTE.

"Bringing the World to the Classroom": Cultural Studies and Experiential Learning

Basak Durgun

As cultural studies scholars and educators, our commitment to understanding and altering oppressive systems of power that shape our lives is a key element of the work we do. Reexamining what Raymond Williams conceived as the project of cultural studies, Couldry (2011: 11–12) writes that at the core of our project is the task of parsing out "the gap experienced between the principles and aims of democracy and the everyday realities of the economy, politics, and social/cultural interaction." It is this critical obligation with which I want to guide my discussion of the methodological merits of experiential learning for cultural studies. The theoretical frameworks we use to analyze institutional and structural power relationships and the historical processes that have advanced these relationships are useful in giving us an analytical lens to organize significant events in digestible forms. They help us make sense of the world around us and imagine other, more just ways of being, doing, relating. By themselves and confined to a classroom without a solid grounding in praxis, theoretical apparatus with which we interpret our social, cultural, economic and political processes that shape our lives, at best does not

B. Durgun (✉)
Miami University, Oxford, OH, USA

© The Author(s) 2019
J. Aksikas et al. (eds.), *Cultural Studies in the Classroom and Beyond*,
https://doi.org/10.1007/978-3-030-25393-6_9

155

stick around long enough and at worst obscures the complexities of the very problems we are trying to resolve. In this section, I offer ideas, techniques and methods for merging theory and practice for teaching cultural studies. I argue that experiential learning strategies are essential to make visible and comprehensible the systemic political, economic and social injustices, to develop long-lasting critical thinking skills and to foster a learning environment grounded in social action and movement building. Experiential learning is a method of learning that facilitates well established scientific research methods in the classroom, transforming it into an active zone of creating new knowledge for greater political impact beyond the classroom and the boundaries of the university. As such, experiential learning expands the radical potential of cultural studies in the classroom.

Experiential learning as a concept originates in John Dewey's (1963) *Experience and Education* (originally published in 1938 by Kappa Delta Pi) where he outlined the general principles of learning through experience. Critiquing traditional education as a top-down and indifferent model that is more concerned with order than the process of learning, rendering students docile, receptive and obedient, Dewey (1963: 18) asserts that learning based solely on textbook instruction is static and passive. He argues for the integration of lived experience into the process of learning. As a strong advocate of learning by doing (Dewey 1963: 25–26) discerns between experiences that diminish one's abilities and those that render themselves to continued growth:

Any experience is miseducative that has the effect of arresting or distorting the growth of further experience. An experience may be such as to engender callousness; it may produce lack of sensitivity and of responsiveness. Then the possibilities of having richer experience in the future are restricted. Again, a given experience may increase a person's automatic skill in a particular direction and yet tend to land him in a groove or rut; the effect again is to narrow the field of further experience. An experience may be immediately enjoyable and yet promote the formation of a slack and careless attitude; this attitude then operates to modify the quality of subsequent experiences so as to prevent a person from getting out of them what they have to give. Again, experiences may be so disconnected from one another that, while each is agreeable or even exciting in itself, they are not linked cumulatively to one another. Energy is then dissipated and a person becomes scatter-brained. Each experience may be lively, vivid, and "interesting," and yet their disconnectedness may artificially generate dispersive, disintegrated, centrifugal habits (pp. 25–26)

These distinctions are essential to the theory of experience that John Dewey constructed. According to Dewey (1963), the "experiential continuum" is a crucial element of learning by doing, against a singular experience without an opportunity to expand. Experiential continuum is the principle that "every experience both takes up something from those which have gone before and modifies in some way the quality of those which come after" (Dewey 1963: 35). The principle of continuity encourages positive growth with opportunities for future expansion of skills and knowledge, rather than static, disconnected habits. According to Dewey (1963), the role of educators is to create the conditions that make continuous and interactive growth possible.

Expanding on John Dewey's legacy and building on common themes and approaches by other foundational figures of experiential learning such as John Dewey, Kurt Lewin, Jean Piaget, Lev Vygotsky, William James, Carl Jung, Paulo Freire, Carl Rogers, and Mary Parker Follett, David Kolb (1984) developed Experiential Learning Theory (ELT) as a systematic framework to address the link between continuous active experimentation and reflective inquiry at the core of experiential learning and to create a holistic model that can be replicated and adapted to fit a variety of educational institutions and circumstances. In this model, learning is understood as a long-term evolving process that moves through moments of resolving conflicts between direct experience and abstract concepts, between observation and action and between theory and practice. He writes:

Learners, if they are to be effective, need four different kinds of abilities – *concrete experience* abilities (CE), *reflective observation* abilities (RO), *abstract conceptualization* abilities (AC), and *active experimentation* (AE) abilities. That is, they must be able to involve themselves fully, openly, and without bias in new experiences (CE). They must be able to reflect on and observe their experiences from many perspectives (RO). They must be able to create concepts that integrate their observations into logically sound theories (AC), and they must be able to use these theories to make decisions and solve problems (AE). (Kolb 1984: 30)

Each of these abilities are developed and nurtured in a holistic process to create new knowledge. Kolb (1984: 38) defines learning as "*the process whereby knowledge is created through the transformation of experience.*" The role of an educator is to design the space suitable for the transformation and to facilitate the development of receptive learners with reflective observation, conceptualization and experimentation skills.

While Dewey (1963) and later Kolb (1984) emphasize democratic social arrangements as the fertile ground upon which experiential learning strategies grow, their model of experiential learning does not necessarily involve a rigorous, critical inquiry and reflection of global power relations. The dialectical relationship between knowledge and power is a key object of inquiry in cultural studies. Knowledge is not a neutral space of equal access. Rather, knowledge is shaped and reconfigured by power. Who gets to have what kind of experience is also determined by structural power relations—a critical node of inquiry built into the cultural studies episteme. Educators who are interested in transformative educational experiences that not only rely on democratic social arrangements but expand the potentials of these arrangements for greater social justice integrate Freire's critical pedagogy with experiential learning strategies. In his influential work, originally published in English in 1970, *Pedagogy of the Oppressed*, Freire (2005) critiqued traditional education, what he called "the banking model of education" in which the learner's agency, experience and creativity are invalidated beneath the authority and expertise of the teacher figure:

> Instead of communicating, the teacher issues communiques and makes deposits which the students patiently receive, memorize, and repeat. This is the "banking" concept of education, in which the scope of action allowed to students extends only as far as receiving, filing, and storing the deposits.

This not only negates the learner's agency, but also "attempts to control thinking and action, leads women and men to adjust to the world, and inhibits their creative power" (Freire 2005). It reproduces the conditions of exploitation, oppression and dehumanization by rendering the learner consistently passive, inferior, and dependent. Against "the banking model of education," Freire (2005) advocated for "problem-posing" as a method whereby the educators and learners as partners in dialogue "develop their power to perceive critically *the way they exist* in the world *with which* and *in which* they find themselves; they come to see the world not as a static reality, but as a reality in process, in transformation." Questioning the figure of authority and committed to liberation, educators and learners collaborate in deepening their consciousness and in creating space for active and reflective learning in order to transform their reality, the oppressive social, political and economic relationships under which they suffer.

I first encountered experiential learning as a graduate lecturer in George Mason University's School of Integrative Studies (SIS).[1] Coming from an activist and community organizer background and as a scholar with research interests in new social movements, experiential learning strategies that drive from a commitment to active and reflective learning inspired me to think of the classroom as an integrated learning community in which we collaboratively imagine and execute our visions for a better world. My training for experiential learning at SIS occurred while teaching two interdisciplinary seminar courses titled "Narratives of Identity" and "Human Creativity: Science and Art." As a team of educators, following experiential learning models, we planned both of the courses together each year as intensive modules that dug deep into students' individual and collective experiences in developing scholarly inquiry and reflection.

The objective of Narratives of Identity was to develop a critical understanding of how social identities are shaped and communicated in a historical context. The course moved along the axis of macro constructions,

---

[1] Formerly known as New Century College, School of Integrative Studies is an interdisciplinary undergraduate school at George Mason University that provides unique, individualized concentrations to prepare students for careers that address contemporary global social, political, and environmental problems.

such as immigration, race, class, gender and sexuality, and strengthened students' critical thinking, literary analysis and communication skills. For many students, this was the first time they encountered issues such as white privilege, heteronormativity, class-based social stratification and undocumented immigration. Their encounters were facilitated through direct experiences with homeless advocates at the Coalition for the Homeless and undocumented day laborers at Centreville Labor Resource center. Posed with a task to identify and interrogate their own identities and social status as lenses through which they understand the world, the students, in dialogue with us, worked on reflective assignments that considered their own race, class, nationality, gender or sexuality as a point of inquiry. The course culminated in a student-organized conference showcasing the synthesis of these investigations and the students' active experimentations with a variety of approaches and media, such as video, photo essay and research paper.

Investigating the integration of fine arts and natural sciences and the essential role of creativity in scientific inquiry and artistic expression, Human Creativity: Science and Art elaborated on major ideas in science and fostered a deep understanding of esthetics, the scientific method and the integral relationship between theory and experiment in providing solutions to contemporary environmental problems, such as climate change and biodiversity loss. During field trips to Environmental Studies on the Piedmont, a research, education and conservation center in Virginia, we made consecutive observations of the natural world, learning to pay attention to subtle changes, sounds and colors and to identify plants and animals as the seasons transitioned from winter to spring. These observations on the transitions of the landscape were reinforced by a self-guided study of evolution at the Smithsonian National Museum of Natural History, facilitation of citizen science experiments in the classroom, conversations with local artists who use the natural world as their inspiration, watching documentaries on climate change, fossil fuels and fracking, and seminar discussions and debates on the urgent environmental problems we are facing.

Each of the course activities were designed to inform and inspire the students toward completing their final projects, an individual visual art piece, called "Visions of Nature," and a group design project. Visions of

Nature required the students to develop and express their relationship to the natural world, going through stages of proposal, execution, presentation and reflection. The group design project was a collaborative research and design task to address an urgent environmental problem the students independently choose to focus on as a group. Similar to the individual visual art piece, the students developed their projects throughout the course in stages, with feedback from me and their peers and inspired by several examples during classroom seminars, culminating in an open fair-like exhibition. At each stage of the projects, the students received feedback, while the course curriculum and my "art of the day" modules offered examples of artistic engagement with the natural world and design solutions to problems associated with climate change and biodiversity loss in order to deepen their experiences. In their projects, the students examined sustainable small-scale food production in their designs of vertical gardens, urban permaculture community gardens and living communities with roof top gardens, while learning how to compost and grow common vegetables in small pots. They explored sustainable building designs and eco-friendly living, waste water treatment technologies and DIY gray water systems for every home. They researched various water purification systems to solve Chesapeake Bay's pollution problem. In both of these courses, activities, field trips and assignments were guided by an unwavering commitment to cultivating learning communities in which students became active agents in their learning, reflecting on their own backgrounds, experiences and unique approaches, while engaging with existing knowledge on the society and the environment. The students, in dialogue with the educators, developed the ability to embrace new experiences, critical observation, conceptualization of problems and corresponding solutions, active experimentation and deliberation, and reflection.

I carried this training into other courses I taught. In particular, I used visual arts as a medium to communicate the key role of gender and sexuality in social institutions in women and gender studies courses that I taught at GMU. "Representations of Women" used representations of women in various forms of media to examine the role of gendered socialization in creating social divisions and interrogate the powerful effects of these divisions in everyday lives of women, while evaluating the visions women have for equality, justice and liberation. "Introduction to Women and Gender Studies" introduced students to key concepts and theories in the field of women and gender studies, such as gender/sex systems, body, labor, motherhood and family, equality, socialization and sexuality in a transnational framework. As introductory survey courses, not designed and scheduled to accommodate for organized or self-directed off-campus activities, these courses did not provide opportunities to fully execute experiential learning strategies. Yet, even under these circumstances, I found it possible to incorporate principles of learning by doing into the course curriculum. In both of these courses I used Visions of Nature as a model to create a final assignment in which the students reflected on a critical element from their learning in the course, utilizing a creative medium of their choice (such as drawing, painting, photography or video, graphic design, sculpture, yarn or textile work), while examining their own lives, histories and experiences at the center of their inquiry. In Representations of Women, the students responded to the prompt "I need feminism, because" with a powerful statement that speaks to their learning experience and socialization inside or outside the classroom. I asked them to think about what kind of a world they want to live in, to imagine that it is possible and to express it using artistic expression as a medium of communication. In Introduction to Women and Gender Studies, inspired by Rivka Solomon's (2002) *That Takes Ovaries!: Bold Females and Their Brazen Acts*, in which Solomon collects stories of ordinary women pushing boundaries and rejecting limitations in various circumstances that range between travel adventures, perseverance through hardship or significant public service, I asked the students to complete "It takes ovaries to" and create a visual arts piece that expresses what, according to their own experiences, observations and histories, takes courage, strength and hard work to accomplish. In both courses the students developed their artworks through the entire semester in stages, culminating in a final exhibit. The assignment was introduced in the first few weeks of the semester, and the students first wrote a short proposal about their preliminary thoughts on what they want to work on, followed by my feedback and if necessary one on one meetings. Along with a finished piece, they also completed a short artist statement on their own work, outlining their vision for the art piece and the statement.

In both courses, the students experimented with all artistic media available to them, ranging from using traditional methods to incorporating new technologies, and even using their own body as a canvas for a performance piece. The topics they dealt with were wide-ranging as well, turning the final exhibit day into a colorful celebration of learning. The students took up issues like gendered discrimination in the labor force and glass ceiling criticizing the wage gap between men and women, and the lack of adequate support and encouragement for women to join the STEM fields. They demanded self-determination of their bodies, full reproductive rights, mental health support, condemning racialized beauty standards, censorship of women's bodies and mainstream expectations of ideal body that create myriad of psycho-social challenges for people. They examined oppressive gender roles, at home and at the work place, and investigated sources of independence, strength and empowerment. They honored their own ancestors—their mothers, grandmothers and aunts—as well as our collective ancestors, the famous rebellious women in history. They condemned police brutality, examined the importance of women icons in the popular culture and advocated for solidarity across movements for liberation. They embraced different expressions of femininity, defended the right of people to use whichever bathroom they choose and educated their peers on consent. Sharing their works with their peers and the larger community of the Center for Women and Gender Studies at GMU at the end of the course, the students demonstrated deeper and long lasting engagement with gender theory, intersectional feminist critique and resistance.

Beyond individualized expressions of engaged learning, what else is possible with experiential learning strategies? As an urban studies scholar and a resident of Washington D.C., I often think about how one might communicate the impact of urban redevelopment and revitalization on urban poor. For instance, imagine a student from an affluent suburb hearing about "food desert" for the first time in the classroom. How are they to understand the real impacts of not having access to affordable, nutritious, quality fresh foods? Imagine another student from a low-income neighborhood. How are they to find a good narrative to describe and contextualize the everyday challenges they face in access to food, transportation, safety and education? The difference between excess and access is quite tangible in supermarkets in different neighborhoods. So, for a unit on intersections of race and class, you might arrange field trips to supermarkets, and ask the students to compose short descriptive reflection essays to guide classroom discussion. What other relationships can a guided observation in the supermarket visualize for us? Gendered marketing strategies? Basic tenets of commodification? Urban planning and dynamics of gentrification? Partnering with organizations that work to alleviate problems of urbanization in the absence of protective policies, for example, homelessness, labor rights, cultural heritage conservation, and directing students toward directly engaging these organizations and reporting back to the classroom community their experiences in creative ways (such as video interviews, website/blog development, photo journalism pieces, program critiques) that require the students to think further about their research problem and new data, is another way to motivate integrative learning while simultaneously developing rigorous research methods. What about games? *Beat the Bourgeoisie* (Norris 2013) provides a great example of actively engaging students in the classroom with a simulated experience of how social, cultural and economic capital shape social mobility.

The lived experiences are an essential part of our learning of the world around us. These experiences are exceptionally poignant for teaching cultural forms, social identities, economic processes, socio-ecological relationships and formation of power and knowledge—issues and problems at the core of cultural studies project. In this section, I gave a summary of the history of experiential learning method and offered some of the strategies I have worked with in the classroom. As a cultural studies scholar and educator, I understand academia as part of a larger system and as a site of conflict and struggle. This helps me maintain a critical position in our role as mediators of conventional educational practices. Moreover, it allows me to continue seeking out new approaches deeply grounded in rigorous intellectual praxis as I, along with my students, learn the contours of systemic context in which we work, learn and grow. It is impossible to make sense of complex social, economic and political processes that shape our lives, offer theoretical apparatus with which to interpret these processes and create space to produce long lasting critical thinking skills that go beyond the classroom and engage with the world around us while confined in a classroom and a static method of education. Experiential learning strategies transform the classroom into exceedingly more integrative and collaborative learning vessel, in which students are not bounded, but rather explore their own histories, commitments and potentials. In the courses I have taught with experiential learning strategies, the students consistently provided feedback on how memorable the course material became as they learned it by getting their hands dirty, sometimes literally. This is key for our educational goals in cultural studies. We want our students to move beyond their grades, and toward remembering and using the frameworks they have learned, through which they make sense of and analyze the world around them.

Acknowledgments I am grateful to the opportunity SIS has given me to expand my pedagogical skills and learn different strategies of experiential learning. My team leaders and colleagues Paul Gorski, Thomas Wood, Karen Misencik Carter, Kris Erickson and Al Fuertes (among many others) were instrumental in the development of these courses and assignments. They introduced me to experiential learning strategies and mentored me through our years of team teaching at SIS. Their dedicated support and generosity in sharing their experiences, knowledge and methods made it possible for me to expand my skills and have something to say about pedagogy and course design.

Works Cited

Couldry, N. (2011). The Project of Cultural Studies: Heretical Doubts, New Horizons. In P. Smith (Ed.), *The Renewal of Cultural Studies*. Philadelphia: Temple University Press.

Dewey, J. (1963). *Experience & Education*. New York: Collier Macmillan Publishers.

Freire, P. (2005). *Pedagogy of the Oppressed* (30th Anniversary ed.). New York: Continuum.

Kolb, D. A. (1984). *Experiential Learning: Experience as the Source of Learning and Development* (1st ed.). New Jersey: Pearson Education, Inc.

Norris, D. (2013). Beat the Bourgeoisie: A Social Class Inequality and Mobility Simulation Game. *Teaching Sociology, 41*(4), 334–345.

Solomon, R. (2002). *That Takes Ovaries!: Bold Females and their Brazen Acts*. New York: Three Rivers Press.

Teaching Cultural Studies in the Undergraduate Curriculum: From the Abstract to the Concrete, and Back Again

Sean Johnson Andrews

Cultural studies and its ancillary fields and projects appear unruly—both antagonistic to systems of authority and breaching the well-hewn boundaries of knowledge, politics, and practice. This unruliness is usually more apparent to its everyday practitioners than its bad faith critics. For every article highlighting the need for theoretical and methodological openness, there is a reductive screed in the *National Review* about the, "spineless, weaselly deans and presidents of America's universities" who kowtow to the "leftist rewrite of history" and police culture (e.g. Gelernter 2016). The culture war dynamic inaugurated with Allan Bloom's 1987 book *The Closing of the American Mind* (2012) is alive and well. Or as Andrew Hartman recently put it: "The Culture Wars Are Dead: Long Live the Culture Wars" (2018). Angela Nagle's book *Kill All Normies* recently made waves in both popular and scholarly circles for effectively blaming the emergence of the Alt-Right—and by extension the election of Donald Trump—on cultural critics who populate their Tumblr feeds with

S. Johnson Andrews (✉)
Humanities, History, and Social Sciences, Columbia College Chicago, Chicago, IL, USA
e-mail: sandrews@colum.edu

J. Aksikas et al. (eds.), *Cultural Studies in the Classroom and Beyond*,
https://doi.org/10.1007/978-3-030-25393-6_10

amateur critiques of racist/sexist/cis-gendered representation and cultural appropriation.

Whatever their political efficacy, versions of the political project of cultural studies—particularly insofar as it highlights the way that systems of representation relate to systems of material exploitation and social oppression—can be found in increasingly popular (and ever more frequent) movements like #MeToo, #BlackLivesMatter, and #Occupy. It could be argued that cultural studies is fundamental to the everyday fare of internet culture, from critiques of racist/sexist/transphobic TV shows on *Buzzfeed* to columns on the errors of cultural appropriation in *Teen Vogue* to Anita Sarkeesian's critiques of the representation of women in video games, self-published on her *Feminist Frequency* YouTube channel. From this perspective, cultural studies as a discipline is Social Justice Warrior 101.

It is true that these critiques mostly focus on what is termed identity politics and that this dimension of the cultural studies (or feminist or anti-racist) project has been most frequently incorporated by the dominant hegemonic culture, even if the theoretical foundation of the incorporated versions of this project remains unstable. As Nancy Fraser (2013a, b) and Chantel Mouffe (Mouffe and Errejón 2016) have highlighted in their recent work on the emergence of Trump and other economic/ethnonationalist politicians, we can see the reactionary panic of white supremacist patriarchy as premature, overstated, and perhaps related to the legitimate economic grievances of the neoliberal subject, but the resurgence of these retrograde ideologies signifies that, whatever one thinks of them, the movements and projects of marginalized subjects' "Emancipation" as Nancy Fraser terms them were necessary and remain incomplete.

Likewise, many universities and colleges have become quite aware of the problems of diversity, equity, and inclusion—even as corporate-minded administrators often evacuate these concepts of any concrete meaning. Yet even after half a century in the academy, and several decades of popular acceptance, cultural studies as a field remains unevenly mapped onto the rigid disciplinary hierarchies of the contemporary Humanities and Social Sciences, which are themselves increasingly marginalized next to emergent "pragmatic" fields of undergraduate education, like the digital humanities, video game design, or business and entrepreneurship.

The politics of austerity following the 2008 financial crisis has been especially unkind to US Higher Education as a whole. In 2012, after 15 straight years of growth, US colleges and universities saw their first declines in enrollment, a downward trend that has continued every year since. The "pragmatic" academic focus and neoliberal intellectual experience has been joined by theories of "Unschooling" promoted by prominent, wealthy right wing libertarians like Peter Thiel (who offers students a scholarship to forgo college and start a business instead) and notions like Anna Kamenetz's (2010) DIY degree, which encourages "edupunks" to take their education into their own hands. Massively Open Online Courses (MOOCs, like those which "teach" 30,000 students at a time on platforms like Udacity and Coursera), badges, and other kinds of informal endorsements (through platforms like LinkedIn) or certificates that primarily target non-traditional students and continuing education were initially intended as replacements for what was declared by pundits as the death of the BA.

In the same vein, there is a sudden explosion of instrumental approaches to educational technology: media darlings like the Khan Academy are poised to replace the potential of critical pedagogy with YouTube videos and online quizzes; for-profit colleges who spend more on marketing than on their predominantly online instruction; large Venture Capital firms investing heavily in virtual colleges and K-12 institutions, marketing themselves as cutting edge, cost-saving, future-oriented models of education; consultants seducing administrators keen to cut labor costs with the latest gadgetry of automated or distance learning; and even sincere attempts at rethinking all of these models, like the competency-based programs of Western Governor's University, which liberals like Barack Obama and his Education Secretary Arne Duncan pointed to as exemplary of the future. In the middle are the majority of faculty and institutions, many of whom feel overwhelmed by the opportunities and defensive of the instrumentalists.

And hovering above all of them is the lingering sense that something is about to change dramatically in higher education and its role in US society at large. At the height of the MOOC mania, Clay Shirky put it more bluntly. Drawing on two data points Shirky says:

Forget private school. Tuition and fees at public four-year colleges went up 72% last decade, even as the market value of a bachelor's degree fell by 15%. [. . . .] This is the background to the entire conversation around higher education: Things that can't last don't. This is why MOOCs matter. Not because distance learning is some big new thing or because online lectures are a solution to all our problems, but because they've come along at a time when students and parents are willing to ask themselves, "Isn't there some other way to do this?" (Shirky 2013)

When we add to this the accumulated student debt in the US, which now stands at over $1.5 trillion, there is pressure to deliver a positive return on investment for students who decide to continue down the traditional path of acquiring a BA at a four-year college or university.

Yet even as colleges and universities are pushing for more instrumental, efficient, commodified pedagogical models, internal critics are surprised to find what they call, "Limited Learning on College Campuses" (Arum and Roksa 2011). They make this judgment based on a test created by The Council for Aid to Education (CAE), a non-profit arm of the RAND corporation, founded in 1952 by executives at General Motors, Exxon, and US Steel, devoted to helping promote corporate charitable giving to higher education. Among other things, the CAE promotes testing and assessment tools so that those corporate donors know what they are getting. The CAE's most well-known test, the Collegiate Learning Assessment (or CLA+) bills itself as, "measuring critical thinking for higher education."

This hegemonic version of "critical thinking" emphasizes "challenging students to address real-life issues presented in performance tasks:" "Beyond simply accumulating facts, [students] must be able to access, structure, and use information." The latter used to be called "thinking," but now even "thinking" is itself in critical condition: thus we must upgrade our terminology. On the other hand, in an era plagued by the ills of fossil fuel use and production, driven by the entire system of automobility, sustained by the global, industrial production of steel, it is unlikely that the CAE's version of "critical" will involve learning about frameworks like the Anthropocene, seeing as though that concept might rub its corporate donors the wrong way. This is a shame since thinking critically about the Anthropocene—or even the more controversial Capitalocene—

would prepare students for the kind of innovative, creative, critical thinking humanity itself needs, now more than ever.

In general the modifier "critical" appears overused: that term should really be applied to only the most relentless, "ruthless criticism of all that exists" as the Young Marx would have it. In practice, "critical thinking" features as a core requirement of most college and university curricula, significantly watering down its meaning. In this context, the work of critical cultural studies is simultaneously more necessary and more difficult than ever before. The difficulty is how to retain this radical kernal even as the dominant culture has incorporated the practice of critical thinking within boundaries that will render it unthreatening to the dominant order. Or to paraphrase Richard Johnson put it, how can we "occupy a critical tradition critically?" (Johnson 1986, p. 40) This is especially the case in arts and media focused institutions like Columbia College Chicago (CCC).

CCC benefited doubly from the echo-boom of college enrollment in the early 2000 and the nearly simultaneous climax of the idea of the "Creative Economy." As the anthropologist Richard Lloyd (2010) chronicles in his book *Neobohemia*, the small- to medium-sized factories in largely minority communities like Chicago's Wicker Park (where Lloyd did his ethnographic work in the late 1990s) served as fertile ground for the gentrification and growth of the creative city—or at least its promise. As in Andrew Ross's book *No Collar* (2003), Lloyd sees most of the growth (including the values for the newly gentrified properties) is made possible by the self-exploitation of creative workers that has now become commonplace: the technology, web design, and editorial firms that thrived in the hollowed-out loft-spaces of Wicker Park were primarily staffed by part-time workers who could "do what they love" (Tokumitsu 2014, 2015) for a pittance because they were supplementing their income by working at the bars, restaurants, bookstores, and concert venues catering to tourists and moneyed hipsters.

With Wicker Park roughly in the middle of the Blue Line train running from Chicago O'Hare airport to downtown, CCC sits at the end, alongside The School of the Art Institute of Chicago (SAIC), and a bevy of other colleges and universities like DePaul and Roosevelt University, which also capitalized on the trend in credentialing the next generation of college students who answer the call Angela McRobbie (2016) discusses in her latest book: *Be Creative*! The school marketing materials echo the hyper-competitive, self-exploitative motto of Tokumitsu says characterizes the creative economy, telling students to "Live the life [they] love." And the recently launched Business and Entrepreneurship department and Career Center reify the notion that students should conceptualize themselves—and "Manage their careers"—in much the same way as the unemployed tech workers interviewed by Carrie M. Lane (2011), encouraging them to see themselves, "as 'companies of one,' entrepreneurial agents engaged in the constant labor of defining, improving, and marketing, 'the brand called you'" (p. 9). Often, this means that otherwise "woke" students—who are highly attuned to issues of race, gender, and sexual orientation—will recite neoliberal platitudes about the need for networking and self-promotion, even as they complain about exhibit A of the effects of neoliberal policy in the US: student loans.

As in the early years of cultural studies' US institutionalization, this context has deeply affected the way the abstract (anti-)discipline has been put into concrete practice. As Stuart Hall put it in his recently published *1983* lectures,

> I also want to emphasise the importance of the institutional moment, which is separate from the bringing together of a set of intellectual discourses. Something additional happens when a set of discourses and practices are institutionalised: They are concretised in a particular form, in a program of activities and a specific socially composed group of people. They are directed to certain targets and projects. In another place, on the basis of a different kind of institutionalisation, different practices emerge. While I will emphasise the fact that the Centre for Contemporary Cultural Studies appeared at a certain moment, in a certain place, I also want to make the more general point that what happens in the evolution of a new field of study must be partly understood in terms of the forms in which those studies are institutionalised. (Hall 2016)

One piece of the work of the US institutionalization of the field occurred first just 150 miles from us—at the University of Illinois at Urbana-Champaign, where Lawrence Grossberg, Cary Nelson, and Paula Treichler helped organize the landmark conference that resulted in their 1992 anthology on *Cultural Studies*. But where their institutional situation led them to declare cultural studies as "actively and aggressively anti-disciplinary," ours at Columbia College Chicago did not allow for such a position: instead it demanded we project a disciplinary coherence to cultural studies that some of its early adherents continue to disavow. Not only did we face local institutional factors—the kind that sit next to you in the departmental faculty meeting—but more importantly, our major served only undergraduate students: in order to provide them with a clear set of parameters, processes, rubrics, courses, and (ultimately) grades, we had to be clear about what cultural studies was, what it meant, and how you could go about teaching a diverse group of students how to *do* cultural studies.

Doing cultural studies has long been the topic of textbooks—most notably the collection by Hall and DeGuy analyzing the Sony Walkman (2013), which takes that topic as its title. But practical guides in conducting or using cultural studies have proliferated well beyond those early Open University publications (Barker 2011; Johnson et al. 2004; McRobbie 2005; Ryan 2010; Sardar 2010; Saukko 2003). With so many recent texts written, published, and evidently sold to students and teachers in the field, it is evident that the contours of the field are more defined than the "anti-disciplinary" reputation would suggest.

In surveying these, the methodology of cultural studies that emerges is close to what Johnson recommends in his 1987 essay, "What Is Cultural Studies Anyway?" Though Johnson argues that, "Cultural studies must be inter-disciplinary (and sometimes anti-disciplinary) in its tendency" (Johnson 1986, p. 43), he ultimately outlines a methodology that is common to the field, if not a specifically disciplinary one. First, it is a radically contextualist methodology, meaning it begins from a coherent and rigorous understanding of the way its objects of study fit into a specific, historical, geographic, political economic, social, and ideological context. To do this, practitioners must marshall a revised version of the methods of disciplines that have an accepted, valid claim to producing partial knowledge about this context: history, geography, sociology, and so on. Here, we can draw from Hall's description of cultural studies and its intervention in the crisis in the humanities:

Serious interdisciplinary work involves the intellectual risk of saying to professional sociologists that what they say sociology is, is not what it is. We had to teach what we thought a kind of sociology that would be of service to people studying culture would be, something we could not get from self-designated sociologists. It was never a question of which disciplines would contribute to the development of this field, but of how one could decenter or destabilize a series of interdisciplinary fields. We had to respect and engage with the paradigms and traditions of knowledge and of empirical and concrete work in each of these disciplinary areas in order to construct what we called cultural studies or cultural theory. (Hall 1990, p. 16)

But whatever methods they appropriate and deploy, cultural studies scholars should account for the specific context out of which the object under analysis emerges. This context will also suggest the methods most likely to illuminate that object.

Second, cultural studies conceptualizes its objects of study as texts, which can be analyzed through semiotic, discourse, literary, or, what Gillian Rose (2016) calls visual methodologies. Whether it is a film, a song, a pair of shoes, or an emergent cultural practice, it can be separated into the signifiers and signifieds that make it function as a meaningful object of culture. Of course, much of the work is in explaining why these specific connotations function in the specific context the analysis is taking place—and for who. Which leads to the third dimension of cultural studies analysis: the reading, the decoding, the audience, and/or the ethnographic. As Johnson puts it, "The text-as-produced is a different object from the text-as-read" (58). Understanding the lived cultures proves to be the most difficult in Johnson's estimation—and ethnographic methods are also the most challenging in undergraduate work in the US as they quickly prick the interest of the human subjects review board. The thick description of a lived reality is often the most satisfying as a narrative that explains what culture is, what it does; but it is also the most partial in both senses of the term, as used by Johnson, et al. (2004): "limited by a particular time, space and social horizon and also motivated, more or less consciously, by desire, interest and power. Moreover, partiality is not only inevitable – a necessary human condition of knowledge production – it is also, potentially, a resource or asset, provided it is made explicit and debated and reflected on" (17).

Taken together, these modes or methods of cultural analysis can be thought of as corresponding to what Johnson and others describe as a cultural circuit. While it is not a linear process, abstracting the text, context, and reading into different methodological paradigms helps highlight both the partiality of each and the way those partialities can be modulated, manipulated, and combined. Or, in Johnson's words, "It is not therefore an adequate strategy for the future just to add together the three sets of approaches, using each for its appropriate moment;" but instead it may be, "transformative to rethink each moment in the light of the others, importing objects and methods of study usually developed in relation to one moment into the next" (73).

Saukko (2003) uses different terms for these methodological distinctions, focusing her energies on the validity rather than "truth" of research. Research into the contextualist moment is shoring up the "contextual validity" of the analyst's work; the textual moment is where we consider the "deconstructive validity"; and the tools of ethnography, and so on, are those which are concerned with the "dialogic validity" of cultural studies research (19–20). Saukko's post-structuralist inflection more centrally highlights the importance of the self-reflexivity of the analyst, but the overall principles of a cultural studies methodology remain the same. We can see echos of this same tripartite division in many other instructional and descriptive texts on the field (cf. Turner 2002).

In short, while many acolytes of cultural studies may paradoxically advise against canon or catechism, there are a set of methodological assumptions that appear to be held in common as core values in the field—or as we call it in the Cultural Studies program at Columbia College Chicago one of Cultural Studies' Core Assumptions (see appendix below for full description of these): **The Need for a Multiplicity of Methods and Interdisciplinarity**. We reiterate this interdisciplinarity throughout our curriculum, but it is especially central to the methodological tenets of our introductory and methods courses, as well as figuring into the final capstone courses, where students design, research, and execute the capstone thesis.

The sequence of courses (see Appendix 2 for sequence of Core Courses) in the major has been developed over the course of a decade, with the most profound changes coming to this final capstone piece. In the early years of the major, students had only one semester to develop their project proposal, assemble the works necessary for a final thesis paper, which they then presented at a forum for family and colleagues the day before graduation. This task was eventually spread out over two semesters, with the bulk of the project development and literature review done in what is now called **Capstone I** and the research and writing left for **Capstone II**. In this second semester, students peer review one another's papers, with careful scholarly and editorial guidance by the professor of the course, supplemented with advice from an external faculty reader at the college.

Our most recent assessment of these papers finds them to be steadily improving, integrating key cultural studies theories, utilizing rigorous textual, contextual, and audience focused methods, and dealing with pressing issues of politics, representation, policy, and culture. Many of these papers have served as students' writing samples for successful graduate school applications in law, public health, communication and media studies, women's and gender studies, social work and critical studies in race and ethnicity. And several have been published with few changes in major media and cultural studies journals, such as *The Journal of American Culture*, which published Columbia College Chicago alumnus Phil Bratta's Capstone paper on nationalism and displays of the flag in the post-9/11 US (Bratta 2009).

The best papers are those that exemplify a deep engagement with the total sequence of classes in the major, and an earnest commitment to the other core assumptions. The object-specific interdisciplinarity complements the other Core Assumptions we argue are common to most Cultural Studies projects and approaches—assumptions that are also threaded through the curriculum. Chief among these is **The Need for Political Commitment and the Analysis of the "Social Whole."** From the perspective of the US mainstream, where one has to take what Donald Trump called "many sides" into account, and where academic objectivity has often served as cover for hidden—or just "common sense"—hegemonic political commitments, this core assumption appears a contradiction in terms: how can one maintain a political commitment while also endeavoring to produce a valid analysis of the social whole? At some point, these are bound to come into conflict, the partiality of knowledge and the partiality of political commitment working to bend the results of the analysis in one direction or the other.

But I would argue this conflict is most acute when this partiality of political commitment remains hidden and the partiality of knowledge is unacknowledged. Hegemonic culture acts as a powerful center of intellectual gravity, endowing its conventional wisdom with the honor of universality *qua* objectivity. It is better that the political commitments—and subjective limitations—of the author be as transparent and the analysis be as broad and open as possible. When I enter a classroom as the white, male, middle-class, married, heterosexual, American, professor, there is no way to shed the partialities, preferences, and biases that have shaped my perspective: I must move beyond the now chic notion of checking one's privilege and be prepared to admit that this privilege has—in some ways irreparably—broken my ability to see beyond my subjectivity. This is the principle that is expressed in **The Need for Self-Reflexivity**, which notes not only that we have implicit biases, but also that, "As cultural researchers, we are 'inside' our object of study." Therefore one of the best ways to understand those biases is to understand and contextualize their significance and power. Ideally, any political commitments would be then be informed and justified by the analysis of the social whole—rather than the other way around!

Though I am skeptical of Lawrence Grossberg's claim (in his chapter in this collection) that there could be a cultural studies informed by right wing or conservative political ideologies, I would say this would only be possible if, with the analysis of the social whole, one saw the left as the hegemonic center, and the critical analysis suggested that the more radical perspective, which would produce useful knowledge for the advancement of a more humane, democratic society, was that of the right. Of course there are a number of alt-right and "men's rights" organizations that now attempt to make roughly this claim: that we are in the grips of a leftist chokehold on the production of knowledge, that feminists and cultural leftists have poisoned the perspective of the mainstream, making a return of patriarchal, conservative, and neoliberal ideologies and social norms necessary and desirable. On the other hand, this assumes the content of the positions right and left are objectively and clearly defined, rather than a product of the context in which they appear. And in this, I share Dr. Grossberg's insistence that whatever one's political ideology is, it will only be served by asking the most probing questions possible in order to best understand the conjuncture in which an object, event, or movement appears.

In practice this core assumption is certainly the most fraught at the undergraduate level, and especially in courses like **Introduction to Cultural Studies**, which serves not only as the gateway to the major as a whole, but also serves the entire college population as a course satisfying a general education requirement (three of six Culture, Values, and Ethics credits all students need to graduate). At one time, this course performed the former purpose much better than the latter, introducing the field of cultural studies, often through an engagement with the Birmingham School and other theoretical legacies of the field. But this approach was not as useful to students taking the course solely for general education credit, who were more interested in developing a conceptual and theoretical toolkit that could be applied to their work in other majors and fields of study. In more recent iterations, the course has focused on introducing key concepts in semiotics and critical cultural studies, for example, mythology, articulation, hegemony, the cultural circuit, and the politics of cultural representation and appropriation. In my sections, I have made it a priority to introduce these concepts as a way of discussing emergent cultural and social movements: Occupy, Black Lives Matters, #MeToo, the protests over the Dakota Access pipeline, the events in Charlottesville, and the larger social issues they help reveal to the broader society.

While most students are familiar with these events, issues, and movements, there are usually more than a handful for whom the slightest exposition of them is a revelation. For them, it is a stretch to ask them to consider the need for a political commitment and the larger range of possible positions. At the same time, in recent semesters, an increasing number of students come to this course with clearly articulated political commitments, in some cases with deep connections with online or hybrid activist communities. For them, the political positions seem obvious—

something like Howard Zinn's observation that you can't remain neutral on a moving train. They have worked out their views in "subaltern counterpublics" (Fraser 1990) on and offline and have a ready-made framework for addressing and interpreting the world around them. In most cases, they help provide useful echoes, enriching details, and instructive nuance to these conversations. But often those already initiated into a community of specific commitments are aided by a broader perspective—historically, spatially, and politically: to the conceptual vocabulary of the field and the analysis of the social whole, we add **the Need to Think Historically and Spatially** and **The Need for and Commitment to Theory**.

These last two core assumptions are introduced in this introductory course, but the latter is developed more comprehensively in the **Cultural Theories** class. The latter is only for students planning to major or minor in cultural studies so can be geared more specifically to their need for a breadth and depth of knowledge in the field, especially in the primary texts of major theorists, from Raymond Williams and Stuart Hall, to Judith Butler and Michel Foucault and more recent theorists of power, race, gender, sexuality, representation, urban, environmental, media, and Marxist studies. While each instructor will give their particular emphasis to the range and selection of theorists, the course generally helps students hone their abilities in recognizing and utilizing different theoretical paradigms—and in thinking with and through theory.

These core assumptions are further developed and problematized in the **Methods and Methodologies in Cultural Studies** course (outlined and described in Jaafar Aksikas's individual contribution to this collection) and in the various elective seminars which students take to round out their major coursework—courses in Queer Theory, Cyberculture, Food and Culture, Marx and Marxisms, and so on. The best **Capstone II** papers are those that are able to utilize theories and conceptual paradigms that are explored in these seminars, rather than being left to the more self-directed literature review in Capstone I.

"All pedagogical reasons aside…"

While this is, to some extent, an idealized rendering of the undergraduate curriculum in cultural studies at Columbia College Chicago, many students who completed a major or minor in the program experienced something close to it. And many of those students went on to be successful in a variety of fields, both in and outside of the academy. It is not a perfect program, but it is consistently improving, often in the face of a great deal of administrative and departmental animosity. As one administrator put it to us "all pedagogical reasons aside," supporting student needs is impossible in the face of institutional politics—in that case it was the need for smaller class sizes in the upper division, writing intensive courses, like Capstone.

Even before enrollment began to decline—both nationally and at Columbia specifically—there were attempts to close or dismantle the program, or key aspects of it. While a few friendly Chairs and Deans sheltered it for the first decade or so of its existence, the second decade has seen biannual—if not bi-monthly—floggings of the program, each time a fresh hell wrought by petty jealousies and ancient grudges weaponized with bureaucratic hierarchies and neoliberal metrics of success. And what account of cultural studies institutionalization would be complete without the vicious, arbitrary, and almost feudal politics of academic departments, colleges, and senior colleagues, where one program's success is seen as a threat to the potential success (or continued mediocrity) of anyone else!

The latter was quite literally the model of institutional overhaul recommended by the consultant Robert Dickeson, whose specialty is helping colleges fire tenured faculty by getting their fellow tenured faculty to argue that they deserve the resources given to their colleagues' department or program, thereby asking the administration to "Prioritize" one another out of a job. When the Cultural Studies program was targeted for closure through that process, around the time Occupy had taken over Zuccati Park, students launched an "Anti-Prioritization" movement, writing missives to academic leadership and the student paper, sitting in on the public forums, using the human mic to disrupt administrative presentations, and even trolling the President at the time into telling a student to "shut up" in a public forum—with all of these exchanges recorded and shared on YouTube and other social media.

Since those heady days of resistance, the major has faced less spectacular but no less damaging threats to its existence. Most recently, an obtuse attempt at curricular revision that intersected with a parasitic vanity project driven by faculty too lazy to develop and defend their own curriculum: a now-failed attempt at squatting on the cultural studies major at a time when there was a moratorium on new majors—and besides, getting a new major approved was a task that required, "too much paperwork," according to an advocate of this strategy at the time. It has nearly seen a death by a thousand cuts and is currently in hospice, with admissions now suspended barring another round of program revision.

The foundation remains strong pedagogically and many of us have faith that we will rise again, perhaps with more of a production focus and with more hooks into other units of the college. In any case, thanks to the valiant efforts of many students, faculty and staff, this cultural studies undergraduate curriculum worked very well and did what curricula are supposed to do: help students think critically about the world and produce useful knowledge that will help make it a better place. With any luck this essay will merely be the end of this chapter of the program, rather than its epitaph.

Appendix 1: Core Assumptions of Cultural Studies

The Need for Political Commitment and the Analysis of the "Social Whole"

Because cultural studies understands culture politically, the notions of "social totality/whole," and, in more dominant versions, that of "articulation" are central in cultural studies. The significance of an event, phenomenon, or practice—be it ideological, political, economic, or cultural—cannot be properly assessed outside a dialectical understanding of its place in society as a whole (which, here, refers to the concrete unity of all interacting spheres of social life), that is, by pursuing their hidden interactions and interconnections in real life. This way we are in a better position to understand how social, economic, and political forces act on cultural production, distribution, and reception; and how cultural forces, in turn, act on the social, economic, and political forces.

The Need for a Multiplicity of Methods and Interdisciplinarity

In most cultural studies, there is a realization that traditional disciplinary methods have their merits and limits, but that they work better when they are deployed together in the analysis of cultural phenomena and processes. No single method is complete; and to get as close as possible to a better and more complex understanding of cultural practices and processes, combining methods becomes indispensable. As Johnson and company put it, "a multiplicity of methods is necessary because no one method is intrinsically superior to the rest and each provides a more or less appropriate way of exploring some different aspect of cultural process." And it is in this nuanced sense that cultural studies is also interdisciplinary. But while cultural studies understands culture in a broad way, as a way of life and encourages interdisciplinary perspectives and strategies, it, at the same time, demands a rigorous engagement with cultural texts, practices, and forms of all kinds.

The Need for Self-Reflexivity

As cultural researchers, we are "'inside" our object of study. We approach our topics with a particular cultural biography. Gramsci notes somewhere that the starting point of critical reflection—in this case, research—is the consciousness of who one is. Far from being negative source of research bias, knowing our partialities enables us to correct our biases. Self-reflexivity puts our work in perspective, highlighting its merits, as well as its limits.

The Need and Commitment to Theory

As Larry Grossberg puts it, "Cultural Studies is always theoretical. It is absolutely committed to the necessity of theoretical work, to what Karl Marx called the detour through theory." It is not committed to theory for theory's sake; it is rather interested in how theory and theoretical work can be deployed to better understand and transform specific historical conjunctures, contexts, and formations.

The Need to Think Historically and Spatially

Cultural research and activity is also temporarily located; it takes place at a certain historical moment/conjecture. The time dimension is an essential perspective in cultural theory and practice. It not only greatly enhances the subtlety with which cultural phenomena is explored, but helps us recognize the historical content and specificity of our work (including the theoretical categories we work with), as well. Cultural research activity is also always spatially located: It takes place somewhere. Issues of space and place are inherent in every research project, and recognizing the particularities of the places we study and where we study them could be enlightening.

Appendix 2: Cultural Studies Curriculum

Core Classes (and Course Descriptions) to Be Taken in the Following Sequence

Introduction to Cultural Studies
Theories of Cultural Studies
Methods and Methodologies of Cultural Studies (Discussed by Dr. Aksikas in this book)
Critical Issues in Cultural Studies
Capstone I and II

Interspersed with Elective Seminars (such as):

Philosophical Issues in Film
Media, Politics and Intervention
Critiquing Children's Culture Power and Freedom on Screen
Urban Images in Media and Film

Nature and Environmentalism in US Culture Cybercultures
Food and Culture
Making and Unmaking Whiteness
Globalization and Culture
Technology and Culture
Post-Colonial Studies
Marx and Marxisms: A Seminar on Marxist Cultural Theory
Queer Theory
Theories of Media, Society, and Culture

References

Arum, R., & Roksa, J. (2011). *Academically Adrift: Limited Learning on College Campuses*. Chicago: University of Chicago Press.

Barker, C. (2011). *Cultural Studies: Theory and Practice* (4th ed.). Los Angeles/London: SAGE Publications Ltd.

Bloom, A. (2012). *Closing of the American Mind: How Higher Education Has Failed Democracy and Impoverished the Souls of Today's Students*. (Reissue ed.). New York: Simon & Schuster.

Bratta, P. M. (2009). Flag Display Post-9/11: A Discourse on American Nationalism. *The Journal of American Culture, 32*(3), 232–243. https://doi.org/10.1111/j.1542-734X.2009.00713.x.

du Gay, P., et al. (2013). *Doing Cultural Studies: The Story of the Sony Walkman* (2nd ed.). Thousand Oaks: SAGE Publications Ltd.

Fraser, N. (1990). Rethinking the Public Sphere: A Contribution to the Critique of Actually Existing Democracy. *Social Text, 25/26*, 56–80. https://doi.org/10.2307/466240.

Fraser, N. (2013a). A Triple Movement?. *New Left Review*. (II), 81, 119–132.

Fraser, N. (2013b). *Fortunes of Feminism: From State-Managed Capitalism to Neoliberal Crisis* (1st ed.). Brooklyn: Verso.

Gelernter, J. (2016). The Liberal Fantasy of Cultural Appropriation, *National Review*. Available at https://www.nationalreview.com/2016/02/cultural-appropriation-leftists-rewrite-history/. Accessed 18 Sept 2018.

Hall, S. (1990). The Emergence of Cultural Studies and the Crisis of the Humanities. *October, 53*, 11–23. https://doi.org/10.2307/778912.

Hall, S. (2016). *Cultural Studies 1983: A Theoretical History*. Durham: Duke University Press.

Hartman, A. (2018). The Culture Wars Are Dead, *The Baffler*. Available at https://thebaffler.com/outbursts/culture-wars-are-dead-hartman.   Accessed 18 Sept 2018.

Johnson, R. (1986). What Is Cultural Studies Anyway? *Social Text, 16*, 38–80. https://doi.org/10.2307/466285.

Johnson, R., Chambers, D., Raghuram, P., & Tincknell, E. (2004). *The Practice of Cultural Studies* (1st ed.). London/Thousand Oaks: SAGE Publications Ltd.

Kamenetz, A. (2010). *DIY U: Edupunks, Edupreneurs, and the Coming Transformation of Higher Education*. White River Junction: Chelsea Green Publishing.

Lane, C. M. (2011). *A Company of One: Insecurity, Independence, and the New World of White Collar Unemployment*. Ithaca: ILR Press.

Lloyd, R. D. (2010). *Neo-Bohemia: Art and Commerce in the Postindustrial City* (2nd ed.). New York: Routledge.

McRobbie, A. (2005). *The Uses of Cultural Studies: A Textbook* (1st ed.). London/Thousand Oaks: SAGE Publications Ltd.

McRobbie, A. (2016). *Be Creative: Making a Living in the New Culture Industries* (1st ed.). Cambridge/Malden: Polity.

Mouffe, C., & Errejón, Í. (2016). *Podemos: In the Name of the People*. London: Lawrence & Wishart Ltd.

Nagle, A. (2017). *Kill All Normies: Online Culture Wars from 4Chan and Tumblr to Trump and the Alt-Right*. Winchester/Washington, DC: Zero Books.

Rose, G. (2016). *Visual Methodologies: An Introduction to Researching with Visual Materials* (4th ed.). London: SAGE Publications Ltd.

Ross, A. (2003). *No-Collar: The Humane Workplace and Its Hidden Costs*. New York: Basic Books.

Ryan, M. (2010). *Cultural Studies: A Practical Introduction by Michael Ryan*. West Sussex: Wiley-Blackwell.

Sardar, Z. (2010). *Introducing Cultural Studies: A Graphic Guide*. (Reprint ed.). London: Icon Books.

Saukko, P. (2003). *Doing Research in Cultural Studies: An Introduction to Classical and New Methodological Approaches* (1st ed.). London/Thousand Oaks: SAGE Publications Ltd.

Shirky, C. (2013). Your Massively Open Offline College Is Broken, *The Awl*. Available at https://web.archive.org/web/20130207202132/http://www.theawl.com/2013/02/how-to-save-college

Tokumitsu, M. (2014). *In the Name of Love, Jacobin.com.* Available at https://www.jacobinmag.com/2014/01/in-the-name-of-love/. Accessed 27 Mar 2016.

Tokumitsu, M. (2015). *Do What You Love: And Other Lies About Success and Happiness.* New York: Regan Arts.

Turner, G. (2002). *British Cultural Studies* (3rd ed.). London/New York: Routledge.

Cultural Studies in Practice: Toward a 'Thick Description' of a Methodology Course in Cultural Studies

Jaafar Aksikas

Cultural Studies and the World of Teaching and Pedagogy: A Missed Articulation

In response to a rather broad, but incisive, question about the relationship between organic intellectuals, teaching, and pedagogy, prompted by the "Cultural Studies and Its Theoretical Legacies" talk Stuart Hall gave at the formative 1990 "Cultural Studies Now and in the Future" conference—which was later anthologized in the well-known collection, *Cultural Studies*, edited by Lawrence Grossberg, Cary Nelson, and Paula Treichler, in 1992, Hall observed:

> When I said that part of what the Centre was about was trying to produce organic intellectual work, I of course had the question of pedagogy essentially in mind. I don't think we can divorce theoretical work from pedagogy. At the Centre for Contemporary Cultural Studies there were only

J. Aksikas (✉)
Humanities, History, and Social Sciences, Columbia College Chicago, Chicago, IL, USA
e-mail: Jaksikas@colum.edu

© The Author(s) 2019
J. Aksikas et al. (eds.), *Cultural Studies in the Classroom and Beyond*,
https://doi.org/10.1007/978-3-030-25393-6_11

three academics, so the organic intellectual we were trying to produce were not only ourselves but our students. So the question of pedagogy as a form of cultural production is crucial. I agree with what I take to be an underlying criticism in your comment, *namely that when we talk about the institutional position of cultural studies, we often fail to talk about questions of teaching and pedagogy.* We talk about intellectual practice as if it is the practice of intellectuals in the library reading the right canonical texts or consulting other intellectuals at conferences or something like that. But the ongoing work of an intellectual practice for most of us, insofar as we get out material sustenance, our modes of reproduction, from doing our academic work, is indeed to teach (290) [My italics].

Hall's recognition of a missing link or articulation between theoretical, intellectual work, on the one hand, and actual teaching labor and practice, on the other, in cultural studies is perspicacious. In fact, while the larger question of critical pedagogy has always been central to the field of contemporary cultural studies since its early formations in post-war Britain, in general, there has hardly been any *published* accounts of actual courses or even classroom practices and activities in the field. While there are some useful teaching materials in the field, most notably the Open University series, and especially since the importation of cultural studies into the US academy, one is generally more likely to encounter moments of critical self-reflection on teaching practices in cultural studies (and in other closely allied) professional annual conferences and meetings. But this has yet to translate into sustained written accounts in the world of scholarly journals and anthologies in the field. It is as if the 'messy,' 'dirty,' and concrete world of teaching and the classroom, on the one hand, and the theoretical, abstract world of cultural studies critique and analysis, on the other, had been kept apart. And yet, most of us have had to face this in the context of the job market, where some general statement or reflection on one's teaching and pedagogical practices is highly encouraged, if not expected, as an essential component of a candidate's portfolio. And even here, the tendency has been to produce 'thin descriptions' of one's teaching at a higher level of abstraction than that of classroom practices and activities. That is why it is not unfair to conclude that teaching and classroom labor have been treated with some implicit contempt and excluded from serious scholarly consideration and robust critical debate.

This is a significant gap that this anthology seeks to address and encourage other cultural studies practitioners to contribute to the emergence of a new genre of writing, centered around 'thick descriptions' and detailed 'reportage' accounts of our classroom teaching and pedagogical practices. Cultural studies is not just a radical intellectual-political project, it is also *in essence* a critical pedagogical project and practice, and there is no doubt that the work of taking seriously and reflecting critically on, as well as of widely documenting and sharing, our concrete teaching and pedagogical practices at the level of courses and classroom activities will yield some important benefits. I would go even further to argue that taking seriously our teaching and pedagogical work is especially urgent at the current conjuncture, where cultural studies and the university are everywhere under increasing attack by fundamentalist, neoliberal forces. Our pedagogy and teaching are now a significant, and sometimes, our only 'way of struggle.'

Therefore, this essay is probably best understood as primarily a call for the need to produce better and more systematic written accounts and 'thick descriptions' of the courses we teach, highlighting the specific kinds of classroom activities, coursework, and projects we deploy in these courses. Only secondarily can it also be seen as an intervention in the growing debates around issues of pedagogy, methodology, and epistemology in cultural studies. This genre or subfield of scholarly work devoted primarily to the description and analysis of the details, practices, and struggles of teaching does not quite exist in cultural studies. I take this moment not to make any grand theoretical claims, but to instead provide a short critical self-reflexive 'thick description' of one of the undergraduate courses I have been teaching at my institution since 2005. The course in question is an advanced research methodology course and is one of a half-dozen core courses in the Cultural Studies Bachelor's Program and is required of every student seeking a cultural studies degree. To take this course, students are first required to take and pass our introductory course, *Introduction to Cultural Studies*, and our critical theory course, *Cultural Theories*. For a more substantive description of the cultural studies curriculum at my institution, please refer to the preceding Chapter by my colleague Sean Andrews.

The Cultural Studies Formation and Curriculum at Columbia College

The formation and changing fortunes of cultural studies at Columbia College, the institution where I teach, might be read through any number of macro- and micro-narratives and struggles, including the increasing corporatization and bureaucratization of the university; the shift from a liberal to a neoliberal mode of education, characterized by the increasing instrumentalization of the university; the paradoxes of working-class, open-admissions institutions of higher education; and the debates about the identity and role of media and arts institutions of higher learning in the United States and in the West; as well as the debates surrounding the relationship between 'career' and 'liberal arts' higher education. Of course, these trends and tendencies are all interconnected and are largely enabled by what the late Stuart Hall has recently called 'the neoliberal revolution,' a social formation that presents an existential threat—especially in times of deep crisis—to a whole range of institutions that refuse to define themselves completely by the logics of commodification, privatization, and marketization. The history of cultural studies at Columbia College, like that of cultural studies in the neoliberal academy, is bound to remain in a state of 'permanent struggle' against the increasing neoliberalization and instrumentalization of the university, which is also in a state of constant struggle for survival, without any guarantees, as is evidenced by the closure and destruction of many successful programs in the field, both at the graduate and undergraduate levels, especially in the United States and the United Kingdom.

Columbia College is largely an arts and media school; it is, in fact, one of the largest and oldest arts and media institution of higher education in North America. And yet, the cultural studies program is generally recognized as one of the more robust and 'more interesting [undergraduate] programs' in the field in the United States and North America (Grossberg 2011, 427). The program was first started in 2002 as an interdisciplinary studies path for a solid block of arts and media students who were no longer happy with the highly specialized nature of other programs, especially those in photography, film, and media arts and who were now seeking a broader critical liberal arts degree. By 2006, the program, thanks to the collective efforts of its faculty, informed by the demands of students, reconfigured its curricula and course sequence to become more specifically cultural studies along the lines I indicated above. Since then, this innovative core curriculum has been taught exclusively by core cultural studies faculty, drawn from across English, the humanities, and social sciences. Since then also, the program has been operating with a very specific understanding of cultural studies and the existence of cultural studies as a field or discipline has been largely and long taken for granted by the institution, even among unsympathetic administrators or colleagues, who largely misunderstand what we actually do. This is clear in the core coursework throughout the program. Every major has to take an introductory course, a theory course, a methodology seminar, and a two-semester capstone seminar (a research proposal and a research thesis course, respectively). *Introduction to Cultural Studies*, the only core course in the program that is open to non-majors, introduces students to some of the key topics, themes, and debates in cultural studies, but did so by focusing on key critical concepts, keywords, and vocabularies in cultural studies. Key critical concepts, such as class, race, gender, agency, subjectivity, and representation, were introduced and employed throughout the course to understand and interrogate larger issues at the intersections of media, politics, and culture.

The syllabus for *Intro* reads:

As the title indicates, "Introduction to Cultural Studies" is designed to introduce students—with very little or no prior background—to the growing academic field of cultural studies, a field which defies easy definition (in fact, cultural studies emerged precisely as an attempt to question, or at least challenge, rigid disciplinary boundaries and institutional constraints), but which is specific enough to warrant a definition. The course operates with the assumption that Cultural Studies is best understood as both a very specific approach within the wider field of the study of culture (one with implicit, but distinctive epistemological and methodological commitments and ways of working), and a political intellectual project and practice (where the desire to want to produce useful political knowledge and to intervene into (and help transform) concrete social conjunctures has always been a guiding commitment in the field from its early formations in the New Left and in the Adult Education and Working Class Movements in post-war Britain). What distinguishes Cultural Studies, among other things, is its commitment to understanding culture and cultural phenomena reflexively, contextually, dialectically, relationally, and materially; and its insistence on the necessity of analyzing the complex mutual constitution of and dialectical relationship between its specific objects of study, on the one hand, and their larger social conjunctures and structures, on the other. The course will do more than introduce students to cultural studies, however. Students should expect to also *do* some cultural studies work themselves. We will bring our discussion of theories and concepts to bear on the practical analysis of cultural phenomena and artifacts, as well as the analysis of the implications of cultural studies work, including our own, for contemporary society and its future.

The topics and questions covered a wide range of cultural and social phenomena, including media and politics; popular culture; youth cultures; women, gender, and sexuality; consumer culture; globalization and culture; and many more. However, what brought all these together was the specifically contexualist and historicizing practice of cultural studies that sought to always place these phenomena in their larger social, political, economic, and cultural contexts.

This specificity of the project of cultural studies is further developed in *Cultural Theories*, which seeks to introduce students to some of the major critical theories and theoretical frameworks that cultural studies has historically engaged. These include Marxism, feminism, critical race theory, queer theory, and post-colonialism, among others. Here, students take what Stuart Hall, drawing on Marx, once called the necessary *detour through theory* and try to get their hands dirty drawing on some of these theories (and with them their core concepts) to understand and analyze specific cultural, political and media objects, practices, and events.

The Methodology Course: Toward a 'Thick Description'

However, nowhere is the specificity of the practice of cultural studies highlighted in a more sustained and systematic manner than in *Methods of Inquiry in Cultural Studies*, the core methodology course in the program, to which I now turn to in an attempt to provide what I called above a 'thick description.' The aim of the course is to focus on the specific epistemology and methodology of research in cultural studies. At the outset, the syllabus insists that:

> This course operates with a very specific understanding of cultural studies, where the latter is seen not only as a particular approach within the wider of field of the study of culture (one with implicit, but distinctive epistemological assumptions and ways of working), but also as a politically committed intellectual project (where the commitment to imagine and help bring about a socialist, humane society and culture has always been a guiding methodology in the field from its early formations in post-war Britain).

This is important because cultural studies is not informed by a specific method or set of specific methods and has tended to draw, more or less, freely on a multiplicity of methods from across the humanities and social sciences fields. Similarly, cultural studies is not limited by a fixed object or set of objects. What is highlighted early on and throughout the course is the fact that the specificity of cultural studies is more closely associated with very specific, and yet largely implicit, set of epistemological and methodological moves, assumptions, and suppositions that remain open to and also question conventional cultural and critical explanations. The seminar thus does two things; first, it introduces students to, and also expects them to think through, the presuppositions, methods, and methodologies appropriate to cultural studies. Second, it expects them to complete several research projects (mini-projects and a final research project) that reflect the specificity of the field of cultural studies. The course and its projects are designed to provide students with ample opportunities to do this in a systematic and methodical manner.

The course starts from the assumption that methods and methodologies cannot be posited as absolute in opposition to their objects and that research methodology must, to quote Adorno from a different context, "stand in a living relationship to this subject matter and must, as far as possible, be developed from it" (Adorno, 72). At the same time, as is common in less careful work in cultural studies, this is not to be taken as a call for absolute openness vis-à-vis method: Any productive cultural inquiry or investigation should be very clear about what it is trying to find out, and the methods should at least be deployed in a way that allows them "to take on emphasis from the meaning of the subject matter, rather than making themselves independent of it" (72). In other words, the relationship between method and object is dialectical, in the sense that they are mutually constitutive of each other. Topics covered include cultural studies' commitment to politics; cultural studies' commitment to materialist dialectics; the dialectic of structural and conjunctural analysis; the place of theory in the field; the uses of self-reflexivity in cultural research; the need for a multiplicity of methods and rigorous interdisciplinarity; and the need for radical contextualism in cultural studies research: social, historical, and spatial.

In general, the methods we examine cover the whole circuit of culture and center on three approaches: several varieties of **textual analysis** (which draw from semiotics, post-structuralism, and deconstruction); a series of **audience reception/consumption studies (including ethnography**, which focuses on the 'lived experience' aspect of culture); and studies of the **political economy of culture** (which have tended to draw on Marxism and focus on the production and distribution of cultural texts and their political economy).

Questions of methodology are approached throughout the seminar using a diverse body of theoretical and applied texts that we examine in terms of the relation between the theoretical questions addressed and the methods and methodologies used to address those questions. The aim here is to show that theoretical questions should always inform the choice of methodology, and that, in turn, methods and methodologies do generate new theoretical questions. Ideally, the course seeks to achieve the following *interconnected* objectives: First, to help students understand the epistemological and methodological foundations of cultural studies and the cultural studies approaches to culture; second, to familiarize students with the wide range of methods and methodologies used in cultural studies research (and to distinguish between those that are appropriate and those that are inappropriate to cultural studies) and provide them with a critical 'how-to' guide to conducting cultural studies research; third, to help students question their methodological assumptions when they approach texts or study practices, that is, to be more aware and critical of the questions they ask about cultural texts and practices, why they ask them, and how these questions might predetermine the methods they use and the interpretations they are likely to produce; and finally, to help students learn to examine cultural phenomena in the context of their social totality (which, here, refers to the concrete unity of all interacting spheres of social life—cultural, economic, and political), that is, by pursuing their hidden interactions and interconnections in real life.

My general pedagogical practice is grounded in my commitment to cultural studies and in my firm belief that cultural studies matters. It is at once critical, self-reflexive, and contextual. Without undermining the authority of knowledge, I try to complicate as much as possible the teacher-student relationship, moving beyond any simple sense in which I am the active teaching subject and students are the passive learning objects. My classes keep lecturing to a minimum and promote critical, generative, but also *structured* and *meaningful* conversations, where the lived experiences and cultural biographies of students are deeply engaged and where epistemological curiosity is fostered in both teaching and learning. And most importantly, my pedagogy strives for praxis and insists on the need to produce useful political knowledge that can help us understand and transform what goes on in the social world we inhabit.

Let me now describe in a bit more detail what happens in the course.

Classroom Work and Assignments

Clearly, all the above assumptions informed my critical pedagogy and syllabus selections. The course is structured around a combination of short (mostly informal, sometimes improvised) lectures, class-wide discussions, and group work activities. Every week, students are expected to complete a short critical reflection on each of the assigned reading materials. The course is an upper-level course, usually taken by students in their third year in the major, and so naturally involves the reading of a variety of difficult and challenging primary texts by key thinkers and theorists for and in the field. The idea behind these short reflections is for students to have something handy before them that they can refer to as we discuss each of the key texts and also something that is meant to help them contribute to and augment classroom discussions. Each reflection is expected to include at least one broad critical question about each of the readings under study. Along with my short lectures, I try to use these broad questions not only to generate other critical questions but also to further organize, structure, and focus our class discussions.

The class is relatively small and generally never includes more than 15 students, all of whom are senior cultural studies major. As such, the class operates like a seminar with lots of opportunities for questions and discussion; and the latter are generally at a pretty sophisticated level. As a research methodology course, students are further expected to conduct several mini cultural studies research projects throughout the course of the semester. Early in the semester, usually during the first or second weekly meeting, the class is divided into four or five smaller research working groups. Each group is tasked with conducting research on one of the assigned cultural objects/texts, engaging cultural studies methodologies or methods covered in class. At the very least, these mini-projects include a critical summary of a recent methodological debate in relation to a pressing social or cultural issue, as well as an analysis of three scholarly articles on the topic. In each of these, the goal is for students to identify the methods and methodology employed in the scholarship and to analyze how well it works or does not work—and how it might work better. For example, in a recent offering of the course, students were expected to complete four collective mini-projects. The first project centered on the US popular show *Sex and the City*. Students were to each watch at least five episodes of the show very carefully; collectively identify and read at least three recent scholarly cultural studies articles/essays on the show (this was in addition to the main analysis of the show by Angela McRobbie, which we use as a core text in the course); and to collectively write a short "Research/Study Proposal" on the show, including a research question/thesis; key concepts; key theories; and central methodologies. The project was meant to get students to apply some of the core methodological presuppositions covered in the first five meetings of the course.

The second project was much more general and dealt with the topic of social media and politics. Again, working in small groups, students had to select at least one textual method/approach (namely, semiotics, narrative analysis, discourse analysis, or deconstruction) and apply it to their group project/study. The third project was equally broad and asked students to employ a political economy/production-based approach in their group project. They had to select an issue related to higher education (student loans, for-profit education, the place of humanities, etc.) and then bring a critical political economy approach to it. The fourth and final group research project was meant to provide students the opportunity to do some fieldwork research. Students were provided three options to choose from, namely the Black Lives Matter 'Movement' in Chicago, The Alt-Right Movement, or immigration and immigrants under Trump. Students were asked to conduct short-term fieldwork research or a mini-ethnography (either a short-term ethnography, a focus group study, or one or two extended interviews and to then write a short paper reflecting on the entire process). Most of them conducted a mini-ethnography, which included a discussion of site selection, access, rapport, field notes, and initial observations, or extended interviews, which included a discussion of issues, such as recruitment, rapport, informed consent, interview schedule, transcript, and initial findings. All these projects were shared with the whole class throughout the course of the semester. Overall, these projects were quite mixed in terms of their quality and level of sophistication and were meant to give me a sense of each of the groups' grasp of the methodologies and methods we had examined. For me, the most frustrating part of these collective research projects has always been how undervalued and misunderstood group research is. In almost every version of the class I have taught over all these years, the 'free-rider' challenge presents itself in these group research projects. Most students begin to resist collective work and group research projects altogether, on the grounds that some of their group members benefit from group grades without doing their fair share of the work. I try to address the issue with the whole class, explaining the merits of truly collaborative work, and also insisting that personal gain from the exploitation of a classmate's work, without contributing anything or very little of their own, is at odds with the cultural studies project, which is intended to make the world a more equitable place. But this hardly makes a difference and students generally continue to resist collective, collaborative work. I will say a bit more about this below.

These smaller projects are meant to prepare them for the major written assignment in the course, the final paper. The final paper is a relatively short (an 8- to 12-page) cultural studies analysis of some object, text or practice, reflecting the *specificity* of the field of cultural studies. This assignment is the main course project and is expected to reflect students' ability to do cultural studies research, systematically thinking through and deploying concepts, theories, assumptions, methods, and methodologies appropriate to cultural studies. I must point out that I also meet with students individually, at least twice, throughout the course of the semester, to provide initial materials to help begin work on this important project. In addition to the written component, students are also required to formally present their research to the whole class during the last two weeks of the semester.

The Early Weeks: Introduction to the Course and to Cultural Studies Research

The first meeting is devoted primarily to a general outline of the whole course, including a discussion of the course syllabus, assignments, and policies and, secondarily, to a broad conversation about what cultural studies is, its histories, current status, and concerns. Students are asked to articulate what they expect to get out of the course in relation to their research interests and also in relation to what would be covered in class. The idea here is for me to see where students are and meet them there. At the same time, I also highlight cultural studies as a specific academic field and intellectual project and provide an overview of its implicit, yet distinct practices and ways of working, that is, its major epistemological/methodological commitments of the field. This opening session usually closes with a small research exercise, meant to give students a 'taste' of research practice in cultural studies.

The second meeting is divided into two parts. The first part is devoted to a broad discussion of the disciplinary identity of cultural studies and its relationships and dialogues with other disciplines and projects in the humanities and the social sciences. This discussion centers on the question of the specificity of cultural studies and how it understands and approaches culture, in a context where all fields in the humanities, the social sciences, and the arts have taken a cultural turn. The discussion is guided by two texts: "Cultural Studies and the Study of Culture: Disciplines and Dialogues" in Richard Johnson (and his colleagues)'s *The Practice of Cultural Studies* and the "Introduction" to Paul Smith's *The Renewal of Cultural Studies* anthology. The former serves as the core text-book throughout the course.

A good deal of time is spent discussing the desire of cultural studies to want to be more than a traditional academic discipline and to want to be politically efficacious. We try to examine cultural studies as a critical intellectual practice that is interested in culture as a site of power and struggle. We talk about what it means for cultural studies to be a critical intellectual project, one that seeks to produce 'useful knowledge' (Hall and Grossberg), 'organic intellectuals' (Hall), and 'intellectual activists' (Ross). I also introduce students here to the key notions of social totality/whole, articulation, and the circuit of culture. In highlighting cultural studies as the intellectually and politically engaged and radical analysis of cultural practices and processes, the notions of 'social whole,' and in more dominant versions, those of 'articulation' and 'circuit of culture' become central in the field. The significance of an event, phenomenon, or prac-tice—be it ideological, political, economic, or cultural—cannot be prop-erly assessed outside a dialectical understanding of its place in society as a whole. The aim here is to put the student in a better position to under-stand how social, economic, and political forces act on cultural produc-tion, distribution, and reception and how cultural forces, in turn, act on the social, economic, and political.

The second part, entitled "Working Practices and the Ethics of Cultural Research," is more technical in nature and focuses on some of the more common moments, strategies, and tactics in the process of cultural research. Here, we mainly focus on "The Research Process: Moments and Strategies," an early chapter in *The Practice of Cultural Studies*. The meet-ing seeks to introduce students to some of the fundamental challenges that conducting, producing, and disseminating cultural research in an ethical manner poses. While it is true that fieldwork/people-based research presents particular challenges (including values, informed con-sent, entry into the field, confidentiality, approaches to data collection, participant roles, ownership of data, writing, representation, and dissemination of results), all cultural research has ethical dimensions that the researcher should be aware of and address. Students are thus introduced to, but also encouraged to be critically self-reflexive about some of the existing ethical codes and research paradigms and procedures, highlighting both their merits and limits. Because cultural studies is interested in culture as 'a way of life' and as a 'way of struggle,' especially amongst marginalized groups, it is important that the representation of cultural complexity, multiplicity of voices/positions/perspectives, and progressive social change are fundamental parts of the cultural research and knowledge we produce. Without undermining the authority of knowledge, we discuss what it means for the research process to be collective, collaborative, participatory, and reciprocal, thus enabling not just researchers to collaborate but also researchers and research participants to work together to shape/constitute the questions and objects of the research.

While many students know where to find materials for their research, most of them do not know how to find them. This is probably the most difficult and most challenging phase of the research process. That is why, a substantive section of the class is devoted to introducing students to the key moments, strategies, and tactics in the research process. These include how to choose and develop a topic (brainstorming); how to begin the research; how to manage time well; how to use libraries, archives, and the internet for research; how to collaborate and work with others (supervisors, peers, research participants); how to review the literature; how to construct a research proposal/prospectus; how to develop a research outline; how to prepare rough drafts; and how to present one's research to others.

The third meeting is devoted to the use of libraries and archives as important resources in cultural research. Here, we start with a general conversation about archives and their implications for cultural studies research. The relationship between cultural studies, archives, and history is discussed in all its complexity and contradictions. The idea here is to highlight how cultural studies is interested in the present and contemporary cultures, while history and archives are interested in the past. At the same time, archives and historical work are also presented as very important resources to cultural student researchers, as long as they are approached contextually and critically. The practice of symptomatic reading, as introduced and developed by Louis Althusser in the context of his analysis of the work of Marx, is especially presented as a productive approach to archives and dominant histories, where both archival and historical texts are analyzed according to what they do not—and indeed cannot—say. The focus is on the silences, noises, gaps, and blind spots of the surface meaning of dominant texts and archives. The meeting usually closes with a library workshop, where students are walked through some of the resources and databases available to them through the college's library and online (surface and deep).

The Core Weeks: The Key Epistemological/ Methodological Commitments of Cultural Studies

The next several meetings are devoted to what I have been calling the foundational epistemological and methodological commitments of cultural studies. The first of these is devoted to the centrality of materialist dialectics, as a form of historicizing relational and contextual analysis and thinking. Here, the lead text is the challenging and generative Marx's 'Introduction' to *The Grundrisse*. Here, materialist dialectics is presented as a method of thinking, interpreting, and understanding the complex social and cultural worlds we live in, with a view of transforming them. The two fundamental propositions of dialectics are introduced: First, that social and cultural phenomena are in a constant process of change, motion, development, and flux; and second, that change, motion, development, and flux involve contradiction and can only occur due to complex contradictions and complex contradictory processes. The meeting closes with a hands-on research activity, where students are provided some examples (Disney, Facebook, reality TV, to give a few examples) and are asked to begin to look at them dialectically. These examples, like other examples and case studies throughout the course, pretty much all depended upon my own levels of knowledge, expertise, and willingness, but were also intentionally and carefully selected to ensure some basic familiarity with them among the students.

The second of these meetings is centered on cultural studies commitment to a multi-perspectival approach and to rigorous interdisciplinarity. In most cultural studies, there is a realization that traditional disciplinary methods/approaches have their merits and limits, but that they work best when they are deployed, more or less, together in the analysis of complex cultural phenomena, processes, and practices. While methods are not equally valid, no single method is complete; and to get as close as possible to a better and more complex understanding of cultural practices and processes, combining methods becomes indispensable. As Johnson and his colleagues put it in *The Practice of Cultural Studies*, "a multiplicity of methods is necessary because no one method is intrinsically superior to the rest and each provides a more or less appropriate way of exploring some different aspect of cultural process" (42). And it is in this nuanced sense that cultural studies can also be said to be interdisciplinary. This meeting is centered around the need of a multiplicity of methods, while at the same time, warning against the opportunistic, eclectic approach to method in cultural studies. I try to revisit the notions of 'social whole/ totality,' 'articulation,' and 'the circuit of culture' and bring them to bear on our discussion of cultural studies' commitment to critical multi-perspectivalism and to rigorous interdisciplinarity. The session also highlights the fact that specific methods have histories, too, and not all of them can be readily and uncomplicatedly combined. The session also engages the notion of interdisciplinarity, making an important distinction between poor interdisciplinarity and robust interdisciplinarity.

The key reading for this session is Angela McRobbie's critical analysis of the US popular cultural show *Sex and the City*, "Young Women and Consumer Culture." Students are asked to read this text very carefully, with the specific aim of identifying the key methods and concepts that McRobbie's employs in her critique of the show. Not only that, students are further asked to consider both the merits and limits of these methods and concepts and to explore alternative methods and concepts that could shed better light on neglected aspects in McRobbie's critique. By way of providing students some theoretical foundation on the topic, I asked them to also read one of the early chapters in the required textbook *The Practice of Cultural Studies*, entitled "Multiplying Methods: From Pluralism to Combination."

The third meeting is a wide-ranging discussion of critical self-reflexivity in cultural studies. As cultural researchers, we are 'inside' and 'part of' our object of study. We approach our topics with a particular cultural burden and subjectivity. Gramsci notes somewhere that the starting point of critical reflection and cultural research is the consciousness of who one is. Far from being a negative source of research bias, knowing our partialities and subjectivities enables us to understand and contextualize our biases. Critical self-reflexivity puts our work in perspective, highlighting both its merits and limits. This meeting seeks to introduce students to the notions of self-reflexivity and positionality in cultural research, showing how cultural research is cultural through and through and how the researcher is part of the object he or she is investigating. The meeting also highlights the importance of paying critical attention to issues of reflexivity, positionality, subjectivity, representation, and power relations in cultural research in order to produce useful and ethical cultural studies research.

Students are asked to revisit Angela McRobbie's essay above, but to now look for moments of critical self-reflexivity throughout the essay on the part of the author. Students are asked to do the same thing with Raymond Williams's well-known "Culture is Ordinary." Finally, students are asked to reflect on their own experiences as researchers and try to tie their particular research interests to their particular cultural biography. The foundational text here was another chapter, "Method and the Researching Self," from *The Practice of Cultural Studies*.

We also devote a whole meeting to cultural studies commitment to radical contextualism. The first part of this meeting is a broad discussion of the notions of context and contextualizing as central to cultural studies work and practice. The discussion is guided by the work of Lawrence Grossberg, especially Chapter I, "The Heart of Cultural Studies," in his *Cultural Studies in the Future Sense*.

Cultural studies insists that cultural texts and practices always occur in specific historical and social contexts and larger social formations. And it is these that cultural studies is interested in intervening into, understanding, and ultimately helping transform. By the same token, any critical studies of cultural phenomena must be radically contextualist. This includes cultural research activity itself, which must also always be contexualized. For example, cultural research is always temporally located; it takes place at a certain historical moment/conjuncture. The time dimension is an essential perspective in cultural and social theory and practice. It not only greatly enhances the subtlety with which cultural phenomena is explored, but also helps us to recognize the historical content and specificity of our work (including the theoretical categories we work with), as well. Similarly, cultural research activity is always spatially located; it takes place somewhere. Issues of space and place are inherent in every research project, and recognizing the particularities of the places we study and where we study them could be enlightening. The second and third parts of the class are more specific and are focused on the notions of time and space. The idea here is to get students to bring both place and time into focus into their own research and to take them seriously as necessary dimensions of cultural studies robust contextualism.

Building on the previous meeting, we devote another meeting to the further development of the practice of radical contexualism and discuss two forms of it, structural and conjunctural analysis. Here, we spend a bit of time with the work of Antonio Gramsci, especially his work on hegemony, relations of force, and historical bloc. Cultural studies is presented as an intellectual practice that is interested less in textual and object-based analysis and more in the larger social structures and conjunctures that texts and objects inhabit. In other words, what is highlighted here is how cultural studies research displays a commitment to conjunctural and structural analysis, where the object becomes (a way to talk about) something much larger and bigger than itself, where the object becomes the very social and historical formation which it inhabits and operates in. Here, I make a distinction between cultural studies research that tends to privilege conjunctural analysis over structural analysis.[1] I take this important theoretical distinction from Antonio Gramsci. In Gramsci's usage, structural aspects of society are organic and relatively permanent, while its conjunctural elements are relatively temporary, immediate, and almost accidental. He writes:

---

[1] Stuart Hall and Lawrence Grossberg, for example, promote an understanding of cultural studies as a practice of conjunctural analysis, but also insist that the latter must include an examination of structural forces and determinations. This is different from how Gramsci theorizes the relationship between conjunctural and structural phenomena.

Meanwhile, in studying a structure, it is necessary to distinguish organic movements (relatively permanent) from movements which may be termed 'conjunctural' (and which appear as occasional, immediate, almost accidental). Conjunctural phenomena too depend on organic movements to be sure, but they do not have any far-reaching historical significance; they give rise to political criticism of a minor, day-to-day character, which has as its subject small ruling groups and personalities with direct governmental responsibilities. Organic phenomena on the other hand give rise to socio-historical criticism, whose subject is wider social groupings – beyond the people with immediate responsibilities and beyond the ruling personnel [My Italics] (201).

Gramsci goes on to say that:

A common error in historic-political analysis consists in an inability to find the correct relation between what is organic and what is conjunctural. This leads to presenting causes as immediately operative which in fact only operate indirectly, or to asserting that the immediate causes are the only effective ones. In the first case there is an excess of 'economism', or doctrinaire pedantry; in the second, an excess of 'ideologism'. In the first case there is an overestimation of mechanical causes, in the second an exaggeration of the voluntarist and individual element (201–202).

For Gramsci, conjunctural analysis is political analysis for action, and is based on the analysis of the immediate social situation and the web of different social forces and relations at a given moment in order to help oppositional social groups determine opportunities for action and act in ways to advance their short-term—and with them their long-term—goals. Structural analysis, on the other hand, seeks to identify the deeper forces and contradictions that determine the structure of society in the long term. While a focus on structural phenomena alone risks being too 'mechanistic,' an analysis of conjunctural elements alone risks being too 'ideologistic,' thus losing sight of the deeper issues and the longer-term struggles. But it is important to stress here that Gramsci—despite this distinction (and dialectic)—also states that "conjunctural phenomena too depend on organic movements to be sure" (201).

The session introduces students to different kinds of structural analysis and conjunctural analysis, highlighting their merits and limitations. In appropriating Gramsci, some actually existing cultural studies work tends to grant priority to the conjuncture and conjunctural analysis becomes the privileged mode in cultural studies, without due consideration of what Gramsci calls the "dialectical nexus between the two categories of movement [the conjunctural and structural]," which cultural and social analysis must try to establish and understand, no matter how difficult that task might be. To be sure, this reworking of Gramsci stems from a certain reading of the work of Louis Althusser, especially his later work, as a confirmation of the need to move away from all and any theories of social structures and to focus instead on the analysis of specific conjunctural articulations of the elements of social life. This displacement and replacement of the notion structure by the notion of conjuncture as articulation misses their dialectical tension and is bound to make the 'common error' that Gramsci warns us against, that is, the "inability to find the correct relation between what is organic and what is conjunctural" and the inability to capture the dialectical nexus between the elements. The meeting argues for the need to find the right balance between the conjunctural and the structural in cultural research.

Theorizing (and in general abstraction) as a practice is central to cultural studies and cultural studies research, and we take a meeting to, first, review some of the work that students had done in this area, especially in the *Cultural Theories* seminar, and, second, to discuss cultural studies commitment to critical-theoretical work. As Grossberg puts it, "Cultural Studies is always theoretical. It is absolutely committed to the necessity of theoretical work, to what Karl Marx called the detour through theory." It is not committed to theory for theory's sake; it is rather interested in how theory and theoretical work can be deployed to make sense of the world, that is, to better understand and transform specific historical conjunctures, contexts, and formations. Our class-wide discussion is structured around the following generative questions: What is abstraction? What is and why theory? Should cultural studies practitioners acknowledge a dominant or foundational theoretical paradigm in their research/work? What should be the place of 'political' theories and approaches, such as Marxism, feminism, queer theory, post-colonialism, disability studies, or environmental studies? What should be the place of more 'philosophical' and 'textual' theories and approaches, such as semiotics, phenomenology, hermeneutics, pragmatism, deconstruction, structuralism, and post-structuralism? What should be the place of traditional institutional disciplines, such as literature, philosophy, sociology, anthropology, history, and other fields? Is there a need to go beyond such disciplines, promoting interdisciplinarity? Why take a detour through theory at all? What would it be like to 'skip' theory? "Theory in the Practice of Research" (a chapter from *The Practice of Cultural Studies*) is used as a critical survey to focus the discussion of some of these issues and questions. Furthermore, two readings are employed here to focus the discussion and to exemplify how cultural studies practitioners practice abstraction and deploy theoretical work in their research: Stuart Hall's "Gramsci's Relevance for the Study of Race and Ethnicity" and Angela McRobbie's "Post-Feminism and Popular Culture: Bridget Jones and the New Gender Regime."

The Final Weeks: Methods of Research and the 'Circuit of Culture'

The next several weeks are spent reviewing, applying, and interrogating a multiplicity of research methods to study the whole circuit of the culture around specific cultural, media, and political objects. The first meeting focuses on a variety of textual-critical methods, mostly those drawn from literary studies and from structuralism and post-structuralism more specifically. These methods include semiotics, psychoanalysis, narrative analysis, Foucauldian discourse analysis, and deconstruction. It introduces each of these methods, highlighting the merits and limits of each of them and providing a brief guide on how to use them, as well as plenty of opportunities for students to use them.

Three chapters from *The Practice of Cultural Studies* are provided as foundational/survey texts: "Reading Popular Narratives: From Structure to Context" (where a general survey on structuralist and post-structuralist approaches is provided); "Reading Texts of or for Dominance" (where the focus is on approaches that are interested in texts and power); and "Reading Fictions, Reading Histories" (where the focus is on the critical interpretation and close reading of fictional texts and popular narratives).

These survey texts can be very useful and informational for undergraduate students and I also warn them throughout against taking these as authoritative texts on the subject. To further nuance the above materials, two key texts are provided as examples of analyses that take texts very seriously: Roland Barthes's "The World of Wrestling" and Rhonda Hammer and Douglas Kellner's "Critical Reflections on Mel Gibson's *The Passion of the Christ.*"

Finally, the meeting closes with a workshop on semiotics and cultural studies, using a rather common and handy topic: tobacco advertising as a case study. Generally, I have found that using examples that students are already familiar with are pedagogically more productive and generative.

The second meeting is a broad conversation about political economy, cultural policy, and cultural studies. The first part introduces students to the critical political economy as an important method of studying cultural phenomena in contemporary society. It shows how critical political economy has tended to draw on Marxism and focus on the production and distribution of cultural texts and their political economy. Here, I also try to make a case for the need of a serious engagement in the kinds of cultural studies work that would make the connections between the production of meanings and subjectivities and the production of commodities, as well as examine the processes of determination amongst and between different levels of social and cultural production.

This section also introduces students to another central form of Marxist analysis, one that is closely associated with critical political economy, namely ideology critique or ideology analysis. It starts with surveying some of the multiple uses of the concept of ideology, focusing on two main uses. The first use, drawn from Marx and his works, understands ideology as a system of false ideas and ideology as the opposite of science and scientific truths. The second use, drawn from Althusser, understands ideology as the inevitable structuring concept that maps all socially relevant aspects of human subjectivity. The conversation then moves to describe how ideology critique (in its two main versions) as a mode of analysis works, highlighting both its merits and limits. Here, we read Douglas Kellner's "Critical Theory and Cultural Studies: The Missed Articulation," along with the "Culture, Power, and Economy" chapter in *The Practice of Cultural Studies.*

To further nuance the above materials, two key texts are provided, one of which we had already looked at, as examples of analyses that take critical political economy very seriously: Rhonda Hammer and Douglas Kellner's "Critical Reflections on Mel Gibson's *The Passion of the Christ*" and Kurt Borchard's and David R. Dickens's "Mystification of the Labor Process in Contemporary Consumer Culture."

The second part of the meeting is devoted to critical cultural policy studies as a sub-field within cultural studies. Tony Bennett's "Putting Policy into Cultural Studies" is employed as a survey piece and is further interrogated and nuanced in light of Robert W. McChesney's "Children, Globalization, and Media Policy" essay.

We also devote a meeting to the study of 'lived experience' and audience studies. The aim here is to introduce students to fieldwork research and different kinds of people-based research in cultural studies. Starting with an important distinction between actual audiences and imagined audiences, between actual consumers and imagined consumers, and between actual participants and imagined participants, this chapter presents a series of methods that can employed in actual audience reception/consumption studies, as well as in critical studies of lived experiences and cultural practices. These methods include ethnography and focus group research, both of which focus on the 'lived experience' and the use aspect of culture.

Two texts are provided as foundational/survey texts on the analysis of lived experience and on studying audiences respectively: "Learning from Experience" in Jim McGuigan's *Cultural Methodologies* and Rosalind Brunt's "Engaging with the Popular: Audiences for Mass Culture and What to Say about Them" in Lawrence Grossberg's *Cultural Studies*.

To further nuance the above materials, James Thomas's "From People Power to Mass Hysteria: Media and Popular Reactions to the Death of Princess Diana" is provided as an example of work that takes actual audience studies and fieldwork very seriously.

Another meeting engages critical ethnography and is presented as a set of general reflections on some key issues and questions in fieldwork and ethnography. Students are warned at the outset against taking our discussion as inclusive of this vast area of research. That is why, while I assign a few contextualizing materials (namely "Doing Ethnography" in

Researching Society and Culture; "New Ethnography and Understanding the Other" and "Between Experience and Discourse" in *Doing Research in Cultural Studies*; and D. S. Madison's "Introduction to Critical Ethnography: Theory and Method" in *Critical Ethnography*), I ask them to read selections from Paul Willis's *Learning to Labor* and selections from Mitchell Duneier et al.'s *Sidewalk*.

Student Research: Final Papers and Presentations

The final class is devoted to students presenting (a shorter version of) their written final research projects. Students were provided with three broad presentation formats and then left to their own devices to select the one that worked best for them. Regardless of the format, each student had 15 minutes to present. The formats included the sharing of a short version/detailed summary of the paper, the sharing of a section or more from and contextualized in relation the whole paper, or the giving of complementary presentation, one that did not simply share a summary or part of the whole paper, but one that was more interactive and employed visual/media texts to walk the audience through the key claims, questions, and findings of the written research paper. The class is divided into three- to four-people panels, determined along the lines of students' project topics and themes. This gives students a glimpse into the world of professional conferences.

Throughout all the years, I have been teaching this course, students' final papers and presentations have always been the most rewarding part of the entire course. The topics that students engage are astonishingly varied and cover a wide range of cultural, media, political, economic, and social phenomena. However, unfortunately, and unlike the mini-projects, the overwhelming majority of them were completed individually, and this despite my insistence throughout on the importance of collaborative work in general and its key place and determining role in early British cultural studies. I must point out that even in the very few cases when students collaborated together on a final project, students would almost always approach me with concerns about how *other* members of the team *did not do enough* or about how most of the work fell to them. It is probably too easy to blame this on their inexperience as undergraduate students, but I think that this raises some fundamental questions about the nature and challenges of collective work in the university and beyond, in a larger social context that addresses, values, and judges us as individuals. However, in most cases, the student work has also engaged—in different ways and to different degrees—the core methodological foundations covered throughout the course. The level of commitment to each of the methodologies varies among students and course offerings, but in general, students seem to develop a deep sense of critical self-reflexivity, political economic analysis, and historical thinking.

A Few Concluding Remarks, or What Is Cultural Studies, One More Time?

It would be misleading to end my essay with any claims about its successes and merits. In fact, the failures and challenges of the course probably outweigh its successes and merits. I say probably because the degree of the success of the course can never be quite established, except by the students themselves and probably in the long term. Instead of approaching this course and this 'thick description' as an ideal to be followed, I think, it is best approached as an instance of what might get covered in a cultural studies methodology course, as one experimental response to the key question: what is cultural studies?

Of course, the course is grounded in my own intellectual and political assumptions about the field as a very specific intellectual practice and a political project. As a vibrant and expansive intellectual project and disciplinary formation, cultural studies cannot be readily and easily contained by definitional fiat. And yet, the field's commitment to transformative and radical politics and to the need to produce 'organic intellectuals' and 'useful knowledges' that can be deployed to understand, intervene into, and transform specific social, historical, and institutional conjunctures and contexts demands a cultural studies that is simultaneously disciplinary, interdisciplinary, anti-disciplinary, and post-disciplinary, all at the same time. Furthermore, such commitments also demand a cultural studies that is methodologically and theoretically robust, coherent, and consistent, while at the same time self-reflexive, open, and attentive to what goes on in other (allied) disciplines, inside the university, and in the larger social world outside.

The claim that cultural studies should be able to draw on the methods and theories of other disciplines and fields in the humanities and social sciences does not and should not necessarily and automatically translate into the extreme view—common in the field—that there is no need for any kind of theoretical cohesion and methodological consistency whatsoever, and even worse, that the latter would be necessarily constrictive, reductive, and non-contextualist. The fact that certain methods, such as semiotics and interpretative textual approaches in general, have come to be associated with most of actually existing work in cultural studies—a fact that has ultimately limited the scope of and further depoliticized the whole field—belies this claim, but it also justifies the need to move beyond this kind of rather undisciplined and constrictive fixation on textual interpretation and interpretive approaches.

Cultural phenomena cannot be approached as mere isolated texts and practices, without due consideration of their conditions of production. And this is what I think cultural studies should aspire to: a serious engagement in the kinds of cultural studies work that would make the connections between the production of meanings and subjectivities and the production of commodities, as well as examine the processes of determination amongst and between different levels of production. This means the rejection of the notion of autonomy (relative or not), and the recognition that cultural phenomenon, far from being autonomous texts, is, even in their specificity, caught in a logic of a contradictory social totality/whole and a logic of the interconnectedness of the different social levels. According to this logic, the significance of a cultural event or phenomenon—be it ideological, political, economic, or cultural—cannot be properly assessed outside a dialectical understanding of its place in society as a whole. If cultural studies wants to continue to make any claims on the political, it must learn to examine cultural forms and events in the context of their social totality (which, here, refers to the concrete unity of all interacting spheres of social life under capitalism), that is, by pursuing their hidden interactions and interconnections in real life. This way, we are in a better position to understand how social, economic, and political forces act on cultural production, distribution, and reception; and how cultural forces, in turn, act on the social, economic, and political. This is especially urgent at a historical conjuncture characterized by a deep economic crisis that has brought to the surface once more and more than ever before (at least in our lifetime) not only the contradictions of global capitalism and the ugly realities and consequences of material inequality in people's lives, but also (re)new(ed) discourses, forms, and possibilities of collective resistance and struggle in the political and cultural realms. The job of a cultural studies that matters—a cultural studies that despite its institutionalization (institutionalization can have its advantages, too, and does not necessarily mean depoliticization!) can still claim to be a radical, political, and intellectual practice—is to understand, study, explain, and help change this state of affairs.

Works Cited

Adorno, T. (1999). *Introduction to Sociology*. Stanford: Stanford University Press.

Barthes, R. (1972). The World of Wrestling. In *Mythologies*. New York: Hill and Wang.

Bennett, T. (1992). Putting Policy into Cultural Studies. In L. Grossberg, C. Nelson, & P. Treichler (Eds.), *Cultural Studies* (pp. 23–37). New York: Routledge.

Borchard, K., & Dickens, D. (2008). Mystification of the Labor Process in Contemporary Consumer Culture. *Cultural Studies ↔ Critical Methodologies, 8*(4), 558–567.

Brunt, R. (1992). Engaging with the Popular: Audiences for Mass Culture and What to Say About Them. In L. Grossberg, C. Nelson, & P. Treichler (Eds.), *Cultural Studies*. New York: Routledge.

Duneier, M., Hasan, H., & Carter, O. (1999). *Sidewalk*. New York: Farrar, Straus and Giroux.

Forgacs, D. (Ed.). (2000). *The Gramsci Reader: Selected Writings 1916–1935*. New York: New York University Press.

Gray, A. (1997). Learning from Experience: Cultural Studies and Feminism. In J. McGuigan (Ed.), *Critical Methodologies*. London: SAGE Publications.

Grossberg, L. (2010). *Cultural Studies in the Future Tense*. Durham: Duke University Press.

Grossberg, L. (2011). Will Work for Cultural Studies. *Journal of Communication and Critical/Cultural Studies, 8*(4), 425–432.

Hall, S. (1986). Gramsci's Relevance for the Study of Race and Ethnicity. *Journal of Communication Inquiry, 10*(2), 5–27.

Hall, S. (1992). Cultural Studies and Its Theoretical Legacies. In L. Grossberg, C. Nelson, & P. Treichler (Eds.), *Cultural Studies*. New York: Routledge.

Hall, S. (2008). The Neo-Liberal Revolution. *Cultural Studies, 25*(6), 705–728.

Hammer, R., & Kellner, D. (2004). Critical Reflections on Mel Gibson's The Passion of the Christ.

Johnson, R., Chambers, D., Raghuram, P., & Tincknell, E. (2004). *The Practice of Cultural Studies*. London: SAGE Publications.

Kellner, D. (1997). Critical Theory and Cultural Studies: The Missed Articulation. In J. McGuigan (Ed.), *Cultural Methodologies*. London: SAGE Publications.

Madison, D. S. (2005). *Critical Ethnography: Method, Ethics, and Performance*. London: SAGE Publications.

Marx, K. (1973). *The Grundrisse*. London: Penguin Harmondsworth.

McChesney, R. (2003). Children, Globalization, and Media Policy. In C. von Feilitzen & U. Carlsson (Eds.), *Children, Young People and Media Globalization* (pp. 23–32). Goteborg: NORDICOM.

McRobbie, A. (2007). Post Feminism and Popular Culture: Bridget Jones and the New Gender Regime. In D. Negra & Y. Tasker (Eds.), *Interrogating Postfeminism: Gender and the Politics of Popular Culture* (pp. 27–39). Durham: Duke University Press.

McRobbie, A. (2008). Young Women and Consumer Culture: An Intervention. *Cultural Studies, 22*(5), 531–550.

Saukko, P. (2003). *Doing Research in Cultural Studies*. London: SAGE Publications.

Seale, C. (2006). *Researching Society and Culture*. London: SAGE Publications.

Smith, P. (2011). *The Renewal of Cultural Studies*. Philadelphia: Temple University Press.

Thomas, J. (2008). From People Power to Mass Hysteria: Media and Popular Reactions to the Death of Princess Diana. *International Journal of Cultural Studies, 11*(3), 362–376.

Williams, R. (1989). Culture Is Ordinary. In *Resources of Hope* (pp. 3–14). London: Verso.

Willis, P. (1977). *Learning to Labour: How Working Class Kids Get Working Class Jobs*. London: Saxon House.

Part III

Cultural Studies Pedagogies in Context: Some Case Studies

Critical (Race) Pedagogy and the Neoliberal Arts in Walker's Wisconsin

Pia Møller

In February 2015, a year and a half into my appointment as a lecturer in the Wisconsin state university system, Governor Scott Walker introduced a state budget, proposing to cut $300 million from the University of Wisconsin (UW) system, the largest cuts in UW history.[1] Walker called it his "Act 10 for the UW," alluding to his infamous "Budget Repair" bill, a multipronged attack on the pensions, salaries, social protections, and collective bargaining rights of public sector employees that trigged a three-week-long occupation of the state capitol in 2011 (Vine 2015). His administration put forward that the UW system be transformed into a "public authority," quite a misnomer as the bill would reduce the state legislature's authority on the UW and vest more power to the Board of Regents, with 16 of 18 members

---

[1] The Wisconsin State Legislature later reduced the cut to $250 million, still by far the largest cut in state history. State of Wisconsin Executive Budget, 2015–2017, p. 589; online: http://www.doa.state.wi.us/Documents/DEBF/Budget/Biennialper cent20Budget/2015-17per cent20Executive-per cent20Budget/2015-17_Executive_Budget.pdf later reduced the cut to $250 million, still by far the largest cut in state history.

P. Møller (✉)
Independent Scholar, Rochester, NY, USA

© The Author(s) 2019
J. Aksikas et al. (eds.), *Cultural Studies in the Classroom and Beyond*,
https://doi.org/10.1007/978-3-030-25393-6_12

appointed by the governor (Marley et al. 2015). The public authority model was abandoned, but the Joint Finance Committee kept substantial elements of the model as they voted to eliminate state statutes on tenure and shared governance, giving the UW Board of Regents and campus chancellors more power to create polices on lay-offs and program discontinuance (Savidge 2016a, 2016b).[2] Wisconsin arguably had the strongest protections of faculty, but now faculty were reduced to at-will employees. Appearing on local right-wing talk-radio, Walker explicitly stated his intent to shift the power within the institution: "Maybe it's time for faculty and staff to start thinking about teaching more classes and doing more work and this authority frees up the [UW] administration to make those sorts of requests" (McCalmont 2015).

Walker's aides also saw fit to revise Chapter 36, the state statute that contains the mission statement for the UW system. This statute, commonly known as the "Wisconsin Idea," articulates a vision of public education as a key element in a healthy and informed democracy: "Inherent in this broad mission are methods of instruction, research, extended training and *public service* designed to educate people and *improve the human condition*. Basic to every purpose of the system is *the search for truth*" (Wisconsin State Statute, Chapter 36 2012). Scrapping these commitments, Walker's aides proposed that its primary mission was to "meet the state's workforce needs" and when this rewording brought public outrage, Walker quickly withdrew it, claiming it was a "drafting error" (Herzog 2015). But Walker's right-hand man Assembly Speaker Robin Vos was undeterred by the criticism and unabashed about his commitment to subordinate public education to corporate needs: "We're working to have more of a market-based approach where we're more responsive to the private sector," Vos told the press in 2016; "There's a long way to go, but we've started the journey" (Savidge 2016a, 2016b). On this view, a fundamentalist pragmatic view, education is nothing more than practical training—hence the need to eradicate the unnecessary "unproductive"

---

[2] In February 2016, the Tenure Task Force submitted its recommendations to the Board of Regents, heated debates ensured, and in March the Board, though deeply divided, passed policies that grant chancellors more flexibility and essentially grants them the right to prioritize fiscal considerations over educations considerations. Among other things tenure may be effectively ended if a chancellor decides to end a program that is deemed fiscally unsound.

(i.e., unprofitable) parts of the university whose value cannot be recognized within a stark economic rationality. The anti-intellectualist ethos that underpins this view was palpable in Vos's remarks at a press conference during the budget negotiations: "Of course I want research," said Vos, "but I want to have research done in a way that focuses on growing our economy, not on ancient mating habits of whatever" (Schneider 2014). The attack compelled researchers to defend their work by emphasizing its value to the state economy; it was practically impossible in this climate to maintain the value of research (or teaching) unless it had a clear, quantifiable economic value or immediate practical application (e.g. Bump 2015).[3]

From my perspective as an instructor in the UW system, Walker's budget priorities and formulations only (if rather brazenly) announced something that had already transpired in the purported liberal arts college, where I held a visiting teaching post, "visiting" being a euphemism for easily disposable. It was ostensibly the very bastion of kind of education that Walker wanted to gut, yet the shift to workforce training was practically a fait accompli in that college. What had begun as a Great Books program some 60 years earlier was now little more than a technical writing program. Assigned readings had gradually shrunken, and, in some courses, consisted of short, easily digestible articles culled from popular science magazines. We, the instructors, might have areas of expertise in art history, cultural studies, ethnic studies, history, literature, and philosophy, but what we should be teaching, administrators regularly impressed upon us, was *writing skills*. Posters in the hallway and articles circulated by administrators informed staff and students that "corporate employers want graduates with good communication skills" and that "many Fortune 500 companies are led by CEOs with liberal arts degrees."[4] In this way, our raison d'être was formulated within a brazen economic rationality and our students were addressed as *homo oeconomicus*—as subjects calculating within a market logic (Brown 2005; 2006). Tellingly, our

---

[3] One notable exception to this line of justification is historian Christine Evans' *New York Times* op-ed "Save the Wisconsin Idea" February 16, 2015; online: http://www.nytimes.com/2015/02/16/opinion/save-the-wisconsin-idea.html

[4] For examples of such takes on the value of the liberal arts, see Adams (2014), Koba (2013), Ray (2013).

online class registration systems had students fill virtual shopping carts similar to those used by Internet retailers. A series of unconnected buzz-words ("academic integrity," "curiosity," "collaborative thinking," creativity," and "passion for learning") scattered on our webpages and program materials was the closest thing we had to a mission statement, and there was no explanation of how we exercised those abilities.

My college exemplified how the liberal arts have become what essayist William Deresiewicz calls "the neoliberal arts" (Deresiewicz 2015). Tasked with increasing enrollment in a time of declining enrollment (in part due to rising tuition), our administrators now recruited mainly among the professional schools and planned to create tailored "tracks" to enable students in nursing, engineering, and social work to select courses more relevant to their majors. In effect, the plan was to save the liberal arts college by discarding the broad-based curriculum that precisely distinguishes the liberal arts, an irony that seemed to escape administrators. Much like a for-profit corporation, the college was set up to keep labor costs down and labor docile: there were no tenure lines, instructors were classified as academic staff, and few held permanent status. Absent faculty governance and departmental status, we existed in a gray area without even a valid charter. Instructors were outnumbered by administrators and supporting staff (advisers and recruiters), and teaching overloads were routine (comparatively low and stagnant salaries ensured that instructors saw overloads as being in their economic self-interest).

The recruitment and retention of high-achieving students took precedence over educational, intellectual, and ethical concerns. The college retained an office assistant to produce data about test scores, grades, and course enrollment; staff meetings were spent crunching numbers and comparing to last year's numbers—numbers that told us nothing about actual student learning or quality of instruction. Instructors were accountable for students who failed to re-enroll and were pressured to inflate grades to keep students above the cut-off bar, either bluntly or through cautionary tales of ill-fated former instructors who were "too tough on grading" to have their contract renewed. Governed by a customer service ethos, instructors were compelled to reduce reading loads, make classes "fun," make themselves exceedingly available (the expectation being that we post 20 office hours weekly for walk-ins), and "respect student opinions," which, as I learned, meant refraining from correcting factually wrong claims, critically engaging flawed assumptions, or addressing hate speech. Course syllabi, texts, and assignments were subject to administrative oversight and revision, and course descriptions were completely rewritten by administrators without expertise in the subject area. Expertise was, in fact, treated as a negative; we were explicitly encouraged to teach outside our area of expertise lest we would come across as "having all the answers." Instead of intellectually challenging study, serious discussion, and critical examination of ideas, our seminars were expected to run like a jovial book club.

In short, the university Walker envisioned was already well into existence in our college, executed by a new strata of administrators who had dispensed with shared forms of governance (or rather, had turned existing forms of shared governance into pro-forma committees, a process aided by the compliance of overworked and tenuously employed staff members). Now, they ran the college using rigid business management models, and they were rewarded in doing so. They were part of the growing layers of professional college managers who control an increasingly contingent labor force and generate assessments ad nauseam, quantifying "outcomes" to "stakeholders" who must be persuaded that education is a worthwhile investment—the presumption being that public institutions are intrinsically inefficient and squander resources without tight oversight. "Flexible" (i.e. precarious) employment arrangements keep labor costs down and servility high, as employees are essentially stifled by their disposability (Chomsky 2014; Giroux 2014).

The corporatized university presents multiple obstacles to a critical cultural studies teaching practice, which is to say a teaching practice wherein the primary task of the scholar-teacher is to engage students in a critical examination of power and domination, in analysis of the social institutions, hierarchies, laws, cultural practices, and ways of thinking through which domination is secured, sustained, or challenged. To my lights, cultural studies goes hand in hand with engaged pedagogy: "a reflexive, experiential, and critical approach in which one's own experience is central to understanding and developing knowledge" (Waring and Bordoloi 2013). For students to develop critical awareness and deep analytical skills, they need to recognize themselves as social actors in a social structure: as both acted upon by that structure and as historical actors capable of shaping that structure. As a job candidate, I'd been clear about my teaching philosophy and described myself as a social justice educator, yet I soon found my commitment at odds with the institutional ethos. It seemed I'd been hired to spice up the curriculum and deliver an easily digestible "cultural studies lite," much like ethnic studies scholars have been hired only to find they're not supposed to be *critical* scholars (King 2008).

It is difficult, especially as a non-tenured instructor, to resist administrative pressure, advocate for changes in institutional culture, and demand academic rigor. In addition, it is difficult to engage and activate students who have graduated from a banking and test-driven K12 education system. At best, my students were unfamiliar with critical inquiry and engaged pedagogy; at worst, they look at those practices with suspicion. As I analyzed my experience, I came to understand that my difficulties were compounded by the passive resistance to critical examination of immigration, race, and ethnicity (my areas of teaching) that my overwhelmingly white students exhibited. Most of them entered my classes with vague expectations of a celebratory multiculturalism void of critical analysis, and there I was, requiring them to study racism, nativism, restrictive laws and covenants, and all manners of other injustices in American society, past and present. Many of them had rarely had to think about these issues before, having grown up in segregated white communities and moved in predominantly white spaces, and their education had not prepared them to examine racism (or rather, had guided them to see it in the more distant past—safely in the era of slavery, typically). Like many other metropolitan areas in the US North, Milwaukee remains profoundly segregated, the result of decades of discriminatory redlining and zoning regulation, since worsened by a severe deindustrialization and urban disinvestment (Causey 2014; Miner 2013). Walker's reign follows decades of anti-social state policies—what Wendy Brown calls a "stealth revolution" (Brown 2015a, 2015b)—which includes the largest and oldest school voucher program in the nation, instituted by the four-time governor and one-time presidential candidate Tommy Thompson and since expanded by Walker. A backdoor privatization program, "school choice" siphons money from public schools into private, for-profit, and religious schools, leaving public schools with fewer resources to serve the student populations who need them most (Lafer 2014; Miner 2015).[5] Other ostensibly color-blind polices (on public education, public transit, and taxes) have helped consolidate the racial order previously secured through explicitly racist policies, and 60 years after Brown v. Board of education, Milwaukee has some of the most segregated (and unequal) schools in the nation (Richards and Mulvany 2014). In Milwaukee, as in many other US cities, there are two separate paths to college: white students, predominantly from suburbs and smaller towns, go to public and private four-year colleges, whereas students of color disproportionately go to community colleges (Fletcher 2013). Token city-to-suburb school integration programs (such as Milwaukee's Chapter 220) are no anti-dote to the intensely segregated realities of the northern metropolis.

In short, the problems I encountered as an academic derived from structural conditions, themselves the result of decades of policymaking. The remedies are also largely to be devised *outside* the classroom: they are political and require sustained and organized mobilization, including the unionization of the faculty and the precariat, and alliances with other workers. We have to insist that another university is possible and we need to work to create it. Yet, at the same time, we have to brace ourselves for the one that *is;* our day-to-day working lives demand that we develop ways of navigating the corporate university. Attending to immediate and practical challenges, this essay first explores how to maintain a critical teaching practice under administrative micro-management and limited academic freedom. Second, the essay considers what critical race educators can do about white racial reaction in the classroom—especially when our re-appointment hinges on "good student evaluations." Third, it analyses the difficulties of pursuing engaged pedagogy with a student cohort accustomed to a passive "banking" style of learning and contemplates the possibility of a "pedagogy of misery."

---

[5] In 2011, after the ACLU found that students with disabilities make up 1.6 per cent of the student body in the voucher schools versus 19.5 per cent in Milwaukee Public Schools, the organization called on the US Justice Department to investigate. The Civil Rights Division of the US Department of Education sent a letter to Wisconsin Department of Public Instruction, 2013, reminding the department to adhere to the American Disabilities Act of 1990. The case is ongoing; see: https:// www.aclu.org/sites/default/files/field_document/04_09_13_letter_to_wisconsin_dpi_0.pdf Wisconsin's non-partisan Legislative Fiscal Bureau estimates that over the decade from 2015 to 2025, the program will siphon $800 million from the public school system into private and charter school; see Legislative Fiscal Bureau, May 26, 2015.

Academic Freedom and Critical Study Under Micromanagement

Precarious conditions of employment not only severely constrain the ability of instructors to influence the academic direction, norms, and culture of our workplaces, they also undermine our ability to uphold academic standards and teach critical studies. What can you do as a precariously employed instructor when customer service-minded administrators intervene in your course design and instruction? This is not a hypothetical scenario. My experience proposing a course on The War on Crime is illustrative here. I devised it as an interdisciplinary and critical study of politics, media representations, and social relations, with ongoing contemplation of how representations of crime and criminal law "shape the modern mind," thus meeting a key course requirement. My proposal detailed assignment requirements, assessment criteria, and overall objectives, all of which were comparable with other topical offerings under the rubric. Yet, the course was not approved as administrators objected to the "ideological perspective of the course."[6] The course description explained that the class would "examine the racial components of the War on Crime" and consider "criminal law from a social justice perspective." These sentences were deemed too "tendentious" and removed. I was asked to replace one assigned book, ostensibly because it wasn't published by a university press (though university press books were practically never assigned in first-year seminars and it was not a requirement). This was hardly a legitimate course approval counsel,[7] but in a corporatized university, non-tenured instructors are not in a position to insist on academic freedom—it is every bit as precarious as our employment. I was encouraged to reconsider

---

[6] Here and in the sentences below, I quote from email exchanges with my former supervisors about my course proposal and from a subsequent meeting with several administrators about the course. The administrators stated they were expressing the positions of anonymous colleagues on the course approval committee. Since the review process was not transparent, I have no way of knowing whose views they expressed, only that my administrators thought them valid objections to my course.

[7] Given that the college had no guidelines for course approval, it was unclear what exactly would constitute reasonable counsel, but my prior experience and perusal of guidelines in other colleges suggest that workload, level of difficulty in texts, fit with course rubric and overall curriculum are considered valid considerations.

so that my courses would fill and my contract could be renewed. Two months into my appointment, I opted to negotiate and worked out a compromise over multiple emails and during a long and uncomfortable meeting. The final course description signaled a disingenuous and embarrassing naiveté about the damage that the War on Crime wreaked in communities across the country ("Is there a racial component to the War on Crime?" the course description now asked, preposterously).

As academics, we take great care in formulating our course descriptions because they express our intellectual, ethical, and methodological commitments. I found it infuriating to see my name associated with such uncritical formulations and having to tolerate that level of interference in my work. Still, there are ways to work around administrative micromanagement and reactionary curriculum policing. In my case, I decided to replace the "banned" book with audio-visual material (lectures and interviews by the objectionable author)—material that I did not have to declare on my syllabus. Seeing that material, several students proceeded to order the book in question, a nice twist of irony since students were now *more* motivated to read it, having "discovered" it on their own. Obviously, this approach requires our classrooms to be wired (or for our students to have reliable internet access at home). Barring that, another option is to create classroom activities using excerpted passages from the "banned" authors to engage students in a critique of the more conventional texts that one is compelled to assign. No doubt many instructors already maneuver like this (if not always for this reason), but those of us coming out of cultural studies, ethnic studies, and other critical fields of inquiry may be unprepared for the reactionary environment of general education and traditional disciplines. We must learn how to navigate such environments and share our experiences.

Critical Race Studies and White Racial Reaction in the Corporate University

Teaching resistant students is another challenge many instructors encounter in general education classrooms. Student resistance to learning is common in courses on race in predominantly white institutions (PWIs) such as mine, and research suggests that this is especially the case for faculty of color who tend to be judged more harshly on student evaluations (Guerrero 2008; King 2008). As a white, cis-gendered woman, I was generally not perceived as threatening by my white students, nor did they tend to see me as aggrieved or biased. I was not labeled an "angry black woman" or "scary black man" because I taught race (complaints made about my colleagues of color); on the contrary, my white students tended to see my whiteness as a guarantee of impartiality. Even so, my students were frequently defensive and occasionally antagonistic, claiming that they didn't "see race" and arguing that if we would "just stop talking about race, racism would go away." Mostly, though, they conveyed their resistance in subtle and passive-aggressive ways: through silence, closed body postures, and exchange of eye-rolling glances among themselves. They complained in their end-of-year evaluation that I exaggerated the extent of racism and focused on it too much (e.g. "She sees racism everywhere," "I wouldn't have taken this class if I had known it was only about race," "why do we have to talk about race all the time?"). This put me in the absurd position of having to defend a focus on race in courses on immigrant experiences, representations of women, and Mexican-US history, among other things. Their reaction spoke volumes about the widespread white denial of the centrality of race (which is to say, *racism*) in US society, past and present.

My white students feared being perceived as racist and expressed frustration with what they saw as a compulsion to self-censor their speech. "I feel like I have to watch what I say, or people might think I'm racist or something," one student observed on a feedback card. Similarly, another student remarked, "everybody should be able to say what they think without others judging them." Other students were vexed about having to be "politically correct" and murmured that others were "too sensitive" or "taking their comments the wrong way." Discernable nods and affirmative sounds in the room suggested that other (white) students shared these concerns and found it reasonable that they be granted such immunity. Some educators see it as part of their job to "mitigate" these fears—ostensibly to provide a "safe space" to all—and it is possible that (white) students develop more goodwill under those conditions (Ninivaggi 2001). But in my eyes, providing them that safety would be unethical regardless of the immediate pedagogical benefit. My white students were essentially seeking a carte blanche—immunity from the consequences of making sweeping, bigoted, and ignorant statements about people of color. Giving them a carte blanche, I'd be complicit in reproducing the white comfort zone they had hitherto been able to take for granted—and which I wanted to disrupt (Henry 1992). As Robin DiAngelo notes, the "entitlement to racial comfort" is a key component of white race privilege (DiAngelo 2011). It was a privilege my students had no intention of giving up, but now it was challenged by the course subject, the professor, and the presence of (even a few) non-white students. The notion of safe space—once the hope and ambition of gay communities (Hanhardt 2001)—has been co-opted; in this situation, safe space meant a safe space for cultural racism or "racism lite" as Eduardo-Bonilla-Silva calls it (Bonilla-Silva 2010, p. 3).[8]

In students' repeated concern about being "misunderstood" (i.e. heard as racist), I heard resonance with the "white injury" speech prevalent in (white) anti-immigrant discourses and explicit in the "illegal alien relief acts" passed across the country in 2006–2009, with *relief* suggesting that white US citizens are victims of something akin to natural disaster (Cacho 2000; Møller 2014). As Barbara Applebaum observes: "the discourse of victimhood by those who have taken their privilege for granted—whites as victims, men as victims, heterosexuals as victims—has become a familiar theme" in social justice teaching (Applebaum 2008).

The claim of victimhood status is part of the white racial reaction to the advances of civil rights as chronicled by Michael Omi and Howard Winant, and, more broadly, it is characteristic of the reactionary politics of the aggrieved which arose in the 1980s and 1990s (Omi and Winant 1989; see also Kaminer 1996). But white injury claims have to be understood also within the socio-geographic conditions in the contemporary United States; ideology cannot be separated from material reality, after all. DiAngelo contends that the intensely segregated lives of (many) whites mean that they "have not had to build the cognitive or affective

---

[8] For a critique of the intellectual limits of "safe space," see Shapiro (2014), Shulevitz (2015). Advocating for the position that "students today are more like children than adults and need protection," see Posner (2015). Related are discussions about whether professors ought to issue "trigger warnings."

skills or develop the stamina that would allow for constructive engagement across racial divides." The result of the racial isolation is "reduced psychosocial stamina," a condition she terms "white fragility" (DiAngelo 2011, pp. 56–57). In a state of white fragility, DiAngelo notes, "even a minimum amount of racial stress becomes intolerable, triggering a range of defensive moves [which] include the outward display of emotions such as anger, fear, and guilt, and behaviors such as argumentation, silence, and leaving the stress-inducing situation" (DiAngelo 2011, p. 57). In my classrooms, I saw all of these behaviors. Students who displayed those behaviors in the first few weeks sometimes transferred to another general education offering. In such an environment, teaching courses on race is difficult and risky for those of us whose contracts hinge on "good student evaluations."

When my students did engage in questions of race, they offered an array of racial stories that contained the primary frames of color-blind racism as described by featured Eduardo Bonilla-Silva: *abstract individualism, naturalization, cultural racism*, and *minimization* (Bonilla-Silva 2010, pp. 76–77). Located in the US North, my students also frequently sought to divert conversations about race with claims about how "it's so much worse in the South," a regional variant of the minimization frame. The lack of other voices—not just students of color but also working-class white students who are statistically more likely to have substantial interactions with members of other racial groups (Frankenberg 1993)[9]—meant that my predominantly white middle-class students could collaborate to establish a consensus among themselves and dismiss racism as something minor and insignificant to the structuring of the US society. In such an environment, it is counter-productive to maintain the student-centered humanist pedagogy that is a key component of a critically engaged pedagogy. Undergraduate seminars in PWIs are especially ill-suited when white students view seminars as spaces where they can "safely" voice their opinions. In practice, this means a few token students of color are compelled to listen to all kinds of claims about people of color, some of which are articulated in a coded language well-documented in scholarship (Bonilla-Silva 2010, pp. 53–77).

---

[9] For what constitutes meaningful interracial relations, see Frankenberg (1993).

Hypothetically, it would be better to postpone such classes until white students have developed more understanding (and more "psychosocial stamina") through interaction and experience with people of color, but when the institution is predominantly white and constitute practically the entire social sphere of students, they are unlikely to gain such experience during their college years. Such is the catch-22 of anti-racist teaching in institutions that are de facto segregated. What is required, of course, is genuine integration at all levels of society which is prevented by institutionalized racism, as discussed earlier in this essay. Institutions permeated by a neoliberal rationality cannot see value in racial integration; all too often "diversity" efforts on campus are not about social transformation but about ensuring a more diverse educational experience for *white* students (or simply about ensuring that the university brand appears unblemished).

In predominantly white classrooms, it may be necessary to resort to more lecturing and screening when teaching on race. I am not alone in reaching that discouraging conclusion. Progressive educator Donald Lazere suggests that in response to students "who have come to think that they can get away with throwing ill-informed, prejudiced opinions off the top of their heads in class discussions and papers," we need to "demonstrate the demonstrability of verifiable truths [...] even if that means a reversion toward the lecture and 'banking' modes of teaching" (Lazere 2006, pp. 21–22). This is a devastating conclusion—it's hard not to see it as an abandonment of critical pedagogy, but perhaps lecturing on racism and racial segregation is the most critical thing we can do under these circumstances. Perhaps it is simply not possible to practice critical (race) pedagogy inside a segregated corporate university that treats students as consumers and instructors as easily disposable workers?

Unwilling to abandon my commitment to critical pedagogy, I devised ad hoc solutions. First, as I kept offering seminars on immigration (and race), I took steps to protect myself. I created an extensive record of my experience, making notes on antagonistic or heated classroom exchanges, copies of student papers (one especially memorable paper was titled "Why don't we just blame it all on white people?"), and studied up on critical race pedagogy in PWIs.[10] I wrote extensively about my experience

---

[10] Especially helpful titles include: Guerrero (2008) and Reddy and TuSmith (2001). On critical whiteness studies and critical pedagogy, see Giroux (1997).

in my annual self-review and referenced research in my review (complete with references). I compiled research on student evaluations—on their limited value and biases against women and faculty of color, especially those who teach on race, class, and gender, and I shared my annotations of this literature with my supervisor.[11] Such an extensive record may be useful if a student files a complaint, in case of undue termination, or as support for departmental initiatives and proposals. Though this maneuver was more about job protection than pedagogy, it enabled me to detach somewhat and become more analytical about my experience and a little less frustrated as I realized it was systemic.[12] Second, I took steps to make the situation more bearable for students of color and others who were troubled by the white consensus but didn't feel comfortable enough to challenge it. I used feedback cards to give students an opportunity to anonymously raise questions and concerns, and I used these in the classroom without putting students on the spot. I did my best to have very different conversations with such students in my office and via email. On some occasions, I shared with them the basic tenets of white racial identity formation, and we contemplated whether what we were witnessing in the classroom was a particular phase of a student's development. Taking such an emotionally detached approach helped make the experience more tolerable (I hope it did for those students too).

I also responded to the situation by designating my upper-level *elective* classes to critical whiteness studies. Rather than being "forced" to take a class on race, these students chose it and were, to some extent, favorably self-selected. Here, too, some students sought carte blanche assurances against being labeled racist, and others sought to change the focus from studying whiteness and racism in the US society, past and present, to talking about "solutions," a move that ethnic studies scholar C. Richard King interprets as "an interruption, meant to detour and disengage" (King 2008, 53). Occasionally, white students saw it as a place to explore how "racism hurts white people too" (psychologically and socially), or as a place to criticize "other white people," specifically more bigoted white

---

[11] This body of work includes: Archibeque (2008); Blattner and Blattner (2003), and Grahame (2004).

[12] For guidance on a reflection journal, see DePalma (2008). Work on academic auto-ethnography is also relevant; e.g. Faith Ngunjiri et al. (2010).

people (the rise of Trump lent itself well to this maneuver). Here, too, my students' moves resemble those described by King: in the former case, students "act out a deeply engrained racial narcissism" (white hurt) and in the latter, they "dissociate themselves from white supremacy, a move that allows them to simultaneously reaffirm their identities (as individuals opposed to racism) and challenge white power (typically in its more extreme manifestation)" (King 2008, pp. 55–56).

As frustrating as it was to see these moves in the classroom, I also witnessed real engagement—especially on two particular matters. First, some students really took to Bonilla-Silva's description of the style of "colorblind racism" because it resonated with what they heard on a daily basis (students recorded their observations in journal entries). They connected his scholarly work with their own lived experience, and through that developed a better understanding of how racism works (and how it *sounds*) in the post-civil rights period.[13] Second, a good number of students became very active online as they posted news stories and other cultural texts that spoke to what we were reading. I encouraged this engagement by making it part of their grade—everyone had to post and comment on a certain number of entries—and I modeled this interrogating practice during the first two weeks of class. Many students went far beyond the requirement, posting multiple times, carrying on discussions over several weeks, referring back to earlier posts, sharing insights from other courses, and in one class, the discussions continued weeks *after* the end of the course. I gave extra points to those who explicitly connected their posts to course texts and in-class discussions, and gave bonus points for posts about local stories/events (I thought it important to pay attention to our city's and state's history and politics). I set aside class time to visit our "archive," highlighting important student discoveries and questions, using the best posts as the basis for further discussion. This required extra work and time investment—hardly a reasonable expectation of term or "visiting" instructors who are something akin to itinerant laborers moving from one location to another, and always in the process of seeking another position. But it was one of the most encouraging experi-

---

[13] The style of colorblind racism may be changing; certainly the popularity of Donald Trump suggests that many (white) Americans have been longing for an unabashed racist style.

ences in my time as an instructor in that college. It was a place of active learning and discussion among students, a place where I saw student initiative and reflection. If I were to re-envision the course, I would use the evolving archive as the anchor of an expeditionary learning experience centered on *race in our space* (including the space of the university itself as recently suggested by NYU professor Pamela Newkirk (2015)). Such an approach is admittedly most useful when students have some identification with and/or stake in the space, likely less productive in college towns.

I must note also that my courses on *Whiteness and Race* were under-enrolled, and in the corporate university, administrators often cancel under-enrolled courses to maximize the expense of labor and facilities. The fact that my courses were not cancelled is perhaps suggestive of the particular historical moment of 2014–2016: the heightened visibility (in white America) of police violence against Black Americans, the rise of Black Lives Matter, the creation of the Ferguson Syllabus, the growing demands by college students of color that university administrators address campus racism and create inclusive spaces and curricula, the rise of Trump and the resistance to Trump (S. Brown 2015a, b; Chatelain 2014a, b; Thomason 2015). All of these developments make it more difficult for administrators and others to dismiss racism as a topic worthy of study.

A Pedagogy of Misery

Besides white racial reaction, student passivity in the classroom was a main classroom challenge. Teaching disengaged and unmotivated students is always draining, but it is especially problematic in seminars which depend on a high level of active participation. My students' involvement with the material was often superficial and mechanical; many had little interest in or patience with in-depth study, exploration, and reflection—some of the core activities of a liberal arts seminar. They asked for reading questions and were frustrated when they couldn't find the answers on the pages assigned, which is to say, they were expecting comprehension questions, not questions that required interpretive, evaluative, or imaginative intellectual work on their part. Their weekly discussion papers asked them to formulate at least one open-ended question about or arising from the text, a task few could execute. Most devised comprehension questions or factual questions—questions unlikely to generate meaningful exploration and discussion. Many students sought extensive guidelines and detailed grading rubrics for assignments, as well as regular updates on their performance. Trying to accommodate them and lessen their apparent anxiety about college, I at first formulated extensive guidelines but this yielded formulaic papers which took the joy out of writing and reading for all involved. Group assignments were met with a barrage of questions about how they would be graded; collaborating with peers was seen as a liability, not an opportunity. There was much frustration in our classroom, on all sides.

The transition from high school to college has arguably never been smooth, and these frustrations are not new, nor were they new to me. But the extent of student disengagement seemed graver. A colleague called my attention to the fact that the cohort I was teaching coincided with the ten-year anniversary of No Child Left Behind (NCLB). These students had been "filled and drilled" since first grade and had had very little opportunity and time to explore, contemplate, formulate, and discuss interpretations, explore complexity, do creative and collaborative work, let alone read for pleasure (Quezada 2008). For most of them, education meant following a very set path and checking off requirements—many were even given summer reading lists. The mix of passivity, disengagement, boredom, neediness, and performance anxiety that I encountered becomes more understandable when seen in the light of the banking model of education and unrelenting testing regime implemented with NCLB (Mora 2011). The banking model requires memorization and regurgitation, and it discourages originality and intellectual risk-taking and leaves little room for self-directed intellectual exploration, higher level thinking, and deep and more complex learning (Berliner 2009).

Most of my students came from well-funded suburban schools and didn't suffer the brunt of NCLB: that has fallen on students in poor urban schools—disproportionately students of color—whose curricula have narrowed as arts, physical education, social studies, and science are deprioritized to focus on math and reading skills (Walker 2014). But relatively privileged public school students are nonetheless also casualties of NCLB (and now of Every Student Succeeds Act (ESSA)[14]) because it denies them of the very best of education: imagination and excitement, being able to follow one's curiosity and internal drive, the feeling of being connected to others and the world (Kohn 2015). As Noam Chomsky put it in a recent talk, "young children are creative, inquisitive, they want to know things, they want to understand things, and unless it's beaten out of your head, it stays with you the rest of your life" (Chomsky 2014). I suspect that NCLB has played a big role in beating those inclinations out of many incoming college students. It may sound overly dramatic, but more than once, I heard students describe themselves as zombies and drones—*their* words, not mine, and they were echoed in other classes.

I recognize that what I am describing is (once gain) symptomatic of larger and deeper structural issues that much be addressed politically and through policy. What's needed is a radical transformation of public education, a real rethinking of K12 schools, and that struggle is on-going.[15] But as we imagine and push for what is possible, we also need to figure out how to deal with what *is*. Seeing my students as casualties of NCLB made me less frustrated with them and made room for empathy: they didn't ask for that kind of education and many had no inkling that other educational philosophies and practices even existed.

Paradoxically, misery may be a productive field insofar as we can tap into that misery and make it a starting point for a critical pedagogy. I first eyed this possibility when I developed a segment on the La Raza studies controversy in Arizona. Besides assigning primary documents and news stories, I screened *Precious Knowledge*, a documentary directed by Ari Luis Palos that examines the eradication of the Mexican American Studies

---

[14] Alfie Kohn notes that the "heart of NCLB lives on" in ESSA, the Every Student Succeeds Act signed by President Obama, see Kohn (2015). For a broader critique of neoliberalized education, see John Bellamy Foster (2011).

[15] The Milwaukee-based organization Rethinking Schools is a great place to start this rethinking; http://www.rethinkingschools.org/index.shtml For curriculum and lesson plans, see Teaching for Change: http://www.teachingforchange.org/

program in Tucson Unified School District K12 schools and features interviews with elected officials, educators, parents, and students. The documentary is unabashedly for Raza Studies but contains interviews with people on both sides. In addition to raising questions about race, class, power, and justice, it prompted students to think about their own educational experience. Seeing the galvanized Raza students defy elected officials as they fought for an inclusive and empowering education exposed my students to a perspective on education that they'd never encountered before. They shared experiences of boredom and emptiness, of Red Bull and Ritalin-boosted test prepping followed by almost instant amnesia about the material studied.

Precious Knowledge sparked discussion about what education *can* be and *should* be; about the political nature of education, and the role of education in a democratic society. This proved to be an opening, a moment of possibility for critical thinking, for even though some students maintained the dominant neoliberal narrative, insisting that the rise of China and India requires American students to shape up, ace the math, stop complaining, buckle down, and so on, other students developed a critical interrogation.[16] I harbor no illusions that I set off a radical movement against the banking model of education, but it was an unexpected entry point to an interrogation of neoliberal rationality—an interrogation with unusually active student participation. In subsequent classes, I used other education-related controversies (e.g. Whiteness Studies in Arizona, AP world history in Jefferson County, Colorado, trigger warnings, and online degrees) to start critical discussions about education, learning, and power—questions that are pertinent in first-year general education classrooms regardless of course subject. Using controversial stories is admittedly a sensationalist approach and arguably also one that appeals to student self-centeredness (since these stories are, in a

---

[16] Examples of such stories include Friedman (2010), Jaschik (2010), and Miller (2009). Similarly, President Obama called on American students to "turn off the TV, stop playing the video games, [and] do your homework." See Schmitt (2011). My point here is not to contest the claim that there are problems in terms of students' study habits, discipline, dedication, priorities, etc., only to challenge the neoliberal tenor of these exhorting accounts which often imply that it is the precariousness of students in, or from, the Global South that explains their ostensibly exceptional drive and discipline (which in turn implies that US students would do better if *their* lives were more precarious).

sense, about them), and certainly we should take on a current controversy only if we are able to properly contextualize it—which means more prep work on our part. This is not to suggest that we have to develop new teaching areas; rather, it is to suggest that we connect through misery wherever we detect it in our encounters with students. We know that neoliberalism produces misery galore; perhaps one task for cultural studies instructors is to find the productive potential—the pedagogic potential—of that misery.

The larger task, however, lies is outside the classroom: in organizing against the assault on the humanities and on the public university as an institution devoted to research and education, to the search for truth, to improving the human condition, and not simply deliver training for the workforce. That assault is ongoing. In Wisconsin, administrators at UW Stevens Point, in an attempt to address the budget deficit resulting from state funding cuts, have just proposed to cut 13 humanities and social science majors, including English, American studies, art, history, philosophy, political science, sociology, geography, and foreign languages, proposing to invest instead in "high-demand career paths" like engineering, chemical engineering, information technology, finance, and marketing (Mensch 2018). University administrators are purposely reducing the institution to a polytechnic, yet maintain that all of their graduates will be "thoroughly grounded in the liberal arts" (Berman 2018). Apparently, a thorough grounding in liberal arts requires nothing much, certainly not the employment of scholars engaged in research in those fields. To turn that tide, academics will need to unionize within universities and organize across occupational fields, along with K12 teachers, public employees, and others whose livelihoods have been rendered increasingly precarious in this regime. And academics must understand that they have a crucial contribution to make to public education activism: we experience first-hand the results of the narrow, banking-style education that has dominated in US K12 schools, and we can apply our skills, as researchers, writers, and speakers to advocate for better public education. Much of the work we need to do lies outside campus, in building coalitions and organizing against the forces that produce the many forms of misery we—and our students—encounter.

Works Cited

Adams, S. (2014). The 10 Skills Employers Most Want in 2015 Graduates. *Forbes,* [online]. Available at http//www.forbes.com/sites/susanadams/2014/11/12/the-10-skills-employers-most-want-in-2015-graduates/. Accessed 10 Mar 2017.

Applebaum, B. (2008). 'Doesn't My Experience Count?' White Students, the Authority of Experience and Social Justice Pedagogy. *Race Ethnicity and Education, 11*(4), 405–411.

Archibeque, O. (2008). *Bias in Student Evaluations of Minority Faculty. A Selected Bibliography.* University of Colorado Denver. Available at http//library.auraria.edu/content/bias-student-evaluations-minority-faculty. Accessed 10 Mar 2017.

Berliner, D. C. (2009). MCLB (Much Curriculum Left Behind) A U.S. Calamity in the Making. *The Educational Forum, 73*(4), 284–296.

Berman, J. (2018, March 18). This Public College Wants to Cut English, History—And 11 Other Liberal Arts Majors. *Marketwatch.* Available at https://www.marketwatch.com/Story/this-public-college-wants-to-cut-english-history-and-11-other-liberal-arts-majors-2018-03-16?&siteid=yhoof2&yptr=yahoo. Accessed 10 Mar 2017.

Bernstein, K. (2013). Warnings from the Trenches: A High School Teacher Tells College Educators What They Can Expect in the Wake of No Child Left Behind and Race to the Top. *AAUP,* [online]. Available at https//www.aaup.org/article/warnings-trenches#.V4JnuKIe64M. Accessed 10 Mar 2017.

Blattner, T., & Blattner, N. (2003). Guarding Against Potential Bias in Student Evaluations What Every Faculty Member Needs to Know. *College Teaching, 51*(1), 27–32.

Bonilla-Silva, E. (2010). *Racism Without Racists* (3rd ed.). New York: Rowman & Littlefield.

Brown, W. (2005). *Edgework Critical Essays on Knowledge and Politics.* Princeton: Princeton University Press.

Brown, W. (2006). American Nightmare Neoliberalism, Neoconservatism, and De-Democratization. *Political Theory, 34*(6), 693–694.

Brown, S. (2015a). Facing Protests About Racial Climate, Another Campus Administrator Steps Down. *The Chronicle of Higher Education,* [online]. Available at http//chronicle.com/article/Facing-Protests-About-Racial/234191. Accessed 10 Mar 2017.

Brown, W. (2015b). *Undoing the Demos Neoliberalism's Stealth Revolution.* Cambridge: Zone Books.

Bump, G. (2015). UW–Madison's Economic Impact to Wisconsin $15 Billion Annually, Study Say. University of Wisconsin-Madison, [online]. Available at http//news.wisc.edu/uw-madisons-economic-impact-to-wisconsin-15-billion-annually-study-says/. Accessed 1 Apr 2017.

Cacho, L. (2000). The People of California are Suffering' The Ideology of White Injury in Discourses of Immigration. *Cultural Values, 4*(4), 389–418.

Causey, J. E. (2014). No Shock, Milwaukee Metro Area Has the Worst Segregation. *Milwaukee Journal Sentinel*, [online]. Available at http://archive.jsonline.com/news/opinion/no-shock-milwaukee-metro-area-has-the-worst-segregation-b99233242z1-252332071.html. Accessed 29 Mar 2018.

Chatelain, M. (2014a). Teaching the #FergusonSyllabus. *Dissent Magazine*, [online]. Available at https//www.dissentmagazine.org/blog/teaching-ferguson-syllabus. Accessed 10 Mar 2017.

Chatelain, M. (2014b). How to Teach Kids About What's Happening in Ferguson. *The Atlantic*, [online]. Available at http//www.theatlantic.com/education/archive/2014/08/how-to-teach-kids-about-whats-happening-in-ferguson/379049/. Accessed 10 Mar 2017.

Chomsky, N. (2014). The Death of American Universities. Remarks at a Gathering of Members and Allies of the Adjunct Faculty Association of the United Steelworkers in Pittsburgh, PA, 2014. *Jacobin*, [online]. Available at https//www.jacobinmag.com/2014/03/the-death-of-american-universities/. Accessed 10 Mar 2017.

DePalma, R. (2008). 'The Voice of Every Black Person'? Bringing Authentic Voices in the Multicultural Dialogue. *Teaching and Teacher Education, 24*(3), 767–778.

Deresiewicz, W. (2015, September). The Neoliberal Arts How College Sold Its Soul to the Market. *Harpers*. Available at http//harpers.org/archive/2015/09/the-neoliberal-arts/. Accessed 10 Mar 2017.

DiAngelo, R. (2011). White Fragility. *International Journal of Critical Pedagogy, 3*(3), 54–70.

Evans, C. (2015). Save the Wisconsin Idea. *New York Times* op-ed. Available at http//www.nytimes.com/2015/02/16/opinion/save-the-wisconsin-idea.html. Accessed 30 Apr 2015.

Finn, A. (2016). Walker Appoints 3 New Members to UW Board of Regents. *The Journal Times*, [online]. Available at http//journaltimes.com/walker-appoints-new-members-to-uw-board-of-regents/article_47233169-242e-56b5-ba62-5203eee471aa.html. Accessed 10 Mar 2017.

Fletcher, M. (2013). Whites and Minorities Follow Unequal Paths to College, Report Says. *The Washington Post*, [online]. Available at https//www.washingtonpost.com/business/economy/minorities-and-whites-follow-unequal-college-paths-report-says/2013/07/31/61c18f08-f9f3-11e2-8752-b41d7ed1f685_story.html. Accessed 10 Mar 2017.

Foster, J. B. (2011). Education and the Structural Crisis of Capital. *Monthly Review*, [online], pp. 17–27. Available at http//monthlyreview.org/2011/07/01/education-and-the-structural-crisis-of-capital/. Accessed 10 Mar 2017.

Frankenberg, R. (1993). *White Women Race Matters: The Social Construction of Whiteness*. Minneapolis: University of Minnesota Press.

Friedman, T. (2010). We're No. 1(1)! *The New York Times*, [online]. Available at http//www.nytimes.com/2010/09/12/opinion/12friedman.html?_r=0. Accessed 10 Mar 2017.

Giroux, H. (1997). White Squall. Resistance and the Pedagogy of Whiteness. *Cultural Studies, 11*(3), 376–389.

Giroux, H. (2014). *Neoliberalism's War on Higher Education*. Chicago: Haymarket.

Grahame, K. M. (2004). Contesting Diversity in the Academy Resistance to Women of Color Teaching Race, Class, and Gender. *Race, Gender, and Class, 11*(3), 54–73.

Guerrero, L. (2008). *Teaching Race in the 21st Century: College Teachers Talk About Their Fears, Risks, and Rewards*. New York: Palgrave Macmillan.

Hanhardt, C. (2001). *Safe Space: Gay Neighborhood History and the Politics of Violence*. Chapel Hill: Duke University Press.

Henry, A. (1992). There Are No Safe Places: Pedagogy as Powerful and Dangerous Terrain. *Action in Teacher Education, 15*(4), 1–4.

Herzog, K. (2015). Walker Proposes Changing Wisconsin Idea—Then Backs Away. *Milwaukee Journal Sentinel*, [online]. Available at http//www.js.com/news/education/scott-walkers-uw-mission-rewrite-could-end-the-wisconsin-idea-b99439020z1-290797681.html. Accessed 10 Mar 2017.

Jaschik, Scott. (2010). Are American Students Lazy? *Inside Higher Ed*, [online]. Available at http//www.insidehighered.com/news/2010/01/04/miller. Accessed 10 Mar 2017.

Kaminer, W. (1996). *It's All the Rage Crime and Culture*. New York: Basic Books.

King, R. C. (2008). Minor Concerns the (Im)Possibilities of Critical Race Pedagogies. In L. Guerrero (Ed.), *Teaching Race in the 21st Century: College Teachers Talk About Their Fears, Risks, and Rewards* (pp. 49–67). New York: Palgrave Macmillan.

Koba, M. (2013). Why CEOs Like Liberal Arts Students. *CNBC*, [online]. Available at http//www.cnbc.com/id/100642178. Accessed 10 Mar 2017.

Kohn, A. (2015). What No Child Left Behind Left Behind. *Alternet*, [online]. Available at http//www.alternet.org/education/what-no-child-left-behind-left-behind. Accessed 10 Mar 2017.

Lafer, G. (2014). *Do Poor Kids Deserve Lower-Quality Education Than Rich Kids? Evaluating School Privatization Proposals in Milwaukee*, Wisconsin, EPI (Economic Policy Institute), [online]. Available at http//www.epi.org/publication/school-privatization-milwaukee/. Accessed 10 Mar 2017.

Lazere, D. (2006). Rethinking Progressive Pedagogy. *Radical Teacher, 77*, 20–24.

Marley, P., et al. (2015). Lawmakers Drop Walker's Plan to Spin off UW Governance. *Milwaukee Journal Sentinel*, [online]. Available at http//www.js.com/news/statepolitics/scott-walkers-proposed-cut-to-owi-treatment-tops-panels-agenda-b99493883z1-302562311.html. Accessed 10 Mar 2017.

McCalmont, L. (2015). Scott Walker Urges Professors to Work Harder. *Politico*, [online]. Available at http//www.politico.com/story/2015/01/scott-walker-higher-education-university-professors-114716. Accessed 10 Mar 2017.

Mensch, S. K. (2018). Professional Organizations Respond to UW-Stevens Point Proposal to Cut Humanities Majors. *Wisconsin State Journal*, [online]. Available at http://host.madison.com/wsj/news/local/education/university/professional-organizations-respond-to-uw-stevens-point-proposal-to-cut/article_77820 6e5-e633-526d-a04c-9365d7e332a3.html. Accessed 1 Apr 2018.

Miller, K. (2009). My Lazy American Students. *The Boston Globe*, [online]. http//www.boston.com/bostonglobe/editorial_opinion/oped/articles/2009/12/21/my_lazy_american_students/. Accessed 1 Mar 2016.

Miner, B. J. (2013). *Lessons from the Heartland a Turbulent Half-Century of Public Education in an Iconic American City*. Ney York: The New Press.

Miner, B. J. (2015, April 17). Vouchers, Religious Freedom and Discrimination. *Milwaukee Journal Sentinel*. Available at http//www.js.com/news/opinion/school-vouchers-in-milwaukee-religious-freedom-and-discrimination-b99480751z1-300392801.html. Accessed 10 Mar 2017.

Mora, R. (2011). 'Schools Is so Boring' High-Stakes Testing and Boredom at an Urban Middle School. *University of Pennsylvania Graduate School of Education, PennGSE, 9*(1), 1–6.

Møller, P. (2014). Restoring Law and (Racial) Order to the Old Dominion White Dreams and New Federalism in Anti-Immigrant Legislation. *Cultural Studies, 28*(5–6), 869–910.

Newkirk, P. (2015, December). Academe Must Confront Its Racist Past. *The Chronicle of Higher Education.* Available at http//chronicle.com/article/Academe-Must-Confront-Its/234534. Accessed 10 Mar 2017.

Ngunjiri, F., et al. (2010). Living Autoethnography: Connecting Life and Research. *Journal of Research Practice, 6*(1), 1–17.

Ninivaggi, C. (2001). Whites Teaching Whites about Race Racial Identity Theory and White Defensiveness in the Classroom. *Teaching Anthropology, 8*(1), 1–32.

Omi, M., & Winant, H. (1989). *Racial Formation in the United States from the 1960s to the 1980s.* New York: Routledge.

Posner, E. (2015). Universities are Right—And Within Their Rights—To Crack Down on Speech and Behavior. *Slate,* [online]. Available at http//www.slate.com/articles/news_and_politics/view_from_chicago/2015/02/university_speech_codes_students_are_children_who_must_be_protected.single.html. Accessed 10 Mar 2017.

Precious Knowledge. (2011). [Film] Tucson: Ari Luis Palos.

Quezada, S. (2008). Critical Pedagogy Dynamic Thinking and Teaching Within the Confines of No Child Left Behind. *Radical History Review, 102,* 35–38.

Ray, E. (2013, July 24). The Value of a Liberal Arts Education in Today's Global Marketplace. *Huffington Post.* Available at http//www.huffingtonpost.com/edward-j-ray/the-value-of-a-liberal-arts-education_b_3647765.html. Accessed 5 Apr/Mar 2016.

Reddy, M., & TuSmith, B. (2001). *Race in the College Classroom Pedagogy & Politics.* New Brunswick: Rutgers University Press.

Richards, E., & Mulvany, L. (2014). Sixty Years After Brown vs. Board of Education. *Milwaukee Journal Sentinel,* [online]. Available at http//www.js.com/news/education/60-years-after-brown-v-board-of-education-intense-segregation-returns-b99271365z1-259682171.html. Accessed 10 Mar 2017.

Savidge, N. (2016a). Changes to Tenure, Budget and Regents Show Extent of Scott Walker's Impact on UW. *Wisconsin State Journal,* [online]. Available at http//host.madison.com/wsj/news/local/education/university/changes-to-tenure-budget-and-regents-show-extent-of-scott/article_90954155-df31-5fdb-bb93-dd93a0f81225.html. Accessed 10 Mar 2017.

Savidge, N. (2016b). Regents Approve New Policies for UW Tenure Over Professors' Objections. *Wisconsin State Journal,* [online]. Available at http//host.madison.com/wsj/news/local/education/university/regents-approve-new-policies-for-uw-tenure-over-professors-objections/article_e0aa29b5-438b-5182-8870-5cd76fb80144.html. Accessed 10 Mar 2017.

Schmitt, T. (2011). *Obama: Immigrants Need Path to Citizenship*. UPI.com, [online]. Available at http//www.upi.com/Top_News/US/2011/09/28/ Obama-Immigrants-need-path-to-citizenship/UPI-83191317229024/. Accessed 10 Mar 2017.

Schneider, P. (2014). UW-Madison Researchers React to Robin Vos' 'Ancient Mating Habits of Whatever' Remark. *The Capital Times*, [online]. Available at http://host.madison.com/ct/news/local/writers/pat_schneider/uw-madison-researchers-react-to-robin-vos-ancient-mating-habits/article_3144b1da-66a7-11e4-93fc-e3c72cb3062d.html. Accessed 15 Mar 2018.

Shapiro, J. (2014). From Strength to Strength. *Inside Higher Education*, [online]. Available at https//www.insidehighered.com/views/2014/12/15/ essay-importance-not-trying-protect-students-everything-may-upset-them. Accessed 10 Mar 2017.

Shulevitz, J. (2015). In College and Hiding from Scary Ideas. *New York Times*. Available at http//www.nytimes.com/2015/03/22/opinion/sunday/judith-shulevitz-hiding-from-scary-ideas.html. Accessed 10 Mar 2017.

Thomason, A. (2015). Students Are Protesting Racism on College Campuses. What Are Their Demands? *The Chronicle of Higher Education* blog The Ticker, [online]. Available at http//chronicle.com/blogs/ticker/students-are-protesting-racism-on-college-campuses-what-are-their-demands/106721. Accessed 10 Mar 2017.

University of Wisconsin System. (2016). *Economic Impact Study Demonstrates Value of University of Wisconsin System to State Economy*, [online]. Available at https//www.wisconsin.edu/news/archive/economic-impact-study-demonstrates-value-of-university-of-wisconsin-system-to-state-economy/. Accessed 2 Apr 2016.

Vine, N. (2015, February 2). Walker: 'Budget Proposal an 'Act 10 for the UW System'. *Stevens Point Journal*. Available at https://www.stevenspointjournal.com/story/news/local/2015/02/04/scott-walker-act-university-wisconsin-state-budget-cuts/22880881/. Accessed 10 Feb 2015.

Walker, T. (2014). *The Testing Obsession and the Disappearing Curriculum*. Published by the NEA (National Education Association) [online]. Available at http//neatoday.org/2014/09/02/the-testing-obsession-and-the-disappearing-curriculum-2/. Accessed 10 Mar 2017.

Waring, C. D. L., & Bordoloi, S. D. (2013). 'Hopping on the Tips of a Trident' Two Graduate Students of Color Reflect on Teaching Critical Content at Predominantly White Institutions. *Feminist Teacher, 22*(2), 108–124.

Wisconsin State Statute. (2012). Chapter 36: University of Wisconsin System. Wisconsin State Legislature, 2017–2018. [Online]. Available at: https://docs.legis.wisconsin.gov/statutes/statutes/36. Last accessed 2 Sept 2019.

Into the Factory: Teaching Cultural Studies as a Critique of Global Capitalism

Pablo Andrés Castagno

The space is fascinating. In a campus of 40 hectares there are two long, warehouse-like facilities containing hundreds of classrooms divided with thousands of partition walls. This academic infrastructure, destined to train about 50,000 students in accounting, administration, law, engineering, communications, medicine, and other predominant disciplines, is located inside the premises of a former Chrysler and Volkswagen automobile factory. A false ceiling separates the classrooms from the impressive roof of metal sheets, iron, and glass dating from the 1950s that encases the new structure like a supra-shell. There are plenty of fluorescent lamps and low-energy bulb lights. When members of the cleaning staff, who know how resistant the old roof is, remove the false ceiling's opaque glasses to clean the latter we can glimpse the whole reality of the setting. Along with a mass of both employed and unemployed, I commute across the metropolitan space of Buenos Aires three hours per day, three times per week to teach cultural studies in the Universidad Nacional

P. A. Castagno (✉)
Universidad Nacional de La Matanza, San Justo, Argentina

© The Author(s) 2019   **243**
J. Aksikas et al. (eds.), *Cultural Studies in the Classroom and Beyond*,
https://doi.org/10.1007/978-3-030-25393-6_13

de La Matanza, established in 1989. We are in the large working-class district of La Matanza, Argentina.[1] This is a national public university.[2]

Background of a Cultural Production

Rethinking my teaching, I reflect here on strategies I used to open a concrete, imaginative debate on radical democracy (Laclau and Mouffe 2001) between 2011 and 2015, in the context of the *marea rosada*, or pink tide of moderate leftist projects that emerged in Latin America after the collapse of neoliberal state regulations in the early 2000s.[3] This discussion in English, however, runs the risk of being cited as the proof of my supposed foreignness to the district. My response to fellow readers (*compañeros*) is that a foreign text is useful if it communicates our hopes as workers and citizens. In contrast, certain national forms (but not all) may be distant to us in terms of their untruth. The reality is that, after the collapse of the neoliberal project in 2001–2002 and the concomitant crisis of state hegemony, the Argentine state managed to manufacture consent. Successive governments claimed that their state policies protect the citizenry against neoliberal capitalism. This state record, however, is debatable.

For Marxist critics, who recognize certain positive achievements, the new "developmental projects" in Latin America actually constituted state mechanisms to reorganize capitalism after the crisis (Robinson 2008; Svampa 2008; Webber and Carr 2013). These authors demonstrated the links between Northern corporations and Latin American ruling classes, revealed the limitations of the social policies implemented, identified gray-state practices directed to co-opt social movements, discussed labor conditions, and illuminated the difficulties to spread democratic reforms. On the contrary, post-Marxist critics concluded that the *marea rosada*

---

[1] La Matanza means the place of the massacre. It is unknown whether the name refers to Spanish colonizers' massacre of indigenous peoples, or indigenous peoples' massacre of invaders.

[2] National public universities are funded by the federal state, administered by an autonomous body of public authorities elected internally by students, graduates, faculty, and staff according to specific power dynamics; and free of tuition for undergraduate students.

[3] It included center-left governments in Brazil, Argentina, Uruguay, Chile, Nicaragua, El Salvador and Peru, and the more radical projects of Bolivia, Ecuador, and Venezuela. The term also refers to the social movements that set in motion those governments.

signified a political sea change in the region. They argued that the *marea rosada* counteracted neoliberal capitalism and imperialism, transformed class and ethnic systems of inequality, introduced democratic innovations, and increased income in the popular classes (García Linera 2006; González 2011; Sader 2011). Indeed, other questions within the purview of cultural studies are important for increasing the light shed on the *marea rosada*, which started to decompose by 2015.[4] For instance, how the social movements that catalyzed the *marea rosada* could not advance in establishing radical democracies. The concern that has most profoundly informed my teaching, however, is that I am not aware of any public endeavor that has addressed this Marxist/post-Marxist debate in my university.

After receiving my doctorate from George Mason University and accepting a part-time, temporary, renewable teaching appointment in Political Science in my home country, I paradoxically felt as though I had fallen into an unfamiliar public arena. As a self-identified Latin American leftist scholar, I found myself in a stronghold of national-popular, but not always leftist, *Peronista* identity. Similar to other cases in the South, in the 1940s Juan Domingo Perón's government materialized a state project of national capitalism that included income distribution policies. Successive dictatorships proscribed the *Peronista* party, while workers reinforced their *Peronista* identity to resist the capitalist assault of the dictatorships against them. Nevertheless, an historical trope of the party has been its rejection of Marxism. La Matanza, the largest district of Buenos Aires state, has always elected *Peronista* mayors. The district remained *Peronista* even when, in the 1990s, the party embraced neoliberalism to fully embed the nation-state into global capitalism, a move that produced skyrocketing unemployment in the factories of the district. Since the pink tide, national and local *Peronista* state administrators advocated a friendly association between the state and private capital.[5] Or, to phrase it in

---

[4] Argentina elected a neoliberal-conservative president, Venezuela fell into a profound sociopolitical crisis, a conservative parliamentary coup destituted president Dilma Rousseff in Brazil, and Ecuador took a conservative path in 2017.

[5] See, for example, the news on the cultural festival Rockea BA organized by Buenos Aires state, a state company holding, La Matanza municipality, the university, and various brands, "Scioli invited thousands of youth to the event of rock and sports" (El1 2015, p. 3, my translation). Scioli was

Gramscian terms, for a state form equivalent to the articulation of political society and civil society.

In this state context, the goal of our university has been to train new working-class generations in well-established disciplines in order to assimilate them into the existing state and market,[6] with success judged in terms of increasing the number of students and graduates (see Secretaría de Políticas Universitarias 2012, p. 87). The mission of the university is, "to satisfy the needs of the community, that is, its inhabitants in general, its firms, institutions, professionals, and other social actors" (UNLaM n.d., my translation). In reading this emblematic public approach from the standpoint of Latin American cultural studies, and notwithstanding its merits to realize the collective right to education, I was struck, however, by the fact that this public approach does not mention the key agents of its cultural policy: students, faculty, women, workers, ethnic groups, or social movements. Instead of referring to these citizens and groups of citizens, for instance, this recurrent state approach abstracts and locates them in a syntactic chain of equivalence, which conceals the reality that such social actors are usually subordinated to firms, the state, and other social institutions.

To put it succinctly, I felt disoriented. Beyond the discourse of the *marea rosada*, I was unable to perceive any affective sign of the working-class district in which we are located. For example, the university took advantage of the functionality of the former factory, but somehow masked its industrial, working-class quality with a post-modernist myriad of up-to-date signs and neoclassical ornamentation, including cybernetic logos, neoclassical columns of cement, Victorian lampposts, and neoclassical white triangular pediments that contradictorily connote innovation and institutionalized knowledge. This constructive materiality invokes the legitimacy of technology and the prestige of prominent academic architecture to communicate with students and faculty. But, in this way, it does not express the old fabric in form, material, and color to enhance academic labor, which is the subjective essence of the setting today. It is as if public administrators, across

---

Buenos Aires' governor and the presidential candidate of Frente para la Victoria (Front for Victory), the party that controlled the national government and *Peronista* politics between 2003 and 2015. Scioli praised the university because it trains a mass of youths who have "the hope of getting a job" (El1 2015, p. 3, my translation).

[6] As is seen, for instance, in the public relevance the university gives to its job fairs.

the state, refrain from conceiving modernist, locally conscious projects to recast the memory of labor struggles as a way to encourage students' critique.[7] Missing the labor of imagination that could keep workers' hopes alive, they block our thinking beyond the factory-like, reifying function of the academic setting today. In other words, instead of revitalizing our working-class patrimony to envision the production of critical knowledge, this recurrent state aesthetic complex conceals the registers of working-class consciousness that would question the state and capital.

Yet, under those conditions, I became finally aware of the *proletarian* specificity of our cultural arena when realistic, working-class students commented to me on the vitality of injured, silenced, and place-based, subaltern identities in the district. Listening to them, I learned to install theoretical, methodological, and pedagogical conditions in our courses that make possible a concrete debate on the state, on its adaptation to the cultural forces of the market and capital. I also understood that the lines of flight we take into theoretical abstraction and translation as intellectuals—to recall Gilles Deleuze and Félix Guattari's (2014) concept of deterritorialization—should be immanent imaginative tools we apprehend from our location in order to intervene dialectically into the latter. We cannot fabricate radical democracy without grasping its necessity within/from our educational situations.

On the Shop Floor

As in a parallax, changing epistemological positions in the space alter the perception we have on knowledge, institutions, and politics. The foundation of this parallax has been an undergraduate writing course I teach as part of the Political Science degree.

Taller de Integración (workshop of integration) previously was a course aimed at engaging students in "scientific knowledge" through the learning of reading and writing skills. I transformed this instrumental goal, contending that we need to reflect on the relationship of our knowledge to culture and politics to make its production critical, self-reflexive and moti-

---

[7] Werner and Aguirre (2009), for example, showed that Chrysler's workers participated in the critical shop-floor organizations and strikes of the 1970s.

vating. This epistemological shift made sense because the workshop follows courses on "elements" of Philosophy, Sociology, Political Science, and History. *Integración* resulted in a teaching practice directed not at assimilating students into mainstream academic grammar but at focusing the production of knowledge onto the social problems of the world we live in. We reflect on our social problems in their global, national, *and* local contexts to demonstrate in comprehensive research essays that social reality is usually different from what hegemonic institutions claim it is. Our workshop became a practical introduction to cultural studies based on an immanent critique of the assumptions of both the discipline and the state context.

My praxis was aimed at reformulating Political Science's assumptions. For example, renowned political scientist Giovanni Sartori argued that his discipline had a crisis of "location" and called on scientists not to excessively expand the field of politics. According to him, "Political decisions involve very different subjects (…) If all these decisions are initially and basically 'political' it is because they are taken by a personnel located in the political domain" (Sartori 2002, pp. 221–22, my translation). My cultural studies reading of this passage is that we cannot define the political domain a priori with the ordinary subjects of Political Science: the political personnel, the State, the political party system, electoral behavior, public policy management, and so on. I opened this field contending to take not official politics, but rather "the political," as the object of research: the relationships of domination, negotiation, resistance, transgression, or indeed revolution that are inscribed in all institutions, practices, and cultural forms. In the words of Ernesto Laclau and Chantal Mouffe, "the problem of the political is the problem of the institution of the social, that is, of the definition and articulation of social relations in a field criss-crossed with antagonisms" (2001, p. 153). Students could pick any political–cultural object they wanted to research.

This methodological perspective is consonant with what are now prevalent trends in cultural studies. As Paul Smith phrased it, our goal is to research "the totality of social relations and cultural productions at given times and in given places" (1997, p. 60); or, in Raymond Williams' words, "the study of relationships between elements in a whole way of life" (2001, p. 63). Throughout the semester I strive to help students situate their research in the historical current. Our objective is to construct our research in terms of a historical and theoretical problematic that would break with the ideological assumptions around the empirical reality we approach. In this sense, we have discussed, for example, how Göran Therborn (2014) analyzed the interplay between political movements and class transformations on a global scale. Or we read Williams' view of hegemony as a process, "a realized complex of experiences, relationships, and activities, with specific and changing pressures and limits" (1977, p. 112). More often we debate the concept of social totality by examining Néstor García Canclini's (2004) cultural analysis.

Following other trends in cultural studies, García Canclini's definition of culture is actually a semiotic one. For him, the concept refers to the production, circulation, and consumption of meanings in social life (García Canclini 2004, p. 34). His understanding is predominant in the Latin American cultural studies field, which is informed by the refusal of contemporary anthropological approaches to take culture as a homogenous whole or totality (see, e.g. Grimson 2010). In my reading, from this perspective it makes sense to criticize analyses that address culture in that way, but in fact cultural studies works have always tended to grasp the contradictions between residual, dominant, and emergent processes within a social totality (Williams 1977). In this Marxist cultural studies sense, as Georg Lukács observed, "the category of totality does not reduce its various elements to an undifferentiated uniformity" (Lukács 2000, p. 12). Or as Marx famously put it, the category of totality "is concrete because it is the concentration of many determinations, hence unity of the diverse" (1993, p. 101). However, this tension between semiotic and dialectical approaches is productive for class discussion. In other words, the point was to connect García Canclini and Therborn.

The latter author argued that, across global capitalism, social movements and political parties articulate or disconnect subaltern classes (industrial workers, workers in the informal economy, peasants, indigenous communities) and middle classes (white-collar masses) who are dissatisfied with their conditions of life under global capitalism (Therborn 2014). While alliances among those social forces support a project of emancipation from global capitalism, ideological disconnection reinforces the dominance of the transnational bourgeoisie. Cultural debates unifying subaltern forces across states then constitute nodes of political signification. This theoretical view is consonant with the reality of our classroom, populated by youth and adults from working-class and middle-class segments.

Our objective is to contemplate how nodes of signification are established or questioned in specific institutional settings. In this sense, following Smith (1997, p. 58), I aimed at keeping a balance between a deductive approach, informed by a theory of historical process, and the research of political–cultural settings. But there has been still a leaning of the classroom toward idealist conceptions that consist in substituting common sense assumptions on the state, capitalism, or culture for theoretical abstraction. A case in point is the view that the *marea rosada* simply replaced neoliberalism with neo-developmental policies. This view ignores the capitalist dynamic across different moments of state regulation, or illuminating the contradictions within the totality of the public policies implemented. In contrast, students produce concrete knowledge when they analyze the multiple determinations at stake in empirical reality, in such a way that this account constitutes another form of knowledge of the political conjuncture. When we arrive at this threshold of representation, the meaning of the object changes. Research becomes a tool to transform reality as we make sense of it.

Essays in the workshop (as we have discussed publicly) examined how state and capitalist forces disconnect subaltern classes and groups among themselves to reproduce the existing social formation. Hegemonic institutions interpellate successful, competitive workers to join the imaginary middle classes; whereas they expose marginal workers to environmental pollution, labor insecurity, minimum programs of social integration (for instance, schools with scare resources, and basic subsistence programs for children of unemployed families), ethnic discrimination, cultural paternalism, and police repression. For example, students demonstrated that state's paternalist cultural policies (such as Programa Envión) address "popular sectors" as beneficiaries that must always be indebted to state managers, instead of conceptualizing youth and working-class families as social actors that press the state to implement social rights. Other essays showed that media representations of social insecurity exclusively focus on crimes committed by youth from working-class slums, failing to classify political or financial corruption as crimes. Hegemonic institutions discursively point to separate "middle-class" subjects from "popular" sectors with representations of fear (as in media representations of delinquency), and communicating commodity-signs of class distinction. The latter also fuse with racial and gender constructions. Students examined how the culture industry interpellates female professionals to embody white North American bourgeois symbols, which are also androcentric representations to grace successful middle-class male competitors in the culture.

But students also revealed practices of subaltern resistance and solidarity. They showed that youth living in slums emphasize pleasure and consumption (e.g. in *cumbia* music) as a way to radicalize their identities and demand equality against neoliberal state forces and the culture industry that segregate, stigmatize, and repress them. They analyzed the emergence of labor unions that build alliances between manual/non-manual workers and professional workers. Or they demonstrated that social movements modulated the public policies of Cristina Fernández's national government (2007–2015), which expanded social rights on gender identities, the media system, or pensions. In rethinking this shifting terrain, however, students also observed how social movements have counteracted the gray networks connecting, for example, oil multinationals and the state.

Around the Workshop

In another seminar I teach on media/cultural studies, while reading Frantz Fanon's *Black Skin, White Masks* (2008), we have realized how official, state "whiteness" permeates our existence, impeding us from expressing our subaltern identities. A state dictum has the appearance of natural law: state and capitalist assimilation is the sole legitimate position within the academic system. This discourse represents knowledge as non-political: engineers modernize infrastructures, political scientists rationalize bureaucracy, lawyers put into effect pure Law, or communicators mediate pleasures. Generally speaking, there is no discussion of how class, gender, race, ethnic, and national structures shape all disciplines. But Fanon's analysis against alienation helps us to be fearless about counteracting representations. Thus, media students discussed Louis Althusser's

(2001) theory on how state repressive and ideological apparatuses, across the state and civil society, reproduce capitalist relations of domination. The insights of this theory are extant in the classroom: under the motto of contributing to citizens' security, between 2012 and 2015 the Buenos Aires state trained 1796 youth in our university to enter the police forces (UNLaM 2015).

In contrast to that cultural studies' approach, mainstream social science conditions the possibilities of Political Science and Media Studies to generate immanent, dialectical, critique. Social science appears as a theoretical enterprise to demonstrate arguments with empirical evidence collected via different methods. Nevertheless, even perspectives that recognize how social interests condition research avoid discussing the political implications of theories. Mainstream social science misperceives how ideology "occupies it, haunts it, or lies in wait for it," as Althusser explained regarding the difficulties of scientific practice (1979, p. 170). It simply refuses to consider the presence of ideology within knowledge. As Max Horkheimer criticized, ideology masks the antagonisms in the social formation, validating the views of certain social groups (1989, p. 55). Alleging a positivist conception of pure, descriptive research, mainstream social science rejects engaging with a critical philosophy: a theory of theoretical practice that is crucial to advance revolutionary research (Althusser 1979).

Mainstream social science actually appropriates Marxist concepts in a liberal way. For example, it takes Gramsci's concept of hegemony as a tool to analyze symbolic tensions as political conflicts, yet it detaches the concept from an understanding of ideology. It wrongly argues that, according to Marxism, ideology is just a distorted system of bourgeois ideas mechanically determined by the economic base.[8] For Gramsci, however, organic and traditional intellectuals, tied to the political parties of the dominant class, mediate bourgeois conceptions into forms of common sense, or hegemonic expectations that subaltern groups often resist

---

[8] For example, in a well-known introduction to anthropology Mauricio Boivin and other authors developed the idea of an "anthropology of inequality" based on a "Gramscian" concept of hegemony that would replace the concept of ideology. For them, the latter is not useful because it supposedly grasps cultural inequalities as exclusively originated in the economic structure (Boivin, Rosato and Arribas 2004, p. 99).

(Gramsci 2000, p. 306). Or, in Williams' reading of Gramsci, hegemony appears as "a whole body of practices and expectations, over the whole of living" (Williams 1977, p. 110), but it is connected to ideology that according to Williams is more formal and articulated. Briefly, for Marxist cultural studies, the concept of hegemony is fundamental to investigate ideology in more profound ways.

My point is that, without thinking how hegemonic practices contradictorily imbricate state apparatuses, political–economic processes, and daily life one into another, it is difficult for students to critically engage with the fragmented knowledge they gain from across the curricula. Instrumental, positivist education realizes the ideological essentialism and economic determinism it alleges against Marxist theory. For example, I observe that courses in Media Studies tend to elide *tout court* Marx's category of capital to approach media history, information rights, or even digital media. Mainstream courses' idealist approaches grasp media transformations as "cultural" phenomena, and as state *or* civil society ethical issues separated from the capitalist processes of value accumulation and crisis. Meanwhile, Political Science's courses on the "economic system" claim to consider the political factors shaping the latter, but they do not approach this formation in terms of social class. As Marx contended, economists consider the economy as the production of things, not as social relationships of labor exploitation and resistance across a world space (Lukács 2000, p. 15). This economism—to substitute the computation of superficial economic data for the analysis of social determinations—and state-centrism even characterize courses on history, which fail to narrate the intersection of labor, ethnic, and women struggles in different political conjunctures. Or, in another positivist fashion,[9] courses on administrative law teach legal instruments—the national budgetary, state's police power, or public hearings—in isolation; without grasping how these state proceedings coerce the capitalist order, and how workers appropriate them to undermine such an order.

Rejecting a critical theory of theoretical practice, conservative education cannot grasp the theoretical innovations necessary to refute assumptions

---

[9] The academic system supports this production of specialized knowledge because it organizes curricula according to a stifling system of fragmented *cathedra* (professorships).

and resolve social problems. Paraphrasing on Neil Larsen's (2009) critique of mainstream pedagogy, conservative education applies theory externally to the objects of study it approaches. It refuses to find the critical theoretical possibilities present in the objects we teach and research, which conservative education always locates outside us. Thus, instead of becoming a dialectical practice directed at transforming our suffering, it produces fetishistic, instrumental contents for the market and the state. As Larsen contended, it does not matter whether the applied theory is "critical"—as sometimes happens in political theory courses—because the method is not. Our academic settings remain paralyzed in their rejection of self-reflection. On the contrary, the dialectical method conceives of theory as the self-knowledge of reality (Lukács 2000, p. 16). It aims to transform our subject of teaching (objects, agents, *and* place) by critically grasping its significance in relationship to the whole social process that theoretical imagination helps us to illuminate.

Cultural Studies and the Social Right to the General Strike

Critical realism and concrete imagination shape our cultural practices in La Matanza. As Nagual, a rock band listened by working-class youth, contends in *El Camino* [The Road], though we shouldn't believe in miracles, we should hopefully learn how "to fabricate them" (Nagual 2013, my translation).[10] In a Gramscian sense, leftist passive revolution—revolution from above—or a frontal working-class maneuver to revolutionize the state is unrealistic in La Matanza and elsewhere at the present. Nevertheless, in another Gramscian sense, we can hopefully take intellectual positions and set conditions to spark public debate on our common needs, resources, and potential for radical democracy. In other words, as Jacques Derrida observed on the social, *proletarian* right to critical interpretation, "there is a possibility of "general strike," a right analogous to that of general strike in any interpretative reading, the right to contest established law" (2002,

---

[10] Nagual takes its name from Mayan culture, according to which *nahuales* are powerful (natural, human, and animal) forces.

p. 271). For Derrida, this interpretative reading is directed to strike the "strongest authority" of the law, the authority of the state (2002, p. 271). On the other side, new forms of control transform and reinforce the authority of the state, sustained in the last two centuries on the spatial and discursive enclosures of disciplinary society, as Deleuze suggested in his postscript on the societies of control (1992).

Not much time will pass until "the installation of the new forces knocking at the door," Deleuze argued (1992, p. 4). However, the concentration of capital in the global North has delayed the complete establishment of the control, flexible mechanisms essential to both the state and capital accumulation in the South. A combination of forms of disciplinary and control societies rules the social formation. For example, the academic curricula are restricted to traditional disciplines that are devalued elsewhere, like the Political Science and Media Studies approaches I criticized. At the same time, educational managers know they need to move toward fluid, communicative, open, and even "affective" mechanisms of control. These modulations are essential to "integrate" the diverse "actors" around the academic setting, as well as to increase the production of research according to global standards. They are also fundamental to train youths into flexible, interdisciplinary approaches so they may work in different fields, or join the white-collar cadres specialized in new managerial ideologies, such as "new media" communications, informational politics, therapy or public policy management.[11]

Despite such efforts, however, academic managers cannot understand the contradictions spanning from the tectonic transformations in the social formation to which they also contribute. In my experience, in the global South I have observed that state managers are overwhelmed with positivist knowledge, ordinary signs of institutional status, and political compromises. Administrators' bourgeois contradiction consists in holding institutional leverage without controlling intellectual capital. This contradiction materializes weak links or institutional points of radical democratic disruption. In other words, educational managers need to employ

---

[11] For example, according to the World Bank (2008), Argentina should abandon traditional education for a model destined to train youths into flexible disciplines, favoring methods that guarantee rapid graduation.

the originality of our comprehensive knowledge, interpretative skills, and ductile approaches to produce alluring symbolic goods and interdisciplinary education in times of furious, implosive capitalist competition. It is in this blind spot of control that our (Latin American) cultural studies practices introduce a striking difference. Teaching cultural studies as a critique of global capitalism means to create public spaces, for a socialist-democratic project, within the very factories of capitalist education.

Works Cited

Althusser, L. (1979). *For Marx*. London: Verso.

Althusser, L. (2001). Ideology and Ideological State Apparatus (Notes Towards an Investigation). In L. Althusser (Ed.), *Lenin and Philosophy and Other Essays* (pp. 85–126). New York: Monthly Review Press. (Original work published 1971).

Boivin, M., Rosato, A., & Arribas, V. (2004). *Constructores de otredad: una introducción a la antropología social y cultural*. Buenos Aires: Editorial Antropofagia.

Deleuze, G. (1992). Postscript on the Societies of Control. *October, 59*, 3–7.

Deleuze, G., & Guattari, F. (2014). *A Thousand Plateaus: Capitalism and Schizophrenia*. London: Bloomsbury.

Derrida, J. (2002). Force of Law: The "Mystical Foundation of Authority". In G. Anidjar (Ed.), *Acts of Religion* (pp. 228–298). New York: Routledge.

El1. (2015, May 18). Scioli convocó a miles de jóvenes en la UNLaM con el rock y el deporte, *El1*, p. 3.

Fanon, F. (2008). *Black Skin, White Masks*. New York: Grove Press. (Original work published 1952).

García Canclini, N. (2004). *Diferentes, desiguales y desconectados: mapas de la interculturalidad*. Buenos Aires: Gedisa.

García Linera, Á. (2006). State Crisis and Popular Power. *New Left Review, 37*, 73–85.

González, H. (2011). *Kirchnerismo: una controversia cultural*. Colihue: Buenos Aires.

Gramsci, A. (2000). *The Antonio Gramsci Reader: Selected Writings 1916–1935* (D. Forgacs). New York: New York University Press.

Grimson, A. (2010). Culture and Identity: Two Different Notions. *Social Identities: Journal for the Study of Race, Nation and Culture, 16*(1), 63–79.

Horkheimer, M. (1989). Notes on Science and the Crisis. In S. E. Bronner & D. M. Kellner (Eds.), *Critical Theory and Society: A Reader* (pp. 52–57). New York: Routledge. (Original work published 1930).

Laclau, E., & Mouffe, C. (2001). *Hegemony and Socialist Strategy: Towards a Radical Democratic Politics* (2nd ed.). London: Verso.

Larsen, N. (2009). Literature, Immanent Critique, and the Problem of Standpoint. *Mediations: Journal of the Marxist Literary Group, 24*(2), 48–65.

Lukács, G. (2000). *History and Class Consciousness: Studies in Marxist Dialectics* (16th ed.). Cambridge, MA: The MIT Press. (Original work published 1968).

Marx, K. (1993). The Method of Political Economy. In K. Marx (Ed.), *Grundrisse: Foundations of the Critique of Political Economy* (pp. 100–108). London: Penguin. (Original work published 1939).

Nagual. (2013). El camino. In *Hacia la montaña* [CD]. Nagual. Available at http://www.nagualrock.com.ar/. Accessed 1 Apr 2018.

Robinson, W. I. (2008). *Latin America and Global Capitalism: A Critical Globalization Perspective*. Baltimore: The Johns Hopkins University Press.

Sader, E. (2011). *The New Mole: Paths of the Latin American Left*. London: Verso.

Sartori, G. (2002). *La política: lógica y método en las ciencias sociales*. Mexico City: Fondo de Cultura Económica.

Secretaría de Políticas Universitarias. (2012). *Anuario de estadísticas universitarias – Argentina 2012*. Buenos Aires: Ministerio de Educación de la Nación.

Smith, P. (1997). *Millennial Dreams: Contemporary Culture and Capital in the North*. London: Verso.

Svampa, M. (2008). The End of Kirchnerism. *New Left Review, 53*, 79–95.

Therborn, G. (2014). ¿Nuevas masas críticas? *New Left Review, 85*, 5–17.

UNLaM. (2015). *Daniel Scioli presentó la flamante policía local en la Universidad*. Available at http://www.unlam.edu.ar. Accessed 22 Apr 2015.

UNLaM. (n.d.) *Misión*. Available at http://www.unlam.edu.ar/index.php?seccion=2. Accessed 1 Apr 2018.

Webber, J. R., & Carr, B. (2013). *The New Latin American Left: Cracks in the Empire*. Lanham: Rowman & Littlefield.

Werner, R., & Aguirre, F. (2009). *Insurgencia obrera en la Argentina 1969–1976: clasismo, coordinadoras interfabriles y estrategias de la izquierda*. Buenos Aires: Ediciones IPS.

Williams, R. (1977). *Marxism and Literature*. Oxford: Oxford University Press.

Williams, R. (2001). *The Long Revolution*. Peterborough: Broadview Press. (Original work published 1961).

World Bank. (2008). *Argentina. Los jóvenes de hoy: un recurso latente para el desarrollo. Informe N° 38825*. Oficina de País: Buenos Aires.

Teaching Conjuncturally: Cultural Studies as the Practice of Conjunctural Analysis

Andrew Davis

Walk into any bookstore in the United States these days and, chances are, you will find a Cultural Studies section filled with a disparate range of titles loosely organized under the banner of "culture." It is easy to understand, then, why students often assume that *cultural studies* refers to any work that analyzes forms and practices of culture in general, or popular culture more specifically. This presents a set of problems not encountered by teachers of (for instance) biology or economics. In fact, the most persistent challenge I and others who share a commitment to a particular political-intellectual project called cultural studies face is getting students to understand what is meant by *cultural studies*. This is due in part to the

---

Portions of this chapter appeared in another form as "A Demonstration of Calculations, or, Cultural Studies as Conjunctural Analysis" in my doctoral dissertation—*The Problem of Sovereignty: Nations, Corporations and Power Relations*—for the Department of Communication at the University of North Carolina—Chapel Hill (UNC-CH) under the direction of Lawrence Grossberg.

A. Davis (✉)
Department of Communication, Appalachian State University, Boone, NC, USA
e-mail: davisag2@appstate.edu

© The Author(s) 2019
J. Aksikas et al. (eds.), *Cultural Studies in the Classroom and Beyond*,
https://doi.org/10.1007/978-3-030-25393-6_14

fact that, as a field, we are hesitant to define what it is we do—why it matters, what counts as cultural studies and (as importantly) what does not count as such. I do not presume to claim authority over what cultural studies should or should not be. My experience teaching Practices of Cultural Studies at UNC-CH, however, has led me to believe that students benefit most from a course designed around an understanding of cultural studies as the practice of conjunctural analysis.

In the following pages, I offer support for this perspective by explaining *conjunctural analysis* as it has developed in the wake of British Cultural Studies (i.e. the intellectual project associated with the Centre for Contemporary Cultural Studies in Birmingham, England) and discussing my experiences developing and teaching an undergraduate course around a practice of cultural studies as conjunctural analysis.[1] I begin by explaining the commitments regarding knowledge and knowledge production that underlie a definition of cultural studies as the practice of conjunctural analysis. From there, I demonstrate how this conceptual and analytical framework has been practically deployed in the development of an undergraduate course in cultural studies, titled COMM 350: Practices of Cultural Studies. After briefly discussing the design of the course's syllabus and reading assignments, I provide a description of the semester-long group research project the students in this course conduct as a foray into the difficult work of conjunctural analysis, detailing how the group project facilitates students' engagement with the practice. Ultimately, this chapter is written in conversation with Megan M. Wood's in this collection ("Conjuncturally Teaching: Cultural Studies Pedagogy Beyond Common Sense"). Her chapter situates the aims of the course I describe here within a perilous context for the promise of both education and the ideals of substantive democracy and offers insights into students' experiences with taking the course as we have designed it. They are best read together.

---

[1] I do not know who originally designed this course, but it is the introductory class for the Cultural Studies major at UNC-CH as advised by Lawrence Grossberg. Before adding my own developments to it, I served as Graduate Research Consultant (GRC) for the course as taught by Adam Rottinghaus. It has since been further developed by Megan M. Wood. My argument here is indebted to both Adam and Megan.

Cultural Studies and Conjuncture[2]

From the perspective outlined above, cultural studies begins with an analytical commitment to "radical contextuality" (Grossberg, "Wrestling with the Angels" 2)—an understanding of reality as being contingently relational, complex and always open to alteration. Each question or problem with which we are concerned is necessarily overdetermined and characterized by an open complexity wherein particular forces, objects, people and so on exist in contingent—non-essential, non-universal, yet also not relative—relations. As such, our mode of analysis must be determined by a commitment to understanding specific relations within specific contexts, instead of being determined by a particular theoretical or methodological commitment. In this way, "cultural studies is always making itself up, reconfiguring itself, in response to the changing configurations of power and the changing possibilities of struggle and resistance, possibility and transformation" (Grossberg, "Wrestling with the Angels" 1). Cultural studies—as the practice of conjunctural analysis—sets as its problematic a contextual system of relations of force characterized by complexity, contingency and overdetermination.[3]

---

[2] It is important to note here that there are a number of crucial distinctions between the Marxist (i.e. in the works of Althusser and Gramsci) and cultural studies (i.e. in the works of Hall and Grossberg) understandings of *conjuncture*. For Gramsci, the conjunctural is ephemeral, nearly incidental and (as such) of secondary importance to structural conditions, which Gramsci understands as being long-term and relatively stable (i.e. the *organic*). For Gramsci, then, conjunctural analysis looks at the "immediate social situation and the web of different social forces and relations at a given moment" in support of tactical and strategic political action (Jaafar Aksikas, personal correspondence). It is, in this sense, distinct from structural analysis, which is concerned with the more constant, determinant features of social organization and historical development. For Hall and Grossberg, however, the conjuncture is precisely the level of abstraction between the immediate and the structural. In this sense, conjunctural analysis is concerned with both the structural and the immediate in order to understand how the contradictions and crises that characterize the immediate situation came to be and what role they play in organic transformations. It is this second (i.e. cultural studies) understanding of conjuncture and conjunctural analysis that I privilege here.

[3] *Problematic* refers to "the objective internal reference system" of a concept or theory that serves as a framework for the "questions commanding the answers given by" that concept or theory (Louis Althusser qtd. in Joshua Barkan 14). In framing the questions, such a reference system consequently limits the possible answers that can be generated by a given concept or theory, thus overdetermining their potential utility.

Cultural studies reconfigures itself analytically from context to context through the practice of *conjunctural analysis*—"analysis which is historically and contextually specific. An exploration of the assemblage, coming together or articulation of particular forces, determinations or logics at specific times and spaces" (Barker 382). Different contexts can be overdetermined by the same vectors of force, but the ways in which these forces become articulated to each other (and the mechanisms and operations by which these forces manifest) depend on the historical and social conditions of the context itself. In order to fully unpack the implications of such a commitment, we need to understand what is meant by the term *conjuncture*.

The concept of *conjuncture* originated as a key political concept in Marxist theory. "As Marx and Engels [thought through] complex and historically transforming social relations in the perspective of a *revolutionary* praxis, they consistently [aimed] to produce a concrete, non-reductionist analysis of specific conjunctures and constellations […] and their structural conditions" (Koivisto and Lahtinen 268). This concept was developed by later Marxist theorists as a means of specifying "the changing forms and contingent interactions of the historical process, while remaining nonetheless anchored in a longer-term hypothesis about the general nature of process in the modern epoch" (Justin Rosenberg qtd. in Callinicos 355). The purpose of developing the concept was in part an attempt to grapple with the "manifest misalignment" between "classical deterministic and economistic Marxist models of change" and the political realities of the twentieth century (Rustin 18). The development of the concept of *conjuncture* is due largely to V. I. Lenin, Antonio Gramsci, Louis Althusser and Nicos Poulantzas—all of whom were concerned with the conjuncture as both an object for concrete, historical-materialist analysis and a point of political intervention.[4]

---

[4] There are (as noted in Koivisto and Lahtinen) other understandings of the concept in Marxist theory, primarily: (1) as being composed of ephemeral surface-level phenomena with the structure of capitalist production being essential and (2) in a narrow, economistic sense as being purely descriptive of a particular historical moment. Additionally, *conjuncture* is understood in business and economics as "the mechanical interaction of law-like cycles," and is used to analyze investments, policies, historical cycles and crisis management (Jessop 12). These perspectives have no bearing, however, on the use of *conjuncture* in cultural studies.

What has come out of the long tradition of Marxist thinking is an understanding of *conjuncture* as indicating:

'the exact balance of forces, [the] state of overdetermination of the contradictions at any given moment to which political tactics must be applied.' Unlike conjuncture in the sense of fluctuation [or in the sense of ephemeral surface-level phenomena], eminently compatible with various teleological philosophies of history, the concept of conjuncture in its developed form is decisively anti-teleological, as well as firmly opposed to economic or class-reductionism. Social changes, also of a structural type, take place in and through conjunctures with many determinations. As an analytical tool, the concept of conjuncture can expand the capacity to act politically by helping to examine the conditions of a political intervention in their complexity, that is, to trace the displacements and condensations to different sorts of contradictions, and thus open up possibilities for action. (Koivisto and Lahtinen 267)

The uptake of *conjuncture* in cultural studies begins with Stuart Hall, whose work is based on (but moves decidedly beyond) the contributions of Gramsci, Althusser and Poulantzas. Hall's understanding begins with the imperative to look reality unflinchingly in the face, regardless of our theoretical presuppositions or political inclinations—to figure out where we are, how we got here and how to re-articulate present conditions to make better futures. Hall considered a conjuncture to be at once political, cultural, ideological and economic, rather than as determinately or predominantly economic. This move beyond the economic preoccupation of Marxist theory attempts to "grasp the 'condensation' of the contradictions that 'are moving according to very different tempos' in the 'particular historical moment' that 'defines a conjuncture'" (Koivisto and Lahtinen 274). For cultural studies, a conjuncture is characterized by "the accumulation and condensation"—the fusing "into a ruptural unity"—of *various* and *different* problems and contradictions within an existing social order, not just political ones (Hay, Hall and Grossberg 16). Moreover, a conjuncture is "a point where different temporalities—and more specifically, *the tensions, antagonisms and contradictions which they carry*—begin to come together" (Clarke, "Of Crises and Conjunctures"

342). As Hall reminds us, it is also where these temporalities fracture—with all their tensions, antagonisms and contradictions.

The analytical move to the conjuncture is intended to help us confront the multiplicity of determinations and contradictions at work in a specific historical formation. Confronting these determinations and contradictions helps us understand both the articulation of organic forces within which a conjuncture operates and by which a crisis calls a conjuncture into existence. This, in turn, helps us understand how the conjuncture operates within organic formations and epochal transformations. In analytical terms, "thinking conjuncturally involves 'clustering' or assembling elements into a formation. However, there is no simple unity, no single 'movement' here, evolving teleologically" (Stuart Hall qtd. in Koivisto and Lahtinen 275).

Rather than seeking causal or deterministic explanations of historical (i.e. organic) transformation in a generalized canon of theories and concepts, cultural studies focuses on the mechanisms and operations of power within specific contexts and employs a variety of concepts and theories based on their analytical value for that context. "Concepts—whether old or new—too often allow us to think we understand the world before we do. We must use concepts but only and always in conversation with the demands of the material realities of the actual" (Grossberg, "Cultural Studies and Deleuze-Guattari, Part 1" 19).

> A conjuncture is constituted by, at, and as the articulation of multiple, overlapping, competing, reinforcing, etc., lines of force and transformation, destabilization and (re-) stabilization, with differing temporalities and spatialities, producing a potentially but never actually chaotic assemblage of articulations of contradictions and contestations. Thus, it is always a kind of totality, always temporary, complex, and fragile, that one takes hold of through analytical and political work. (Grossberg, *Cultural Studies in the Future Tense* 41)

A conjuncture, then, is not something that exists as an object independently of its construction through analytical choices—choices which are at once epistemological and political. Epistemologically speaking, conjunctural analysis presupposes that "knowledge is understood as an act within the world rather than a representation of the world" (Grossberg, *Cultural Studies in the Future Tense* 57). We assemble a conjuncture through the articulation of contingent, contradictory and fluid forces that converge in a particular problematic or set of problematics in relation to an organic crisis. This type of intellectual practice requires a "conjunctive logic of multiplicity" which can account for the contradictory complexity of the operations of power on people's lives (Grossberg, "Learning from Stuart Hall" 6). The mechanisms and operations of power upon material reality are socially and historically provisional. "Specific historical moments are the site of entanglements between multiple formations and tendencies," thus requiring a serious consideration of analysis on the ways in which "the residual and the emergent" forces become articulated to "the dominant struggles" of the context instead of focusing solely on those dominant struggles (Clarke, "Of Crises and Conjunctures" 340). The political character of conjunctural analysis arises from this understanding as a commitment to construct knowledge that tells a compelling narrative about the complexity of reality (while always recognizing the inevitable failure of such a project)—all with the expressed goal of producing change in the world. These are the epistemological and political foundations on which the project of conjunctural analysis as understood within cultural studies is built. The great value of a conjunctural perspective is not simply that it allows us to analyze complex determinate relations within specific socio-historical contexts (although it certainly does allow this) but that such analysis can serve as a basis for understanding the relation of the conjunctural to organic transformations in ways that avoid essentialism, teleological determinism and economic reductionism.

Conjunctural Analysis

As with the concept of conjuncture, there are variations between Marxist and cultural studies versions of conjunctural analysis. Marxist conjunctural analysis tends to be more temporal and causal in orientation. For both Gramsci and Althusser, it is an attempt to understand the causes and movements of problems within a conjuncture while remaining "anchored in a general theory of the abstract tendencies of the capitalist mode of production" (Callinicos 355). Cultural studies, on the other hand, understands that the abstract tendencies of capitalist production are only one factor in the development of organic forms as indicative of epochal transformations (i.e. long-term historical developments such as "Modernity"). They are also only one factor in the operations and mechanisms of power as they affect "the ordinary lives of located and embodied subjects" (Stacey 45).

This is what characterizes conjunctural analysis as the work of exploring the articulation of particular forces into assemblages, with an eye to identifying "how the balance of forces is being worked on, shaped, directed in the search for a 'solution' and a 'way forward'" (Clarke, "Still Policing the Crisis?" 125).[5] Conjunctural analysis, then, is a theoretical-analytical-political practice (Gunkel), guided by a conjunctive logic wherein "each additional clause transforms the meanings and effects of all the previous ones" (Grossberg, *Cultural Studies in the Future Tense* 17). Taken together, these considerations direct us to the major components and operations of conjunctural analysis: context, articulation, problematic and a concern with political utility.

It is this notion of context that indicates the strength of conjunctural analysis as practiced in cultural studies over that of Marxist traditions. To focus on a context is to be concerned with the "specificity of particular practices" in socio-historical locations (Slack 117). Within the practice of conjunctural analysis, a context is constructed through the process of "radical contextuality" (Grossberg, "Standing on a Bridge" 318)—the analytical mapping of the relations of force that produce certain conditions of power within a closure of social reality. "The work [of radical contextuality] is done by historical specificity, by understanding what is specific about certain moments, and how those moments come together, how different tendencies fuse and form a kind of [temporarily sustained]

---

[5] *Articulation* refers to "the contingent connection of different elements that, when connected in a particular way, form a specific unity," with elements understood as ideas, things, words, institutions, practices, and/or affects (Slack and Wise 127). *Assemblage* refers to "the ways that these practices, representations, experiences, and affects articulate to take a particular dynamic form [...] a particular constellation of articulations that selects, draws together, stakes out and envelops a territory that exhibits some tenacity and effectivity" (Slack and Wise 129).

configuration of contradictions" (Hall and Back 664). As an object of analysis *context* refers to the historically specific, concrete yet contingent "organization—by power—of the social formation as a configuration of unequal positions and relations" (Grossberg, "Does Cultural Studies Have Futures?" 3).

Analytically speaking, the context is constructed as an assemblage (i.e. a specific yet contingent unity of ideas, practices, etc.) through the practice of articulation. In a basic sense, *"articulation can be understood as the contingent connection of different elements that, when connected in a particular way, form a specific unity"* (Slack and Wise 152). But this understanding carries with it a multiplicity of implications—theoretical, epistemological and political. Theoretically speaking, articulation can be thought of as a theory of contexts and a way of making and remaking them—a way of thinking about social formations without lapsing into forms of reductionism or essentialism (Slack). Epistemologically, articulation serves two purposes. First, the practice of articulation helps to fragment perceived unities in order to demonstrate how social structures are composed of "correspondences, non-correspondences and contradictions" (Slack 113). The articulation of an assemblage "begins by discovering the heterogeneity, the difference, the fractures in" what is perceived to be whole (Grossberg, *Cultural Studies in the Future Tense* 22). In other words, articulation begins with the dis-articulation of relations that have been made to seem normal, essential and/or necessary. Second, articulation becomes a project of reassembling those relations into different unities that can produce (however temporary and contingent) other (and hopefully more equitable and productive) possibilities for social relations. This practice of re-articulation serves as an attempt to resettle "the social, political, economic and cultural contradictions in any particular" context in order to analyze the conjuncture ("Editorial" 5). Articulation, then, is the epistemological process of dis-articulation and re-articulation. In this sense, articulation is not only a method of cultural studies, but also a method of constructing reality—"the project of looking at the continuous production of relations which are never guaranteed in advance" and, as such, are open to contestation and intervention (Grossberg, "Cultural Studies and/in New Worlds" 4). This speaks to the political implications of articulation, whereby articulation becomes a strategy for pushing to the forefront the mechanisms and operations of power in a given social formation in order to find tactics for intervening in and contesting those mechanisms and operations (Slack).

But in and of themselves, articulations do not constitute a context as a conjuncture. It is only when these articulations are considered as overdetermined lines of force in an assemblage of power that they can be said to constitute a conjuncture. Epistemologically, the conjuncture trains our focus on the ways in which "an organization of power is being constructed through the disarticulation and rearticulation of relations" (Grossberg, *Cultural Studies in the Future Tense* 24). After all, power is constantly being (re)produced in different contexts under different conditions through different mechanisms and operations; it is "complexly and contradictorily organized, along multiple axes and dimensions that cannot be reduced to one another" (Grossberg, *Cultural Studies in the Future Tense* 29). As such, modes of power are themselves assemblages of mechanisms, operations and terrains of struggle within and through which force relations can be articulated anew into different contexts, which highlights the necessity of maintaining a commitment to radical contextuality throughout the process of analysis.

The analytical assembling of the problematic "is what constitutes the conjuncture" in that the problematic reproduces the accumulated and condensed articulations of the force of a crisis as articulated to a particular context. Although the problematic is determined through the process of conjunctural analysis, "what constitutes the unity of the conjuncture then is its problematic(s), which [are] usually lived (but not necessarily experienced per se) as a social crisis of sorts" (Grossberg, *Cultural Studies in the Future Tense* 41). One's understanding of the problematic determines the questions on can ask about "the messy and complex political realities of the world," as well as the methods and types of empirical evidence that are required to grapple with those questions (Grossberg, *Cultural Studies in the Future Tense* 52). To say that a conjuncture is constituted by a problematic is not to say that a problematic is the essence of a conjuncture; any problematic is the result of a choice of how to analyze the articulation of contradictions and crises that become "lived as a singular political crisis or struggle" (ibid). The construction (at once epistemological and political) of the problematic determines the socio-historical context one then seeks to further analyze.

The insistence on radical contextuality—as a simultaneous working-through of context, articulation and problematic—leads to an understanding of conjunctural analysis as a methodological framework for mapping and constructing conjunctures through practices of dis- and re-articulation, the purpose of which is to "configure a larger structure of relationships, contradictions and contestations" (Grossberg, "Modernity and Commensuration" 313).[6] A conjuncture is not a historical moment but a "condensation, an *accumulation* of tendencies, forces, antagonisms and contradictions" (Clarke, "Of Crises and Conjunctures" 341). This type of analysis immerses us in the complexity of contingently articulated relations in hopes of mapping out the fractures, gaps and uncertainties of existing power relations.

> Mapping a conjuncture makes it possible to begin to see where and how interventions might be desirable and successful, and how different inter-ventions might influence change in one direction or another. [...] In this way, cultural studies acknowledges that scholarship does more than merely report on or describe what is supposedly already out there, but always nec-essarily intervenes in the production of knowledge about the struggles that constitute the social formation, thereby contributing potentially to cultural change. (Slack and Wise 218)

This is not to suggest, however, that the politics of cultural studies (as the practice of conjunctural analysis) are presupposed (Grossberg, *Cultural Studies in the Future Tense*). Instead, the political commitment of conjunctural analysis is the "attempt to understand and intervene into the relations of culture and power" (Grossberg, "Cultural Studies and/in New Worlds" 2), while constantly placing "our own assumptions, obser-vations and values to the test of empirical complexities and political pos-sibilities" (Grossberg, "Cultural Studies and Deleuze-Guattari, Part 1" 12). Conjunctural analysis is a strategic, tactical and (hopefully) logistical politics without guarantees—one that takes stock of the relational

---

[6] "Structure" is understood here as a system of processes rather than as an object.

complexity of the terrain of power, the points of weakness among lines of force that characterize the terrain, the available resources for exploiting those weaknesses and the moves necessary for (re)producing vectors of force in ways that do not reproduce the existing power relations of subordination and domination—always with a self-reflexive humility that recognizes our own positions as limited, contingent and open to revision in light of new evidence and better perspectives. Conjunctural analysis is a way of answering Marx's imperative to move between levels of abstraction in order to get from the empirical to the concrete in a specific socio-historical context—always with the question of power in mind.

Designing a Course Around Conjunctural Analysis

You should be aware first of all that Cultural Studies is NOT the "study of cultures." Rather, Cultural Studies is an interdisciplinary approach that takes up the context of any given moment in space (country, state, neighborhood, corporation, etc.) and time. And though Cultural Studies has been an arena where popular culture and media have been heavily explored, one might just as easily find a scholar of cultural studies "doing" economics, feminisms, literary studies, anthropology or otherwise. Methodologically, Cultural Studies focuses on what is known as conjunctural analysis—analysis of the interrelation of particular problems in a particular time and social space as they relate to questions of power.

This was the first paragraph of the Course Overview in the syllabus for Practices of Cultural Studies when I taught it.[7] Although it requires explanation, it does contain a consideration of the elements involved in

---

[7] Since then, Wood has altered the opening slightly to read: "*Practices in Cultural Studies* is an introduction to the intellectual and political practice of Cultural Studies. Cultural Studies is NOT the 'study of culture' in the way you might imagine; rather, it is an effort to understand the context of any given moment in space and time. It investigates how people's everyday lives are structured and organized in contradictory ways by social, economic, political, and cultural relations of power, as well as the historical possibilities of changing those lived realities—the ways we imagine(d) life could be otherwise. Methodologically, Cultural Studies uses various tools to do this work, an assemblage of approaches more formally called conjunctural analysis. Topically, cultural studies scholars have variously taken up popular culture, feminism and antiracism, literature and film,

developing and teaching a course on cultural studies as the practice of conjunctural analysis. The first objective of this statement is to direct students away from the common assumption that cultural studies is about studying culture. Second, it orients them to the two core components of conjunctural analysis: context and power. Admittedly, this statement is insufficient to explain *cultural studies* to a group of undergraduates who have never encountered it, but it achieves the necessary task of unsettling their presuppositions while also getting them to begin to think about knowledge production that is problem- or question-driven rather than object-oriented. In order to demonstrate how this practically works in the classroom, the rest of this chapter discusses syllabus design, reading assignments and student research projects.

In addition to a discussion of expectations that are part of the first week of any class, my version of Practices of Cultural Studies introduces students to *communication* and *culture* by assigning early on James Carey's "A Cultural Approach to Communication." The benefit of Carey's ritual (or cultural) model of communication is that it helps students understand that communication is not simply the transmission of information, but the ritual construction of cultural reality. This is important for students to grasp from the onset because (in this sense) communication and culture are recursively related within the construction of contexts. Beyond the course introduction, Practices of Cultural Studies is divided into two main parts: "What Is Cultural Studies?" and "Defining the Conjuncture." "What Is Cultural Studies?" defines the project of cultural studies as conjunctural analysis by exploring its origins at the Centre for Contemporary Cultural Studies (CCCS), introducing students to key vocabulary and discussing the theoretical and conceptual foundations of the field. In this section, we look at how scholars have attempted to answer the questions of what makes cultural studies different from traditional academic disciplines and how one actually goes about practicing cultural studies. In addition to the original working papers from CCCS, texts that have proven especially useful in this section include the introductory chapter of Chris Barker's *Cultural Studies: Theory and Practice*, and "Cultural

---

economics, technology, and other areas of import as necessary for studying the interrelation of problems in a particular time and social spaces."

Studies: Two Paradigms" and "The Emergence of Cultural Studies and the Crisis of the Humanities" by Stuart Hall.

This provides a framework for considering the theoretical background of cultural studies, especially the historical formation of the discipline and how that formation relates to the production of knowledge. Through readings such as Stuart Hall's "Signification, Representation, Ideology: Althusser and the Post-structuralist Debates" and Lawrence Grossberg's "The Heart of Cultural Studies" (a chapter in *Cultural Studies in the Future Tense*), students begin to develop an understanding of what it means to think about and study a conjuncture or a context rather than an object. The "What Is Cultural Studies?" section of the course ends with an actual case study in the tradition of British Cultural Studies. For example, *Doing Cultural Studies: The Story of the Walkman* by Paul du Gay et al. and *Policing the Crisis: Mugging, the State and Law & Order* by Stuart Hall et al. are good representations of what it means to think conjuncturally and how to approach a cultural analysis. In Wood's version of the course, she added a sub-unit within "What Is Cultural Studies?" called "Doing Cultural Studies." This set of readings (which include, for instance, Ann Gray's *Research Practice for Cultural Studies* and Rachel Hall's short essay "Letting the Object of Study Lead: A Cultural Studies Ethics") offers students the opportunity to explore some practical considerations about contextual issues like method and voice as part of the work of conjunctural analysis. This unit helps students to understand the difference between "methodology" and the radically contextual practice of conjunctural analysis.

The remainder of the semester is dedicated to the section "Defining the Conjuncture," which takes students through a range of problem spaces one might possibly need to consider when analyzing a conjuncture (e.g. discourse, publics, race, popular culture, politics, gender, economics, history, labor, technology and class). Of course, not every conceivable problem space can be considered in one semester. Choices regarding the nature of these problem spaces and the readings selected to represent them vary according to a number of factors, including the particular teacher's own research expertise, students' areas of interest and the relevance of particular problem spaces to current events. Regardless of which problem spaces are covered in a semester, the point of this section is to help students develop an understanding of the complex and contingent articulation of any context by having them engage with a variety of theories, concepts, methods and perspectives. I have found (and Wood agrees) that combining scholarly work with popular literature and art is especially useful for helping students understand the connection between theory and everyday life.

For example, during the section on popular culture, I have students read theory—specifically "What Is Popular Culture?" from John Storey's *Cultural Theory and Popular Culture: An Introduction* and Stuart Hall's "Notes on Deconstructing the Popular"—alongside Hunter S. Thompson's *Hell's Angels: A Strange and Terrible Saga*. The main benefit of bringing in a non-scholarly work such as Thompson's is that it demonstrates the relevance of conjunctural thinking beyond academic practices. In *Hell's Angels*, Thompson brings together sociology, popular film, journalism, ethnography and political culture to construct an understanding of a particular context in America in a way that is more accessible to undergraduates than much of academic writing. As another example, Wood has paired classic readings in cultural studies on youth, style and generational politics with popular media by or about "millennials" and "Gen Z." In addition to the readings, we also engage with forms of popular culture that speak to the role of popular culture in terms of both the organization of social relations and practices of everyday life (e.g. the Banksy documentary *Exit through the Gift Shop* and episodes of Charlie Brooker's *Black Mirror* or *How TV Ruined Your Life*).

Organizing a cultural studies course in this way is not only beneficial in terms of the knowledge that students gain, but also in terms of the knowledge they produce. The centerpiece of Practices of Cultural Studies is a semester-long group research project. In order to provide a concrete understanding of how this process works, I will combine an overview of the process with a discussion of a specific group project that resulted from the class—a group I refer to here as the Detroit Group, for reasons that will become clear.

Students are divided into groups of four or five based upon their stated research interests. During the second week of class, students are asked to turn in a list of about four topics that they are interested in studying and are then divided into groups based on overlapping areas of interest. At this point, topics tend to be quite general (e.g. gender, music and technology). The process of formulating research questions begins with each group discussing the specific phenomena and/or issues that led each student to list a particular topic. In the case of the Detroit Group, the members were brought together initially through a shared interest in technology, although their specific interests ranged from electronic/noise music, information and data, coding and the repurposing of old/broken technologies for use beyond the intention of their original design and production.

This initial step leads to the first of a series of checkpoints that each group is required to submit at regular intervals throughout the semester. The first checkpoint describes the group's proposed project, providing a rough sketch of the ideas, contradictions, problems or phenomena that the group wants to tackle. Groups are given feedback on their ideas so that they can narrow and refine the project proposals. The second checkpoint is a revised proposal that formulates a specific yet open-ended research question, one concerned with *how* something occurs, not *why* it does so. For the third checkpoint, students meet with either the teacher or Graduate Research Consultant to strategize the development of their research question into a research plan. For the Detroit Group, discussion of the members' various interests led to an understanding that each of their specific interests could be addressed by focusing on various technological imaginaries concerning the city of Detroit, Michigan. For example, one student highlighted the role of Detroit artists in the development of electronic and techno music. Another became interested in how the residents of certain housing developments in the city repurposed old machinery for urban farming. Another brought up the ways in which images of Detroit are constructed in television ads for the automobile industry. The convergence of these concerns resulted in a research question based on the difference between how a particular image of Detroit is constructed in public discourse (e.g. advertising, film and journalism) and the actualities of everyday life for Detroiters as indicated by the technological practices mentioned above.

Each of the remaining checkpoints deals with essential components of the research process: a project rationale (i.e. why and to whom the project matters, as well as the implications of the research question on the research practices/methods required to deal with the question); a background summary of the context of the project (i.e. a consideration of how the issues relevant to the research question have been discussed in academic, journalistic and popular sources); an annotated bibliography explaining the relevance of the sources to the project and how the project contributes to existing knowledge; an outline of the groups methodology; a summary of the theoretical literature to which their research is relevant and an outline with initial findings. These checkpoints serve two main purposes: they (1) teach students the components and stages of rigorous research and (2) ensure that consistent progress is made throughout the semester, culminating in a completed research project. Although most of these projects take the form of traditional research papers, I have allowed students to experiment with the form their final projects take, as long as the form is appropriate to the content.

In order to understand how this works, I want to turn briefly back to the research project developed by the Detroit Group. Regarding project rationale, the group was able to make a convincing case that their research would be of interest not only to residents of Detroit, but also fans of electronic music, practitioners of urban agriculture and scholars in urban studies and media & technology studies. The group designed and wrote each section to appeal to each particular audience, but with the overarching goal of the entire project being understandable to a lay audience while demonstrating the connections between each section. One section dealt with the construction of a technological imaginary in public discourse of Detroit as a city in ruins—decayed, deindustrialized and riven with crime, poverty and racialized divisions. For evidence of this, the group looked at a variety of sources, including news reports, advertisements, depictions of the city in film and television (e.g. *RoboCop*) and social media posts falling into a category commonly referred to as "ruin porn" (i.e. tourists taking photos of decayed urban areas in which people actually live). The rest of the research project analyzed actual practices of everyday life that contradict this popular narrative about the history and current condition of life in the city (e.g. the development of techno music and the repurposing of discarded industrial machinery and other old technologies in the recreation of urban space). The final project itself was presented as an interactive digital zine, which presented each section with embedded hyperlinks to academic and journalistic sources for more detailed information, online video content referring to popular culture representations of Detroit and a musical timeline demonstrating the city's role in electronic music.

This is but one of a number of vital projects that were developed during my time teaching the course. For instance, one group researched the experiences of migrants from Sudan, adjusting to living and working conditions in Durham, NC. Much of their research consisted of interviews, so they produced a short documentary video that incorporated these interviews with a discussion of contemporary conditions in Sudan and the process of migrating from there through Europe to the United States. Other examples include a podcast about the experiences of female executives working in the music industry in Los Angeles and a research paper about the political decisions involved in the disbursement of lottery revenue to county school boards in North Carolina. Regardless of the form or subject matter, these projects present analyses of power relations in particular contexts and their overdetermining role in the experiences of everyday life in these contexts. Ultimately, this type of analysis results from the organization of the course around the concept of *conjuncture* and the practices of conjunctural analysis.

Of course, the course discussed in the previous pages is an open-ended framework. We regularly revise the course based on changes in both our own understanding of conjunctural analysis and our students' experiences with learning such a form of analysis. Through all of the revisions to Practices of Cultural Studies, we have become more convinced that organizing the course around *conjuncture*—from syllabus design to reading assignments to student projects—best serves our students' understanding of cultural studies as a political-intellectual project. Megan M. Wood discusses this in more detail in "Conjuncturally Teaching: Cultural Studies Pedagogy Beyond Common Sense."

Works Cited

Barkan, J. (2013). *Corporate Sovereignty: Law and Government under Capitalism.* Minneapolis: University of Minnesota Press.

Barker, C. (2000). *Cultural Studies: Theory and Practice*. London: Sage.

Callinicos, A. (2005). Epoch and Conjuncture in Marxist Political Economy. *International Politics, 42*, 353–363.

Clarke, J. (2008). Still Policing the Crisis? *Crime Media Culture, 4*(1), 123–139.

Clarke, J. (2010). Of Crises and Conjunctures: The Problem of the Present. *Journal of Communication Inquiry, 34*(4), 337–354.

Davison, S., & Jonathan, R. (2010). Editorial: Everything to Play for. *Soundings, 44*, 4–9.

Grossberg, L. (1993). Cultural Studies and/in New Worlds. *Critical Studies in Mass Communication, 10*(1), 1–22.

Grossberg, L. (2006). Does Cultural Studies Have Futures? Should It? (or, What's the Matter with New York?). *Cultural Studies, 20*(1), 1–32.

Grossberg, L. (2010a). *Cultural Studies in the Future Tense*. Durham: Duke University Press.

Grossberg, L. (2010b). Modernity and Commensuration: A Reading of the Contemporary (Economic) Crisis. *Cultural Studies, 24*(3), 295–332.

Grossberg, L. (2010c). Standing on a Bridge: Rescuing Economies from Economists. *Journal of Communication Inquiry, 34*(4), 316–336.

Grossberg, L. (2014). Cultural Studies and Deleuze-Guattari, Part 1. *Cultural Studies, 28*(1), 1–28.

Grossberg, L. (2015). Learning from Stuart Hall, Following the Path with Heart. *Cultural Studies, 29*(1), 3–11.

Grossberg, Lawrence. (Forthcoming). Wrestling with the Angels: Cultural Studies in Dark Times (Cultural Studies and Deleuze-Guattari, Part 3). In Eric Maigret & Martin Laurent (Eds.), *Cultural Studies Beyond Identity*. Presses Universitaires de Lyon.

Gunkel, A. H. (2011). On *Cultural Studies in the Future Tense*: Pedagogy and Political Work in Cultural Studies. *Communication and Critical/Cultural Studies, 8*(3), 323–329.

Hall, S., & Back, L. (2009). In Conversation: At Home and Not at Home. *Cultural Studies, 23*(4), 658–687.

Hay, J., Hall, S., & Grossberg, L. (2013). Interview with Stuart Hall, June 12, 2012. *Communication and Critical/Cultural Studies, 10*(1), 10–33.

Jessop, B. (2012). Left Strategy. *Transform: European Journal for Alternative Thinking and Political Dialogue, 10*, 8–17.

Koivisto, J., & Lahtinen, M. (2012). Historical-Critical Dictionary of Marxism: Conjuncture, Politico-Historical. *Historical Materialism, 20*(1), 267–277.

Rustin, M. (2009). Reflections on the Present: A Conjunctural Analysis of the Current Global Financial Crisis. *Soundings, 43*, 18–34.

Slack, J. D. (1996). The Theory and Method of Articulation in Cultural Studies. In D. Morley & K. H. Chen (Eds.), *Stuart Hall: Critical Dialogues in Cultural Studies* (pp. 113–129). London: Routledge.

Slack, J. D., & MacGregor Wise, J. (2015). *Culture and Technology: A Primer* (2nd ed.). New York: Peter Lang.

Stacey, J. (2015). The Unfinished Conversations of Cultural Studies. *Cultural Studies, 29*(1), 43–50.

Conjuncturally Teaching: Cultural Studies Pedagogy Beyond Common Sense

Megan M. Wood

It is difficult to imagine a more urgent moment than this one—marked by an assemblage of crises of knowledge, agency, public memory, politics, and more—for developing critical pedagogies able to confront the challenges facing us. In the context of the U.S. academic community, I've seen this urgency manifest in a number of ways. For example, consider the emergence of what N.D.B. Connolly calls the "#syllabus" movement,[1]

This essay is most indebted to my mentor and friend, Larry Grossberg, who bears the greatest responsibility for gifting me Cultural Studies. Whether or not he agrees with my words and ideas, his presence in my life saturates them all. I also thank my fellow COMMrades at the University of North Carolina at Chapel Hill, who regularly influence my practice—my learning-doing-teaching—of Cultural Studies. Great and many thanks also to the editors, Jaafar Aksikas, Sean Johnson Andrews, and Donald Hedrick, whose diligence made this piece possible.

[1] "2.0" or "3.0" versions of these syllabi are sometimes authored by others who mean to rectify egregious omissions in previous iterations, or offer disciplinary- or topic-specific spins on the original crisis/issue. Katie Pearce, "Understanding Trumpism: Syllabus Co-Compiled by Johns Hopkins

M. M. Wood (✉)
University of North Carolina Chapel Hill, Chapel Hill, NC, USA
e-mail: megwg@live.unc.edu

© The Author(s) 2019
J. Aksikas et al. (eds.), *Cultural Studies in the Classroom and Beyond*,
https://doi.org/10.1007/978-3-030-25393-6_15

279

where academics and publishers circulate mock course syllabi (typically, organized reading lists) in response to significant cultural phenomena or current events such as the election of Donald Trump, the Black Lives Matter movement, the Standing Rock protests, or the "#MeToo movement." Additionally, online and conference-based pedagogical discussion forums often feature anxious debates on whether and how one should "be political" or "teach (with) political topics" in the classroom in a moment where it seems both difficult to do (given the present hostility toward educators and education) and difficult to get by without doing. These are certainly useful—and crucial—points of departure. However, in the proliferation of products like these (reading lists, stories of political "successes or failures" in classroom conversations), I get the sense that, in times of national and cultural crisis, it is easy for (critical) pedagogy to become limited to a question of how teachers can immediately and emergently respond to this collectively felt sense of crisis—how do we satisfactorily answer our students' questions about specific and politically charged events? What existing tools (readings, theories, emotional speeches by media personalities) should we round up to arm them and ourselves with? All too often, this is framed by other questions: How do we teach to win for "our side"? Or, "How do we help teaching feel better or more comfortable for ourselves as teachers or for our students in these difficult times?"

This, I argue, is not the sense of pedagogy with which Cultural Studies operates.[2] In fact, it is moments of collectively felt crisis in which Cultural Studies has historically emerged and taken hold (in various national con-

---

Historian Goes Viral Post-Election," *Hub* December 16, 2016, https://hub.jhu.edu/2016/12/09/connolly-trump-syllabus/

[2] In this essay, I capitalize "Cultural Studies" as a way of indicating my reference to a particular version of cultural studies: the political-intellectual project typically first associated with the Centre for Contemporary Cultural Studies in Birmingham, England that was/is primarily concerned with "describing and intervening in the ways cultural practices are produced within, inserted into, and operate in the everyday life of human beings and social formations, so as to reproduce, struggle against, and perhaps transform the existing structures of power. ... It investigates how people are empowered and disempowered by the particular structures and forces that organize their everyday lives in contradictory ways, and how their (everyday) lives are themselves articulated to and by the trajectories of economic, social, cultural, and political power." This version of Cultural Studies understands itself as "responsible to the changing context (changing geographical, historical, political, intellectual and institutional conditions) in which it works." Lawrence Grossberg, *Cultural Studies in the Future Tense* (Durham, N.C.: Duke University Press, 2010), 8–9.

texts and not necessarily in formal educational institutions) as an intellectual formation premised precisely on a different kind of relationship with pedagogy.[3] Cultural studies does not *have* a pedagogy, it *is* a pedagogy: its purpose, through its intellectual work and within the conditions of its given context, is to invigorate critical thinking and praxis, knowledge production, and change in new and important ways. In this sense of pedagogy, the classroom is but one site within a larger (and inherently complex and ever-changing) pedagogical terrain where people learn to imagine and define themselves as social and political agents, and where struggles over defining and organizing politics happen.[4]

To treat Cultural Studies in the first instance as a pedagogical sensibility (rather than, perhaps, its usual primary tags as an "intellectual project" or a "political commitment") is, I think, in line with Raymond Williams's reflections on the futures of Cultural Studies just prior to his passing. His remarks concerned what he saw to be the constitutive core of Cultural Studies, its "crucial theoretical invention," which should now be legible as Cultural Studies' particular version of conjunctural analysis—a form of analysis which links thinking and pedagogy and which involved constantly subjecting the practice of Cultural Studies itself to its own intellectual and analytical frameworks. He writes:

> I want to begin with the quite central theoretical point which to me is at the heart of cultural studies but which has not always been remembered in it and this is—to use contemporary terms instead of the rather more informal terms in which it was originally defined—that one cannot understand an intellectual or artistic project without also understanding its formation; that the relation between a project and a formation is always decisive; and

---

[3] For an interesting take on the histories of different national formations of cultural studies and their respective relations with academic institutions and with social movements, see Jon D. Cruz, "Cultural Studies and Social Movements: A Crucial Nexus in the American Case," *European Journal of Cultural Studies* 15, no. 3 (2012).

[4] This way of framing pedagogy has its roots in the work of Henry Giroux, Stuart Hall, Lawrence Grossberg, and others who have worked to develop the notion of "public pedagogy" in their efforts to understand the workings of cultural politics. Giroux considers public pedagogy to be a "referent for analyzing how knowledge, values, desire and social relations are constructed, taken up, and implicated in relations of power in the interaction among cultural texts, institutional forms, authorities, and audiences." It concerns how and where culture operates both symbolically and institutionally as an educational, political, and economic force. Henry A. Giroux, *Public Spaces, Private Lives: Democracy Beyond 9/11* (Lanham, Md.; Oxford: Rowman & Littlefield, 2003), 83.

that the emphasis of cultural studies is precisely that it engages with both, rather than specializing itself to one or the other [as this requires] the refusal to give priority to either the project or the formation. We have to look at what kind of formation it was from which the project of cultural studies developed and then at the changes of formation that produced different definitions of that project. We may then be in a position to understand existing and possible formations which would in themselves be a way of defining certain projects toward the future.[5]

With this frame in mind—in short, that cultural studies as a practice is both determined by and determining of a contextual system of relations—rather than approaching the question of pedagogy and Cultural Studies as the need to develop (or formalize or assess) methods, texts, assignments, or forms of authority in the classroom *for* cultural studies, I approach the question in terms of what it might mean to teach and practice Cultural Studies as a particular pedagogical sensibility, as the art of tacking back and forth between project and formation to determine, in the midst of things, what methods and practices and knowledges and skills are to be built and how to build them, if we are to "understand and intervene into the processes of power that determine the future."[6] This approach presumes that pedagogy concerns a realm of force extending well beyond formal education and the classroom, and so the responsibility of practitioners of cultural studies is much broader than the classroom, even as the classroom is a very specific site in which public pedagogy takes place. In what follows, I describe some of what this responsibility to conjunctural thinking has looked like for my own and my undergraduate students' experiences practicing cultural studies in the "Cultural Studies classroom."[7] Specifically, I survey here just a few of the things engaging in the conduct of cultural studies as a conjuncturally specific pedagogy has meant to me.

[5] Raymond Williams, "The Future of Cultural Studies (1989)," in *Raymond Williams on Culture & Society: Essential Writings*, ed. Jim McGuigan (London: Sage, 2014), 151–2.

[6] Lawrence Grossberg, "Rage against the Dying of a Light: Stuart Hall (1932–2014)," *Truthout* February 15, 2014.

[7] This chapter is written to be in conversation with Andrew Davis' chapter in this book. We have both taught the same course, COMM 350: Practices of Cultural Studies, and so share responsibility for the design of the course on which my commentary here is based. Andrew's piece addresses the significance of the conjuncture concept to Cultural Studies and describes in more detail than I do here the collective conjunctural analysis research practice we engage in with our students.

Cultural Studies *in Media Res*

In his story about its formation in the U.S., Jon D. Cruz notes that Cultural Studies entered *in media res*: in the middle of a very different "troubled and deeply conflicted moment" than that which characterized its emergence in Birmingham.[8] Just as it did in the U.K. (but with a different tone of reception, different problems, and different organization), Cultural Studies in the U.S. found itself institutionalizing in the educational sphere. The Academy became an important site where, amid a larger juncture of changes (the solidification of post-war capitalism, new and rapid developments in mass communication, the continuation of Cold War politics and the transnational realignment of major political and ideological associations), various social antagonisms were brokered and new formations of cultural politics (feminisms, anti-racisms, youth, and anti-war movements) found different forms of presence and voice in alliance with, and sometimes against, the intellectual formation of Cultural Studies. Reflecting on the history of Cultural Studies in the 1990s, Stuart Hall echoed Williams' earlier view on the relation of context and intellectual project by noting that, since its inception in Birmingham, Cultural Studies "has been ever since, an adaptation to its terrain; it has been a conjunctural practice. It has always developed from a different matrix of interdisciplinary studies and disciplines," and even within Britain, the "three or four places bold enough to say they are offering courses in cultural studies have different disciplinary roots, both in the humanities and the social sciences."[9]

The idea that Cultural Studies is always already *in media res* has become a defining principle of my approach to *practicing* (a verb which I use to at once mean learning-doing-teaching) it. It is a principle which shapes experiences with/in my Cultural Studies course offerings. Practicing

---

[8] There are several different stories that are told about Cultural Studies' identity in the U.S. (e.g. its origins in the work of pragmatists and media scholars, its relationship with Birmingham or social movements in the U.S.). While this essay is not the space for reflection on these stories (their contradictions, why they matter, etc.), suffice to say that, in whatever story, the point that Cultural Studies "enters *in media res*" stands.

[9] Stuart Hall, "The Emergence of Cultural Studies and the Crisis of the Humanities," *October* 53 (1990): 11.

Cultural Studies *in media res* means presuming in my role as a teacher the arrival of a community of students and research assistants who are squarely and full-force "in the middle of things" themselves. By this, I mean that although it is often unacknowledged (as if our students are blank slates walking into a conversation of which they have not been a part), what we might call the nucleus of a Cultural Studies sensibility, or of a developing conjunctural analysis, is already present in *all* participants' own conscious engagement with and response to the context in which they find themselves personally, educationally, and—especially clear in times of national crisis—socially and politically. As a way to activate this development, I try to introduce students to Cultural Studies "head first": we do not begin day one with an introductory textbook chapter on contemporary issues or theories in cultural studies or a lecture on the history of cultural studies formations. Instead, we consider a few short pieces on the American university, on being a student, on ignorance, reason, and civic politics.[10] We may also read an email from our university Chancellor that gives insight into the meaning of "student" and how the public university sees itself and its role, or excerpts from the University's newest "Master Plan," and/or some basic empirical data on student debt and the conditions of student work/labor. What often happens is that the materials we're engaging drop out of view and what emerges is a heady (and sometimes therapeutic!) discussion centered on participants' relationship with their education and the "idea" of education. It is full of contradictory anecdotes about the felt accumulation of cultural, political, and social change in the present: how people think childhood and emerging adulthood has changed; how it seems anxiety-management, security and preparation, credentialism, and instrumentalism are the core of educational experiences; what it is like as a student to be over-worked, debt-ridden, isolated, or emotionally overcharged; and how a sense of extreme social and political polarization leaves everyone feeling rather breathless, ambivalent, or even hopeless.

---

[10] While new ones are written all the time, one pair well-received by my students has been a viewpoint essay by basketball player Kareem Abdul-Jabbar in *Time* magazine called "American Students—and Politicians—Need to Stop Waging War on Reason" and the (less insightful, more polemic) piece by Greg Lukianoff and Jonathan Haidt in *The Atlantic* titled, "The Coddling of the American Mind."

Different ways of being a "student"—those who come wishing to see Cultural Studies as a course offering a politically focused (or politically confirming and comforting) sensibility, those who are looking for a course to simply and efficiently fulfill their "Diversity" or "Research-intensive" requirement, and those who aren't quite sure why they're there (or in college, for that matter)—all seem to have *something* to say. Contrary to some of the arguments we read in those op-eds which suggest college students are homogenously lazy, coddled, disrespectful, uncritical, unmotivated, too motivated, too political, or not political enough, what becomes clear is that they are instead heterogeneously cynical (but idealistic), drained, and nervous. When it comes to politics, and in contradistinction to the caricatures of students and politics represented in media, those who would usually be labeled "liberal" voice their uncertainty regarding how to reconcile their own (sometimes primitive) sense of progressivism with their valid critiques of the Left,[11] and those typically labeled "conservative" emphasize feeling that "the government" has failed them and their hopes for the future. They all share concerns and ambivalence about what education is for today, and what they are equipped to do or be as a result of having earned a degree. Some are content to see it as a means to somewhere else—an expensive, credentialing hurdle; others are disenfranchised by the ways in which the current educational paradigm has failed to measure up to the expectations they had of it as preparation for civic life (for example, this manifests as a frustration with having to be too busy or too grade-focused to actually take the time to learn).

The conversation eventually becomes, to some degree, a self-evident (though very incomplete) microcosm of the complex and incongruous conditions, social antagonisms, and structures of feelings that make up contemporary political struggles. More importantly, it becomes an opening for an introduction to the promise of Cultural Studies—its concern with actually existing experiences, passions, and positions; its discomfort with logics of opposition, reduction, and universalism, and its premise that troubling taken-for-granted political visions and the work they do opens up possibilities for a better future. At the peak of this conversation,

---

[11] These include concerns with blind celebration of activisms; ambivalence toward "identity politics" regarding either its successes or failures, class-based critiques, and more.

before the natural point where analysis would generally begin, we pause. I ask them to bracket the "deep habits of the university" they've learned on the one hand (their actually existing expectations of their role as students, of mine as teacher, of grades and of the idiom of student debt) and the "strident demands of political urgency" on the other and consider what it might look like to engage both of these in a different way.[12]

Thus, I do not claim to teach what Cultural Studies "is"; rather, I claim to teach the contexts in which Cultural Studies formations have emerged and the ways in which they have and continue to develop epistemologically, methodologically, politically, and institutionally. My students begin to learn Cultural Studies through engaging primary texts (and the stories I tell about them)—namely, Cultural Studies' foundations (excerpts from the works of Marx and Gramsci, the early efforts to work with these inheritances by Raymond Williams, E.P. Thompson and Richard Hoggart), selections from the "gray" archives of the Center for Contemporary Cultural Studies, and more contemporary reflections on the histories and practices of Cultural Studies by various leading practitioners.[13] They also learn Cultural Studies through the way the whole of our course (what we read and how we research) is organized around units claiming to help "Define the Conjuncture": these units, based initially on my assessment of "working areas" that may need to be considered in a present conjunctural analysis, include theoretical, empirical, and popular materials on topics such as "Economies and Economics," "Policy and Politics," Race and Empire, "Genders and Feminisms," "Affect and Cultural Feelings," "Media and Information," or others. While some of these have staying power, it is not uncommon for specific materials or

[12] Lawrence Grossberg, "On the Political Responsibilities of Cultural Studies," *Inter-Asia cultural studies* 11 (2010): 241. Key here is the idea that at the level of this "conjuncture," the questions change, and the terms of political engagement and possibility change as well. A visual representation of the first few weeks of our work in my cultural studies course where we build up to this "different way" can be found in the "Asking Questions in Cultural Studies" handout I provide for my COMM 350: Practices in Cultural Studies students. See Appendix for the most recent version.

[13] In particular, Stuart Hall, Lawrence Grossberg, John Clarke and Janet Newman, Ann Gray, and Gil Rodman are some of those whose accessible, introductory pieces on topics like the notion of the conjuncture and conjunctural analysis, on cultural studies' relationship to politics, on concepts like neo-liberalism, on the question of method, and so on. I tend to incorporate, as well as excellent excerpts from the work of lesser known or newer practitioners.

even a whole unit to be thrown out mid-semester in favor of something else we collectively identify as more pertinent to our developing conjunctural investigation.[14] We also spend time early and regularly on the question of "doing" Cultural Studies—from where are particular epistemologies appropriated and why? Why is it that we, situated in this moment, read or engage something in a particular way? What combination of methods help shape what kinds of questions? What does a contemporary Cultural Studies pedagogy need and what should it seek to accomplish?

In other words, they meet Cultural Studies in the conduct of Cultural Studies: through the beginnings of a conjunctural analysis where a context, "often viewed with some sense of pessimism and even despair," is set up to be reconfigured as "one of possibilities" through the rejection of "all forms of simplification and reduction" and the embrace of "the complexity, contradiction and contingency of the world."[15] If it is still the case, as Hall suggested via Gramsci, that part of the politics of the work of Cultural Studies formations is the production of "organic intellectuals" who would help shape a necessary and "emerging historical movement," practicing cultural studies *in media res*—as an articulation of the intellectual and the actually existing political—seems to me a necessity for Cultural Studies pedagogy.[16]

Cultural Studies' Politics as a Responsibility, Not a Commitment (and/or, How to Think, Not What To)

As several reflections on the formations of Cultural Studies and their contexts have articulated, one concern about the emergence of Cultural Studies in the "highly ratified and enormously elaborated and well-

---

[14] For example, once, we transformed a unit on "Resistance" into a unit on "Adulting," in order to examine the construction of "millennials" changes in the youth experience, and cultural politics. This new unit included both classic Cultural Studies work on style and youth culture, but also "adulting" internet memes, a revisit of theories of class, and a look at empirical generational U.S. social policy data.

[15] Grossberg, *Cultural Studies in the Future Tense*, 241.

[16] Stuart Hall, "Cultural Studies and Its Theoretical Legacies," in *Cultural Studies*, ed. Lawrence Grossberg (1992), 282.

funded professional world of American academic life," particularly when compared to the difficulties faced by the organization of "a marginalized Centre in a university like Birmingham," was the fact of its theoretical fluency.[17] As Hall described of the state of Cultural Studies in the U.S. in the early 1990s:

> There is no moment now, in American cultural studies, where we are not able, extensively and without end, to theorize power-politics, race, class, and gender, subjugation, domination, exclusion, marginality, Otherness, etc. There is hardly anything in cultural studies which isn't so theorized. And yet, there is the nagging doubt that this overwhelming textualization of cultural studies' own discourses somehow constitutes power and politics as exclusively matters of language and textuality itself … [where] power [is constituted] as an easy floating signifier which just leaves the crude exercise and connections of power and culture altogether emptied of any signification.[18]

There are two cautions implied here that each influence my approach to the practice (again, as learning-doing-teaching) of Cultural Studies. The first, described by Ien Ang as having to do with the inherent tension between academic and intellectual work, concerns the danger of theoretical over-sophistication, or when theory becomes a pedagogical end in itself. It is understandably appealing—especially in an educational context so focused on legitimation, metrics, and influence—to want to structure a Cultural Studies course around a survey of the vast canons of political and cultural theory.[19] Indeed, this is the approach that some of the most popular reactionary #syllabi I mentioned in the introduction take. This approach asks: who from the Frankfurt School, from Postmodernism, from Feminism (with the capital F), from Political Economy or Postcolonial Theory or the New Materialisms offer the concepts and theories that will give us the answers? How should we organize them together? However, as Ang notes:

---

[17] Ibid., 286.

[18] Ibid., 287.

[19] Ien Ang, "Stuart Hall and the Tension between Academic and Intellectual Work," *International Journal of Cultural Studies* 19, no. 1 (2016).

This pursuit of theory for theory's sake was (or is) [only] possible in the U.S. because of the enormous capacity of the American university system to absorb new intellectual trends within its dense frameworks of professional scholarly production, especially through its expansive infrastructure of graduate schools. In this context, ever more complex and proficient talk of power, race, class, gender, otherness, etc. could go on and on feeding on itself indefinitely, without ever having to be grounded within, or connected to, actual practices outside the walls of academia. For Hall, this kind of academism, with all its radical posturing and erudite display, falls far short of his own vision of cultural studies as an intellectual and political practice. Key here is the critical distinction Hall makes between intellectual work and academic work: 'they overlap, they abut each other, they feed off one another, the one provides you with the means to do the other. But they are not the same thing'.[20]

This approach does not often forefront questions like: how does this concept or theory change when it is asked to confront this particular concrete, empirical material reality? What does this concept itself (and not just its author) or its many mobilizations take for granted, if we consider contexts? Is this concept made to be an "answer," and what questions does it purport to address? Are those the questions the conjuncture even demands? Without these considerations, even or especially at the moments of choosing course material, one is not practicing Cultural Studies. That does not mean, of course, that the contents of these canons are not useful or even necessary in the practice of Cultural Studies. It is from these canons that I share pieces with my students for them to grapple with and for us to discuss as they work on their specific conjunctural research problematics. However, more important than the content of these canons, at least in the first instance, is the contents' immediate insertion into our conjunctural analysis: What work does a concept do?

Following John Clarke (whose piece, "Living with/in and without neo-liberalism," is one I frequently use to teach this particular kind of a relationship with theory), when we encounter an important canonical theory or concept, I ask students to try approaching theory as a tool—to contemplate its weight, its utility, its price, and its appeal. Borrowing

---

[20] Ibid., 31.

from Clarke, they consider a concept's density (is it useful in its current form), its promiscuity (is it used in seemingly contradictory ways), its omnipresence (is it treated as a universal, global, or ahistorical phenomenon), and its omnipotence (is it identified as the cause of a wide array of social, political, and economic changes).[21] Their given goal is to consider how a concept or theory might be, rather than a closing of their work, an opening: is it/can it be contested, usefully mobile, flexible, and above all part of a process of contextual assemblage, articulation, and translation? In short, Cultural Studies pedagogy is meant to challenge the institutional and epistemological order of things. With regard to theory, this means to consider theory a constitutive part of culture and not just a description of it, and therefore something that must always be approached with an experimental ethos rather than reverence.

The second caution implied in the above reflections on Cultural Studies' formation in the U.S. academic context regards the tension between intellectual and political work, or put more concretely, the relationship between teaching Cultural Studies (in academic institutions) and politics. An early and central concern for Cultural Studies had/has been transcending the separation between education and publics—from an early focus by British cultural studies on how to invigorate adult education in working- and middle-class communities to the ongoing role of U.S. Cultural Studies in mediating crises that resulted from the surges of various social movements—feminisms, civil rights, gay liberation, anti-war protests, responses to economic decline, and so on. and their pressures on the educational sphere, particularly on institutions of higher education.[22] Today, the question of Cultural Studies as a formation in the U.S. academy (with its particular institutionalized modes of doing intellectual work such as teaching topical courses, organizing degree programs, publishing manuscripts) and its relationship to the conditions of politics in the present makes the following question a crucial one for a contemporary Cultural Studies pedagogy: "What is the place of political values and ethical commitments in scholarly work, especially in the light of the powerful contemporary mandate, even the demand, in contempo-

---

[21] John Clarke, "Living with/in and without Neo-Liberalism," *Focaal* 2008, no. 51 (2008): 135.
[22] Cruz, "Cultural Studies and Social Movements: A Crucial Nexus in the American Case," 258, 73.

rary academic and intellectual spaces, to be political (and 'politically correct') at any and every moment?" This demand, as Grossberg
characterizes it,

> takes its most benign form in the claims of engaged scholarship and activist
> research, and its most malignant forms in the saturation of all knowledge
> with political identifications. It is the product of two independent commit-
> ments: first, a necessary rejection, embodied in cultural studies and else-
> where, of the claims of epistemological universalism and objectivity; and
> second, an unfortunate and rather unreflective polarizing practice of criti-
> cal analysis, which replaces the complexities of Foucault's theory of the
> inseparability of knowledge and power with the simple assumption of a
> guaranteed relation between explicit political agendas and identities on the
> one hand, and the forms and contents of knowledge claims on the other.[23]

Against the all too common assumption that describes Cultural Studies
as (equivalent to) a "political *commitment*," I've come to teach "the politics of Cultural Studies" as a *responsibility*. "Commitment" ("*the state or
quality of being dedicated to a cause, activity*") and "Responsibility" ("*the
state or fact of being accountable or to blame for something*") are both vague,
promiscuous concepts, often used interchangeably, and are both
mobilized discursively to do certain kinds of social and political work in
a variety of contexts. However, treating them in much the same way as
any other useful concept for Cultural Studies, my purpose for distinguishing between them is to help students carefully consider what it
means to say that Cultural Studies is political. A commitment, as the
state or quality of dedication, is a state of *desire*—one commits because it
feels good or right to do so, but also a state of certainty—in which one
knows not only the content of the commitment but also its (moral) correctness. A responsibility, as the state or fact of being accountable, is not
a state of desire or certainty, nor does it necessarily imply agency—one
can be or become held responsible for—held accountable to—something
despite ones' desire or to one's surprise.

In my experience, this small adjustment has meant that the practitioners of Cultural Studies in my course are able to shift in focus from the

---

[23] Grossberg, *Cultural Studies in the Future Tense*, 95.

feeling and *content* of politics to the *moments* when the political is felt or is given content. One exercise I have used to demonstrate this difference is to roughly diagram the politics of the practice of cultural studies itself. After having read excerpts from Lawrence Grossberg's piece, "On the Political Responsibilities of Cultural Studies," we consider in visual abstraction (e.g., we make an actual concept map on the whiteboard) where political desires, obligations, or positions may be encountered, bracketing for the moment the possible content of that politics.[24] Our starting point is often this claim:

> In the first instance, [Cultural Studies] is political in relation to the questions it asks. While conjunctures pose their own questions, what we hear is partly determined by our political positionalities. In the last instance, its politics appear at the end of its story, which fabricates the context anew and, in addressing its problematic, opens new possibilities, both imaginative and strategic, for getting somewhere else. But conjunctural analysis does not have a single, guaranteed ethico-political foundation, nor can the political implications of its analyses be guaranteed in advance. At the very least, one cannot control how the stories one tells will be taken up in the name of political struggles.[25]

The goal of this exercise is to get to a point of acknowledgment that it makes sense for ones' concrete political commitments to influence, but not determine, the political responsibility of the intellectual work of conjunctural analysis—and vice versa.

While this is a useful beginning for getting students to see the difference between a Cultural Studies pedagogy and other approaches to critical theory and analysis they may encounter, it is only as students work through their own conjunctural analysis projects in the class that some vocalize or demonstrate in their writing the realization that the distinction between political and intellectual work is not clear but strategic. It is strategic in the sense that it is always a contextual articulation of the political and the intellectual, it involves attempting to both de-naturalize

---

[24] "On the Political Responsibilities of Cultural Studies."
[25] Ibid., 243.

the present and open it up to the possibility of a better future, where better does *indeed* imply an ethico-political desire to "seek a world in which all people have the material conditions of survival, the political conditions of freedom and justice, and the intellectual conditions of education and expression, as the basis for such a task."[26]

Cultural Studies and the Metaphor of Conversation

Finally, my practice (learning-doing-teaching) of Cultural Studies has focused on the utility of the metaphor of *conversation*.[27] One of my favorite images of Cultural Studies was conjured by Charlotte Brunsdon in her writing about her time as a student at the Centre for Contemporary Cultural Studies. She remembers Stuart Hall arriving to seminars with arms full of books, which he would pile on the table ahead of the seminar starting. Hall "was bringing with him," says Brunsdon, "making available, what might be useful in the coming discussion. And he had to bring lots of books because, depending on the way the discussion went, different scholarship would be relevant."[28] Brundson's image of Hall and his books[29] have been used to highlight the "interdisciplinary promiscuity" and "transdisciplinary excess" that have long characterized Cultural Studies' relationship to research.[30] Yet, it also illustrates something about what it means to teach Cultural Studies as pedagogy: it is a responsibility to hold open the debate, to accept the contingency of knowledge produc-

---

[26] Ibid., 244.

[27] Larry Grossberg elaborates on what the conversation means to Cultural Studies in his introduction to this collection.

[28] Charlotte Brunsdon, "On Being Made History," *Cultural Studies* 29, no. 1 (2014): 95.

[29] I must say this image rather reminds me of spending time in *my* mentor's (Larry Grossberg's) office: There is not a square inch of that room that is not touched by the floor-to-ceiling archive of books, newspapers, manuscripts, notes, and journals spanning half a century's time of collection. When discussing new ideas in that space, I always look around and feel as if the whole story of this conjuncture can be found in that office.

[30] Brunsdon, "On Being Made History," 95; Ang, "Stuart Hall and the Tension between Academic and Intellectual Work," 33.

tion and to plan for surprise, and to facilitate conditions in which practitioners are able in some measure to keep "going on theorizing."[31]

With regard to the classroom conversation, in my own practice of Cultural Studies, I first acknowledge the ways in which this kind of experimental, intellectual ethos runs counter to the "deep habits" of U.S. academic institutions. I find myself often reiterating to the practitioners in my class that some of the risks they take in their research may ultimately fail, but that doesn't mean they shouldn't take them and that doesn't mean they "fail Cultural Studies." It is a significant challenge to get them to see that "success" in the course (a unit of education where learning is assessed) is a measure of changes in *how* they know and do rather than what they know and do. I strive to incorporate the openness of Cultural Studies pedagogy in the actual classroom conversation by leaving space in the reading list for new directions, integrating the materials read "on the outside" for research projects, and perhaps most importantly for many, providing a template for treating the process of intellectual work (reading, research, debate) as engagement in a larger conversation. Specifically, this template consists, first, of a frank lesson on what it means to be a "demanding reader." The relationship students have with the idea of education (discussed early in this essay) profoundly shapes their approach to reading and research. I've had students describe reading as "painful," "frustrating," "boring," and as akin to "a scavenger hunt." None of these descriptions of engagement with material are compatible with Cultural Studies inquiry as a flexible and curious mode of critically productive thinking. In an effort to rehabilitate some students' relationships with reading and research, we discuss practical techniques offered by popular authors and poets on the art of reading, such as how the different marks one makes in a book express differences and agreements with the author, (mis)understanding, big feelings, or new ideas.[32] We talk about how one sets intentions for reading and research, and how doing so

---

[31] Lawrence Grossberg, "On Postmodernism and Articulation: An Interview with Stuart Hall," in *Stuart Hall: Critical Dialogues*, ed. David Morley; and Kuan-hsing Chen (London: Routledge, 1996), 150.

[32] For example, I use very short excerpts and stories from Mortimer Adler's and Charles Van Doren's *How to Read a Book: The Classic Guide to Intelligent Reading*, particularly from the section on "How to Be a Demanding Reader."

enables a different read or find each time. Finally, I structure an opening toward conversation in the reading assignment given in my courses, which I call the "Choose Your Own Adventure" reading assignment. This assignment, due each week, offers a range of experimental reading prompts as a way to engage material on one's own terms and with a different set of intentions each time. These range from creating graphical abstracts of concepts or theories, to playing devil's advocate with an author's claim, to considering everything *but* the reading (who wrote it, when, where, why) to describing "The Thing I Couldn't Stop Thinking Of" while reading, to just asking questions. The prompts require responses which take different forms (written, visual, experiential, etc.), and these responses serve as entry points into the classroom conversation about the material. As a result of this assignment, students are generally well-prepared and confident about their novel contributions to the classroom conversation, and we often wind up moving our collective conjunctural analysis forward by hashing out contradictions within their responses, finding new areas of disciplinary or professional expertise represented in the room, and fielding surprise connections or insights that we otherwise wouldn't have made with a more basic "close-reading" discussion. In the current educational context, this template helps students learn how to read as more than students—as participants in the ongoing *process* of intellectual work as conversation.

While Cultural Studies still finds itself primarily situated within disciplinary spaces in the U.S. academy, operating as it does at the level of the "conjuncture," Cultural Studies pedagogy must acknowledge that as contexts change, the questions change, and the terms of political engagement and possibility change, as well. The present raises important questions, then for the larger conversation of Cultural Studies, which Cruz put this way:

> how attuned might cultural studies be today to the social moments and movements that swirl in many places in the world? The remarkable social movements of the moment – environmental struggles, expanding women's struggles, economic justice, mass mobilizations against political authoritarianism, communication-enabled new publics and others– raise [another] question: what kind of intellectually flexible mode of critically productive

thought will be [or must be made!] available to enable the much-needed comprehending, combining, and juxtaposing capable of bringing new conditions (combining formations and projects) into critical visibility and dialogue?[33]

I concede that the diffusion of Cultural Studies within the academy across disciplines and degree programs has made this set of questions difficult for Cultural Studies as a formation to address. In some ways, its concern with being visible and legible as a project in conjunction with dialog implies the question of whether and how Cultural Studies can "succeed" without a recognizable and desirable kind of institutionalization (whatever that might be). In my position teaching Cultural Studies primarily to an undergraduate population (and as the foci of my teaching choices above might make clear), I am aware of the limits that institutional constraints have imposed on our ability as teachers who practice Cultural Studies to directly facilitate the kinds of engagement in a broader public conversation that Cultural Studies calls for. However, I am also aware that Cultural Studies has never really controlled the role it plays in the broader public conversation, and that, because of the necessary and productive tension between the shape of a project and its context, there are possibilities that a different or marginalized position for Cultural Studies in the academy affords.

As an elective course within a Communication degree program that also fulfills an elective research requirement, my Cultural Studies course is populated by students studying media with intention to enter the cultural industries, with management and economics students confronting unignorable crises of major economic inequality, with business students hoping to start social enterprises, with students in the biological and medical sciences concerned with climate health, and students from disciplines like Art and English and History and Geography who are budding activists, performance artists, and teachers themselves. I do not teach Cultural Studies to "Cultural Studies students," I *do* and *share* Cultural Studies pedagogy (understood as an approach to intellectual work whose purpose, within the conditions of its given context, is to invigorate criti-

---

[33] Cruz, "Cultural Studies and Social Movements: A Crucial Nexus in the American Case," 299.

cal thinking and praxis, knowledge production, and change in new and important ways) with diverse individuals in the process of building vital links to social movements, industries, institutions, and organizations beyond the academy. And so, the questions, the intellectual and research skills built collaboratively, and ideally even in some cases, the vision of what's next for the project of Cultural Studies are brought to the elsewheres they go.

Works Cited

Ang, I. (2016). Stuart Hall and the Tension between Academic and Intellectual Work. *International Journal of Cultural Studies, 19*(1), 29–41.

Brunsdon, C. (2014). On Being Made History. *Cultural Studies, 29*(1), 88–99.

Clarke, J. (2008). Living with/in and Without Neo-Liberalism. *Focaal, 51*, 135–147.

Cruz, J. D. (2012). Cultural Studies and Social Movements: A Crucial Nexus in the American Case. *European Journal of Cultural Studies, 15*(3), 254–301.

Giroux, H. A. (2003). *Public Spaces, Private Lives: Democracy Beyond 9/11.* Lanham/Oxford: Rowman & Littlefield.

Grossberg, L. (1996). On Postmodernism and Articulation: An Interview with Stuart Hall. In D. Morley & K.-h. Chen (Eds.), *Stuart Hall: Critical Dialogues* (pp. 131–150). London: Routledge.

Grossberg, L. (2010a). *Cultural Studies in the Future Tense.* Durham: Duke University Press.

Grossberg, L. (2010b). On the Political Responsibilities of Cultural Studies. *Inter-Asia Cultural Studies, 11*, 241–247.

Grossberg, L. (2014, February 15). Rage Against the Dying of a Light: Stuart Hall (1932–2014). *Truthout.*

Hall, S. (1990). The Emergence of Cultural Studies and the Crisis of the Humanities. *October, 53*, 11–23.

Hall, S. (1992). Cultural Studies and Its Theoretical Legacies. In L. Grossberg (Ed.), *Cultural Studies.*

Pearce, K. (2016, December 16). Understanding Trumpism: Syllabus Co-Compiled by Johns Hopkins Historian Goes Viral Post-Election. *Hub.*

Williams, R. (2014). The Future of Cultural Studies (1989). In J. McGuigan (Ed.), *Raymond Williams on Culture & Society: Essential Writings.* London: Sage.

The Ethics of Postgraduate Supervision: A View from Cultural Studies

Liam Grealy and Timothy Laurie

Introduction

To make the comparison that one should never otherwise make, Higher Degree Research (HDR) supervision shares one thing with parenting: it is a topic about which every person has an opinion. Watching other people supervise can be as excruciating as observing a nonchalant parent whose child is throwing food in a café. When postgraduates fail to meet expectations, we might imagine that better training was possible, that bad choices were made at crucial junctures and that somewhere sits a parent reading the newspaper while the floor is covered in spaghetti. The neglectful supervisor, like the neglectful parent, is easily viewed as a person of a certain type, and quotidian discussions of supervision practices

L. Grealy (✉)
The University of Sydney, Camperdown, NSW, Australia
e-mail: liam.grealy@sydney.edu.au

T. Laurie (✉)
The University of Technology Sydney, Ultimo, NSW, Australia
e-mail: Timothy.Laurie@uts.edu.au

© The Author(s) 2019
J. Aksikas et al. (eds.), *Cultural Studies in the Classroom and Beyond*,
https://doi.org/10.1007/978-3-030-25393-6_16

quickly deteriorate into moral appraisals of virtues and vices. Although providing short-lived pleasures, the impulse to piety can distract from uneven historical transformations in higher degree training *tout court*. Supervision practices need to be understood not as expressions of a moral disposition (friendly, mean and forgiving) or achievements of profound intelligence (the cult of the eccentric genius), but as provisional responses to a turbulent global industry that produces many contradictory messages about the purposes and outcomes of higher degree programs.

This chapter links the development of teaching skills around HDR supervision to broader institutional issues around working conditions and knowledge production. In particular, we identify key questions facing higher degree supervisors in the humanities and social sciences, citing Australian cultural studies research as an example. By drawing from the contemporary sociology of education, we examine different forms that supervision can take, the professional expectations placed upon supervisors, the impacts of affective accumulation in the production of social capital and the challenges associated with HDR supervision for cultural studies practitioners in Australia. In doing so, the chapter draws together literature on research learning communities to sociological studies of class-based stratification and increased casualisation within the tertiary sector, noting the ways that intersecting issues around expertise, hierarchy and interdependency can shape supervisors' teaching practices.

The chapter begins by comparing critical approaches to HDR supervision, including the recent turn towards supervisors' ethical responsibilities in relation to what Christine Halse and Peter Bansel (2012) call 'learning alliances'. While endorsing conceptions of learning as a collective practice, we foreground instances where the language of moral obligation can risk displacing important conversations about affective labour and contractual precarity in an increasingly casualised tertiary sector. Building on these observations, we argue for critical engagement with the value- and community-making functions that HDR supervisors perform. Finally, specific challenges are identified for postgraduate (a.k.a. 'graduate') students working in cultural studies, especially when faced with interdisciplinary restlessness and methodological experimentation. Throughout, the chapter does not make strong prescriptions about what best practice supervision should look like, because the diversity of institutional circumstances makes the 'actionable quality' of such prescriptions somewhat negligible (Morris 2008, p. 433). Nevertheless, we do identify points of tension between what good supervision practices hope to achieve and the changing institutional contexts within which these practices take place.

Collective Responsibility and Learning Alliances

Across the last two decades in Australia, doctoral populations have expanded significantly (Pearson et al. 2008) and government funding bodies have placed increased pressures on supervisors to produce timely postgraduate completions.[1] In this context, attention has been directed towards producing more efficient and reliable postgraduate pathways (P. Green and Usher 2003; McCallin and Nayar 2012; Harrison et al. 2017), leading to institutional changes in admission requirements (e.g. elaborated metrics for assessing candidate suitability and reliability),[2] forms of assessment (e.g. a proliferation of interim reviews and presentations during candidature) and models of supervision (e.g. larger, interdisciplinary supervision panels). Yet, despite the proliferation of support systems, supervisors are still primary nodes of guidance and responsibility for the HDR students. Supervisors continue to orchestrate thesis timelines, endorse special administrative provisions, select examiners and act as formal and informal referees.

Unfortunately, few universities provide reliable opportunities for disseminating good supervision practices. In most instances observed, formal induction sessions linked to supervisor accreditation eschew sustained discussion of 'bad' supervision experiences, supervisors' 'self-protective measures' (Halse 2011), negotiation strategies in the allocation of students, or labour considerations around supervision workload. Feedback

---

[1] A recent evaluation of trends in postgraduate performance is the Australian Government Department of Education and Training's "Key findings from the 'Completion Rates of Higher Education Students – Cohort Analysis, 2005–2015' report" (2017).

[2] On metrics and HDR supervision, see Grealy and Laurie (2017).

mechanisms around supervision are less developed than those for undergraduate teaching and, in this respect, the private character of supervision is both its strength and its weakness. On the one hand, supervision can sometimes create unique spaces for students to be intellectually vulnerable and to work through any complications arising from personal experiences. On the other hand, poor supervision relationships are often tolerated by supervisees and supervisors alike because few comparative yardsticks are available. Furthermore, while postgraduates' negative experiences can travel quickly by word of mouth (Tsai 2008), supervision horror stories easily become naturalised as inevitable failings of already imperfect institutions. In the Australian postgraduate sector, few avenues are provided to identify systemic failures in supervision practices at an institutional level. For these reasons, many academics can have little awareness about the spectrum of available supervision practices. Among these practices and conceptions, Anne Lee lists five:

> (1) functional: where the issue is one of project management; (2) enculturation: where the student is encouraged to become a member of the disciplinary community; (3) critical thinking: where the student is encouraged to question and analyse their work; (4) emancipation: where the student is encouraged to question and develop themselves; [and] (5) developing a quality relationship: where the student is enthused, inspired and cared for. (Lee 2008, pp. 270–271, see Table 1, p. 268)

Those supervisors who prioritise functional outcomes and critical thinking fit comfortably within the 'master-apprentice' model discussed by Christine Halse and Peter Bansel (2012), and to which we briefly turn.

The master-apprentice model is described by Halse and Bansel as 'based on a hierarchical power relationship whereby the doctoral student is constituted as requiring instruction and discipline by an academic supervisor who is able and authorised to accomplish this task by virtue of his or her knowledge, skills and expertise' (2012, p. 379). Taking a psychoanalytic approach, an oblique argument for the master-apprentice model of supervision has been made by John Frow, who characterises the process for PhD students as involving a temporary loss of ego, entry into 'a community of novitiates', a period in a liminal state and the crossing of multiple thresholds into academic maturity (1988, p. 318). Higher degree research cultures are commonly shaped by supervisees' desires for the approval of senior staff members; by libidinal investments in disciplinary figureheads, texts and journals; and by the wonderfully Freudian tendency for postgraduates to dismiss their original thesis proposals as 'shit'. In the humanities and social sciences, the plethora of theoretical frameworks available is matched only by the ever-expanding repertoire of criticisms and dismissals that could be directed towards one's work. The disorienting collision of assertions and criticisms heightens the demand for reliable signs of mastery to secure one's sense of intellectual credibility. The supervisee must therefore place faith in the existence of a 'subject who is supposed to know' (Frow 1988, p. 314). In this context, the supervisor can perform an important prohibitive function while providing intellectual securities in the face of unknown risks: 'you *cannot* say this, but it *is* possible to do that'.

The master is neither infinitely brilliant nor infinitely generous, and obedience to the supervisor's every whim does not necessarily make for a healthy supervision relationship. Eve Sedgwick's observation about undergraduate students may resonate with HDR teaching: 'There are students who view their teachers' hard work as a servile offering in their honor – a distasteful one to boot. There are other students who accept the proffered formulations gratefully, as a gift, but without thinking to mimic the process of their production' (2003, p. 154). Insofar as learning can take place through well-timed disagreement and discord, it may be more appropriate to heed Gilles Deleuze's suggestion that '[we] never learn by doing *like* someone, but by doing *with* someone, who has no relation of resemblance to what we are learning' (1972, p. 22, emphasis in original). Furthermore, as the widely circulating cliché would have it, postgraduates upon completion will know more about their topics than their supervisors. This shift can happen much earlier—too early, sometimes, for the supervisor to adopt the position of master. In such cases, supervision may require creative dialogues that allow both supervisee and supervisor, 'apprentice' and 'master', to learn.

The drawbacks of the master-apprentice model are well documented. Supervisors can feel overly responsible for supervisees' progress; the dyad can be isolating and dysfunctional practices can remain invisible to others; and the fetishisation of mastery can cement existing institutional hierarchies, working 'to shore up outdated knowledge, traditions and practices by replicating the supervisor's prior work and reproducing an exclusionary elite' (Halse and Bansel 2012, p. 379). Travelling anecdotes about disaster supervisions often involve supervisors strictly asserting mastery and escalating disagreements into irresolvable antagonisms (Grealy 2016). As an alternative to the master-apprentice model, supervisors may tend towards a 'socio-cultural' approach by facilitating access to a shared world of practicing teachers and researchers (Halse and Bansel 2012, p. 378), integrating students into learning communities that can sustain them throughout candidature (see Amundsen and McAlpine 2009). David Boud and Alison Lee shift their focus away from 'supervision' and 'provisionism' and focus instead on 'distributed' and 'horizontalized' pedagogies, 'with an associated dispersal of responsibility and of agency' (Boud and Lee 2005, pp. 501–502; see also B. Green 2005). Peer-activated learning communities can provide forums for discussing projects, for sharing institutional knowledge and for personal support (Connell 1985). Boud and Lee recommend 'programmes of seminars and workshops, supervisor selection and training and linking of students with active research groups', as well as 'monthly meetings of research students around topics of concern, the use of an online environment and, notably, a research student conference' (Boud and Lee 2005, p. 506). Postgraduate writing groups also have demonstrable benefits for research students (McCallin and Nayar 2012).

One of the most developed models of collective learning practices is what Halse and Bansel call 'the learning alliance'. The learning alliance prescribes 'an ethical approach for the "morally-committed" actions necessary for praxis' linked to 'the moral grammar of doctoral education' and structured by 'ethical relations of responsibility' that require scholars to consider 'relations among multiple actors, and their practices and policies' (Halse and Bansel 2012, pp. 384–385). The goal of doctoral supervision, Halse and Bansel suggest, is 'praxis' involving an alliance 'between multiple institutional agents grounded in a relational ethics of mutual responsibility' (p. 377). The concept is elaborated as follows:

> Praxis is concerned with the shared practices, including policies, procedures and processes, of individuals and organisations 'who are conscious

and self-aware that their actions are "morally-committed, and oriented and informed by traditions" – like the traditions that orient the work, the being and the becoming of people' (Kemmis and Smith 2008, p. 5). Thus, the learning alliance is much more than a pedagogy of doctoral education. (Halse and Bansel 2012, p. 378)

Supervision work is expanded beyond outcomes-based learning to a more holistic model of care. Drawing on Hannah Arendt, the notion of 'work' deployed is intended to signal a 'fruitful, creative activity that produces long-lasting objects and effects' and as 'the prerequisite for the possibility of action – the unique and visible acts that produce change and constitute the realm of great deeds and words' (Halse and Malfroy 2010, p. 83). Supervision work can foster extended social relationships; cultivate habits of mind that maintain interest in the student's needs; enhance students' 'techne' as 'the creative, productive use of expert knowledge to bring something into existence or accomplish a particular objective'; and implement contextual expertise to facilitate the student's progress and achievement (p. 87).

The learning alliance is a moral community to be distinguished from the alienation engendered by university bureaucracy. Halse and Bansel appear to advocate overlaying professionalised social structures with unmediated social attachments guided by principles of responsibility:

> Whilst we may not be responsible for the design and implementation of the policies and managerial practices through which doctoral programmes, candidature and supervision are regulated, they create the conditions under which we must assume responsibility and that responsibility is collective rather than individual.... This is not an ethics where a certain end justifies the means to achieve it – timely completions, publications, etc. – but an ethics of responsibility that is attuned to the consequences of human conduct in the existing context and willingness to take responsibility for them. (Halse and Bansel 2012, p. 387)

The learning alliance enlarges the scope of what 'good supervision' looks like and expands the university's obligations well beyond 'administrative matters of risk control, audit, surveillance or crisis management when a problem arises with a student, supervisor, or in the supervisory relationship' (Halse and Bansel 2012, p. 384). Ethical learning communities promise alternatives to market-based logics of competitive enterprise; as Raewyn Connell and Catherine Manathunga put it, 'a supervisor's role is to protect the student from the institution, as far as one can, and encourage originality and radical thinking' (2012, p. 8).

The learning alliance urges academics to diversify the resources and relationships available to supervisees. However, the appeal to ethical justifications for forming learning communities can cut in multiple directions. Learning alliances are not formed through collective consensus: professional communities are assembled through uneven desires, compromises and coercions, wherein informal gift economies may consolidate nestled enclaves of power and influence. Brown, Goodman, and Yasukawa (2010) suggest that casual and sessional staff can feel wedged between feelings of ethical obligation to continue teaching and mentoring others, and the unreasonable demands of workplaces in which 'managers enjoy a relatively secure income flow, but choose to impose income insecurity on an increasing proportion of the staff responsible for face-to-face teaching' (p. 170). We cannot endorse learning communities without remaining attentive to the cumulative effects of such wedgings. The following section argues that learning alliances are embedded in professional communities fractured in two ways: inwardly, through the uneven distribution of labour within social hierarchies; and outwardly, through processes of social capital accumulation. Reflecting on the necessary move made towards collective responsibility in Halse and Bansel, we argue that learning alliances need to be understood in tandem with tendencies toward individualisation and casualisation in the academy.

The Casual Supervisor

Working conditions vary widely among those charged with building learning alliances. These variations are frequently masked by the 'myth of egalitarianism' (see Gill 2014, p. 24) cultivated by the university's upper management through the rhetoric of 'shared' purpose and 'collective' enterprise. In seeking to go beyond the dyadic form of supervision, Halse and Bansel make important connections between academic duties and other kinds of 'ethical' social relationships. This is, however, a risky move. Casual, sessional and contract-based employees are particularly vulnerable to exploitation. 'Lacking income security,' write Brown, Goodman, and Yasukawa, 'casual teachers become a highly responsive and manipulable pool of labour, bent to the will of the contract' (2010, p. 179). In 2012, it was estimated in Australia 'that less than 36% of university employees are employed on a secure basis' (Mayhew 2014, p. 265),[3] and for Mayhew, the attendant 'culture of anxiety and resentment has a pernicious effect on academic research cultures' (p. 268). In institutions where women are 'overrepresented in lower grades and temporary positions' (Gill 2014, p. 19), increased casualisation can also be a crucial pivot in the reproduction of gendered organisational hierarchies. Evidence from the United States suggests that similar imbalances can hold around the intersections between race, class and gender, albeit with discipline-based variations (see the studies collected in Muhs et al. 2012).

Casualisation produces a labourer that is simultaneously the subject of responsibility (in relation to students) and the object of responsibility (in relation to senior staff). This can impact HDR students directly, who—alongside Early Career Researchers (ECRs)—are frequently 'charged with delivering mass undergraduate programs without training or support' (Gill 2014, p. 19). Supervisors are required to train HDR students in more skills across shorter durations, or what Pam Green and Robin Usher call 'fast supervision' (2003, p. 44), and the same institutional pressures that shorten research candidature also contribute to employment insecurity for supervisors themselves, as well as placing HDR candidates in competition for future employment. Supervisors can often experience contractual precarity within the communities that their students hope to join, and the notion of 'opening doors' for supervisees becomes fraught for those supervisors who do not yet have office doors.

Furthermore, the labour of those academic workers within the 'learning alliances' of HDR supervision is not evenly distributed. Casualisation individualises responsibility for the quality of university services, and

---

[3] These figures refer to academic and professional staff, where 'secure' refers to employment on a permanent (or 'tenured') basis. Similar figures hold in the United Kingdom and the United States (see Gill 2014, p. 19).

casuals may engage in 'self-exploitation' either out of a sense of personal obligation to students, or because they need to over-perform their competency in anticipation of possible contracts in the future (Brown et al. 2010, p. 179). Furthermore, in the United Kingdom, those who are perceived as embodying social diversity within the university (e.g. around class, gender, race, sexuality and religion) are frequently required to do informal and affective labour in supporting marginalised HDR students, legitimating diversity initiatives and diversifying curricula, and navigating colleagues' conflicting expectations around the 'diversity work' required of them (Ahmed 2012; Taylor 2013). Affective labour performed by supervisors, especially in instances when they have been singled out to work with vulnerable or marginalised students, can remain invisible within the extant 'metric assemblages' around academic performance (see Grealy and Laurie 2017). For example, the capacity for interpersonal care is commonly treated as a requirement for women but a special achievement for men, and this produces imbalances in the amount of work expected of female supervisors and the professional recognition received for such work.[4]

The professional subjectivities of inexperienced supervisors also merit special consideration. Most academics receive little formal training in supervision practices and find themselves 'becoming a supervisor' as an improvised by-product of becoming an academic (see Barcan 2015). The preparation processes that do exist are largely informal and tacit and often unsatisfactorily addressed by institutional training focused on 'techne' and 'contextual expertise' (Halse and Malfroy 2010, p. 88). Elspeth Probyn notes that 'feeling like a fraud is routine in the modern university' (cited in Barcan 2013, p. 192), and Ruth Barcan argues that such feelings of fraudulence are exacerbated by post-disciplinarity (the porous borders of conventional disciplinary expertise), globalisation (the geographical mobility of researchers), productivism ('one can never, by definition, have done "enough"') and casualisation, where 'overworked permanent staff and the undervalued casual staff are two sides of the same coin' (Barcan 2013, pp. 199–200). Claims that 'a deep substantive knowledge of their discipline or specialization [is] essential for supervising doctoral

---

[4] On gender and affective labour in the modern university, see Gregg (2010).

students', and about the importance of professional networks for facilitating supervisees' examination and future employment (Halse and Malfroy 2010, pp. 86–88; Lee 2008), can further consolidate a sense of incompetence for ECR supervisors.

Feelings of fraudulence can sometimes be useful. The relative vulnerabilities of junior supervisors can provide opportunities to build bridges across institutional gulfs, in keeping with Barcan's analysis of academic insecurity: 'refusing to allow our students to feel that they are not the only person in the room who doesn't know enough, or shouldn't be there, or doesn't understand, or isn't convinced, or doesn't have the right background for this, is not only an ethical imperative, but also a political pedagogical challenge' (Barcan 2013, p. 193). Acknowledging insecurity may allow supervisors to model important lessons about limitation, failure, humility and intellectual generosity, as well as to affirm a collective confidence in the 'right to be somewhere' (203). This can be particularly important for doctoral students whose communities and cultures have been historically excluded from Western tertiary institutions and hierarchies of knowledge production (see Trudgett 2011, p. 393; Gidley et al. 2010). Elsewhere, studies of primary and secondary education have noted that students can benefit from adopting the position of teacher (Harris and Lemon 2012), and some higher education researchers recommend that the 'breaking down of barriers between the "experts" and the learners is … necessary for engaging in a genuine dialogue' (Durden et al. 2014, p. 150).

Given these tensions around the conditions shaping supervision as a labour practice, our argument is not simply that the pedagogical problem of good supervision can be solved by improving industrial relations—although it would certainly help. By pointing to what Rosalind Gill (2014, p. 25) calls 'the hidden injuries of academic labouring in the Western University', we also heed her caution about not disavowing the privileges and desires of academic workers. Teaching work can involve many unexpected pleasures and always contains some 'room for manoeuvre' or even possibilities for 'exhilaration' (Ross Chambers in Morris 2013, p. 450). Nevertheless, the labour of community building is uneven in its social distribution and imbalanced in the rewards it can deliver. The first step in producing viable learning alliances may not necessarily be collective altruism but rather pragmatic self-interest. We need to create security and balance in the working lives of teachers, and to ensure that any 'relational ethics of mutual responsibility' is grounded in sustainable relationships with the university itself.

The Social Life of Knowledge

The issue of working conditions for supervisors leads to a second issue for learning alliances concerning the formation of disciplinary communities. In extant literature on supervision practices, the rewards of completing a thesis are often couched in humanist terms for the student (who contributes to knowledge), to the supervisor (who guides and learns from this contribution) and to the discipline (which is reinvigorated with new perspectives, approaches and concepts). Some studies also frame the production of higher degree knowledge as a contribution to 'knowledge economies' intended to make 'a significant contribution to change and development in the workplace' (McCallin and Nayar 2012, p. 69). When noted at all, ambiguities around the virtue of knowledge production are mostly attributed to external influences, like 'economic competitiveness' (Halse and Bansel 2012, p. 387) or 'adversarial models' of education (Bartlett and Mercer 2000, p. 197).

However, knowledge is always produced in a particular place, for a particular professional community, and within the parameters of what is already considered to matter culturally, historically and politically (Trudgett 2011; Connell 2007). Universities are classifying machines: they rank and punish, emplace and displace, include and exclude. Practices of HDR supervision and research accreditation bring together historically specific ways of certifying and remunerating knowledge production; of separating individuals on the basis of authority (e.g. tutors, lecturers and professors), discipline (e.g. archaeology and cultural studies) and institutional tier (e.g. technical colleges, 'Oxbridge', the enterprise university); and of stratifying non-tertiary spaces in relation to mandatory educational qualifications (e.g. professional gatekeeping). The possession of knowledge does not automatically place an individual in an academic 'class' (Devlin 2013; Gidley et al. 2010), and correspondingly, those claiming membership in the 'knowledge class' do not necessarily possess more knowledge than others (Frow 1995, p. 117). Nevertheless, some persons are equipped with resources—social capital, cultural capital and embodied capital—that allow them to make stronger claims over knowledge in bounded institutional settings (Bourdieu 1997). Research in Australia has considered the trajectories of students from Low Socio-Economic Status (LSES) areas passing into higher education, noting the impact of both cultural and social capital in students' university experiences (Devlin et al. 2012; Devlin 2013). John Frow characterises this relationship in the following way:

> The knowledge class acquires legitimacy through the acquisition of credentials, and at the same time achieves a measure of class closure by integrating the community of those with appropriate credentials and excluding those without it; it structures its Other in terms of its own claim to knowledge. (1995, p. 126)

To paraphrase Pierre Bourdieu (1984), the knowledge class is defined by its capacity to classify knowledge, and in doing so, to classify itself in relation to the institutions that authorise such claims to knowledge.

In the context of academic communities formed through the classification and authorisation of specialised knowledge, HDR trajectories are strongly marked by social capital, or 'the aggregate of the actual or potential resources which are linked to possession of a durable network of more or less institutionalised relationships of mutual acquaintance or recognition' (Bourdieu 1997, p. 51). The HDR dissertation is not a commodity as such, but functions rather as an instrument of commoditisation in an inter-institutional market formation, and can thus be understood 'as a process of becoming rather than as an all-or-none state of being' (Kopytoff 1984, p. 63). For those situated in Australia's research-focused Group of Eight (Go8) research-intensive universities,[5] the latent value of a dissertation is frequently converted into social and cultural capital, both through the immediate tie between supervisor and supervisee, and what

---

[5] The University of Sydney, the University of Melbourne, the University of Adelaide, The University of Western Australia, The University of Queensland, The University of New South Wales, Australian National University and Monash University.

Granovetter (1985) calls the 'weak ties' of extended professional affiliations to which senior supervisors may grant access. For the postgraduate student, social capital is crucial in 'providing access to key scholarly networks or opportunity structures, and investment in deciphering the unwritten rules of the institutional culture and the larger discipline' (Zambrana et al. 2015, p. 5). Consider Lee's account of supervision as a pivot of institutional power:

> [Supervisors] will provide some specific expertise, but will also be a gatekeeper to many more learning resources, specialist opinions and networks. The supervisor can choose which gates to open, particularly in the early stages of the researcher's life .... The struggle can be political on several levels. The student needs to be aware of how powerful (or not) their supervisor is in the institution, and discussion about enculturation as a concept or an expectation could help the student to make realistic decisions. (2008, p. 272)

Supervisors must balance a sense of responsibility to supervisees with the risk of heightening or consolidating their own investments in what Philippe Ariès, commenting on bourgeois education, concisely characterised as 'a host of little societies' (1962, p. 414). Relatively little is known about the relationship between HDR research trajectories and social capital accumulation, despite a handful of longitudinal studies pointing toward these issues (e.g. Walpole 2003; Zweigenhaft 1993). The aggregated labour market effects of embedded social networks have not been studied at the level of an entire discipline, but we can find clues about tendencies. Recent research in the United States indicates that scholars from 'minority' backgrounds 'are hindered by limited access to material resources, social capital, and prior experiences in segregated or underserved neighborhoods and schools' (Zambrana et al. 2015, p. 44). Comparable nation-wide research is yet to be conducted across the Australian tertiary sector, but evidence suggests that social and cultural capital may be significant factors for Aboriginal and Torres Strait Islander HDR students (see Trudgett 2011). In saying this, we do not want to posit a simple deficit model, wherein students understood to 'lack' social capital and cultural capital must automatically seek to overcome this lack.

Rather, we must take into account 'the lived realities of such students as subjects of particular histories, social situations and affective states that have a significant impact on their expectations and aspirations with regard to higher education' (Low 2013, p. 20). In this context, we might treat social capital as part of an analytics of power, without presuming that social capital acquisition is the telos of all student subjectivities.

As noted in our discussion of casualisation above, discipline-based social capital is something that a supervisor may offer. Institutional expectations that supervisors support supervisees' social and institutional progress (see Connell 1985, p. 41) are buttressed by an affective component linked to memory and trauma. Most students experience the supervision relationship as ground zero for the accumulation of social capital in its disciplinary aspect (or 'disciplinary capital'), as distinct from existing social networks. The interpersonal tribulations between supervisor and supervisee—deferred and missed deadlines, arguments and tears, prohibition and warning, conciliation and congratulations—accumulate as shared affective memory. If the student pursues an academic career, the spoils of affective accumulation may be converted into mobile social capital. Even fraught supervision relationships can produce enduring social connections, because traumatic supervision can heighten the supervisor's own investment in the candidate and the project. Affective labour in supervision therefore has two distinct faces. Facing inwards is the uncounted social work by supervisors who subscribe to what Lee calls the 'quality relationship' model of practice. Facing outwards is the extraction of social capital from HDR candidature enabled through affective accumulation. These may be two expressions of the same general tendency. As market-based interactions are increasingly embedded within academic life,[6] affective relations and informal circuits of social capital provide relative securities in otherwise volatile and unpredictable environments. Affective connectivity is not only a site for strategic exploitation by the neoliberal university, but is also a tactical response to the social erosions and displacements of an unpredictable labour market.[7]

---

[6] See Granovetter (1985) on socially embedded markets.

[7] On this distinction between strategies and tactics, see Michel de Certeau (1988).

For some of the issues raised so far, a range of simple correctives may be available. When supporting peer-based networks of learning among postgraduates, staff could make sure to include part-time students, students off campus, international students or interested students from other universities. When casual or sessional staff are engaged in supervision, other staff could make sure to include them in 'teaching alliances' that provide social supports and offer opportunities for difficult supervision relationships to be mediated by supervisors with greater job security. In this final section, we outline specific issues around research supervision for cultural studies practitioners, noting the ways that social relationships can acquire disciplinary value.

Higher Degree Research in a Cultural Studies Context

Cultural studies can find itself unexpectedly conflicted in the HDR environment. On the one hand, higher degree research programs can be formative spaces where students develop critical approaches to knowledge production itself, and for those not intending to pursue academic careers, such critical approaches can contribute to a broader public good elsewhere. On the other hand, the supervision dyad and the gatekeeping functions of doctoral assessment challenge cultural studies to confront practices seemingly incongruent with its own political orientations. These latter include the articulation of strict hierarchies between institutional and non-institutional forms of expertise; the exercise of institutional authority often linked to punitive mechanisms; the commonplace reification of 'knowledge for knowledge's sake' in some (primarily humanities) HDR programs; the valorisation of the mind over the body, or the being of ideas over the pragmatic doing of ideas; and the enforcement of distinctions between what cultural studies is and what cultural studies is not. To support this line of inquiry, we need to first pinpoint distinctive features of cultural studies as a research framework.

Cultural studies in Australia is described by Frow (2007) as both a 'common project' (p. 72) and as 'a kind of "clumping" of intellectual energies at key places and times' (p. 71), including the formation of a number of new academic journals and the communities that under-pinned them; increased government investment into the culture indus-tries in the 1970s and 1980s; and new (or 'non-sandstone') education institutions which sought to distinguish themselves from the established universities through their interdisciplinary programs. It matters whether we transmit the history of cultural studies through the legacy of the Centre for Contemporary Cultural Studies,[8] or through those critical social movements that created the political and intellectual spaces that cultural studies now fruitfully occupies, including feminism (e.g. Morris 1988) and critical responses to multiculturalism, often themselves framed in feminist terms (e.g. Gunew 1988). For the sake of brevity, we will focus on features of cultural studies most relevant to teaching.

Let's say that if the social sciences are defined by their methods, cul-tural studies is defined by its problems. Cultural studies' problems require drawing from 'whatever fields are necessary to produce the knowledge for a particular project' (Grossberg et al. 1992, p. 2), and the resulting prob-lem spaces become 'an interrelated set of questions that generates a body of knowledge – with the proviso that the singularity of this problematic is as much self-consciously constructed as it is given in advance' (Frow 2007, p. 68). For this reason, cultural studies does not appear to have attachments to particular facts or fact-gathering methods. And yet, in order to sustain its own radical heterogeneity, cultural studies must have attachments to the circumstances that support its own existence, namely, the circumstances of institutionalised education. Cultural studies has firm intellectual investments in cultivating institutional spaces where unexpected ideas can be explored. For this reason, Graeme Turner fore-grounds undergraduate teaching as an important base from which cul-tural studies programs have developed in Australia, and as a crucial site for the pedagogical interventions that cultural studies is readily, if not uniquely, equipped to make. '[Early] cultural studies programmes were taught in ways that explicitly and deliberately built on their own stu-dents' popular cultural capital', suggests Turner, and 'their focus upon the media and popular culture enabled students to immediately engage in

---

[8] See, for example, recent commentaries in Bennett (2015), Frow (2007) and Turner (2011).

conversation with the discipline' (2011, p. 79). Just as cultural studies research takes seriously the phenomena of everyday life—its pleasures, frustrations, contradictions and aspirations—so too should the discipline enable students 'to learn something new about their own experiences, location or patterns of consumption' (p. 87). In this way, cultural studies' pedagogical orientations dovetail with John Dewey's philosophy of education, which prioritises the 'capacities, needs, and past experiences of those under instruction', and seeks to articulate 'purposes' through 'cooperative enterprise' and 'social intelligence' (Dewey 1997 [1938]).[9] For similar reasons, some cultural studies scholars have expressed concerns about canon formation in the discipline (e.g. Grossberg 2010; Rodman 2014), and Turner strongly recommends against the 'mystificatory approach to the teaching of cultural studies theory that privileges the authority of the knowing teacher rather than enables the curious student' (2011, p. 78; see also Turner 2013).

The scandal of cultural studies teaching is that it does not necessarily require the existence of cultural studies texts or cultural studies subjects. Problem spaces and intellectual conjunctures can emerge from the intersection of many different disciplines, where 'cultural studies' may simply name the transit across this intersection. If, as Tony Bennett argues, 'cultural studies matters as a meeting place for heterogeneous forms of sociocultural and cultural-economic analysis that have diverse forms of practical engagement' (2013, p. 439), the cultural studies pedagogue takes on the role of traffic conductor in a busy metropolitan intersection. Successful cultural studies teaching may therefore involve introducing a philosophy student to sociology, or a documentary film-maker to postcolonial literary theory, rather than enacting a conversion to cultural studies *tout court*.

Higher Degree Research programs accentuate the challenges of undergraduate cultural studies teaching. While research students may continue to benefit from the adage that *learning is doing* (see Durden et al. 2014,

---

[9] What education researchers call problem-based learning (PBL) follows principles already welcomed by cultural studies scholars working with this Deweyian disposition. Universities are now more holistically placing emphasis on the development of HDR students' transferable skills, such as 'problem solving, collaborative work, leadership and knowledge application' (Green and Usher 2003, p. 39).

p. 149), the kinds of reflexive identity work and peer-based discussion commonplace in cultural studies' undergraduate classrooms are unlikely to fulfil the criteria for HDR projects. Supervisors cannot always engage supervisees through the same kinds of experience-based learning activities that continue to inspire and exhilarate undergraduates, and ongoing coursework is rarely a feature of HDR experience in Australian universities. This marks an important point of difference between the Deweyian ideals of the 'bottom-up' undergraduate classroom, and the more unwieldy demands of the cultural studies postgraduate space. Just as importantly, cultural studies cannot know in advance what kinds of research projects will be relevant to its purposes. Supervisors and supervisees must place a great deal of confidence in 'immanent' criteria linked to the particular problems posed by the research piece at hand. Undergraduate teaching can accommodate a degree of intellectual dilettantism, linked in part to the pedagogical device of exploring everyday experiences and adapting scholarship to suit these purposes. Where undergraduates are invited to explore different methods and approaches, postgraduates are expected not only to demonstrate mastery over one or several methods, but also to justify their methodological choices in historical terms: how is this problem being approached in and for the present? Producing convincing answers to such questions can also become important for facilitating candidates' transitions into non-academic labour markets (Frow 2013), and we must remember that these links outside the university are important for sustaining cultural studies as a lively social and political project.

From the issues discussed thus far, it should be evident that cultural studies research can produce unique forms of intellectual vulnerability. In the absence of a mandated suite of methods, postgraduates must learn to navigate tacit collective understandings of which problems are currently viable, which pathways have been exhausted and which concepts remain salvageable from adjacent humanities and social science disciplines. Criticisms of canonical authority in cultural studies can be re-evaluated in this context. In contrast to Stuart Hall's formulation of a 'Marxism without guarantees' open to the 'relative indeterminacy' of 'political action given by the terrain on which it operates' (1996, p. 44), HDR programs produce terrains where guarantees are most furiously sought after and where indeterminacy creates the greatest anxiety for those most vulnerable to failure. The researcher who is encouraged to draw on phenomenological or auto-ethnographic ways of knowing must remain confident in the authority of those who are seen to license these methods. The prized canonical names of cultural studies, its 'host of little societies', and the authority of a supervisor can be indispensable resources for those seeking to secure a voice within the discipline. In this context, the phylogenetic development of cultural studies—the emergence of great names and works over the last five decades—provides a speculative roadmap for the ontogenetic growth of the postgraduate's own research identity.

Postgraduate learning trajectories in cultural studies also involve complex social attachments. Academic communities produced through networks of affiliation and association can be joyful in addition to their 'capitalising' functions, and in the context of cultural studies, Meaghan Morris notes the importance of 'any self-motivating group that is sustained, within as well as without the silos of highly industrialized sectors, by a shared commitment to an educative project that acts as a source of ethical and emotional value for those involved' (2011, p. 126). As indicated in our discussion of learning alliances above, we must introduce a small caveat to such claims. In order to promote ethical and emotional values within educative projects, we must also promote sustainable and non-precarious industrial arrangements, wherein the ravages of casualisation can no longer 'capture' emotional and ethical investments as sites for further exploitation.

Conclusion

This chapter has moved between two distinct kinds of discourse that circulate within the sociology of higher education. One discourse considers the practices required to achieve a single broad outcome: best teaching practice. For those teaching HDR students, the criteria for best practice may involve progressing students toward a timely completion and creating the best conditions for the student to pursue a career. At the same time, we have interrogated the perceived outcomes of higher degree research in broader institutional contexts, noting key points of tension across the tertiary sector. In addition to focusing on the phenomenological experiences of teaching and learning, we must keep in view the patterns and cycles that shape the reproduction of programs, disciplines and institutions. There is no absolute separation to be made between teaching as a discrete activity and its broader institutional contexts, and boundaries are frequently blurred between teaching and socialising, instruction and collaboration and mentorship and exploitation. This blurring can produce unexpected joy, relief, excitement, security, anticipation and disappointment. For this reason, when promoting learning alliances as responses to deficiencies in the master-apprentice model of supervision, we also need to be sensitive to the organisational structures and working conditions within which such alliances are embedded. The informal allocation of pastoral responsibilities for supervisors can disproportionately affect casual or sessional workers, for whom professional aspirations can mix unpleasantly with the concrete challenges of precarious employment. Acknowledging the demands placed by universities on postgraduate productivity, supervisors should remain committed to multiplying the diversity of resources to support supervisees, while remaining prepared to engage with the institutional politics that continue to distribute teaching obligations and rewards unevenly across the tertiary sector.

Works Cited

Ahmed, S. (2012). *On Being Included: Racism and Diversity in Institutional Life*. Durham/London: Duke University Press.

Amundsen, C., & McAlpine, L. (2009). "Learning Supervision": Trial by Fire. *Innovations in Education and Teaching International, 46*(3), 331–342.

Ariès, P. (1962). *Centuries of Childhood: A Social History of Family Life* (Robert Baldick, Trans.). New York: Afred A. Knopf.

Australian Government Department of Education and Training. (2017). *Key findings from the 'Completion Rates of Higher Education Students – Cohort Analysis, 2005–2015' report*. URL https://docs.education.gov.au/node/46121. Last Accessed 1 Apr 2018.

Barcan, R. (2013). *Academic Life and Labour in the New University: Hope and Other Choices*. London: Ashgate.

Barcan, R. (2015). Learning to be an Academic: Tacit and Explicit Pedagogies. In G. Noble, M. Watkins, & C. Driscoll (Eds.), *Cultural Pedagogies and Human Conduct* (pp. 129–143). London: Routledge.

Bartlett, A., & Mercer, G. (2000). Reconceptualising Discourses of Power in Postgraduate Pedagogies. *Teaching in Higher Education, 5*(2), 195–204.

Bennett, T. (2013). The Multiplication of Cultural Studies' Utility. *Inter-Asia Cultural Studies, 14*(3), 438–441.

Bennett, T. (2015). Cultural Studies and the Culture Concept. *Cultural Studies, 29*(4), 546–568.

Boud, D., & Lee, A. (2005). "Peer Learning" as Pedagogic Discourse for Research Education. *Studies in Higher Education, 30*(5), 501–516.

Bourdieu, P. (1984). Conclusion: Classes and Classifications. *Distinction: A Social Critique of the Judgement of Taste* (R. Nice, Trans.). (pp. 466–481). Cambridge: Harvard University Press.

Bourdieu, P. (1997). The Forms of Capital. In A. H. Halsey et al. (Eds.), *Education: Culture, Economy, and Society* (pp. 46–58). Oxford: Oxford University Press.

Brown, T., Goodman, J., & Yasukawa, K. (2010). Academic Casualisation in Australia: Class Divisions in the University. *Journal of Industrial Relations, 52*(2), 169–182.

Connell, R. W. (1985). How to Supervise a PhD. *Vestes, 2*, 38–40.

Connell, R. W. (2007). *Southern Theory: The Global Dynamics of Knowledge in Social Science*. Cambridge: Polity.

Connell, R. W., & Manathunga, C. (2012). On Doctoral Education: How to Supervise a PhD, 1985–2011. *Australian Universities' Review, 54*(1), 5–9.

Coughlan, S. (2014, October 12). Labour's Hunt Urges "Hippocratic Oath" for Teachers. *BBC News*. URL http://www.bbc.com/news/education-29482160

De Certeau, M. (1988 [1974]). *The Practice of Everyday Life* (S. Rendall, Trans.). Berkeley: University of California Press.

Deleuze, G. (1972 [1964]). *Proust and Signs* (R. Howard, Trans.). New York: George Braziller.

Devlin, M. (2013). Bridging Socio-Cultural Incongruity: Conceptualising the Success of Students from Low Socio-Economic Status Backgrounds in Australian Higher Education. *Studies in Higher Education, 38*(6), 939–949.

Devlin, M., et al. (2012). *Effective Teaching and Support of Students from Low Socioeconomic Status Backgrounds: Practical Advice for Teaching Staff*. Sydney: Office for Teaching and Learning, Department of Industry, Innovation, Science, Research and Tertiary Education.

Dewey, J. (1997 [1938]). *Experience and Education*. New York: Touchstone.

Durden, E., Govender, E., & Reddy, S. (2014). Higher Degree (Un) Consciousness. In A. Wardrop & D. Withers (Eds.), *The Para-Academic Handbook: A Toolkit for Making, Learning, Creating, Acting* (pp. 140–163). Bristol: HammerOn Press.

Frow, J. (1988). Discipline and Discipleship. *Textual Practice, 2*(3), 307–323.

Frow, J. (1995). *Cultural Studies and Cultural Value*. Oxford: Clarendon Press.

Frow, J. (2007). Australian Cultural Studies: Theory, Story History. *Postcolonial Studies, 10*(1), 59–75.

Frow, J. (2013). On Knowing and Mattering. *Inter-Asia Cultural Studies, 14*(3), 447–448.

Gidley, J., et al. (2010). From Access to Success: An Integrated Approach to Quality Higher Education Informed by Social Inclusion Theory and Practice. *Higher Education Policy, 23*(1), 123–147.

Gill, R. (2014). Academics, Cultural Workers and Critical Labour Studies. *Journal of Cultural Economy, 7*(1), 12–30.

Gilroy, P. (1993). *The Black Atlantic: Modernity and Double Consciousness*. Cambridge: Harvard University Press.

Granovetter, M. (1985). Economic Action and Social Structure: The Problem of Embeddedness. *The American Journal of Sociology, 91*(3), 481–510.

Grealy, L. (2016). Cliché, Gossip, and Anecdote as Supervision Training. *The Review of Education, Pedagogy, and Cultural Studies, 38*(4), 341–359.

Grealy, L., & Laurie, T. (2017). Higher Degree Research by Numbers: Beyond the Critiques of Neoliberalism. *Higher Degree Research and Development, 36*(3), 458–471.

Green, B. (2005). Unfinished Business: Subjectivity and Supervision. *Higher Education Research & Development, 24*(2), 151–163.

Green, P., & Usher, R. (2003). Fast Supervision: Changing Supervisory Practice in Changing Times. *Studies in Continuing Education, 25*(1), 37–50.

Gregg, M. (2010). Working with Affect in the Corporate University. In M. Liljeström & S. Paasonen (Eds.), *Working with Affect in Feminist Readings: Disturbing Differences* (pp. 182–192). London/New York: Routledge.

Grossberg, L. (2010). *Cultural Studies in the Future Tense*. Durham: Duke University Press.

Grossberg, L., Nelson, C., & Treichler, P. (1992). Cultural Studies: An Introduction. In L. Grossberg, C. Nelson, & P. Treichler (Eds.), *Cultural Studies* (pp. 1–16). London: Routledge.

Gunew, S. (1988). Authenticity and the Writing Cure: Reading Some Migrant Women's Writing. *Poetics, 17*(1), 81–97.

Hall, S. (1996). The Problem of Ideology: Marxism Without Guarantees. In K.-H. Chen & D. Morley (Eds.), *Stuart Hall: Critical Dialogues in Cultural Studies* (pp. 24–45). London: Routledge.

Halse, C. (2011). "Becoming a Supervisor": The Impact of Doctoral Supervision on Supervisors' Learning. *Studies in Higher Education, 36*(5), 557–570.

Halse, C., & Bansel, P. (2012). The Learning Alliance: Ethics in Doctoral Supervision. *Oxford Review of Education, 38*(4), 377–392.

Halse, C., & Malfroy, J. (2010). Retheorising Doctoral Supervision as Professional Work. *Studies in Higher Education, 35*(1), 79–92.

Harris, A., & Lemon, A. (2012). Bodies that Shatter: Creativity, Culture and the New Pedagogical Imaginary. *Pedagogy, Culture & Society, 20*(3), 413–433.

Harrison, N., Trudgett, M., & Page, S. (2017). The Dissertation Examination: Identifying Critical Factors in the Success of Indigenous Australian Doctoral Students. *Assessment & Evaluation in Higher Education, 42*(1), 115–127.

Kopytoff, I. (1984). The Cultural Biography of Things: Commoditization as Process. In A. Appadurai (Ed.), *The Social Life of Things: Commodities in Cultural Perspective* (pp. 64–91). Cambridge: Cambridge University Press.

Lee, A. (2008). How Are Doctoral Students Supervised? Concepts of Doctoral Research Supervision. *Studies in Higher Education, 33*(3), 267–281.

Low, R. Y. S. (2013). Can the "Under-Represented" Student Speak? Discerning the Subjects Amongst the Objects of Widening Participation in Higher Education. *Australasian Journal of University-Community Engagement, 8*(1), 1–24.

Mayhew, M. (2014). Marginal Inquiries. In A. Wardrop & D. Withers (Eds.), *The Para-Academic Handbook: A Toolkit for Making, Learning, Creating, Acting* (pp. 263–290). Bristol: HammerOn Press.

McCallin, A., & Nayar, S. (2012). Postgraduate Research Supervision: A Critical Review of Current Practice. *Teaching in Higher Education, 17*(1), 63–74.

Morris, M. (1988). *The Pirate's Fiancée: Feminism, Reading, Postmodernism.* London: Verso.

Morris, M. (2008). Teaching Versus Research? Cultural Studies and the New Class Politics of Knowledge. *Inter-Asia Cultural Studies, 14*(3), 433–450.

Morris, M. (2011). Commentary: Coping with Cynicism. *Cultural Studies, 25*(1), 123–127.

Morris, M. (2013). On the Power of Exhilaration. *Inter-Asia Cultural Studies, 14*(3), 449–452.

Muhs, G. G., Niemann, Y. F., González, C. G., & Harris, A. P. (Eds.). (2012). *Presumed Incompetent: The Intersections of Race and Class for Women in Academia.* Boulder: University Press of Colorado.

Pearson, M., & Brew, A. (2002). Research Training and Supervision Development. *Studies in Higher Education, 27*(2), 135–150.

Pearson, M., Evans, T., & Macauley, P. (2008). Growth and Diversity in Doctoral Education: Assessing the Australian Experience. *Higher Education, 55*(3), 357–372.

Rodman, G. B. (2014). *Why Cultural Studies?* West Sussex: Wiley-Blackwell.

Sedgwick, E. K. (2003). *Teaching Feeling: Affect, Pedagogy, Performativity.* New York: Duke University Press.

Taylor, Y. (2013). Queer Encounters of Sexuality and Class: Navigating Emotional Landscapes of Academia. *Emotion, Space and Society, 8*, 51–58.

Trudgett, M. (2011). Western Places, Academic Spaces and Indigenous Faces: Supervising Indigenous Australian Postgraduate Students. *Teaching in Higher Education, 16*(4), 389–399.

Tsai, E. (2008). Learning to Labor: Thesis Supervision and Academic Work in the Graduate School. *Inter-Asia Cultural Studies, 9*(3), 451–468.

Turner, G. (2011). *What's Become of Cultural Studies?* London: Sage.

Turner, G. (2013). Practising Cultural Studies Today. *Inter-Asia Cultural Studies, 14*(3), 463–467.

Walpole, M. (2003). Socioeconomic Status and College: How SES Affects College Experiences and Outcomes. *The Review of Higher Education, 27*(1), 45–73.

Zambrana, R. E., et al. (2015). "Don't Leave us Behind" the Importance of Mentoring for Underrepresented Minority Faculty. *American Educational Research Journal, 52*(1), 40–72.

Zweigenhaft, R. L. (1993). Prep School and Public School Graduates of Harvard: A Longitudinal Study of the Accumulation of Social and Cultural Capital. *Journal of Higher Education, 64*(2), 211–225.

Public Pedagogy and Private Programs: Practicing Cultural Studies in Professional Education

R. Gabriel Dor

So the enormous explosion of cultural studies in the U.S., its rapid professionalization and institutionalization, is not a moment which any of us who tried to set up a marginalized Centre in a university like Birmingham could, in any simple way, regret. And yet I have to say, in the strongest sense, that it reminds me of the ways in which, in Britain, we are always aware of institutionalization as a moment of profound danger. (Stuart Hall 1992: 286)

In today's neoliberal academy, cultural studies as a mode and method can only exist through institutionalization, with all the attendant dangers noted by Stuart Hall over 25 years ago only amplified by the current commercialization and commodification of higher learning. However, cultural studies can also still provide a site of critique and challenge within the structures and conditions of its academic study. Responding to the growth of "Professional Studies" programs marketed to returning adult undergraduates, this paper explores the critical potential of cultural stud-

R. G. Dor (✉)
Independent Scholar, Chicago, IL, USA
e-mail: gabrieldor2011@u.northwestern.edu

© The Author(s) 2019
J. Aksikas et al. (eds.), *Cultural Studies in the Classroom and Beyond*,
https://doi.org/10.1007/978-3-030-25393-6_17

325

ies to disrupt normative pedagogies and institutional hierarchies and create a space for theory and praxis in programmatic professional education. Unlike the corollary development of online learning, also designed to make the university more "accessible" to a broader consumer base, the Professional Studies programs can enable truly interactive learning with smaller class sizes, less departmental supervision, more motivated and mature students, and required courses face-to-face on a campus.

Although critical pedagogy and adult education were foundational influences in the development of cultural studies as an academic discipline, its incorporation into neoliberal university departments has frequently meant re-inscription in the very academy it sought to challenge. Acknowledging the importance of these issues in the pioneering scholarship of Richard Hoggart, Raymond Williams, and Stuart Hall, critics of cultural studies education have continued to insist on the need for reflexive radical practice against institutional disciplinary norms (Giroux 1994, 2000, 2004, 2005; Grace 2001; hooks 1994, 2003, 2010b; Maton and Wright 2002).

Theorizing Public Pedagogy as Political Praxis in Cultural Studies

In "Cultural Studies and Its Theoretical Legacies," Hall asks the field: "[W]hat happens when an academic and theoretical enterprise tries to engage in pedagogies which enlist the active engagement of individuals and groups, tries to make a difference in the institutional world in which it is located?" (1992: 284). In her three books on the subject, *Teaching to Transgress, Teaching Hope*, and *Teaching Community*, bell hooks elaborates on Hall's question with a radical humanization that engages teacher and learner as subjects not just of reason but also emotion. Her "engaged" pedagogy prioritizes feeling, embodiment, and subject positioning. Building learning communities among diverse students enables them to learn from each other while critiquing dominant ideologies. They collaboratively challenge authority, hierarchy, objectivity, and neutrality. She situates critical thinking as political practice for educators and students alike to transgress the disciplinary divisions, social status, and cultural norms of institutional higher learning.

Henry Giroux' "Cultural Studies, Public Pedagogy and the Responsibility of Intellectuals" likewise articulates a democratic approach to public pedagogy which broadly critiques structures and practices of cultural power:

> Cultural studies theorists have greatly expanded our theoretical understanding of the ideological, institutional and performative workings of culture, but as important as this work might be, it does not go far enough ... in connecting the most critical insights of cultural studies with an understanding of the importance of critical pedagogy, particularly as part of a larger project for expanding the possibilities of a democratic politics, the dynamics of resistance, and the capacities for social agency. For too many theorists, pedagogy often occupies a limited role theoretically and politically in configuring cultural studies as a form of cultural politics. (2004: 60)

Like hooks, Giroux recognizes in his expansive definition that: "Pedagogy is not simply about the social construction of knowledge, values, and experiences; it is also a performative practice embodied in the lived interactions among educators, audiences, texts, and institutional formations." (2004: 61). Taking teaching out of its formal location in institutional hierarchies, Giroux thus indicates how the mobile transgressive practice of the educator can promote democratic engagements in, around, and beyond the classroom.

In his earlier essay, "Public Pedagogy as Cultural Politics: Stuart Hall and the 'Crisis' of Culture," Giroux points to Hall having embodied these principles: "I argue that Hall's attention to the relationship between culture and politics provides a valuable theoretical service to educators by contributing to a notion of public pedagogy that makes the pedagogical a defining principle of cultural politics" (2000: 342). Likewise, Leslie Roman introduces a special issue of *Discourse: Studies in the Cultural Politics of Education* devoted to the late scholar by identifying "Hall's primary legacy... as an extraordinary educator and public intellectual" (2015: 162). She elaborates: "Hall helped us to see that education is at once a site for contesting the yet unfinished practices of 'cultural becoming' and sites of struggle over power, knowledge, publics, and in whose name education registers" (2015: 165).

Over a decade ago, Karl Maton and Handel Wright subjected the 2000 Crossroads Cultural Studies Conference held in Birmingham to a quantitative content analysis of sessions and hours of discussion showing pedagogy to have been highly neglected and marginalized despite calls to acknowledge its centrality to cultural studies (2002: 381). In contrast, the 2015 Cultural Studies Association Meeting, "Another University is Possible: Praxis, Activism and the Promise of Critical Pedagogy," was devoted to foregrounding educational reflexivity in panels, plenaries, roundtables, and workshops against the hegemony of neoliberalism dominating institutional formations of the contemporary academy.

Giroux's reflections on the neoliberal academy have only come to gain more meaning with the increased corporatization of learning and labor in higher education. "Cultural Studies in Dark Times: Public Pedagogy and the Challenge of Neoliberalism" crystallizes his ongoing critique of the privatized public sphere:

> Under neoliberalism, dominant public pedagogy with its narrow and imposed schemes of classification and limited modes of identification uses the educational force of the culture to negate the basic conditions for critical agency… As collective agents recede under neoliberalism, market forces incessantly attempt to privatize or commercialize public space… As public spaces disappear, it becomes more difficult to develop a democratic discourse for educating collective social agents capable of raising critical questions about the limits of a market-driven society… (2005: 7)

As an example of this, university extension programs once designed to offer classes to the general public on and off campus, have given way to semi-autonomous degree-conferring continuing and professional studies programs with their own campus buildings and program offerings linked to other undergraduate departments and programs. These programs are designed and marketed to find additional consumers of private education seeking a degree as a means of conferring personal and professional distinction towards better career opportunities.

Practicing Public Pedagogy in Professional Studies Programs

Degree-granting Professional Studies programs offer privatized university resources with cultural distinction to an additional consumer population of undergraduates with a professional income, affiliation, or sponsorship to finance tuition. Some departmental faculty teach these classes as a form of supplemental income. Frequently though, these courses are taught by adjunct professors who either maintain separate professional lives to support themselves or are graduate students and junior academics struggling for work in the oversaturated pool of precarious labor.

In my recurring position as an adjunct professor in one such program, I had multiple opportunities to teach a once weekly, three-hour media contexts course to returning undergraduates enrolled in the elite university's evening and weekend courses designed for working adults. While the school serves neoliberal corporate purposes of generating revenue and conferring status, it also enables mature professionals, university employees, day students, and community members to access programs, materials and resources to enrich their studies and pursuits according to their schedule. More diverse and intimate than their main campus equivalents, these classes tend to represent a broader community cross-section across age, race, class background, and national origin. Such differences are celebrated, explored, and brought to bear on class content, issues, and assignments.

Taking into account cultural studies both as critical theory and pedagogical practice, I have structured the introductory course situating media texts within larger social, economic, and political systems and structures which shape their functions, meanings, and values as an intensive seminar unpacking primary texts in film and television research, Frankfurt School materialism, French cultural theory, Birmingham School cultural studies, Anglo-American empiricism and effects research, and methods of study in industry, audiences, gender, sexuality, race, and globalization. Not only does the assigned reading, detailed below in the references, enable students to learn how to engage primary scholarly texts rather than summary textbook surveys and illustrate the comparative implementation of research methodologies, the heterogeneity of writing allows them to understand the textural range of scholarly styles and invites them to develop their own analytical voices.

Central to the readings, discussions and assignments is a critical view of cultural industries, reception practices, and identity formations. Students learn to place individuated commodities and personal experiences into broader frameworks of contemporary capitalism and the cultural construction of racial and sexual difference which implicate their own social identities and consumer practices beyond the classroom.

André Grace argues for the importance of "queer cultural studies to transgress adult educational space" as labor which "situates a critical practice of adult education with an ecology of learning that is sensitive to responsible individualism, honored Otherness, and the politics of building democratic communities of difference in living, learning, and work spaces" (2001: 262). My pedagogy prioritizes personal experiences and social relationships in a scholarly community over short-term mastery of course material. Class size has ranged between 3 and 13 students. The smaller the class size, the more opportunity there is for student input and social cohesion. Because the course is a major requirement, it has been saved from cancellation despite small enrollment.

While students tend to be straight white men and women between the ages of 25 and 40, the class also may include one student of color, a gay or lesbian student, a senior from the community enrolled out of interest, or even a day student who needs the elective at that time. In the small seminar, such representation tends to lead to multiple perspectives on the material and issues engaged. Older students necessitate a different pedagogical approach than the typical undergraduate population. Rather than requiring classroom management and monitored work, students are capable of greater initiative, independence, and investment.

Reflexive Pedagogies of Close Reading, Classroom Community, and Critical Writing

Meetings are heavily discussion based, grounded in close readings of assigned essays but also tying the texts to broader cultural issues and objects. I present a brief lecture supplying background information to readings, and guide discussion. In order to deconstruct pedagogical hierarchies and my position of teaching authority, I insist on students calling me by my first name and feeling comfortable sharing their own subjectivities as I do. As Hall writes, "Autobiography is usually thought of as seizing the authority of authenticity. But in order not to be authoritative, I've got to speak autobiographically" (1992: 277). I try to model a critical reflexive stance on my own positions, problems, and privilege.

Frequently, class lessons are redesigned to meet the questions and needs of the students as they struggle through the disciplinary canon trying to assign their own meanings to technical and theoretical jargon. Students choose a set of readings on which to present during several class meetings across the term. Instead of a formal presentation, they guide close reading of assigned texts adding their own questions, research, and observations to help stimulate individual ownership of their learning experience. Email communications with each student before the class meeting in which they present help give students important points on which to focus, added confidence and clarity, and ways to integrate their part into the broader lesson.

While my knowledgeable participation helps explain, connect, and keep discussion on track, students are constantly reminded that it is their contribution and takeaway which matter the most. In addition to lively discussion and dialogue in the classroom, emails to individuals and the class keep the conversation going across weekly meetings, help students focus their reading, writing and presentations, and provide ongoing feedback, attention and reinforcement of the lessons. Throughout, humor and human connection as pedagogical tools help challenge the hierarchical passivity of the traditional classroom, engaging students personally to join discussion, ask questions, and draw from their own interests and experience.

Reading, writing, and speaking on chosen topics of interest, the students are encouraged to engage the difficult disciplinary readings by applying them to contemporary cultural examples in order to assess critically the comparative benefits and limitations of competing methodologies in media and cultural studies. A progressively structured sequence of short assignments enables students to work with difficult material, research their own media interests, practice critical writing, and gain ongoing feedback on their work. For their final papers, students propose and prepare their own case studies analyzing particular media objects and relevant core articles in the applied contexts, with guidance and feedback to support their independent research projects.

The course structure and syllabus set out a flexible teleological arc for the learning curve. We begin by addressing dialectical materialism, base and superstructure, and Marxist foundations challenged and revised in the turn to culture. This structure is an intentional defamiliarization exercise for American adult students to grapple with their own epistemology and position in history, society, and culture. The difficulty of the readings and the intensive participation take these students out of their comfort zone. Frequently students lack a philosophy background, and are unused to treatises this opaque or advanced. There is great resistance to the dense language, and first contact with Hall's "Encoding/Decoding" is often marked by frustration and distance.

I remind them that while the curriculum is graduate level, the grading is introductory level. Nonetheless these disciplined, motivated and achievement-oriented learners struggle with lack of comprehension, clarity, and mastery. Thus, lectures and emails frequently give background and clarify points of summary, as well as supply pep talks and praise for the daunting challenges undertaken. The interpersonal element is key to keeping students engaged against the density of the materials and the distractions of everyday life.

Following these theoretical foundations, the syllabus shifts to more accessible discussions of audience research, reception studies, and spectatorship. It is at this point that students confront the empirical legacy of media effects and cultivation studies in the Anglo-American social science research tradition. Having de-centered such epistemological formations and institutional paradigms most familiar to American ideologies and public discourses through exposure to critical European theories and models, students are able to appraise more critically the institutional complicity of the methods, knowledge, and common sense that quantitative research offers. This process demands reflexivity on the part of these students on consumer technologies and higher education, and their own implication as subjects in these epistemologies. They become conscious of the institutions, formations, and ideologies which inform, produce, validate, and circulate knowledge, the very conditions which bring them to the classroom and the classroom to them.

Building on these critiques of mass media empiricism, the successive lesson on qualitative theoretical interventions offers a more critical approach to reception studies through ethnography, resistant appropriation, and embodied spectatorship. Addressing gender and sexuality, the next readings cover feminism and queer theory. Diverse approaches to racial issues in media studies are introduced with reference to Hall's "New Ethnicities" and a screening of the 1997 documentary, "Stuart Hall in Lecture: Representation and the Media." At this point, students finally come to understand his importance to critical studies of popular culture, and are able to connect with his pedagogy in the recorded lecture more easily than his theoretically dense writings. They are now working toward cultural studies as auto-ethnography, using the frameworks and models to situate their own experiences and interests, and then to reflect back on the theory through these case studies. They are also understanding their personal investment in these political struggles over fields of culture.

In this way, the overwhelming theoretical introduction leads into increasingly concretized and instantiated issues and themes which are easier to grasp, drawing from and reflecting back on the abstract course foundations. Short papers integrate the lessons from the students' own critical perspectives, relying on a certain number of personal choices of assigned, listed essays in order to compare and contrast methods. A number of open-ended prompts suggest ways of connecting and differentiating particular readings while allowing students to supply specific media examples. The cycle of writing assignments, increasing in page length and required number of assigned essays, provide a feedback loop for both students and myself. Closely reading, engaging, and commenting on their work, I am able to help them ascertain their interests and strengths, as well as to identify individual and collective gaps in understanding to be remedied in class or through personal communications. I encourage them not only to reflect, but also to ask questions, take risks, challenge assumptions, and be creative.

Together the class builds a collective community of socially engaged, self-aware learners. The interpersonal relationships built through the group provide a structure of trust and support to encourage each on their respective journeys and challenges. The classroom environment and its online supplements, not substitutes, along with the writing assignments which frequently develop from presentations or participation, allow for such multiple trajectories through a standardized syllabus that opens up and personalizes research agendas for each student. One size does not fit all, a learning mode that is easier to implement in a smaller class with more independent students and less standardization in testing, here becomes an opportunity for correction and ownership by each of the learners, including myself. Situating myself as a learner alongside them, albeit with more experience and knowledge with which to mentor, the class is free and empowered to address procedural and substantive obstacles in the progression of the course structure and term. It also creates the basis for trust from which to share personal and academic interests, concerns, ideas, and experiences. Thus, peer collaboration occurs not through group projects with their own problems for busy competitive professionals, but in the classroom as part of the learning process.

Critical Conclusions: Cultural Studies, Course Methods, and the Corporate Academy

The final assignment, guided through smaller assignments, entails a concentrated case study of a particular controversy surrounding a media object of the student's choice. The preliminary project outline is designed to focus students on the relevant course readings and methods, popular and production discourses surrounding the media object, and problems and questions encountered in preliminary research. Students are asked to look into the particular case history surrounding the controversy, focusing attention on media documents such as newspaper articles, promotional materials, and fan sites. Engaging the assigned readings in response to their interests, students are thus encouraged to build meaning by returning to prior material with a new understanding and purpose.

Final papers have covered a variety of topics drawing on the cultural interests, methodological affinities, and social experiences of individual students, including: gendered taste cultures of commercial wrestling; ideological, social, and economic effects of embedded digital advertising;

status and subjectivity in the discursive construction of celebrity star-figures; queer impacts of gay-themed sitcoms; race and feminism in the production and reception of films featuring African-American women; cinema architecture and consumer subjectivities; and critical ethnography of adult female fandom around popular vampire film franchises.

The repetition and difference of reading on their own assigned essays which successively reference prior ones, close reading and discussion of these essays in class, writing assignments reflecting on the reading, presentations mandating personal responsibility for guiding class discussion and understanding, and the final case study enable students to gain critical reading, writing, thinking, and analytical skills with which to confront complex cultural questions and methodologies from a meaningful perspective. Rather than simply "applying" theories, students are asked to reflect critically across the methodologies covered, integrating issues of industry, reception, and identity into their analysis and evaluating the relevance and limitations in relation to their chosen media objects.

Students thus learn to bring their "real world" experiences to the classroom implicating their own identities, positions, and preferences in broader systems of culture and power, and to reframe their consumer practices with critical analysis bringing classroom skills to bear on everyday spaces outside the university. This course design of shortened dense readings, intensive seminar discussions, and personalized writing and presentation assignments adapts a media major requirement in a private program for returning undergraduates seeking social, economic, and intellectual advancement into a public pedagogy for collective democracy and critical citizenship along the terrain of cultural politics. In this way, while the cultural capitalization of the elite adult education program socializes students into neoliberal economic and professional mobility, the transgressive modes, methods, and materials challenge easy assimilation into contemporary capitalist hierarchies and empower reflexive consumption of popular cultural commodities mindful of their implication in structures of power.

Such a rigorous and challenging seminar of close reading may be a tough sell to students *cum* consumers and thus institutional departments competing for funds, performed often by adjunct labor that is highly available, cheap, and disposable. However, the reward to the students and the teacher and the easy adaptation of course requirements or attractively themed offerings can allow practitioners of cultural studies to remain true to the mission of public education against the privatized demands of the neoliberal corporate university through its own professional marketing programs. The cultural distinction of having taken such a class is itself a marketing tool to serve much more radical pedagogical strategies. In a new era of higher education and media technologies, cultural studies must adapt to survive while maintaining its pedagogical aims. There are students out there with diverse backgrounds and life experiences who welcome the opportunity to be more than passive satisfied consumers of higher education.

Adult pedagogy is live guidance and facilitation, and online tools connect beyond the classroom in ways which can personalize and extend the limits of scheduling at the same time that technology in or as the classroom can get in the way of being human against the disciplinary apparatus of cultural reproduction. Adult learners don't need power-points, exams, and policing. They need structured discussion circles and assignments which engage the readings in application. They need a teacher who cares about their projects. They need to be treated like an integrated hybrid of graduate students and undergraduate advisees, nurturing their intellect while eschewing the excruciating expectations and neglect which cripple doctoral students. They need intellectual handholding and cheerleading, but they don't need babying and rigid management. They talk freely and do the reading for the most part. More than that they are a diverse group, each case and personality quite unique. At worst, that means a demanding or monopolizing voice, but a teacher skilled in classroom management and unafraid of challenging older students can channel the enthusiasm and engagement into productive responsibility for discussion.

The challenge is institutional, and in fact, adult learners are more willing to find value in the curriculum and pedagogy than the neoliberal university and its departmental apparatus. The space of adult learners, the incubator of Stuart Hall's practice, is endangered by the institutional changes in budgets, contracts, departments, distribution, digitization, branding, and labor. At the same time, it is this very space of adult education which provides the pedagogical opportunity to humanize and engage against a backdrop of professionalizing neoliberal corporatization in higher education. In this liminal space, students can be empowered to interrogate the epistemological conditions of consumer culture that situate their own place in the academy and society. As such, critical pedagogy in cultural studies can continue through adult education branded as professional studies despite the economic restructuring of the neoliberal university. At the same time, these students can increase their reflexivity and critical response to the disciplinary apparatus of corporate professionalization, continuing the mission of everyday relevance.

It is easy to be pessimistic and cynical about cultural studies in the mass market model of neoliberal education. The market has certainly not responded to my methods. But cultural studies calls and inspires us to permeate the cracks and the fissures, to adapt, modify, and subvert the consumer discourses and disciplinary practices of hierarchical corporate institutions. In this way, the contingent labor pool and the student consumer population can be mobilized in resistant alliance against the institutional forces that commodify intellectual praxis and higher learning while relying on our collective financial indebtedness to raise their own profit margins. To the extent I have been able to navigate the academic market and bureaucratic hierarchies, it is thanks to other educators who invested their belief and faith in guiding and supporting me and the students who cared enough to truly profit from the experiences. Together we create a community of engaged, reflexive teachers and learners challenging the divisive and denigrating institutional conditions of our independent and collaborative academic labor.

Works Cited

Adorno, T. (2010). Culture Industry Reconsidered. In S. Thornham et al. (Eds.), *Media Studies: A Reader* (pp. 16–21). New York: NYU Press.

Ang, I. (2010). Wanted: Audiences. On the Politics of Empirical Audience Studies. In S. Thornham et al. (Eds.), *Media Studies: A Reader* (pp. 451–461). New York: NYU Press.

Barker, M., & Petley, J. (2010). From Bad Research to Good – A Guide for the Perplexed. In S. Thornham et al. (Eds.), *Media Studies: A Reader* (pp. 418–429). New York: NYU Press.

Baudrillard, J. (2010). The Masses: The Implosion of the Social in the Media. In S. Thornham et al. (Eds.), *Media Studies: A Reader* (pp. 52–62). New York: NYU Press.

Bourdieu, P. (2010). Some Properties of Fields. In S. Thornham et al. (Eds.), *Media Studies: A Reader* (pp. 94–99). New York: NYU Press.

Brunsdon, C. (2010). The Role of Soap Opera in the Development of Feminist Television Scholarship. In S. Thornham et al. (Eds.), *Media Studies: A Reader* (pp. 341–349). New York: NYU Press.

De Certeau, M. (2010). The Practice of Everyday Life. In S. Thornham et al. (Eds.), *Media Studies: A Reader* (pp. 76–88). New York: NYU Press.

Doty, A. (2010). There's Something Queer Here. In S. Thornham et al. (Eds.), *Media Studies: A Reader* (pp. 471–480). New York: NYU Press.

Dyer, R. (2010). The Role of Stereotypes. In S. Thornham et al. (Eds.), *Media Studies: A Reader* (pp. 206–212). New York: NYU Press.

Foucault, M. (2010). Truth and Power. In S. Thornham et al. (Eds.), *Media Studies: A Reader* (pp. 63–75). New York: NYU Press.

Gilroy, P. (2010). Between the Blues and the Blues Dance: Some Soundscapes of the Black Atlantic. In S. Thornham et al. (Eds.), *Media Studies: A Reader* (pp. 291–301). New York: NYU Press.

Giroux, H. (1994). Doing Cultural Studies: Youth and the Challenge of Pedagogy. *Harvard Educational Review, 64*(3), 278–308.

Giroux, H. (2000). Public Pedagogy as Cultural Politics: Stuart Hall and the 'Crisis' of Culture. *Cultural Studies, 14*(2), 341–360.

Giroux, H. (2004). Cultural Studies, Public Pedagogy, and the Responsibility of Intellectuals. *Communication and Critical/Cultural Studies, 1*(1), 59–79.

Giroux, H. (2005). Cultural Studies in Dark Times: Public Pedagogy and the Challenge of Neoliberalism. *Fast Capitalism, 1*, 2. Available online: http://www.fastcapitalism.com

Gorman-Murray, A. (2010). Queering Home or Domesticating Deviance? In S. Thornham et al. (Eds.), *Media Studies: A Reader* (pp. 302–313). New York: NYU Press.

Grace, A. (2001). Using Queer Cultural Studies to Transgress Adult Educational Space. In V. Sheared & P. Sissel (Eds.), *Making Space: Merging Theory and Practice in Adult Education* (pp. 257–270). Westport: Bergin and Garvey.

Hall, S. (1992). Cultural Studies and its Theoretical Legacies. In L. Grossberg, C. Nelson, & P. Treichler (Eds.), *Cultural Studies* (pp. 277–294). New York: Routledge.

Hall, S. (2010a). New Ethnicities. In S. Thornham et al. (Eds.), *Media Studies: A Reader* (pp. 269–276). New York: NYU Press.

Hall, S. (2010b). Encoding/Decoding. In S. Thornham et al. (Eds.), *Media Studies: A Reader* (pp. 28–38). New York: NYU Press.

Hall, S., Critcher, C., Jefferson, T., Clarke, J., & Roberts, B. (2010). The Social Production of News. In S. Thornham et al. (Eds.), *Media Studies: A Reader* (pp. 645–651). New York: NYU Press.

Halloran, J. (2010). On the Social Effects of Television. In S. Thornham et al. (Eds.), *Media Studies: A Reader* (pp. 384–388). New York: NYU Press.

Hermes, J. (2010). Media, Meaning and Everyday Life. In S. Thornham et al. (Eds.), *Media Studies: A Reader* (pp. 514–522). New York: NYU Press.

hooks, b. (1994). *Teaching to Transgress: Education as the Practice of Freedom.* New York: Routledge.

hooks, b. (2003). *Teaching Community: A Pedagogy of Hope.* New York: Routledge.

hooks, b. (2010a). The Oppositional Gaze: Black Female Spectators. In S. Thornham et al. (Eds.), *Media Studies: A Reader* (pp. 462–470). New York: NYU Press.

hooks, b. (2010b). *Teaching Critical Thinking: Practical Wisdom.* New York: Routledge.

Kitzinger, J. (2010). A Sociology of Media Power: Key Issues in Audience Reception Research. In S. Thornham et al. (Eds.), *Media Studies: A Reader* (pp. 405–417). New York: NYU Press.

Maton, K., & Wright, H. K. (2002). Returning Cultural Studies to Education. *International Journal of Cultural Studies, 5*(4), 379–392.

McClintock, A. (2010). Soft-Soaping Empire: Commodity Racism and Imperial Advertising. In S. Thornham et al. (Eds.), *Media Studies: A Reader* (pp. 751–765). New York: NYU Press.

McQuail, D., Blumler, J., & Brown, J. R. (2010). The Television Audience: A Revised Perspective. In S. Thornham et al. (Eds.), *Media Studies: A Reader* (pp. 389–404). New York: NYU Press.

McRobbie, A. (2010). Post-Feminism and Popular Culture. In S. Thornham et al. (Eds.), *Media Studies: A Reader* (pp. 350–361). New York: NYU Press.

Morley, D. (2010). What's 'Home' Got to Do with It? Contradictory Dynamics in the Domestication of Technology and the Dislocation of Domesticity. In S. Thornham et al. (Eds.), *Media Studies: A Reader* (pp. 523–535). New York: NYU Press.

Radway, J. (2010). Reading the Romance. In S. Thornham et al. (Eds.), *Media Studies: A Reader* (pp. 440–450). New York: NYU Press.

Roman, L. (2015). 'Keywords': Stuart Hall, an Extraordinary Educator, Cultural Politics and Public Pedagogies. *Discourse: Studies in the Cultural Politics of Education, 36*(2), 161–170.

Said, E. (2010). Introduction to *Orientalism*. In S. Thornham et al. (Eds.), *Media Studies: A Reader* (pp. 111–123). New York: NYU Press.

Thompson, J. (2010). The Globalization of Communication. In S. Thornham et al. (Eds.), *Media Studies: A Reader* (pp. 138–151). New York: NYU Press.

Thornham, S., Bassett, C., & Marris, P. (2010). *Media Studies: A Reader* (3rd ed.). New York: NYU Press.

Williams, L. (2010). Skin Flicks on the Racial Border: Pornography, Exploitation, and Interracial Lust. In S. Thornham et al. (Eds.), *Media Studies: A Reader* (pp. 277–290). New York: NYU Press.

Williams, R. (2010a). Programming as Sequence or Flow. In S. Thornham et al. (Eds.), *Media Studies: A Reader* (pp. 192–198). New York: NYU Press.

Williams, R. (2010b). Advertising: The Magic System. In S. Thornham et al. (Eds.), *Media Studies: A Reader* (pp. 704–709). New York: NYU Press.

Index[1]

---

[1] Note: Page numbers followed by 'n' refer to notes.

© The Author(s) 2019

J. Aksikas et al. (eds.), *Cultural Studies in the Classroom and Beyond*,
https://doi.org/10.1007/978-3-030-25393-6

CPSIA information can be obtained
at www.ICGtesting.com
Printed in the USA
LVHW040011191219
640944LV00011B/180/P